A FAITH FOR MODERNS

BOOKS BY ROBERT GORDIS

THE BIBLICAL TEXT IN THE MAKING

THE JEW FACES A NEW WORLD

THE WISDOM OF ECCLESIASTES

CONSERVATIVE JUDAISM

KOHELETH: THE MAN AND HIS WORLD

THE SONG OF SONGS

JUDAISM FOR THE MODERN AGE

THE ROOT AND THE BRANCH:
JUDAISM AND THE FREE SOCIETY

THE BOOK OF GOD AND MAN—A STUDY OF JOB

JUDAISM IN A CHRISTIAN WORLD

LEAVE A LITTLE TO GOD

A COMMENTARY ON LAMENTATIONS

POETS, PROPHETS AND SAGES—
ESSAYS IN BIBLICAL INTERPRETATION

A FAITH
FOR MODERNS

Revised and Augmented Edition

By

ROBERT GORDIS

BLOCH PUBLISHING COMPANY
New York

Copyright © 1971 by Robert Gordis

Published by Bloch Publishing Company
31 West 31st Street
New York, New York 10001

Library of Congress Catalog Card Number 76-136424
SBN 0-8197-0001-0

TO OUR CHILDREN—
AND TO THEIRS

Preface to the New Revised Edition

As the horrors of Hiroshima and the Holocaust have receded in time, their legacy of unspeakable agony and the other colossal problems spawned by the Second World War have become increasingly evident. The dead have not yet buried the dead, but new mountains of corpses in a dozen new wars desecrate the earth anew. The darker-skinned races of mankind, long oppressed and despised, are rising up in revolt against their former exploiters. Yet all too often they are satisfied merely with reversing the role of master and slave and are substituting new tyrannies for old. For the first time in history man possesses the scientific knowledge and technological skill to provide all human beings with the resources needed for an abundant life. Instead, war, poverty and disease continue to destroy or to maim millions of children and adults in every corner of the globe. The most affluent of nations has gone furthest in impoverishing the land, polluting the air and poisoning the waters. The curse of Cain is descending upon the human race.

In the face of the mounting crises everywhere, men have found that the great historic religions, at least in the forms in which they were generally expressed in the past, have no meaning or value for them. Many have, therefore, turned their backs on organized religion and sought to find substitutes in a half dozen secular faiths. Sooner or later, they may discover that the new idols demand heavier sacrifices than the God whom they had rejected. Others have sought escape by reviving primitive religious cults, clinging to ancient superstitions or experimenting with drugs, the full consequences of which are still unknown. What unites all these disparate groups is a feeling of powerlessness, a sense of burdens too heavy to be borne, of crises defying solution.

Fortunately, not all our contemporaries have "copped out," as the current phrase has it, and resigned from the basic human enterprise of building the world. Some are seeking to re-discover the faith they need for life and action by exploring untapped resources in the great religious traditions, which prove to be richer and more varied than was often suspected. To be sure, there are many who are seeking the warmth and snug comfort of "the good old religion" of yesteryear. They have achieved a blissful euphoria by insulating their faith from the challenges of the real world and from the insights of science and philosophy, which they dismiss as irrelevant and immaterial. But there are others who are unable or unwilling to set up an iron curtain between the heart and the mind, between faith and knowledge, between the sacred and the secular. They cannot compartmentalize their lives, because they hear the great commandment, "You shall be whole before the Lord your God." For them integrity, intellectual as well as moral, is the basic imperative. They regard a fragmentation of the spirit, whether schizophrenic or "normal," as the ultimate tragedy.

Today, there is deep ferment in both historic religions of the Western world. The horrors of atomic destruction, the unspeakable bestialities of the crematoria and concentration camps, and the impotence of conventional religion have created a veritable revolution in Christianity. The extent of the upheaval is not fully recognized only because organized religion is not as powerful today as it was in the Middle Ages. Actually, the dimensions of the struggle going on in all branches of the Christian Church are greater than those of the Reformation in the days of Luther and Calvin.

For Jews the crisis in faith goes even deeper. On the one hand are the unbearable memories of the Holocaust and its aftermath, and on the other the opportunities, real or imagined, that Jews see in the free, or at least, the open society. Hence they tend to desert the Jewish community and be absorbed into the majority group. These elements of recent Jewish experience whether positive or negative, raise agonizing questions both with regard to God's place in the world and Israel's place in God's plan. To put it in non-theological terms, increasing numbers of sensitive men and women are concerned with the possibility of genuine faith in our age and with the nature and need for Jewish identity. These issues within both the Christian and the Jewish communities go far beyond doctrinal differences among sects and denominations. It is the future of God among men that hangs in the balance.

It was to aid in this task of discovering the elements of a vital and relevant faith for modern men and women that this book was written a decade ago. As is indicated in the Foreword and the Introduction to the first edition, *A Faith for Moderns* was intended as a presentation of the fundamentals of all vital religion and not as an exposition of Judaism. Hence, this book does not concern itself with such issues as Jewish law and observance, the relationship of religion and nationalism in the Jewish tradition, the role of the State of Israel, or the nature of Jewish identity. To these problems I have addressed myself in several other books, notably *The Jew Faces a New World* and *Judaism for the Modern Age*. The specific insights that may be derived from the Jewish tradition for meeting some basic ethical problems in modern life are treated in *The Root and the Branch* and *Sex and the Family in the Jewish Tradition*.

The present work is concerned with the abiding issues of human life and destiny in the universe, which transcend particular ethnic, cultural or religious backgrounds and, by that token, are common to all men because they are human. Before turning to these perennial concerns, the book seeks to grapple with the road-blocks posed by the role of religion as an institution. Having been part of "the Establishment" for millennia, religion has untold sins of commission and omission to answer for. The book then analyzes the possibility and the need for faith in God in a scientific and technological age. Among the elements of a religious world-view then discussed are the nature of man, the foundations of the moral order, the meaning of history, the mystery of evil, and the possibility of hope in the future which lies at the heart of the Messianic vision. We then turn to the concrete manifestations of the religious life, and examine the function of ritual and the role of prayer.

All these are problems of profound concern to Christians as well as to Jews, whether they stand within their respective traditions or without. But while the themes of this book are those upon which Judaism and Christianity have thought and said much—and even done a little—its aim is to discuss and explicate the attitudes and insights that I believe are essential to all vital religion.

In this connection it should be added that this book is written from the perspective of Western religion, rather than from the standpoint of the great faiths of the Orient. As many passages in this book attest, I have a high regard for many aspects of the world-view embodied in the religions of India, China and Japan, which can help to correct and balance the errors and excesses of Western religions. Nevertheless, this book is rooted in the Hebraic tradition. In my book, *Judaism in a Christian World*, I have sought to demonstrate that Judaism has had a uniquely intimate and ambivalent relationship with Christianity. This shared experience during two thousand years of history has often been denied; it cannot be erased.

I have spoken of the ferment in Christianity during the past decade. To many observers it has seemed to be the mark of chaos and dissolution. On the other hand I have discerned in these very phenomena of revolt and change an emerging pattern, a far-flung process of return to the Hebraic sources of the Christian faith. This interpretation of the tensions in contemporary Christianity was presented in a paper "The Re-Judaization of Christianity," which appeared with scholarly documentation in *Buffalo Studies* (Vol. 4, No. 5, 1968), a publication of the University of Buffalo, and in somewhat shorter form in the *Center Magazine* (September 1968), published by the Center for the Study of Democratic Institutions in Santa Barbara, California. The paper also appeared in a Hebrew version published in the State of Israel as well as in America.

The twentieth century may be described as the most momentous era in Jewish history. The tragically long debit side of the ledger includes the destruction of East-European Jewry, even before the advent of Hitler and the Nazi Holocaust. On the credit side, we may reckon the rise and development of the American-Jewish community and the birth and growth of the State of Israel. Both the lights and shadows of Jewish experience in our day have added new dimensions to the age-old problem of the survival of Judaism and the Jewish people. In a paper, "The Meaning of Jewish Existence," which first appeared in the *Shazar Jubilee Issue* of the *Jewish Frontier* (January 1970), I have sought to approach these issues in the light of my understanding of Jewish religious thought and contemporary life.

My warmest thanks are extended to the editors of the periodicals in which the two papers first appeared for their permission to include them as Chapters 18 and 19 in the present augmented edition of *A Faith for Moderns*.

I am deeply grateful to my good friend Charles E. Bloch, the young and dynamic President of Bloch Publishing Company, whose enthusiasm for the book led to the publication of this new edition, both in cloth and as a paper-back.

It is my hope that men and women of every background, and above all, young people, will be stimulated by this book to set out themselves on the unending quest for a viable philosophy of life. We live in a world where faith is practically impossible—it is merely indispensable.

ROBERT GORDIS

March 1971.
New York, N. Y.

Foreword

The story is told of two disputants in an East European village who came to their learned rabbi for judgment. After hearing the plaintiff, the sage nodded his head in agreement and said, "You, my friend, are right." "Wait until you hear my side, rabbi!" the defendant insisted, and after he had presented his story, the rabbi turned to him and said, "You are right." When the rabbi's wife, who had overheard the proceedings, remonstrated with her husband, "How can they both be right?" he answered, "You, too, my dear, are right." This tale is apropos of the much discussed "revival of religion" in our day, which has been decried by many observers as superficial and hailed by others as rich in promise.

The truth is that by and large what we are witnessing is less a revival of religion than a revival of interest in religion. Its most concrete manifestation is the growth of membership in American churches, which has far outstripped attendance at services or religious observance. Its most public expression is to be found in the notion that religion is good for the country and that the absence of some kind of faith, it matters little what its content or character, ఎ somehow subversive of society.

This "religiosity" takes on many forms. For some, it is a preoccupation with the color and pageantry of religious ritual, which they view as a kind of play-acting, particularly "good" for the children. Others are fascinated by the drama, genuine or synthetic, that may be found in religious personalities and events. A long list of best-selling novels, successful plays, and films bears testimony to the limitless lodes of gold that can be extracted from the pages of the Bible. For others, conformity to religion is a passport to social acceptance, a cachet of respectability. And there are many who turn to religion in desperation as promising peace of mind in their troubles or an avenue of escape from the problems of reality.

There is, however, another, deeper level in this new interest in religion. In an age of dissolving standards and vanishing values, a growing number of intelligent and sensitive men, women, and young people are interested in exploring for themselves the resources of religious tradition, hoping that it may help them live with insight and courage in an age rich both in peril and in promise. They would like to discover for themselves the values that are found in religion by those who are committed to its interpretation of life.

To be sure, there is no shortage of books, many of them eloquent and moving, that call for a return to religion. All too often, however, they ignore the new dimensions of existence in the modern age, and insist that the tradition of the past needs only to be repeated in order to be adequate for the present. This approach does not meet the need of those men and women who are seeking an understanding of the content of religion, but are unwilling to resign from the twentieth century in the process. There is much in contemporary life that is desperately in need of reconstruction. But there is much, too, in the achievement of the age, in the scientific discovery, philosophic analysis, and ethical striving of our century, which modern men regard as authentic and worthwhile. Hence they find themselves unable to make the leap of faith, which, they are told, involves the surrender of reason and at times even the suspension of the ethical. They are seeking an introduction, if not yet a commitment, to a vital religion. The faith they seek will not be a cloak of passivity and withdrawal from the arena of conflict and struggle which is the real world, nor an island of refuge for those who insist that loss of confidence in man is the prerequisite for faith in God.

It is my profound conviction that such a wise, open-eyed, hopeful-hearted world-view is eminently possible. I have not attempted to create a new philosophy of religion (assuming that I should be capable of it), though I hope that the attentive reader will discover some originality in insight and novelty of approach in the ideas expressed in these pages. Nor have I sought to demonstrate the truths of religion *more geometrico,* through mathematical proofs, as Spinoza sought to do in his *Ethics.* Actually, the present volume is a spiritual autobiography in disguise, the distillation of the insights and attitudes on God and man, life and death, the individual and society, at which I have arrived, on the basis of my personal experience and my understanding of the religious tradition, as refined in the crucible of the scientific and philosophic quest for truth. It is my hope that the record of the paths by which I have traveled, and the description of the spiritual home at which I have arrived, will be useful to other travelers on the same journey.

This book is not written for specialists or technical students of religion on the one hand, nor does it present a course in "religion in five easy lessons." It is intended for men and women who are willing to think seriously about the enduring issues of life. Drawing upon the insights of Biblical and post-Biblical religion but in no sectarian spirit, I have sought to set forth the basic elements of a religious view of life that will be tenable for modern men and women, whatever their formal religious affiliation, or even if they have none.

It is these ideas and insights which I have sought to transmit during my career as a rabbi in the American Jewish community, and as a teacher of Bible at the Jewish Theological Seminary of America for nearly three decades, as well as in lectures on college campuses and countless other forums throughout the country. My views have been challenged and deepened by a decade of teaching as Adjunct Professor of Religion at Columbia University and by a year as Visiting Professor of Old Testament at Union Theological Seminary.

That this book emerged at all, in the midst of a much too active career, was due to the warm fellowship and understanding of my beloved Congregation, Temple Beth-El of Rockaway Park. I am very thankful to David Ritter and other Temple leaders, who gave me the assurance that this and other fruits of my thought and labor would see the light of day.

I am deeply grateful to my secretaries, Bella Cohen and Shirley Kabakow, whose loyalty and friendship for the author have inspired their patient and devoted labors on the book.

I am particularly pleased that this book represents another milestone in the deep friendship which I have long enjoyed with Dr.

Abraham I. Shinedling. Drawing on his wide knowledge in many fields, and his matchless penchant for accuracy, he has prepared the manuscript for publication, proof-read the text, and furnished the Index. I am happy that my son David has assisted him in these arduous tasks.

My thanks are extended to Mr. Edward H. Bloch, Mr. Charles E. Bloch, and Mr. Solomon Kerstein, of the Bloch Publishing Company, whose enthusiasm for the book is reflected in its attractive format.

My wife's understanding and her boundless devotion have been a pillar of strength and a beacon of light to me throughout the years. Her own intellectual integrity and her spiritual sensitivity have impelled me always to rigorous thought and the quest for honest conviction, qualities which I hope will be evident in these pages.

Long as these credits may seem, they do not begin to exhaust the debt of gratitude which I owe to a vast and anonymous company. To them the ancient sage referred, "Much have I learnt from my teachers, more from my colleagues, and most of all from my pupils." Freely have I received and freely would I give.

ROBERT GORDIS

Belle Harbor, L. I.
May, 1960

Contents

MAN AND GOD

A FAITH FOR MODERNS

Warning to the Reader

Very few books can lay claim to universal significance, with a message for all times and all men, a truth of which honest authors are painfully aware. Most writing is much more restricted in its appeal. Nonetheless, authors do not generally seek to frighten off would-be readers at the outset. In prefacing this book with the notice *caveat lector*, "let the reader beware," we may seem to be doing just that. Actually, we are following the example of the medieval philosopher, Maimonides, who in the introduction to his masterpiece, *The Guide to the Perplexed*, declares that there are two classes for whom he is not writing: the naive believers and the sophisticated skeptics, upon both of whom he bestows unflattering epithets. We lay no claim to his magisterial authority, but should like to indicate the spirit of our quest for a modern faith by noting several classes of readers for whom our far more modest work is *not* intended.

The first group consists of untroubled believers, who are, perhaps fortunately, beset by few doubts and therefore find no difficulty with traditional religion. Even in our skeptical age, there are substantial numbers of men and women who accept the faith of their fathers as taught to them in childhood, finding no contradiction between the attitudes of tradition on the one hand, and modern insights and problems on the other. If a contradiction does arise that they cannot ignore, they solve the problem by a device which has been called the "compartmentalized mind," insulating their religion in one corner and their modern attitudes in another. Men of this

1

stamp avoid the conflict between the two simply by preventing a meeting. This is the position of a distinguished leader in traditional religious education in our day. He declared that the harmony of science and religion, which is widely regarded as a desirable goal, does not mean that the religionist should draw upon the conclusions of science or that the scientist should reckon with the insights of religion, but that the same individual should be trained to be loyal to religion, while being familiar with the content of science. That such a partition of the spirit is psychologically feasible is clear from the large number of men and women who have found an island of spiritual security in various types of religious orthodoxy, Christian and Jewish. From the days of Francis Cardinal Newman to Gilbert K. Chesterton and Heywood Broun, there have been spectacular conversions to the Roman Catholic Church by distinguished figures who have grown weary of the perpetual quest, the gnawing uncertainty and the apparently unending speculations which are the hallmarks of the modern temper. With a variety of motivations, such converts have sought shelter in a faith which offers total assurance and demands total acceptance. In our day, many a disillusioned communist has simply transferred his habit of unquestioning obedience from one system to another. Protestantism and Judaism, like Catholicism, can point to other, though perhaps less sensational, examples of former nonbelievers who have found spiritual sanctuary in their respective systems of belief. The proverbial "zeal of the convert" derives from the same compulsion, the need to banish all lurking doubts and suppress all inner discussion.

Be this as it may, the fortunate minority for whom no religious doubts or problems exist will have no need of a book such as this. For it is our basic assumption that doubt is not only natural to thinking and sensitive men, but also an essential instrument for attaining spiritual maturity. If religion has anything of value to offer men in their quest for a satisfying world-view, as we profoundly believe, it is because of those who dared to challenge the accepted patterns of faith in their day. The greatest exponents of living religion were fearless iconoclasts like Abraham, troubled doubters like Moses, passionate protestants like the Prophets, intrepid inquirers after truth like the sages and philosophers in all the great religions of the Orient and the West.

Moreover, the only religion that matters is the personal religion of each individual, which is never identical with that of any other, because each human being is unique. To be sure, a man's personal religion will normally be derived in largest measure from the specific tradition to which he is heir. But the particular insights which he will select from the sum total of the tradition, the emphasis which he will give to some of its aspects, as well as the elements which he will modify, soft-pedal, or discard, all constitute a personal interpretation of the group heritage. He who is prepared to accept his religion ready-made and neatly packaged, who has no patience with speculation, doubt, and uncertainty, will surely not find this volume of interest.

There are several other groups who will doubtless avoid this book. There are those at the opposite pole, whose hostility to religion in all its aspects is so intense that they have closed the door on any serious discussion of religious belief and practice. They, too, fall into several categories. Some have become convinced, on the basis of personal misfortune or frustration, that life is meaningless and that "vanity of vanities, all is vanity." Viewing life, as is entirely natural, solely from their personal vantage point, they are unwilling to see the world from any broader or more balanced position. There are others who are so enamored of the achievements of science that they deny the reality of whatever cannot be weighed, counted, or measured. That science itself rests, as we shall see, upon a far-reaching act of faith, they have never stopped to notice. They deny the need or possibility of any metaphysical outlook whatsoever. Still other opponents of religion consist of people who have broken with the orthodoxies in which they were reared, but are still chained to the assumption that the only religion worthy of the name is "the old-time religion" that was beaten into them in their impressionable years. Unable to accept that body of doctrine and practice, they insist that there is nothing at all in religion for them. Frequently, they justify their antagonism to religion in the name of science, blissfully unaware of the fact that science itself has progressed far beyond the materialistic views dominant a half century ago.

Besides, if we are to be entirely frank, it cannot be denied that there are some who derive pleasure from flouting the sensibilities of their conventional fellow men. A case in point is afforded by the tale of the old Jewish atheist in an East European village, who was wont to teach the falsity of religion to an admiring band of disciples. When the day of his death approached, he turned to them and said, "My dear pupils, now that I am at the threshold of death, I repent my past. I should like you to know that God is in Heaven and what Moses and the Sages taught was the truth." "Master," they exclaimed in astonishment, "What has happened? All your life you have emphasized how false the teaching of religion is, and now you recant!" "Far from it, my dear friends," the dying man answered, with a smile. "I am simply trying to prove that the Talmud is wrong even in its statement that 'Sinners do not repent, even on the threshold of death.'" Whatever the motivation, such orthodox opponents of religion will find little comfort in these pages.

Finally, there is another group who, far from being hostile to religion, are among its most pervid advocates. Many of them are men and women who, after years of indifference or hostility to religion, recently found their way back to a passionate faith in God, primarily because of the pressure of the multiple crises of our time. Because of the nature of their spiritual journey, most of them are probably unwilling to embark on another, hazardous intellectual adventure, to which this book is dedicated. For them, not objective truth, but subjective commitment, is all that matters. Now, existentialism has made a signal contribution to the revitalization of religion. It has revealed the dimension of depth in many an insight of Biblical thought. It has stressed the importance of undergoing religious experience rather than merely explicating religious concepts. It has underscored the truth that religion must be felt, not merely analyzed, that God must be sensed as a living presence, who is loved and obeyed, and not deduced as a great Abstraction, "sicklied o'er with the pale cast of thought." It has properly insisted that it is impossible to "prove" the existence of God; men cannot be argued into faith. It has reminded us that religion cannot be taught, it must be caught.

These are invaluable contributions to the life of our times, for which all lovers of religion must be grateful. Unfortunately, existentialism suffers from grave drawbacks, which are largely inherent in its virtues. All too often, it has vitiated its truths by exaggerating them. Frequently, its advocates are disillusioned veterans of secular faiths, "tired liberals" or disillusioned radicals. In the face of the complexities of modern life and the bitter frustrations of totalitarianism, they have lost their ardor for the struggle for a better world and have surrendered their confidence in men's capacity to conquer the evils of society through their own activity. They have therefore sought refuge in a God who is "totally other," whose kingdom is entirely beyond man's present arena of conflict and defeat. Their loss of faith in man seems to them to be the surest foundation for their new-found faith in God.

Their lack of confidence in man's efforts to rebuild the world is matched by their lack of respect for man's intellect as an instrument for understanding it. From a background of rationalistic disbelief in God they have made "the leap of faith" and decided that religion is possible only through the suspension of the rational. When confronted by a logical contradiction, they rechristen it a "paradox," and they regard it as an error of a "simplicistic" mind to strive after consistency of thought. They are convinced that any effort to discuss the ideas and beliefs of religion by the canons of reason is bound to prove fruitless.

Undoubtedly, the will to believe is fundamental to the religious life, but it cannot establish its dimensions and limits. We live in a miraculous and mysterious world that we can apprehend, even if we cannot fully comprehend it. A reasonable faith will recognize the bounds of man's reason and will necessarily go beyond it in its vision of reality, but it will not scorn reason or contradict it, for it remains man's indispensable guide.

There are several compelling grounds for honoring reason. What men's intelligence can discover about the world must be relevant to what lies beyond its ken, because the universe is one, so that what is known is a clue to what is unknown.

Moreover, if reason is disallowed in religion, men are bereft of the capacity to distinguish between truth and error, between a life-giving faith and the manifold perversions and counterfeits of religion. Hence the Hebrew Prophets, whose visions are basic to vital faith, and who were at the farthest possible remove from philosophers, spent at least as much of their energies in castigating false religion as in expounding true religion.

The claim is often advanced that the antirationalistic approach of existentialism is "Biblical religion," because the Scriptures do not argue their basic postulates about God and man. The contention is mistaken. It is true that the Biblical mode of thinking is different from the Socratic method. The Bible never seeks to·debate the existence of God, but only because no one in ancient times denied it, not even the heretic and the sinner. Being sensible men, the Prophets and Sages argued only those issues that were controversial in their day. Did the gods of the heathens live and rule? Can God be given physical representation? What reward is there in the virtuous life? Can man see God? Does God interfere in human affairs? Why do the wicked prosper and the righteous suffer? What are the destiny and role of Israel? On all these issues Biblical religion debated, questioned, and agonized, in its quest for a mature and vital faith. Because most of these questions are perennially alive, the Bible still speaks with matchless relevance to our generation. Some of our problems today admittedly go deeper, such as the very existence of God or the reign of law in the universe. That is all the more reason for not abandoning reason or despairing of it. The truth is that *les extrêmes se touchent*. The religious existentialist who insists that religious truth need not be rationally demonstrated is virtually at one with the antireligious thinker, who insists that religious teaching cannot be rationally justified.

The lack of respect for reason has another drawback. If religion is to be transmitted from one generation to another and communicated from one human being to his fellows, it must operate with the canons of rational discussion, for communication presupposes rationality. Unless there is a common universe of discourse, there can be no meeting of minds. If religion consists solely or even principally of indescribable experiences of the ineffable, there can be no community of belief and of action linking men together. All that can be hoped for is a scattered number of individuals, each caught up in his own experience, which he cannot describe to himself, let alone share with his fellow men. But it is precisely the social character of religion which has been most marked in all the great classical Western faiths, Judaism, Christianity, and Islam. The existence of a Sacred Scripture in all Western religion testifies both to the need and to the possibility of religious communication between men. Similarly, the creation of the institutions of the Synagogue, the Church, and the Mosque bears witness to the possibility and the need of establishing a religious community.

That is not all. The denial of the validity of reason and the lack of respect for man's capacities raise unanswerable problems with regard to the goodness of God. A world where man's efforts are doomed permanently to failure is hardly a world created by God who, according to *Genesis*, "saw all that He had made and behold, it was very good." A creature whose basic trait is sinfulness scarcely qualifies as the apex of God's creative power, fashioned in the image of his Maker and serving as God's copartner in the universe.

We recognize the important contributions which existentialism and crisis-theology have made to the revitalization of religion in our day. But the point of view of the present work is that of the mainstream of Western religion, which has long insisted that reason and faith are not antagonists, but partners in comprehending the world. This is not to suggest that we can take over ready-made the systems of an Aristotle, a Maimonides, or an Aquinas. We believe that what they achieved for their day, we must strive for in ours. For us, God and His world are not perpetually at war with one another. If God is in His place, all must ultimately be right with the world. Life can be meaningful, without our looking at existence through rose-tinted spectacles.

In sum, the present work is not likely to interest the untroubled believers who find traditional religion, the heritage of their ancestors, thoroughly adequate to their spiritual life. Nor is it likely to pierce the hard shell of dogmatic nonbelievers, whose orthodoxy of disbelief belies their pretensions to open-mindedness. Finally, it parts company with that earnest band of men and women who, through agony and doubt, have found their way back to religion, but who believe that the price of admission to the Temple is the surrender of reason, or at least its suspension, at the entrance. Varied as these groups are, they share the conviction that a deep and impassable chasm divides faith from reason, religion from science, and ancient wisdom from the modern temper. Hence, they conclude, each man must take his stand on one or another side of the barricade.

For whom *is* this book intended? It would seem that the circle of its potential readers is very restricted, particularly if we consult current theological fashions. Actually, the readers whom we have in mind are a vast number. Maimonides called them "the perplexed"; today we might perhaps better describe them as "the seekers." Since the twelfth century, when Maimonides wrote, the ranks of those who are sincerely troubled and are seeking to assay the validity of the religious answer to the riddle of existence have increased tremendously. They include untold numbers of men and women who are both sincere and intelligent, and are to be found both within the religious camp and without. There are those who, in greater or lesser degree, practise the religious way of life, whether out of ancestral piety or because of deeply ingrained habit, or out of a deep love for the ancient ways, but who are aware of the challenges posed by the modern world, in some of its noblest attitudes and deepest insights. Though they cleave to religious tradition, they are unwilling to withdraw from the world or resign from the twentieth century, both because they could not if they would, and they would not if they could. The travails of the age have not blinded them to its achievements and values. Yet they are in search of a rational basis for the practices which they observe and the deeply rooted emotional ties which they feel to their religious background.

On the other hand, there is a vast army of idealistic and knowledgeable men and women who feel themselves at home in the modern world, but who have found no place for themselves in organized religion. Yet they are aware of the doubts and confusions of our age, of its moral collapse and spiritual emptiness. They know that in the past traditional religion proved a source of strength and a beacon of light to men, guiding them safely between the shoals of folly and despair. They would like to discover whether this heritage can still have meaning for them, or whether its values have been dissipated or disproved. They see about them some of their contemporaries, who find light and delight in their faith, but they themselves stand outside the charmed circle into which they yearn to enter.

The present work is the record of a journey of rediscovery by one who believes that there is no necessary conflict between the heart and the mind, between faith and reason, between tradition and truth. On the contrary, for us, religion and the other great enterprises of the human spirit, science, philosophy, and art, are allies and not foes in man's struggle to attain humanity. We believe that the timeless truths of the past cannot be in conflict with the vital insights of the present. Liberalism has been defined as the conviction that all legitimate goals are in harmony with one another. In this basic sense, this book is an expression of religious liberalism.

It is our hope that its pages will reveal the life-giving values which are to be found in traditional religion, when it is interpreted with sympathy and insight.

Both groups of seekers, both those who stand within religion and without, are invited to discover whether the answers that one of their fellow men has found can help them in their quest. Their lot has been graphically described in a parable attributed to the founder of Hasidism, Israel Baal Shem Tov. A lively wedding dance is going on in a small village to the strains of the village fiddler. A totally deaf stranger comes accidentally upon the scene. Since no strains of the music reach his ears, and he notes the strange behavior of the guests, capering about and grimacing, he is persuaded that the villagers are mad. The analogy is obvious. Perhaps some of our fellow men who are troubled by the apparent chaos and meaninglessness of existence will pause and try to recapture the melody of faith which they have ceased to hear. If they succeed, they will experience anew the joy of the Psalmist in the Presence of God: "Thy laws have been a song to me in the house of my sojourning." The notes which we have here set down on paper will then take wing and be transmuted into music in the heart of the reader. This is our purpose—and our hope.

THE NATURE OF RELIGION

CHAPTER I

Why Religion?

One of the most pervasive signs of the temper of our time is the widespread interest that religion now elicits almost everywhere. Books, plays, radio and television programs dealing with religion, whether on a simple or on a sophisticated level, are exceedingly popular, some even attaining the ultimate glory of the best-seller lists. Serious periodicals, including literary and philosophical journals, are concerned with religion to a degree undreamt of two decades ago. The teaching of religion on college campuses has been expanded, and continues to interest an ever larger number of students. For the first time in our own century religion has become intellectually respectable. Outstanding religious thinkers, like Kierkegaard, Tillich, Niebuhr, Rosenzweig, Heschel, and Buber, to mention only a few, are read today by persons who, two decades ago, would have regarded all religion with scorn. It is equally symptomatic of our times that the rationalistic thinkers in religion, and particularly the advocates of naturalism and humanism, are at least for the moment in eclipse, while the exponents of the mystical and the ineffable enjoy the greatest prestige.

Americans are a practical people, and this new-found interest in religion is reflected in the increased growth of church membership in the country, both absolutely and proportionately. Thus, in 1850, only 16% of the American people were church members. As the frontier receded and established communities became the norm, the percentage continued to rise, reaching 36% in 1900. From 1900 to 1953 the process continued, so that at the end of the sixth decade of our century the percentage is in excess of sixty.

This expansion of church membership derives in large measure from social motives rather than from a new-found sense of religious commitment. This conclusion is clear from several facts that have been emphasized by many observers. The process of growth in church membership is not recent, but goes back at least a century. Hence it cannot be attributed entirely to the mood of crisis induced by the horrors of two World Wars or the perils of the atomic age. Moreover, the new interest in religion by broad masses of people is noticeable principally in America. It is considerably less marked in Great Britain, and is almost nonexistent on the Continent. Undoubtedly, the rise in church membership has been stimulated by the development of new suburban areas and the growth of smaller cities. As people have moved into suburbs and bought homes of their own, millions who previously lived in rented quarters in the cities, "enjoying" a kind of spiritual facelessness and anonymity, have sought a sense of status. Many who were formerly caught up in the maelstrom of the great cities are now eager to find an anchorage in their new communities. Nearly everywhere the church dominates the landscape as the central social institution. For this reason, as well as because of the desire to give their children some religious education, the new families, by the hundreds of thousands, have become church members.

Undoubtedly, there is a great measure of truth in this sociological interpretation, but it does not plumb the depths of the phenomenon, because it fails to ask some fundamental questions. Why is it that the house of worship is the central institution to which people gravitate, and not the community center, the fraternal order, the civic club, the parent-teachers' association, or even the local country club? Moreover, many of these "areas of settlement" are totally new, residential developments erected on recently vacated farm lands or even on filled-in soil. Here, obviously, no religious institutions pre-empt the scene. Why do the new families almost invariably, as the first step, create congregations, religious fellowships, rather than secular organizations? Granted that most families which join a congregation may be actuated by social reasons, or by the wish to participate in the "activities" sponsored by the institution. Yet even in the majority, there must be a religious nucleus alive in the social protoplasm, an impulse, however obscure, drawing them toward the spiritual content of the contemporary church and synagogue. As for the elite minority—and there is such a minority, too—they will be concerned not merely with social factors, but also with the cultural program of the institution, and of them at least a fraction will be interested in the religious message emanating from the pulpit, the lecture platform, and the study group.

Finally, in estimating the degree of genuine religious interest in the current "revival," another factor must be taken into account. It is obvious that to a large degree, when intellectuals become interested in the content of the religious tradition, they are slow to seek active affiliation with a church or synagogue. The reason most often assigned is that so much of the energies of modern religious institutions is spent in areas remote from religion, varying from social service to folk-dancing. But there are other hindrances as well. Often there are social lines and economic barriers not easily crossed by those coming from without. At times, considerable differences in cultural level prevail between the ranks of the faithful and those who have lost faith in doubt and yet are doubtful about faith. For reasons such as these, the search for God is often pursued with greater earnestness outside of the official precincts of religion than within its halls.

It is, therefore, clear that the extent of the revival of interest in religion in our time is both less and more than the statistical rise of congregational membership; it includes only part of the new affiliates, but also many more who have not signed any membership application.

This widely varied group of sensitive and intelligent men and women represents the saving grace of the contemporary return to religion and the ultimate hope for its genuine revival. What are the motivating factors that lead them to explore the resources of religious tradition? In a phrase, what are they seeking in religion?

First and foremost is *the quest for psychological security*. It is not a guarantee of personal safety they seek, but the assurance that the human adventure is no accident, destined to be wiped clean from the earth's surface. Our age had divested itself of the mantle of faith in what seemed the beginning of a perpetual springtime, only to stand shivering before the chills and blasts of an endless winter.

Let us hasten to point out that the religion which our age has lost was not the creed preached in the pulpits of church, cathedral, and synagogue. *That* faith had ceased to be a living and relevant reality for many modern men long before our day. At best, the pomp of ritual and the sonorities of Scripture were intended for decoration and not for use. The faith which really dominated the landscape of the Western world during the past half-century and more, and which now has crumbled, is the worship of science as the ultimate source of truth and the fountain of all good. The cornucopia of scientific discovery and technological advance made it easy not only for the unreflective masses, but for the intellectual leaders of the age as well, to look to science as the great god from whom all blessings flow. Whatever was not known, science would disclose; whatever was lacking, science would grant.

In our day, the tide of blessings has continued to flow, but it is dwarfed by a greater inundation of catastrophe, generated in the same kind of scientific laboratories. An earlier generation, perhaps more naive than ours, would have stood in silent awe before the miracle of the discovery of nuclear energy and would have seen in it a manifestation of the Divine. Had not the first words flashed across the telegraph by its inventor, Samuel F. B. Morse, been, "What hath God wrought!"? Instead, the birth of the atomic age was heralded by no paeans of thanksgiving, but by the horrors of Hiroshima and Nagasaki. Even the sense of wonder has been dwarfed by abject, helpless terror. It is noteworthy that the destructive capacities of atomic energy have been explored far more successfully and exploited far more effectively than have its peaceful uses, which are still largely in the blueprint stage.

This is no criticism of the scientific process or of its practitioners. By its very nature, science is concerned solely with the disinterested quest after truth, and not with the application of its results to human life. By the same token, it is not within its function or capacity to determine the goals of life, or to offer any assurance that they will be attained.

To achieve these purposes, many are turning to the area of religion, where men through the ages sought and found a basis for security. It is noteworthy that in Hebrew *bitahon* means both "security" and "faith." It is a truism today that the power of mankind to manipulate the forces of nature has so outdistanced its capacity to govern its own impulses that the survival of the race is in peril. Men desperately want to believe that the fate of mankind is not entirely dependent on the blunders, follies, and crimes of the pygmies all too often ensconced in the seats of the mighty. Even if as individuals men are doomed to perish, they want to know that humanity will endure, and that the dreams and ideals by which men live are no wraiths of the imagination, doomed to dissolve like smoke.

To be sure, not all men yearn for this assurance. A contrary conviction about life was expressed by Bertrand Russell with rare eloquence and pathos:

> "Brief and powerless is Man's life; on him and all his race the slow, sure doom falls, pitiless and dark. Blind to good and evil, reckless of destruction, omnipotent matter rolls on its relentless way; for Man, condemned today to lose his dearest, tomorrow himself to pass through the gate of darkness, it remains only to cherish, ere yet the blow falls, the lofty thoughts that ennoble his little day; disdaining the coward terrors of the slave of Fate, to worship at the shrine that his own hands have built, undismayed by the empire of chance, to preserve a mind free from the wanton tyranny that rules his outward life; proudly defiant of the irresistible forces that tolerate, for a moment, his knowledge and his condemnation, to sustain alone, a weary but unyielding Atlas, the world that his own ideals have fashioned despite the trampling march of unconscious power" (*A Free Man's Worship*).

Its sonorities aside, Russell's position suffers from inherent logical difficulties, which will be discussed elsewhere in this volume. These are not our concern at this point. What should be noted here is its psychological weakness, its inadequacy as a viable philosophy for mankind. Undoubtedly, some few men can extract a grim comfort from the spectacle of inevitable doom confronting man's hopes, and can derive an ethic of compassion from the vision of man's destiny as meaningless and endless suffering. But most men cannot live permanently in a state of glorified despair. They are not likely to be nerved to struggle and sacrifice, unless they have the conviction that their martyrdom and agony are not in vain.

Heroism, particularly in the face of defeat, is at best a rare trait. But the universal testimony of experience is that the martyr is sustained by the conviction that, ultimately if not now, his cause will be vindicated. Job, surrounded by uncomprehending friends, cried out in the hour of his agony:

> "I know that my Redeemer liveth,
> Though He be the last to arise upon earth."

Joan of Arc, condemned by the Church, whose loyal daughter she felt herself to be, went to the stake convinced that the cause of a liberated France would triumph, because that was God's will. The nameless masses, murdered in the Nazi crematoria, fashioned a tragic song that served as their death march, from the words of Maimonides' creed:

> "I believe with a perfect faith that the Messiah will come,
> and though he tarry, yet will I daily await his coming."

Through the ages, men have found that religious faith alone could bring to them this security, this sense of the permanent behind the flux of life, this assurance of the triumph of the ideal. In the words of the Psalmist, "The Lord is my light and my life; whom shall I fear? the Lord is the fortress of my life; of whom shall I be afraid?"

Confronted by fears unimagined by the Psalmist, modern intelligent people are therefore led to ask themselves whether faith in God is possible for them. Such a faith becomes more than a distant hope, once men disabuse themselves of the error of believing that only that which can be weighed and measured is real. The crucial step is to recognize that what counts in life usually cannot be counted.

A second goal impels men to turn to religion—*the deeply felt need for a satisfying philosophy of life.* They are beginning to discover, after a long period of neglect and even of scorn, that the insights of religion are indispensable for a world-view by which they can live. It should not be necessary to argue that in building one's vision of reality, the conclusions and methods of science play a basic role, so that any religious system which turns its back on science, however emotionally satisfying it may appear to be, will ultimately prove stultifying and self-defeating. It is, however, important to understand both the functions and the limitations of science. For the purpose of mastering the complexities of the universe, science divides the world into distinct areas, such as astronomy, geology, physics, chemistry, biology, and many others. After decades and centuries of dedicated and brilliant investigation in his chosen field, the scientist is able to point to a substantial body of information. This material, however, is not of uniform value. Much of it is undoubtedly true, some is doubtful, while other elements, now accepted as valid, will turn out to be mistaken. Finally, there is a considerable area where the scientist still stands on the frontier and has not succeeded in bringing it into the domain of law and order. As scientific progress continues, the contents within each category, the known, the doubtful, the erroneous, and the unknown, continue to change, but the categories themselves remain permanent features of the landscape. This is true, because each new scientific discovery solves some problem, to be sure, but opens up new, previously unsuspected vistas of the unknown. Not only is *ignoramus*, "we do not know," a constant of the human situation, but also *ignorabimus*, "we shall not know," the conviction that the totality of the universe will continue to elude man's intellectual grasp.

That is not all. The necessary specialization of science, without which its progress would be impossible, exacts a heavy price. One of the great problems of our time is the fact that the various disciplines find it increasingly difficult to communicate with one another. This creates scientific problems of the first magnitude, and efforts are therefore being made to bridge the gaps by means of "frontier sciences" like biochemistry and biophysics. Yet each of these new disciplines, valuable as it is, simply becomes another unit in the seemingly endless series of research specialties that amass details in the portrait of the universe, but complicate the task of seeing the total pattern. The result is that man, who is an integral and organic unit, finds himself confronted by a plethora of knowledge and a dearth of wisdom. Life must be lived in the world as a whole, not in the limited area of biology or physics or psychology, into which the scientist must divide reality for purposes of analysis. At best, science can supply the bricks for the edifice of a world view; it cannot serve as the architect.

Finally, each man living in the here and now must achieve an outlook on life that will encompass chaos as well as cosmos, tragedy as well as joy. He must evolve an approach to life which will make it possible for him not only to accept the elements of the world

that "make sense" because they are rational and pleasant, but also
to come to terms with those aspects which are negative and painful,
impossible to grasp and all but impossible to bear. Living beings
cannot always be drinking of the cup of self-fulfillment and joy;
frustration, suffering, and death are universal elements in experience.
Indeed, for most men the shadows linger longer than the sunlight.

In sum, the facts supplied by science constitute a necessary, but
not a sufficient, condition for constructing a world-view. In other
words, after the scientist has completed his work, each man, scientist and layman alike, is faced by the task of evolving his personal
philosophy of life. The problems posed by the mutual relationship
of science, philosophy, and religion will be elucidated below. Let
it be noted here that increasing numbers of men and women today
are asking whether the insights of religious tradition, in whole or
in part, cannot help to create a philosophy by which they can live,
work, and hope, in the face of the chaos and peril of the age.

Perhaps the most powerful motivation for the religious quest
today lies in *the desire to find a firm basis for ethical standards.*
Immorality, in all its protean forms, is no modern invention, but
in the past the generality of men, including the sinners themselves,
knew right from wrong and thus had a firm basis for holding themselves and their neighbors accountable in judgment. One of the
hallmarks of the modern age is the increase in the number of men
who lack any moral convictions, any belief in the existence of
ethical standards, by which they could evaluate the acts of individuals and of nations. To expect science to discover ethical standards betrays anew a failure to comprehend the character of science.
Its function is fulfilled in the elucidation of reality, which includes
both the natural world and the data of human experience. To achieve
its purpose, science must be morally neutral in its approach. Many
scientists, as we know, have been stricken with remorse at their
contribution to the development of nuclear weapons and the wholesale destruction that has been wrought. Their emotions are understandable, yet the guilt is not theirs. The physicist in his work
on the atomic bomb is not a whit more immoral than the biologist
seeking a cure for cancer. What society does with the results of
scientific discovery is not the responsibility of science, which is
governed by only one moral principle: loyalty to the truth. To

demand that science be held responsible for the uses to which its results are put by society is as fatuous as to demand that music stimulate moral behavior, that poetry advance social reform, and that arithmetic make men honest.

The amoral character of science, however, makes it a superb servant but a dangerous master. It is like a high-powered automobile that can bring us swiftly where we wish to go, but obviously cannot determine where we ought to go. Which goals in life are worth while? What is the ideal man? What traits are to be cultivated in men, and which are to be redirected or restricted? What are the qualities of the ideal society, and what means shall be adopted for approaching the goal? On all these questions science, *qua* science, can have no answer.

Does that mean that science has no contribution to make to the good life? Far from it. The one ethical imperative on which science is based, the love of truth for its own sake, is one of the noblest of all human attributes, raising men above the accidents of their personal destinies, breaking down the barriers of race, nation, and class, creating a universal fellowship of humanity. This is a unique ethical achievement.

Moreover, science makes one other invaluable contribution to morality by indicating the true nature of man and his world. It thus stakes out the boundaries within which man must live and function. In other words, science performs the negative, but indispensable, function of demonstrating that certain proposed goals are impractical or unnatural or harmful, because of the character of the world or of man.

Beyond indicating these broad limits, however, science has no answer as to the goals of human behavior. Is the active life the highest good, because "to live is to function," as Justice Oliver Wendell Holmes declared, or is life an illusion to be avoided and is activity to be minimized in favor of passive meditation? Should man's ultimate goal be his self-fulfillment as an individual, or the interests of the group? Should man's highest loyalty be given to his family, his class, or his nation, or to the higher rung of humanity? On all these questions the scientist, as a human being, will undoubtedly have his opinions, but science *per se* has no decisive answer to give. At best it can offer some hints. Even on so fundamental a question as to whether or not there are direction and meaning in the evolutionary process, qualified scientists quite legitimately can differ. The divergence lies not in the content of the data but in their interpretation.

That science is a morally neutral enterprise is clear from the fact that substantial research was carried on even in Nazi Germany, as is emphatically the case in Communist Russia today, as well as in the lands of the democratic West. Some of the most extensive investigations on the physical and mental limits of human endurance were conducted by accredited scientists in the horrible laboratories of the Nazi crematoria.

Since anthropologists have revealed a vast variety of moral standards and customary behavior among the peoples whom they studied, those who look to science as the great arbiter have often drawn the conclusion that right and wrong are merely matters of social convention, that morality is no more than *mores*, the customs and taboos of a particular society. The rise of totalitarianism disclosed the ominous consequences of this approach. Hitler and Stalin used the same ethical vocabulary as the democratic West, except that "truth," "justice," and "freedom" were equated with whatever advanced the might of the state or furthered the interests of the dictatorship of the proletariat. Concepts such as "kindness," "pity," "fair play," and "sympathy" were completely eliminated from the moral code. "Virtue" and "sin," being heavily drenched in religious associations, were the first to be expunged from the modern vocabulary, but "right" and "wrong" were not far behind. When the Nazi-Communist pact was signed in 1939, it was possible for Molotov to justify the act by saying that "fascism is a matter of taste." In spite of the Latin proverb which declares that there is no arguing over tastes, here was a matter of life and death over which men disputed bloodily—an indescribable World War, half a dozen smaller conflicts since that time, with thirty million casualties, and a world poised on the brink of a third world holocaust, as the results to date. As Malcolm Cowley wrote: "That 'modern' world to which we have grown accustomed and which lasted for such a brief moment of history—that world where evil had apparently ceased to exist, where sin was explained as maladjustment and there was nothing that could not be cured by gland extracts, vitamins and psychoanalysis . . . that world has been utterly destroyed by the German invasions. Hitler's bombs and his broken promises have taught us to believe in virtue again, by restoring our faith in evil."

Where shall a basis for ethical behavior be sought? Looking upon the collapse of international morality and the wholesale decline of moral standards at home, men are beginning to discover that there is nothing innate about the so-called basic human virtues. Elementary decency, love of justice, devotion to the truth, consideration for the weak, a sense of personal honor, a hatred of cruelty, a respect for human personality, opposition to vandalism and genocide—these and similar qualities had long been taken for granted as inborn in all men. The tragic history of the twentieth century has shown that far from being "self-evident" or "natural," these ethical norms represent the precious distillation of the religious ideals cherished by past generations. Our modern age has been the spendthrift heir of virtuous, hard-working ancestors, who created the heritage that their children have now all but squandered. All the decencies of human nature today were nurtured by the creeds of yesterday. Justice, mercy, and truth became human imperatives, because they were felt to be the attributes of God, whom men were commanded to imitate. Ethical culture is possible only in a soil rendered fertile earlier by religious faith.

Modern science suggests a parable. According to the astronomers, there are stars in the heavens, located many millions of light years away, that have disintegrated in the past and ceased to be. Yet the light rays of those stars are still traveling toward the earth, so that men see what no longer exists. At last, however, the final beams from those stars reach the earth and then there is darkest night. So, too, in the modern world, men have continued for a spell to walk by the light emanating from the star of faith that had ceased to exist for them. All too often, they have been heedless of the fact that their moral standards derived from habits of thought and patterns of action inculcated by religion and that these values could survive the decay of faith only for the brief interval of a generation or two or less. Now the period of grace is past and the all-encompassing darkness has descended upon our generation.

The frightening reality of proliferating evil has persuaded growing numbers of men that a firm basis for moral striving must be found, if life itself is to survive on anything beyond the animal level. Men are accordingly seeking a basis for ethical living where it has traditionally been anchored, in religious faith.

These are the three basic motivations for the new interest in religion in our time. Men are seeking support for the hope that humanity is not poised on the brink of annihilation. They are seeking to buttress the faith that the human adventure will not end, either in a bang or in a whimper. Moreover, they are searching for the assurance, which undergirds all the religious and ethical systems of mankind, that man is not alone in a meaningless, unfeeling universe, and that morality is not an invention of man, but his discovery of a law of life, which is rooted in the cosmos and therefore destined to emerge victorious. Finally, it is only such a faith that can give men the courage to sacrifice for the good life and to do battle for the right.

The quest for a clear-eyed yet hopeful view of life, both for the individual and for society, that will see the forest as well as the trees, is not simple; there are many pitfalls along the way. Yet as we explore the resources of religion, we may hope to discover how such a goal can be attained and man may fulfill his destiny. It is true that each of us must build his own sanctuary of the spirit. Yet each man's personal testament of faith may prove helpful to his neighbor. It is my deepest conviction that these objectives may be found within religion, if we approach its altar with openness of mind and humility of spirit. Nor is there any need to divorce the mind from the heart, to isolate faith from reason, or to insulate religion from the other great enterprises of the human spirit. Those who are alive in the twentieth century, in spirit as well as in time, have it within their power to achieve a faith by which to live.

CHAPTER II

The Sins of Religion

We have noted the vast increase of interest in religion in our day and the powerful motives that have led men to seek to discover its message. It is, however, a far cry from an attitude of respect for religious teaching, on the one hand, to a personal commitment to religious living on the other. It is hard enough to change long-cherished views, especially if all the forces of one's environment conspire against it. To transform the pattern of one's life, by breaking long-established habits and creating new and unfamiliar modes of behavior, requires nothing less than a gigantic spiritual revolution. Of this, relatively few men are capable.

The Talmud, which declares that even the wholly righteous cannot attain to the level of the penitent, is at one with the New Testament parable which teaches that the shepherd rejoices over the one sheep that has strayed and been restored more than over the ninety-nine in the flock that have never wandered away. Such passages bear witness to the excruciating agony involved in inner reconstruction. To "return," especially to a spiritual home which many modern men never knew at first hand, requires not only intellectual courage, but also ethical attributes of great rarity. It is not enough to be logically convinced that there is greater wisdom in the old paths than on the new highways; one needs also profound humility and strength of will to make the turn. In this fearsome battle of the soul, each man must fight alone. Little can be done to aid him, except perhaps to clear some obstacles from the way.

Such a road-block, confronting many sincere and intelligent

persons as they struggle to achieve a living, active faith, is the tremendous chasm that yawns between religion in theory and in reality. The preachments of religion, as embodied in its sacred Scriptures, its world-view, and its ethical imperatives, seem noble and persuasive. But the practice of religion, as seen in human experience, both past and present, stands in tragic contrast to its pretensions. That religion as an ideal is beautiful may be granted, but the evidence is impressive that as a reality it has all too often served as an obstacle to human progress.

Religion may be dedicated to the worship of God, but Rabelais' old couplet about the Devil seems more applicable to its role in human life:

> "The Devil was sick—the Devil a monk would be,
> The Devil was well—the devil a monk was he!"

It is not difficult to draw up a powerful bill of indictment against religion as a force in history. It is undeniable that war through the ages has been blessed by virtually every religion. In the Biblical period, the Israelites carried the Ark of the Covenant forward against the enemy in battle; the classic Hebrew phrase for "declaring war" is to "sanctify war." The young Mohammedan religion swept across Asia and Africa and stormed the citadel of Europe, offering to the conquered population the choice of the Book or the Sword. Its fanaticism is far from spent today. Christianity, too, is not free from guilt. The religion of the "Prince of Peace" has a long record of violence and destruction to atone for. The Crusades proved a significant milestone in history, but both their conscious motivation and their direct results were a human holocaust for the glory of God. The Crusades were initiated by massacres of the age-old Jewish communities of the Rhineland, were accompanied by the death en route of untold thousands of Crusaders through disease and hunger long before Palestine was reached, and were climaxed by centuries of warfare in the Holy Land. The Thirty Years' War between the two chief branches of the Christian church devastated Germany and embroiled much of Europe for three decades, from 1618 to 1648.

Closely allied to the blessing of war by religion has been its fomenting of persecution and intolerance. Not only were campaigns organized against the infidel Turks in the Holy Land, but the Catholic Church carried out crusades of extermination against the Christian sect of the Albigenses in 1229 and all but decimated the Waldenses for maintaining heretical doctrines. On St. Bartholomew's Day in 1572, some 10,000 of the Protestant leaders of France were massacred in a massive blood bath that saved France for the Catholic Church. The Bohemian Reformer John Huss had been given a solemn safe-conduct by the Emperor Sigismund, so that he might present his case before the Council of Constance in 1415. But the Emperor was assured by his spiritual advisers that a promise made to a heretic was not binding, and Huss was seized and burnt at the stake for his ideas. Even the dead were not safe. During his lifetime, John Wyclif, the translator of the Bible into English, had powerful protectors, but in 1428, forty-four years after his death, church officials exhumed his bones and burnt his remains. The Inquisition has long been a byword for unrelenting cruelty set in motion by religious fanaticism. To be sure, the Church was technically guiltless of the blood of its victims. Moved by "love" for the heretics and by the zeal to save their souls, it turned over the living bodies of thousands of men, women, and children to the secular arm of the State for torture and burning. The ten-volume *History of the Inquisition,* by Henry C. Lea, is a tragic record of man's cruelty to man induced by the love of God.

Nor is this sorry record limited to any single religion. During the greater portion of its history, Judaism was the religion of a people in exile, and hence too weak to enforce its way of life upon others, even if it had been so minded. But during the brief heyday of Jewish independence achieved by the Maccabees (142–63 B.C.E.), the Jewish king, John Hyrcanus, and his son Aristobulus, forcibly compelled the Edomites in the south and the Gentile inhabitants of the Galilean cities in the north to accept Judaism as their faith.

In our irreligious age, persecution in the name of religion has given way to newer motives. Yet even in the twentieth century it is not dead. During the period of the Mussolini-Hitler pact, the fascist regime of Anton Pavelik was set up in Yugoslavia with the blessing of Archbishop Aloysius Stepinac, who offered three choices to the Serbs: to accept the Catholic faith, or to "move out" (of Croatia), or "to be cleansed with the metal broom" (i.e., to be shot). In his report to the Vatican on May 8, 1944, he announced that 240,000 Serbs had been converted as a result of his zeal.

The number of Jewish children sheltered in non-Jewish homes during the fury of Nazi persecution will probably never be known. It represents one of the brighter pages in the dark history of twentieth-century man. Yet even upon these episodes of light some shadows have fallen. In many instances these children were raised in the dominant faith and thereafter prevented from returning to their people and family. The case of Robert Finaly in France, in which the child was forcibly denied to his relatives, became a cause célèbre, but it is not unique.

The most striking instance of the role of religion in fomenting persecution is afforded by the ubiquitous social disease of antisemitism. In recent years, the phenomenon has been subjected to study from every conceivable angle. It is clear that its virulence derives from the fact that it goes back to no simple or superficial cause. Antisemitism is a complex of psychological, religious, social, economic, and cultural factors. In part it is the result of genuine prejudice, but it has been stimulated not a little by the cynical charlatanism and the cold-blooded self-interest of individuals and groups who seek to ride to power and wealth by setting the demon loose. With so complicated and deep-seated an etiology, it is no wonder that antisemitism does not easily yield to social therapy.

In this complex of evil, it cannot be denied, organized Christianity has played a large role, stimulating and maintaining anti-Jewish prejudice, even if it did not create it. Countless efforts have been made by scholars to refute the charge that the Jews are responsible for the death of Jesus, on the basis of evidence adduced from the political, religious, and social conditions of Palestine in the Second Temple period. It has been pointed out that the Jews lacked the motive, the means, or the opportunity for executing a religious dissenter. Moreover, Jesus' religious ideas probably differed less from normative Judaism than did those of many other Jewish groups and sects, upon whom attention has been focussed anew by the discovery of the Dead Sea Scrolls. Apostles of good will have sought to stress the obvious truth that not only Jesus' opponents, but all his disciples, were Jews. Nonetheless, the cry of "Christ-killer" still continues to reverberate through time. One recalls the bitterly ironic remark of Israel Zangwill that many a Christian who does not believe that Jesus ever existed is sure that the Jews killed him! Studies by Drew University and other institutions have demonstrated that the deeds of prejudice are often sown for many well-meaning Christians in their Sunday school instruction, which they never outgrow.

In our modern age, secular rather than religious factors seem to predominate in antisemitism. Nonetheless, the religious source of prejudice is far from extinct. In 1952, nearly a decade after Hitler, when the Austrian League for Human Rights appealed to Cardinal Theodore Innitzer of Vienna, to remove from some churches in the Tyrol tablets and paintings which depicted Jews as using blood for the Passover ritual, he referred the matter to the local Bishop Rusch of Innsbruck, who answered that "the Jews have not yet proved that they never did such a thing." The Church can point to many great-souled leaders and followers who have nobly sought to atone for such darker phases by their heroism, sacrifice, and genuine love for their fellow men, but the record of the past cannot be entirely blotted out.

The indictment against religion is not limited to its contribution to war, persecution, and intolerance. In a casual review of a book on law, an obscure writer, a century ago, struck off a phrase that has not been forgotten. Religion, Karl Marx declared, is the opiate of the people. The epigram has persisted because it cannot easily be dismissed as false. All too often organized religion has served as an instrument for social exploitation and political tyranny. More than once, the teacher of religion has stood side by side with the oppressor, casting a halo of sanctity over the tyrant's misdeeds and teaching the people that submission to evil is the will of God. Every student of French history knows of the extensive line of privileges and emoluments enjoyed by the Church, along with the nobility. In Czarist Russia the Greek Orthodox Church taught the peasant that he owed reverence equally to the Great Father in Heaven and to the "Little Father" in the Kremlin. It has been maintained that the habit of total obedience to tyranny which seems to characterize the Russian people under communism became ingrained in the national character by centuries of religious indoctrination. The close alliance of the Church with Franco, and its role as one of the great landowners in poverty-stricken Spain, need no documentation today. In our own country the flag and the cross are among the two most popular symbols used by reactionary groups and agencies.

Moreover, organized religion has again and again opposed scientific progress. In the Middle Ages the Church was strongly hostile to the translation of the Bible into the vernaculars of Europe. The fate of John Huss and of John Wyclif has already been referred to. The classic instance is that of Galileo, imprisoned by the Inquisition for daring to suggest that the earth moved around the sun, murmuring under his breath, as he recanted, *e pur si muove*, "And yet it moves." To avoid a similar fate, the publication of the findings of Copernicus, the father of modern astronomy, was delayed for a half a century until after he was dead. With the weakening of the power of organized religion since the eighteenth century has come a lessening of its ability to hinder scientific progress. The Scopes trial in Tennessee was a tragicomic epilogue to a bitter struggle that had been waged for centuries.

This bill of particulars against the role of religion in human affairs could be extended with little difficulty. That the indictment is true, every fair-minded observer will be compelled to admit. But, as is often the case, it is not the whole truth, and half a truth is often worse than none. It would be extremely shortsighted if, after the prosecution was heard, the case were to be closed and the hasty verdict handed down that religion is a bad business.

Even before any defense is attempted, a few considerations ought to be made clear. In the first instance, the religious believer has no obligation to defend all manifestations of religion in history, any more than a lover of literature, music, or art is called upon to praise every poem, song, or painting that has been created. To believe in religion does not mean to declare that all religions are true or even that everything in any given religion is good. Apologists for religion who have failed to recognize this truth have done their cause no service. By distorting the record, they have left religion vulnerable to the charge that it is an enemy of progress. Even if the origin of religion is divine, its conduct and organization are human, with the well-known propensity of men to error and sin. There is no need, therefore, either to deny or to minimize the sins of religion throughout history. The greatest exemplars of religion the world has ever known, the Prophets of Israel, spent at least as much energy castigating the wrongs of religion as in expounding its truths.

It should be conceded, freely and honestly, that all religions during their checkered history have been guilty of grave offenses against the human spirit and by that token have sinned against the Divine Presence, to which they owe allegiance. But, like any defendant before the bar of judgment, religion deserves to be viewed in its proper perspective.

Here a basic consideration should be noted—very often religion has been the instrument of evil, but not its cause. Ours is an age when religion has lost much of its influence and even more of its power. This has not led to a reduction in the sway of evil in our time. All that has happened is that today evil tends to be secular in motivation and expression. Compared to Nazism, the worst forms of religious persecution and massacre in the past seem almost idyllic. The Kishineff pogroms in 1903, which aroused the indignation of the civilized world, were organized by the Czarist regime as a diversionary tactic and enjoyed the blessings of the priests of the Greek Orthodox Church. The total casualties were forty-five dead and five hundred and eighty-six wounded. How these riots pale into insignificance in comparison with the cold-blooded, systematic destruction of 175,000 human beings in the Nazi gas-chambers in Dachau alone! During its history extending over several centuries, the Inquisition encompassed the death or torture of several thousand men and women. Contrast this with the meteoric career of Nazism which, within two decades, brought about the murder of millions. Communist dictatorships have slain hundreds of thousands and condemned millions more to slave-camps and lifelong imprisonment. The motivation of modern totalitarianism is violently anti-religious, seeking to justify its practices by the pseudo-scientific theory of race in one case and by the doctrine of the dictatorship of the proletariat in the other. No one will rightly condemn science because of its perversion by the totalitarians. So, too, religion cannot justly be held accountable for the perversion of its insights by the practitioners of bigotry and ill-will, whether past or present.

Religion, it is true, has not only been used to bless war, but has served in ancient and medieval times both as a cause and as a pretext for war. The roots of modern war, on the other hand, are undisguisedly nationalistic and economic in character, and the fruits are indescribably more horrible than in past conflicts.

In sum, oppression and fanaticism are not monopolies of religion. They are coefficients of the lust for power from which few men are free. We may meet it in a Cardinal Richelieu, to be sure, but not because he is a Prince of the Church—simply because he is human. The Biblical sage, Ecclesiastes, had noted this tragic proclivity of human nature long ago: "This too have I seen under the sun, where one man rules over his brother to do him harm." The root of the evil, both within religion and without, was expressed by Lord Acton in a historical axiom that has become a truism: "Power corrupts, and absolute power tends to corrupt absolutely."

Why has religion so often been in alliance with the powers of oppression? The answer lies in its strong hold on the souls of men. The tyrant will use every available instrument to rule the spirit of his victims, the more effectively to enslave their bodies. For centuries religion constituted virtually the entire world-view of the masses. No other instrument could prove so efficacious in keeping them contented with their lot, particularly since religion offered the consolations of a happier existence in the world beyond. For all its bitter sarcasm, the old I. W. W. song reflected fairly this role of religion:

> "By and by,
> You'll eat pie,
> In the sky."

Even today, religion possesses tremendous power, but it is no longer the only expression of group-culture. Tyrants and dictators will therefore use the school system, the press, the radio, literature, the arts, and, above all, national patriotism to buttress their position of power. The remedy for the abuse of culture is obviously not the abolition of culture. Similarly, in the area of faith. Religion is not the opiate of the people; it *may be*, and often has been, a drug, but its role depends upon the people and the religion in question.

We have cited the sins of religion in the indictment; it is only fair to note that religion has also been a powerful force for good. From its inception, religion was the mother of the arts and sciences. Astronomy and geometry were first cultivated by the priests in the Nile and Euphrates Valleys. The art of writing, the origins of which are veiled in obscurity, was almost surely an invention of the priests and it long remained virtually their monopoly. The word "theatre" still reminds us that drama was originally part of the ritual of the Greek religion, dedicated to the Olympian gods and the myths which enshrined their deeds. In the chaos of the Middle Ages, it was the Christian monks who copied and thus preserved the great classics of antiquity, secular as well as religious. The text of the Hebrew Bible was safeguarded against corruption by the labors of untold nameless scholars called the Masoretes, who erected a dike against the flood of changes and errors that would have inundated the text of Scripture. The ancient Biblical manuscripts recently discovered among the Dead Sea Scrolls have underscored the yeoman achievement of those Guardians of Tradition whose pious labors extended over a thousand years and to whom the world owes the preservation of the Book of Books. It would be interesting to survey the contribution that both the Catholic and Protestant Churches have made to human culture by providing "livings" for the clergy, thus making it possible for gifted sons of the lower and middle classes to have both the leisure and the education for creative work in literature, music, art, and science. In Judaism, the relationship between religion and culture is organic. "Rabbi" means "master, teacher," and the basic concept, *Torah*, is untranslatable, embracing law, lore and learning, culture and faith. Divine in origin, Torah is constantly enriched by man's activity.

As against the use of religion to buttress privilege and oppression there must be set its role as a valiant force for freedom. Not only the prophet and the preacher, but many a revolutionary leader as well, drew his inspiration from religion and spoke in the name of God. In the preface to his translation of Scripture, Wyclif declares that "the Bible believes in government of the people, for the people, and by the people," four hundred years before the phrase was used by Abraham Lincoln, who was himself molded principally by the Book.

The close relationship of religion and democracy in American history has been frequently pointed out. The Puritan motto declared: "Rebellion to tyrants means obedience to God." When a seal for the United States was under discussion in Congress, a committee consisting of John Adams, Benjamin Franklin, and Thomas Jefferson proposed the adoption of this apothegm, together with a scene depicting the escape of the Israelites and the destruction of their Egyptian pursuers at the Red Sea. The Puritans have been described as "Old Testament Christians," because they sought to build their polity on the basis of the Hebrew Book, with its unmistakable emphasis upon freedom from subjection to man as the right of all God's children. The emergence of American political institutions testifies to the truth of W. H. Lecky's frequently quoted words, "Hebraic mortar cemented the foundations of American democracy." When the American Revolution broke out, it was the book of *Exodus* to which the Founding Fathers of the American Revolution turned for inspiration and hope, comparing George Washington to Moses, George III to Pharaoh, the British to the Egyptians, and the Atlantic Ocean to the Red Sea.

The Bible has been a source of inspiration in the far-flung struggle for human liberation on many fronts. The enslaved Negro on the Southern plantation undoubtedly found it easier to bear his lot because of his simple faith in the hereafter, but he also drew courage to await ultimate liberation on earth from the Biblical saga of Moses and the Exodus, which he recalled in the moving spiritual:

> "When Israel was in Egypt land,
>   Let my people go,
>   Oppressed so hard they could not stand,
>   Let my people go."

The deeply moving spectacle of dignity and courage which American Negroes are setting before the world in their present struggle against segregation owes much to religion both in its inspiration and its mode of expression.

A Jewish contemporary of Marx, Moses Hess, wrote a work, *Rome and Jerusalem*, which appeared in 1862 and was all but forgotten, because it appeared before its time. In this book, Hess proposed a synthesis of the noblest features of Biblical religion, social justice, democracy, and ethical nationalism, all of which he traced back with substantial reason to the Prophets of Israel. The American social reformer, Henry George, creator of the single-tax philosophy, selected for the fly-leaf of his well-known work, *Progress and Poverty*, the great verse of *Leviticus* (25:23): "The land shall not be sold in perpetuity, for the land is Mine, and ye are but dwellers and sojourners with Me." This verse occurs in a chapter setting forth a far-reaching program of social legislation designed to prevent the concentration of wealth in the hands of a few and the expropriation of the many. It is significant that this section is to be found not in the Prophets, but in the Law, which was the province of the priests, the "professional" custodians of religion. Eighteen centuries before Henry George, Rabban Johanan ben Zakkai, who maintained that all human bondage was an affront to the Sovereignty of God, found scriptural warrant for his view in another verse in the same chapter (*Lev.* 25:55): "'For unto Me the children of Israel are servants'—and not servants unto servants! (i.e. human beings)."

It is undeniable that in the period since the French Revolution, when religion began retreating from its position of centrality in human life, its active zeal for righteousness in society has abated more than a little. Its energies have largely been absorbed in the struggle for its own survival. Yet the emergence of the "social gospel" in the first decades of the twentieth century bears witness to the enduring vitality of this emphasis in the tradition. With the appearance in our day of the new tyranny of totalitarianism, red, brown, and black, religion has emerged with new vigor as the champion of the freedom of man, which is rooted in the Fatherhood of God. The innate dignity of every man, the absolute sanctity of the individual, the equality of all races, and man's inalienable right to freedom as well as justice in God's world—all these seemed platitudes in the halcyon days before the First World War, but have become searing truths in this age of crisis. These principles have been rooted in religious teaching and have often been defended by religious spokesmen with vigor and courage, even when victory seemed hopeless.

Indeed, religion has been one of the few bulwarks left to defend human dignity and freedom in this age of the tyranny of the monolithic state. During the days of the Second World War, when President Franklin D. Roosevelt was asked to define the issues of the conflict, he answered: "We are fighting on behalf of one verse of the Book of Genesis: 'God created man in his own image'." This conviction was no mere homiletical conceit. Albert Einstein has been cited as saying, "When the Nazis came to power, I looked to the German universities to speak out, but they were silent. I turned to the press, but there was no word from them. I turned to the great labor unions, but found them speechless as well. Only in the church, which I had completely dismissed, were valiant voices raised to speak out on behalf of the freedom of man." In the bitter struggle waged in South Africa to depress and isolate the "non-white" population permanently, the only force among the white settlers that has spoken out with any vigor against the policies of "apartheid" has been the Anglican Church.

The role of the Church in Europe and Africa has its parallels in America. Before the tide of repression began to recede in America, it was the Federal Council of the Churches of Christ, the Central Conference of American Rabbis, the Rabbinical Assembly of America, and similar bodies that dared to speak out against the menace of McCarthyism. A constructive role is being played by organized religion in the long and complex struggle for desegregation in the South. Undoubtedly, many Southerners are heartily opposed to the myth of "white supremacy," but few have dared to speak out, for thoroughly understandable reasons. The Roman Catholic Church, however, was the first strong voice that denounced Jim Crowism in its churches and schools and that has remained determined to uphold its doctrine of human equality. Protestant ministers and Jewish rabbis in the South have been among the leaders in the struggle for justice and sanity. Undoubtedly, most churchmen, being men, are heir to all the weaknesses and prejudices of their fellows. It is therefore understandable why the majority remains inert. What is significant is that religion is the source and shelter of the saving minority.

We can now grasp the full truth with regard to the role of religion in human history. Both the indictment and the defense are justified—religion has been an instrument for reaction, as well as a force for progress, a defender of tyranny and darkness, but also a stimulus to freedom and light.

What explains this ambivalent role of religion in the life of man? In large measure the answer lies in the fact that religion has two aspects—it is both an ideal and an institution. If an institution is the lengthened shadow of a man, the sad truth is that as the ideals of the man are lengthened, their image inevitably becomes distorted. Yet the growth of organization, for all its perils, is not only unavoidable, but essential. If religious values are to survive and to elicit loyalty from one generation after another, educational processes must be created for transmitting the content of religious teaching. Rituals must be developed and *sancta* established that will dramatize and concretize the ideal. The kernel of religion can be preserved only within the shell of institutions, which stand guard over rites and practices. Undoubtedly, the founders of the great religions are nobler figures than their followers, who catch only an echo of the heavenly voice and seek to embody them in synagogue, church, and mosque. Being manned by ordinary individuals for the most part, with vested interests to preserve, institutions often fall below the high plane of vision of their founders. What is the alternative? Moses was incomparably greater than his brother Aaron, yet it was the Aaronic priests who preserved the Law of Moses. Without Buddhism, Gautama would never have been remembered; were it not for Christianity, Jesus would have been as nameless as the unknown "teacher of righteousness" in the Dead Sea Scrolls, and of as little influence. Without institutions, the very memory of ideals, let alone their influence, would perish. Undoubtedly, the price that must be paid is high, but no one has offered a lower rate. The custodians of a religious institution easily fall into the error of regarding the temporary advantage of their group as a permanent victory for their cause, identifying the interests of their hierarchy of power with the glory of God. That is unfortunate, but the destruction of the institution would be worse.

That an institution which is created to preserve an ideal then threatens to suffocate it is a tragic paradox in human experience, not restricted to the area of religion. The custodians of institutions always tend to defend the status quo, not merely because the familiar is more comfortable, but also because it is infinitely easier to sail in sheltered waters than to brave uncharted seas. That is why one cannot equate original research with scholarly organizations, scientific progress with the universities, or artistic creativity with the academies. The history of literary and musical achievement is an unbroken record of rebellion by young, creative spirits struggling against the influence and power of the entrenched conventional custodians of the arts. The schools of classicism, romanticism, realism, naturalism, impressionism, and symbolism have each had to contend with the hostility of their predecessors; once established, they have fought against their successors with equal stubbornness. Yet somehow the path of growth and creativity in literature, music, and art remains open. In the grim art of warfare, the same principle may be observed. Such "advances" as the airplane, the submarine, the tank, and the nuclear bomb were first

opposed, then belittled, and only at last grudgingly admitted into
the arsenal of modern war by the official heads of the armed forces.

Even the field of science, which puts a premium on originality,
discloses this flaw of human nature. Today, scientific research has
grown extremely complicated and costly, requiring elaborate and
expensive equipment. Hence important discoveries are likely to
emerge in the future less frequently from the work of private inves-
tigators than from academic and industrial laboratories. Yet we are
not so far removed from the events as to forget that such revolutionary inventions as the steamboat, the telephone, the telegraph,
the electric light, and the airship were all the work of scientific
amateurs.

When Benjamin Franklin discovered that lightning was a form
of electricity, he sent a paper on the subject to be read for him by
a friend before the Royal Society in London. This friend reported
that it was "laughed at by the connoisseurs." When, in 1837, Row-
land Hill proposed a postage stamp for Great Britain, instead of
the cash payments made on the delivery of a letter by the recipient,
the Postmaster General, Lord Lichfield, declared that it was "entirely repugnant to reason."

Whatever will be the ultimate verdict of science, psychoanalysis
is undoubtedly one of the great scientific discoveries of the century.
Yet Sigmund Freud never rose above the rank of an assistant professor in Vienna, while the universities were cluttered with non-
entities and conventional mediocrities. After the new drugs used
in the war against tuberculosis had dramatically demonstrated their
efficiency, the experts of the National Tuberculosis Association,
who had previously warned that they could actually prove "a
step backward," now declared that "isoniazid does not appear to
be superior to previous treatments and may be inferior."

Additional illustrations are needless. Institutions are essential in
order to preserve the achievements of the past, but the original
creative impulse in every age comes from the amateur, the rebel,
the breaker of idols. What is true in art, music, literature, and
science is pre-eminently true in the field of religion. True progress
depends upon the creative tension between the ideal and the institution, between the forces of progress and the agencies for con-
servation. Only the interplay between the two can distinguish
between what is significant in the new and what is merely shocking.

Without the ideal there would be stagnation; without the institution there would be chaos. The passionate rebel, the glowing creative spirit, are essential, but the cool conservator, the skeptical critic, are also needed, if society is to be marked by orderly growth and stability.

Religion in the Western world has attained its lofty position because it is the resultant of both factors in its history, the inter-action of the prophet, sage, and martyr, who enlarged the bound-aries of the religious ideal, and the priest, the officiant, the teacher, who stood guard over the annexed territory. On the other hand, the primitive and ancient religions, which never attained to the level of the great faiths, were all marked by a preponderance of institutional factors, such as priesthood, rite, ceremony, and fixed patterns of worship, while they lacked the influence of the great religious leader and ethical teacher.

The uniqueness of the Biblical heritage lies in the central role which the "non-professional" leadership played in its development. Biblical religion began its career with authority vested in the hands of the Temple priests, a hereditary caste not fundamentally differ-ent from the priests of all ancient cults. But by the side of the hereditary priesthood, who served as the custodians of the sacred shrines and as the officiants in the Temple, there arose the dynamic, non-hereditary movement of the Prophets.

When the prophet Amos was driven from Beth-el by the priest Amaziah, because he announced the doom of the state and the royal house, he was told, "Go back to Judah and do your prophesy-ing there and there earn your bread." Amos answered indignantly, "I am neither a prophet nor the son of a prophet." He was no pro-fessional member of the guild, like those stigmatized by Micah: "The prophets, who lead My people astray; who, when they have food between their teeth, proclaim, 'Peace,' but whoever does not feed their maws, against him they declare war" (3:5).

Similarly, the birth of the Christian Church was the achievement of the simple, unlettered men who called themselves disciples of the Master, and the work of the passionate Apostle to the Gentiles, Paul. Its later growth was the work of similarly dedicated men and women. The blood of martyrs is the seed of the Church, for it is they who die for a cause who bear witness to its truth.

One of the abiding glories of Judaism lies in the fact that through-

out the greater portion of its history, it has fought institutionalism
and rarely given way to the clerical spirit. The priests of the house
of Aaron, who were the official custodians of Israel's faith during
the days of the First Temple, spoke in the name of an ancient and
honored tradition going back to Moses. But when the Jews were
exiled to Babylonia in 586 B.C.E., no temple remained on Zion's
hill, and no altar was ready now to receive their offerings. As a
result, two new forms of worship, study and prayer, replaced animal sacrifice. Thus the custom arose of meeting regularly on the
sabbaths at the home of a prophet or an elder for the reading and
exposition of God's word, supplemented by prayer and religious
exercise.

Thus the synagogue, the threefold house of assembly, study,
and prayer, arose. What began as a substitute for the Temple induced by necessity became a beloved institution, treasured for its
own sake. When the exiles were permitted by Cyrus of Persia in
538 B.C.E. to return at will to Jerusalem, they brought back the
passionate desire to rebuild the resplendent Temple on Zion's hill,
but also their love for the modest, unassuming synagogue which
came into being whenever ten men assembled for prayer. The process was completed nearly a century later by Ezra, who was a
priest by descent and a Scribe or "Master of the Book" by vocation.
Ezra transferred the spiritual leadership in Judaism from the hereditary priesthood to a new democratic class of scholars, who were
recruited from every level of society, from the lowest to the highest.
In the millennium that followed, the rabbis of the Talmud, num-
bering several thousand, were all non-professional teachers of religion, earning their livelihood by every calling, including the
humblest.

Not until the Middle Ages, when the duties of administering
communal affairs required the complete time and energy of trained
functionaries, did the practice arise of paying salaries to the rab-
binate. Even then the religious authorities had difficulty in validating the practice, since the traditional Jewish doctrine quoted God
as saying, "As I teach freely, so teach ye freely." One recalls the
similar New Testament injunction: "Freely have ye received,
freely give" (*Matt.* 10:8). The payment of salaries to rabbis and
teachers was finally justified on two grounds: they were deprived,
by their duties, of the opportunity of earning a living at some other

occupation ("payment for enforced idleness"), and were taking care of the children entrusted to them ("payment for guarding the young"), a medieval predecessor of modern baby-sitting!

This situation has, of course, grown infinitely more demanding in the face of the complexities of modern life. It would be extremely unrealistic to expect the conduct of religious activities to be practised exclusively by non-professionals today. The skills and experience required necessitate a total absorption in religious work as a full-time calling, and not merely as a leisure-time vocation. Yet once again the old peril appears—institutionalism leads to the development of professional vested interests, the perfunctory repetition of rites, the stress upon conformity to long-established patterns—in a word, the hardening of the arteries of the spiritual life.

Is there no escape from the dilemma? The answer, in theory at least, is simple. To be sure, all cultural institutions are subject to abuse, but men do not on that account proceed to destroy the universities, academies, and museums. Rather, men are called upon to stand constantly on guard in order to revive the proper functions of these institutions. Similarly, in order to make religion a vital instrument of human salvation, it is necessary to recapture the spirit of the amateur, in its original and authentic sense as the lover and devotee of the ideal. Both the professional leaders and the laity need to be imbued with this spirit of dedication to religion both as an idea and as a commitment. Only thus can men attain the ability to rise above the private goals and vested interests of their particular group, for the sake of the greater cause. The Hebrew root "to know," *yada*, means also "to love." What is required, therefore, both in the laity and in the clergy, is the rebirth of the knowledge and love of God, which the institution is designed to further. That this is not easy to achieve is clear from the fact that the prophet Isaiah includes these last-named virtues among the attributes of the ideal Messiah (11:2)! Yet the goal must be striven for unremittingly, and a measure of success may be attained.

Another principle for the vital functioning of religion must be kept in view. Those who love religion truly must labor to enhance its influence and at the same time stoutly oppose its pretensions to power. Here the specifically American ideal of the separation of church and state has a unique contribution to make to modern life. The doctrine was originally embodied in the American constitution for the purpose of strengthening the young republic by eliminating the strife of contending religious factions. But what was intended as a protection for the state has proved a blessing for religion. Possessing no official status and deriving no direct aid from the state, religion has fared far better here as a voluntary activity than it has in Europe, where state churches and the compulsory teaching of religion in the schools have been the rule. Its influence on all phases of American life and culture has certainly not been dominant, but neither has it been negligible.

Thus, no organized anti-clerical movement has arisen in America such as arose on the Continent, where the church buttressed itself by means of the state. Wherever religious leaders succeeded in seizing power, the reaction proved decisive sooner or later. Communism, nazism, and fascism, with their violent anti-religious bias, arose precisely in those countries where the church and the state were in closest alliance, and where discrimination against other groups was most flagrant. The lesson of history is plain—religion as a power has proved a peril; as an influence, it can be a unique force for good.

Undoubtedly, organized religion, like organized science, music, art, and literature, poses a perpetual challenge to the ideal. The path of reason lies not in denying the ideal because of its abuse by the institution, but in laboring devotedly to make the institution responsive to the ideal. The Talmud tells of the great sage, Rabbi Meir, who had been a pupil of Elisha ben Abuyah. In the midst of his career, Elisha became a heretic, publicly flouting the faith and culture to which he had previously been devoted. Meir continued to show him the deference due a master, and to draw instruction from him. When Meir was upbraided by his colleagues for these marks of respect to an enemy of religion, he answered: "I found a pomegranate; its fruit I ate, its rind I cast away." To mix our metaphors, he did not pour out the baby with the bath. It is this wisdom which is called for in every aspect of life. Religion has many sins to answer for, but, like humanity itself, its future still lies before it.

Our basic concern in this volume is to deal with the body of ideals and beliefs which are the essence of vital religion, the fruit of the soul-struggles of its prophets, sages, and lawgivers. But the road block created by institutional religion and by the perils inherent in its structure could not be ignored. We have tried to assess these negative factors fairly, while noting the positive contributions that an institution makes to the preservation of the body of the ideal. What is worth having is worth preserving.

At this point the chapter ended in the earlier edition of this book. We had noted that all cultural institutions are subject to abuse. We then went on to say, "Men do not on that account proceed to destroy the universities, academies and museums." This is no longer an accurate description of the facts! The growing sense of desperation in our age has driven increasing numbers of youths, both of the under-privileged and of the over-privileged groups, to unfurl the banner of violence as the only effective instrument for gaining attention and "getting things done."

Until clear proof is available that the destruction of the universities and other cultural institutions is the only effective way of curing their ills, we reaffirm the position maintained above—what is required is perpetual vigilence in quest of the re-vitalization of institutions. To be sure, there may be more emotional release in the intoxicating wine of violence. Genuine progress is a less heady potion, being compounded of patience and intellectual clarity, respect for differences and humility before the unknown, coupled with a faith in man's capacities and the courage to experiment with the new and the untried.

The record of history, supported by the testimony of common sense, makes it clear that the destruction of the religious "Establishment" will not spell the end of religious institutionalism. It will merely replace it by another set of functionaries and vested interests. The onslaught on religion by authoritarian dictatorships during the Nineteen Thirties merely transferred the allegiance of the masses to the new gods of fascism and communism. The widespread disaffection with religion today has not made emancipated philosophers of the people. On the contrary, it has spawned mystical cults and pseudo-Oriental sects, not to speak of occultism, astrology and devil worship.

In every aspect of human life, including religion, there is no shortcut to the New Jerusalem, no substitute for the path of genuine renewal, the goal of which was charted by Rabbi Abraham Isaac Kuk, "The old must be made new and the new must be made holy."

CHAPTER III

Why Not One Religion?

Our glance backward at the role of religion in human history has revealed both lights and shadows. Any fair reading of the record must disclose countless examples of religious bigotry and persecution. But that is not all that history teaches. Religious hostility has been visited more often upon religious believers of another persuasion than upon total nonbelievers. The differences among Christian, Jew, and Mohammedan, the divergences of Catholic and Protestant—these have been the greatest causes of religious intolerance.

It is therefore by no means unfair to ask whether the future must recapitulate the past. Is it not possible to preserve the values of religion and avoid most of its evils by adopting one creed for mankind? Obliterate the lines of demarcation among the historic creeds, and religion would cease to be a divisive factor and become a genuine force for unity in the world.

The ideal of a universal religion has undeniable appeal. It has captured the imagination of prophet, philosopher, and statesman, as well as that of humbler folk. When the prophet Zechariah declared that the day would come when "the Lord shall be One and His name one," he thought of all men as worshipping the One God under one Name, apparently that of the God of Israel. This seems clear from the fact that he describes the universal observance of the Hebrew Feast of Tabernacles by all the nations. The missionary movement in Christianity, from Paul to the present, testifies to the goal that has actuated the Church in its endeavors to be catholic, inclusive of all men. Islam made the same claim to universality, validating it by conquest or by conversion and extending its sway from the Philippines to Gibraltar.

Bluntly put, however, the ideal of one religion for mankind is little more than a form of religious imperialism. Just as Winston Churchill advocated one language for the world and proposed Basic English for the role, so those who cherish the ideal of one religion for mankind are usually thinking of their own particular creed. It is noteworthy that advocates of religious unity are often quite unconscious of the religious imperialism which they preach. Judaism, Buddhism, and Islam have each been offered in good faith for the role of world religion. The missionary character of Christianity is an expression of lofty universalism, but it cannot be dissociated from the exclusivism of the declaration in the Gospel of John (14:6), "No man cometh unto the Father, but by me." Nineteen centuries later, a distinguished Swiss theologian, in an impassioned plea for Christians and Jews to close ranks against the inroads of paganism, declared that "just as Christians understood and accepted the Old Testament, so Jews should accept the New." He was quite oblivious of the fact that in this partnership he was proposing that Christians retain their Christianity, but that Jews surrender their Judaism. A long time ago Israel Zangwill perspicaciously noted that if Jews and Christians were to unite and create one religion based on the best elements of both, each group would argue that it had contributed more significantly to the new faith than the other!

Obviously, however, such claims by the historical religions cancel each other out. A religion that could hope for universal acceptance would need to be free from any entanglements with the past and from any roots in a given group-experience. In other words, it would need to be a *novum*, as most creators of would-be universal religions have recognized. Such an attempt was made in the days of the French Revolution. The Catholic Church had been gravely weakened because of its alliance with the royal Court and the feudal system during the Bourbon regime. Jean Paul Marat and other revolutionary leaders created a "Religion of Reason," with a ten-day week and new temples to the Divine goddess everywhere. The new cult lasted for a shorter time than even the French Revolution. In the middle of the nineteenth century, the French sociologist,

Auguste Comte, maintained that mankind had gone through the
two stages of religion and metaphysics and was now ready for
the mature faith of positivism, which would be built solely upon
science. He therefore strove zealously to create what he called
"the religion of humanity." Its success, too, was not impressive.
Toward the close of the nineteenth century, Ethical Culture was
developed in the United States by Felix Adler, who sought to found
a movement dedicated to moral living, in which Christians, Jews,
and nonbelievers might find a common basis. Various contemporary
cults like Theosophy, New Thought, and Bahai also appeal to the
ideal of universal religion and claim to transcend the frontiers of
the great historical creeds.

Yet for all its apparent attractiveness, the ideal of a new universal
religion is neither feasible nor desirable. Its lack of practicality is
clear from the total failure of most of these new churches, which
have disappeared completely. Others have had very limited success, surviving simply as additional religious cults and supplement-
ing the varieties of traditional religious experience announced in
the Saturday or Sunday newspapers.

The failure of these attempts to create a universal religion stems
from various causes, which shed significant light upon the nature
of faith and its modes of expression. The more highly rational systems have failed to recognize the emotional sources from which
religion draws, the all-pervasive sense of the mystery of life, the
deeply rooted feeling of the dependence and weakness of man,
which, coupled paradoxically with the conviction of his significance
and worth, constitutes the essence of man's relation to God. Precisely because some of these cults have eschewed metaphysics, they
have not been able to nourish the sense of awe, or satisfy the yearning of the human heart to feel itself in harmony with the universe.

Even those movements, however, which do propose some God-
concept have not struck deep in the hearts of men, because religion
is not a body of abstract doctrine to be learnt from books or lectures. A vital faith, with a grip on the life of a human being, is
always the outgrowth of the personal experience of a man or of
the historic expression of a group—otherwise it is nothing. Science
can be, and should strive to be, universal in its content, because it
is the essence of the scientific method to exclude the subjective
factor in arriving at its conclusions. But religion, while drawing

upon all that can be known objectively about the world, as we shall see, fashions its own subjective view of life, and this will necessarily be based upon the experience of each individual and group. Hence a religion cannot be created artificially, any more than an artificial language can replace the exasperatingly illogical tongues and dialects spoken by the children of men. It may be maintained almost as a universal law that on every important issue life transcends logic and it is folly to depend on reason alone.

The differences among religions are, moreover, neither artificial nor unimportant. Ritual is no minor element, either in religion or in life as a whole. It gives dramatic expression to the beliefs and ideals cherished by the individual and by the society of which he is a part, and it keeps alive the memories upon which they rest. Only in the rarest of cases can a man act any role but his own. The Frenchman reveres liberty no less than an American, but he associates it with the Fall of the Bastille on July 14th, while the American recalls the signing of the Declaration of Independence on July 4th. The Jewish religion pays its tribute to the ideal of human freedom on the Passover festival; Christianity sees victory over death in the Resurrection commemorated on Easter.

It may be that the anthropologist sees the Mohammedan kneeling on a prayer-rug, the Jew garbing himself in a prayer-shawl, and the Christian kissing a crucifix as engaged in parallel religious exercises, but these sacred objects vary widely in their importance and meaning for the different communicants, and above all in the sanctity attaching to them.

That is not all. The differences among religions, and the values inherent in them, go beyond the rituals. It simply is not true that all religions are expressing the same truths, or even that at their highest level all religions will meet. Undoubtedly, the higher men's plane of vision rises and the more unobstructed their view of reality becomes, the greater will be the area of ideals that they can hold in common. But it does not follow that total agreement will result. For religion represents an attitude toward the world as a whole, and must, therefore, in greater or lesser degree, go beyond the evidence of man's senses and the reasonable conclusions which he bases upon them. On the contrary, the unproved hypothesis, the scarcely hoped for surmise, the personal reaction, the faith beyond the evidence—all these are the warp and woof of religion. It therefore follows that men equal in their idealism and wisdom will continue to differ fundamentally as to what is the highest good or the deepest truth.

These differences are indeed reflected in the great historic religions. The Christian may draw from his faith in his Savior the classic and compelling source of inspiration for nobler living and dying. The Jew, on the other hand, may see in the doctrine of the Incarnation an attenuation of the spiritual nature of God and of His uncompromising unity. Indeed, Maimonides declared that "whoever conceives of God in physical form denies his Maker."

Nor are these differences limited to varying conceptions of the Godhead. On the question of the *summum bonum*, the ultimate goal of human striving, every shade of the spectrum is represented in the great religions. At one extreme, Buddhism teaches that the highest goal of man is Nirvana, the conquest of desire, and, by that token, the avoidance of frustration and bitterness. At the other end, many forms of pagan religion regarded the enjoyment of the senses as the highest good. Closer to Buddhism, but far from identical with it, is the standpoint of Paul, who set up the ideal of celibacy as the ultimate level of holiness. Much further toward the center is the viewpoint of the Talmud, which, on the one hand, declares, "Every man is destined to give an accounting before God for every pleasure in the world that his eyes beheld which he did not enjoy," and which at the same time maintains that contentment is the secret of happiness: "Who is rich? He who is happy in his portion." A Hasidic teacher, Rabbi Michael, expressed this balance between asceticism and the enjoyment of life when he said, "I thank God that I never needed anything until I had it."

So, too, there is no unanimity on the question of how men are to react to the existence of evil. Shall they hate evil and fight to destroy it, or shall they turn the other cheek, lest they themselves be contaminated by the evil which they oppose? There is Scriptural warrant for both attitudes.

On all these ultimates, there is room neither for dogmatism nor for uniformity. In each of these opposing attitudes there are both life-giving truths and the seeds of error. Only the tension of contradictory views helps to correct the error and prevent the truth from being exaggerated into a falsehood. It is undeniable that self-abnegation is an essential element in living the good life, yet so, too, is the enjoyment of the world's blessings. Similarly, life demands that men both transform evil and transcend it. Only by striving after the proper balance between the two alternatives can we hope to attain the highest wisdom. The dogmas of Christianity enshrine profound mysteries for the Christian believer, though they may seem unacceptable, if not incomprehensible, to the Jew. On the other hand, while the Jew may see in the injunctions of the Torah a matchless instrument for disciplining and refining human nature, the Christian may feel that the observance of the minutiae of the Law is a heavy burden, while it is the faith in Jesus that gives wings to the human spirit. This is far more than a debate—it is a dialogue, in which each group is stimulated and challenged by the other to fulfill the high claims which it advances for its respective insights.

To speak of a universal religion, therefore, means to fail to reckon with the complexity of the world and the multiplicity of man's attitudes toward life. What is needed is not deadening uniformity, but fruitful coexistence, based on mutual respect and mutual influence, created by keeping open the lines of communication.

Every religion, be it noted, includes three elements: beliefs, rituals, and an ethical system. The degree of universality will differ for these three elements. At one extreme stand the rituals, which are the most strongly particularistic element in every religion. At the other extreme is the sphere of ethics, in which the largest measure of similarity among the various religions may be found, though even here there will be significant variations. Sharing many features in common, but with recognizable and important divergences, each religion possesses a body of ideas and beliefs, which have emerged from the interaction of events and personalities in the life of the particular community.

Those who advocate a universal religion thus ignore two of the three elements that enter into religion, the beliefs and the rituals, and they generally content themselves with urging little more than an ethical code. Yet even this circumscribed goal is not attainable through a universal religion. As we shall note in greater detail later, an ethical code which does not rest upon a system of beliefs and is not kept vivid and alive by ritual patterns will be weak and anemic. Lacking vitality and staying power, it will be unable to face the challenge of man's weakness or meet the competition of other seductive philosophies that preach the contradictory gospels of aggressiveness or self-indulgence, of self-deception or despair.

In sum, conformity is neither possible nor desirable. What is needed is universal understanding based upon knowledge, and an openness of the spirit resting upon humility, the recognition that loyalty to one's own faith need not preclude an appreciation of the insights and values cherished by others, but, on the contrary, gains in depth and meaning from such empathy.

In life, the short-cut may prove all too long, and the longer path the only sure road to the goal.

The weaknesses of religion can be overcome and its power for good can be strengthened, but not through a simple panacea, like "one religion for all," which proves to be neither simple nor a panacea. Eternal vigilance of the mind and of the will is the price that men must pay for life as well as for liberty, for faith as well as for freedom.

CHAPTER IV

The Roots of Religion

It is possible to maintain the thesis that the history of civilization is the record of the gradual emancipation of culture from the thralldom of religion. Originally religion included every basic enterprise of the human spirit. The arts, literature, drama, music, sculpture, and painting were all sacred in the ancient world, since they served to preserve the myth-content of religion and to give it vivid expression through ritual. The earliest branches of science were cultivated by the priests of the Nile and Euphrates valleys. As for speculations on the nature of reality, it is true that not only in ancient days, but also throughout the medieval period and up to the very threshold of the modern age, philosophy was the hand-maiden of theology. Yet step by step, each of these activities, art, science, and philosophy, has freed itself from the fetters of religion and become a secular and autonomous aspect of culture.

It is therefore by no means impertinent to ask whether or not religion today is not merely the vestigial remnant of an outgrown stage of culture. Perhaps, it may somewhat irreverently be suggested, religion is like the Cheshire cat, which disappeared, leaving only its grin behind. What, if anything, remains as the special province of religion? Cannot its functions be performed more effectively today by philosophy and science? To answer these questions properly, it would be necessary to discover the origin of religion and then proceed to establish its scope and content. Unfortunately, however, this is more easily said than done, for all origins are veiled in obscurity. We do not know the origin of language, music, or art; for that matter, the beginnings of life and of the universe itself are veiled from us. Theories, of course, exist in abundance. A similar situation obtains with regard to the origins of religion.

In the eighteenth century, the philosophers of the Age of Reason, who were generally antagonistic to the Church as the enemy of "Enlightenment," declared that religion was an artificial creation of self-seeking priests who invented religion in order to batten on the labor of others. Through the institutions of religion, the argument ran, the masses were fleeced economically and kept in bondage intellectually. This view of religion as organized charlatanism has been generally abandoned, as anthropologists have studied the life of the most remote human groups, the aborigines of Australia, the savages of the African jungle, and the primitives of the Arctic wastes, nowhere finding a society in which religion is lacking. Some type of religious life exists among the most primitive as well as the most advanced of peoples.

Recently, for example, anthropologists reported on a pygmy race in Thailand, which represents perhaps the most undeveloped group of men known to science. They lack almost all the marks of social organization, and have virtually no tools. Yet even here the rudiments of religion exist. The scientists reported: "The tribesmen did not know how to work stone or metal. They had no games, music or art. They didn't even draw pictures in the dirt with their fingers. They had no leader. They spent all their waking hours avoiding tigers or human huntsmen and trying to find something they themselves could kill and eat. They worship a spear spirit. If anyone touches another man's spear, there must be an animal sacrifice to satisfy the spirit. Illnesses are a sign that the souls of dead relatives have not been able to find food, and again an animal sacrifice is called for" (New York Times, October 5, 1955).

At the other extreme of the cultural spectrum, the most sophisticated societies have not dispensed with religion. Even where the great conventional religions lose favor, the vacuum is filled by new cults, which demonstrate that man is incurably religious. The history of an avowedly nontheological movement like Ethical Culture is most instructive. At the turn of the nineteenth century Felix Adler organized the Ethical Culture movement, so that, in his words, men of every religious viewpoint, and of none, might unite for the purpose of cultivating the ethical life. But Ethical Culture, which originally arose as a movement outside of organized religion, has become a religious sect in every significant sense of the term. It has its ministers (called leaders), its services (called meetings), its rituals of marriage and death, its schools. Most recently, the Ethical Culture Society of Washington demanded, and ultimately received, tax exemption as a bona-fide religious group. It is, incidentally, listed always on the Religious Pages of metropolitan newspapers. Part of the failure of Ethical Culture to expand, as Felix Adler himself recognized before his death, lay in the fact that it failed to make adequate provision for a system of ritual, which answers to deep, nonrational needs of the human spirit and by that token is indispensable for transmitting the values of the group to coming generations.

A system as violently antireligious as communism is itself a religion. In actuality, its hostility to conventional religion derives in largest measure from the fact that it presents itself not as a political or economic order, but as a system of absolute values. Communism has its God, the socialist state; its lawgiver, Karl Marx; its Bible, *Das Kapital;* its major prophets, Lenin and Stalin (or Khrushchev, or whoever reigns at the moment); its minor prophets, Engels and Bukharin. It believes in the Last Judgment (the social revolution), when the righteous (the proletariat) will at length triumph over the wicked (the bourgeoisie). In its missionary zeal, its impassioned hatred of heresy, its sectarianism, the psychological phenomenon of its conversions, and the capacity of its devotees for self-sacrifice, communism is the Church Militant of our age.

The conclusion is clear: if religion is driven out of the door, it enters through the window. It cannot be airily dismissed as an artificial concoction, created by charlatans and intended for fools. Whether for good or for ill, it represents part of man's innate endowment, and must be reckoned with as a constant in human nature.

What is the heart of the religious impulse? A contemporary scholar, writing on "Man's Religions," J. B. Noss, declares: "The essence of the religious spirit is the attitude that the relation between man and nature is organic and vital, not accidental and external. Man depends for life and the fullness of being on forces outside himself, which share, in some sense, his nature, with which he must be in harmony." Religion, therefore, may be beneficial or harmful, but it is natural.

How did religion arise? On its origin, there is no lack of theories. One highly popular view maintains that fear is the source of religion. Primitive man was afraid of the world, which he found full of perils lurking everywhere, in the fastnesses of the jungle, in the wild beasts and in the unpredictable forces of nature. Taking himself as a starting point, man assumed that the world about him was peopled with sentient beings like himself, but far more powerful than he. Animism is the first stage in the evolution of religion. Since life was essentially dangerous and unpredictable, his attitude toward these spirits was one of fear. He tried to ward off evil by placating these forces, as he would a dangerous fellow man, by praising them, which is flattery, and by bringing them gifts, which is bribery. Thus there arose the typical religious acts of worship and sacrifice.

This theory undoubtedly has elements of truth within it, but the sciences of comparative religion and anthropology have indicated that it is only partially adequate. Undoubtedly, fear played a good part in the life of primitive man, who was afraid of his environment and therefore peopled the universe with evil beings. These hostile spirits he sought to neutralize and coerce into a type of "do-nothing" neutrality through rites of magic.

We must not, however, exaggerate the sense of fear and insecurity of ancient man. If he lived solely and perpetually in terror, life would have been insupportable. There were aspects of nature which, from the very beginning, impressed our earliest ancestors as favorable. There were the rainfall and the sunshine, the cool white moon and the silent stars, the trees with their fruits and the welcome shelter of their boughs, the quickening stream and the green oasis in the wilderness, and undoubtedly, too, the beauty of a fertile valley, and the awesome sight of a lofty mountain. To all these, in however rudimentary a fashion, primitive man responded with gratitude and a joyful recognition that the world was not hell, but home. He believed that all these happier elements of his environment were also peopled by living spirits, and these were at least potentially friendly. These beings he sought not merely to neutralize through magic, but to win over positively through religion. Animism thus gave rise to a dualistic view of the universe: it contained beings that were friendly to man, and these were the gods; and also demons, or evil spirits, who had to be coerced or cajoled into ineffectiveness. It was the worship of the gods, not the placating of demons, that constituted the twin bases of ancient religion.

Primitive fears have, of course, by no means disappeared from men, because perils and pitfalls still beset man's path. The power of superstition is an index of the strength of these fears in the hearts of modern men. And since fear belongs to the most primitive layers of the human soul, superstition often outlives religion. People will knock wood who do not believe in the saving power of the cross, and will avoid the number thirteen without even thinking of Judas, the thirteenth person at the Last Supper, from which the current superstition is derived. Magic is not to be confused with religion. Even in its earliest forms, religion represents a sense of hope in life, a spirit of harmony with nature, a sense of at-homeness in the world.

Another view as to the origin of religion regards the sense of wonder as the basic impulse. Primitive man, we are reminded, differed far less from his modern descendants than he did from the beasts that were his ancestors. As soon as ancient man could think and feel—and both these attributes were part of his inheritance— whenever the rigors of the struggle for existence abated for him, however temporarily, he found himself caught up by a sense of wonder. Standing under a moonlit sky, with the panoply of the heavens overhead, enthralled by the beauty of a mountain covered by green forests or mantled by snow, or viewing the quiet charm of a brook in a forest glen, he experienced an indescribable feeling of awe. Man was filled with a sense of his own relative weakness and insignificance, by the side of the majesty and grandeur of the world about him. Thus religion was born out of a sense of wonder. Albert Einstein has described this cosmic religious experience, which he regards, incidentally, as the strongest driving-force behind scientific research. He defines it as the seeking on the part of the individual "to experience the totality of existence as a unity far beyond existence. The most beautiful and profound emotion we can experience is the mystical. It is the source of all true art and science. He to whom this emotion is a stranger, who can no longer pause to wonder and stand rapt in awe, is as good as dead; his eyes are closed. This insight into the mystery of life, coupled though it be with fear, also has given rise to religion. To know that what is impenetrable to us really exists, manifesting itself as the highest wisdom and the most radiant beauty which our dull faculties can comprehend only in their primitive forms—this knowledge, this feeling, is at the center of true religiousness. In this sense, and in this sense only, I belong in the ranks of devoutly religious men." (Quoted in *New York Times*, April 19, 1955.)

It may seem a far cry from Einstein, representing one of the noblest embodiments of man's civilized nature, to his primitive ancestors, and yet he himself notes that the line of descent is clear and unbroken. The religious experience finds its classical expression in the Biblical tale of the youthful Jacob, fleeing his home, finding no shelter, and finally taking a stone as his pillow in the open field. As the lad slept, he saw a vision of a ladder reaching from earth to heaven, with angels ascending and descending upon it. When he rose in the morning he called out: "How awesome (*nora*) is this place; indeed, there is God in this place, and I did not know it" (*Gen.* 28:16). The Hebrew word *nora* means both "fear" and "awe." It has been noted that there is no word for "religion" in the Bible. The closest approximation to such a term in Biblical Hebrew is supplied by the same root in the phrase *yirat Adonay*, usually translated as "the fear of God," but encompassing fear, reverence, and awe.

A third view seeks the origin of religion, not in the notion of fear or in the feeling of awe, but rather in the realm of religious activity. For these scholars, the source of religion is best sought in what is the oldest act of religion, namely, sacrifice, and its essence lies in man's quest for companionship in the world. Sacrifice itself, however, has given rise to a variety of theories as to its meaning among students of the history of religion. Thus Robertson-Smith believes that the sacrifice represents a communion, a binding of the god and the worshipper through the sharing of the body of the sacrificed animal in a common meal. Taylor regards sacrifice, on the other hand, as a gift by the worshipper to his god in order to induce him to act on his behalf. Related to it is the view of Eichrodt, that it is a gift to the god in order to sustain his strength. In other words, the gods are pictured in human guise, possessing appetites and needs that must be met, in order that they may be able to fulfill their task of protecting the worshipper and his clan. A third view is that the act of sacrifice releases vital powers through the animal's death. This explains the great emphasis in the sacrificial rite upon the blood, which is the vital principle in all living creatures, "for blood is the life." It is probable that all these factors played a part on the oldest levels of religion. (See H. H. Rowley, *The Meaning of Sacrifice in the Old Testament* 1950, pp. 76 ff.)

Significantly, all these views are at one in regarding the gods as actually or potentially friendly. Thus sacrifice, the oldest religious act, supports the view that religion arises, not out of a sense of fear of a hostile universe, but out of a feeling of fellowship with the world. Conscious of his weakness before a mighty universe, primitive man had the sense of awe. Yet in the good hours of life—and he had these, too—in times of rest and satiety and comfort, he felt that life was good, that he "belonged" in the world. That sense of fellowship gave him the conviction that there were beings like himself in the world, except that they were stronger, more powerful, endowed with immortality, similar to men in their traits, but with a higher potential. The Greek philosopher Anaxagoras laughed at man's propensity to create gods, and declared that if horses could think, their gods would be in the form of horses. Yet the naiveté of paganism, which the philosopher mocked, enshrines a fundamental truth: water cannot rise higher than its source, and the presence of man in the universe indicates that the world must have been fashioned by a power that is at least not inferior to man. Anaxagoras himself bore unconscious witness to this truth, by teaching that a supreme intelligence (*nous*) was the cause of all things—another illustration of a man "creating" his God in his own image! The speculations of philosophy are thus not far removed from the earliest stirrings of animism in primitive man, or from the pagan myths of ancient religion.

Speculations about the origins of religion are likely to remain perpetually fascinating and perpetually inconclusive. This is, however, not fatal to our quest. Though knowledge of the beginnings of an institution can shed welcome light on its history and nature, one must be on guard against the genetic fallacy, the assumption that the origin of a given phenomenon is an adequate guide to its later function and use. The history of man and of his culture demonstrates again and again how origins are radically transcended by later experience. Only willful blindness can equate man with his animal ancestry—he is, Ecclesiastes notwithstanding, far more than a beast. Music, literature, and art may be, as Freud insisted, sublimations of the sexual impulse itself—they are by no means identical with it. Since development is the law of life, our inability to discover the origin of religion is not fatal to our purposes. It is far more germane to study the role of religion in the life of contemporary man.

The hundreds of definitions of religion current today demonstrate that, like every important concept, it is all but impossible to define. The word itself, *religio,* of Latin origin, is to be derived from the verb *religere,* which means "to pay heed, to be concerned with rites," and is the opposite of the root *negligere,* "to overlook, neglect." For the practical-minded, nonspeculative Romans, religion was a matter of performing the stated rites of worship. In connection with the term, however, a folk-etymology is perhaps more significant than the more rigorously exact etymology. Popularly, the word is derived from the Latin verb *religare,* meaning "to bind." Religion has therefore frequently been described as the sense of man's link, or bond, to the world.

We may perhaps be forgiven for adding one more definition of the complex phenomenon called religion. We should like to define *religion as man's sense of his place in the world, including his relationship to his fellow-men, and the forms, both individual and collective that he has created for expressing this relationship.* Our formulation is broad enough to embrace all forms of religious expression and organization, including religions that do not maintain the belief in a Supreme Being or God, such as Buddhism. It recognizes that religion is a universal human characteristic. It calls attention to the group-character of religion, for, as we shall see, there is no such thing as an individual religion except in a purely derived sense. Finally, it includes the three basic elements in every developed religious system: a structure of beliefs concerning life in the world, a corpus of ritual acts through which the believer expresses these beliefs vis-à-vis the god or gods in whom he believes, and some system of ethical behavior, which he regards as divinely ordained, and for which he will be held responsible.

The most famous religious code in the world, the Ten Commandments, reflects this tripartite character of religion. The first of the

Ten Commandments, "I am the Lord thy God who brought thee out of the land of Egypt, out of the house of bondage," is an article of belief, which declares not only that God is one, but ethical in character, espousing the cause of freedom against slavery. The next three Commandments—"Thou shalt have no other gods before me," which forbids the worship of a plurality of gods and the creation of images; "Thou shalt not take the name of the Lord thy God in vain," which enjoins reverence for the Divine name and its various manifestations; and "Remember the Sabbath day to keep it holy"—are ritual in character. The Sabbath commandment, however, with its great emphasis upon the right of slave and animal to rest, already possesses a strong ethical character, which is stressed in the Deuteronomic version, in which the commandment is directly linked to the experience of Egyptian bondage: "And thou shalt remember that thou wast a servant in the land of Egypt, and the Lord thy God brought thee out thence by a mighty hand and by an outstretched arm; therefore the Lord thy God commanded thee to keep the sabbath day" (*Deut.* 5:15). Thus the Sabbath command serves as an excellent transition to the last six of the Commandments: "Honor thy father and thy mother," and the prohibitions of murder, adultery, theft, bearing false witness, and covetousness, which are obviously ethical in character. The structure of the Ten Commandments thus reflects on a high plane what is to be found in every religion. If religion may be compared to a tree, the roots are the system of underlying beliefs, the branches are the ritual and ceremonial acts, and the fruits symbolize the ethical code, which flows from the pattern of creed and rite.

Any serious definition of religion, such as the one proposed above, will raise the question as to the relationship of religion and philosophy. Undoubtedly, they have much in common, both being concerned with elaborating a world-view, an attitude expressing man's relationship to the universe. One may therefore often use a phrase like "a man's religion" or "a man's philosophy" almost interchangeably. There are, however, significant differences. A philosophy may be purely individual; religion always expresses itself collectively. When the devotees of a given philosopher become conscious of the link among them and create forms for expressing that bond, they evolve a cult, which may develop into a full-fledged religion. A philosophy may content itself with formulating abstract thought and go no further; a religion must invariably be embodied in a program of concrete action, both ritual and ethical. Because philosophy appeals purely to the intellect, at least on the conscious level, it often seems cold and remote; true religion is infused with feeling and warmth. Hence the differences may be described epigrammatically: religion is philosophy touched with emotion, or, religion is philosophy in action.

History indicates that while some rare individuals may find sufficient shelter for their spirit in pure philosophy, this is not true of the generality of mankind. Most men—and by no means the lowest among them—are not satisfied by the rarefied, detached atmosphere of philosophy. Confucianism began as ethical teaching by a man who scrupulously sought to avoid any entangling alliance with the gods. "To recognize the gods, and to avoid any contact with them, that is the path of wisdom" was the teaching of Confucius. Yet he himself became the source of a new religion and ultimately its central figure. In modern times, as we have already seen, Felix Adler created an ethical philosophy of life, which has evolved into virtually a full-blown religion.

It is true that some modern thinkers have suggested a more far-reaching distinction between religion and philosophy. Philosophy, it has been argued, represents man's intellectual quest for truth about the universe, buttressed by the conviction that no complete assurance can be hoped for. Religion, on the contrary, assumes that the truth is already revealed and is capable of being known. The hallmark of philosophy is doubt; of religion, faith. Or to put it otherwise, philosophy stresses the everlasting questions, religion claims to have the eternal answers. Now, this distinction could have arisen only in an age of widespread skepticism like our own. Hence, many professional philosophers in our day have been content to limit their field of interest, restricting philosophy to a *method*, rather than regarding it as a *body of thought*. The widespread preoccupation with semantics, useful as it is, is symptomatic of this approach. This conception of philosophy as a means to truth rather than as the end makes no demands on life and requires no commitments in action. In largest degree, the sense of irrelevance and remoteness from reality in modern philosophy, of which many philosophers themselves complain, is the result of this approach, the tendency to make of the search an end in itself, as though a racer were to strain every muscle in the contest, but were studiously to avoid reaching the finishing-line.

The truth is that all the great philosophic systems in history have been much more than mere methods. Such varied thinkers as Aristotle, Spinoza, Thomas Aquinas, and John Dewey differed in their views as to the means whereby men could attain to truth, but all of them were convinced that the truth was attainable and that, when attained, it would prove intelligible and life-affirming. Hence, each attempted to formulate his vision of reality into a system of thought. We shall see below that the method of rational inquiry characteristic of science and philosophy does not differ so radically as it is often supposed from the approach of religion.

Yet the difference between religion and philosophy is real, even if it be principally in emphasis. While both enterprises are concerned with the quest for certainty, philosophy is more conscious of the quest and religion of the certainty. Yet to minimize the element of conviction in philosophy is as misleading as to ignore the role of doubt in religion. Because religion is rooted more deeply in the emotions than philosophy, men find it less painful to surrender their philosophy than their religion.

Basically, however, philosophy and religion are both concerned with man's relationship to the universe, and both are deeply personal. We may call a man's version of the truths which he shares with his fellow men his philosophy. With equal justice, we may call these same elements a man's religion, his individual selection and structuring of the content of his group tradition. In both cases, the interpretation which he gives these ideas and the hierarchy of values into which he organizes them make them truly his own. This is far from unimportant, for all truth, as Renan has reminded us, lies in the nuances. A man's outlook on life, call it his religion or his philosophy, will determine his character and fate.

CHAPTER V

The Scientific Challenge

A century ago, the French thinker, Auguste Comte, pigeonholed very neatly what he called the three stages of human development. First came the theological or the religious epoch; then the metaphysical, or philosophical; and finally, the apex, the scientific. In the face of the rich complexity of human experience, the scheme was attractively—and deceptively—simple. But Comte himself proceeded to subvert his classification by inventing a new religion for humanity in the scientific era, the temper of which may be judged from some of the provisions which he laid down. In the new faith, Comte would be the dictator, surrounded by a body of priests; all independent thought and the desire for change were to be extirpated, and all books, except for a hundred of his own choosing, were to be burnt in a gigantic conflagration.

Comte was mistaken in assuming that religion, philosophy, and science represent three successive phases of the human adventure. They are, and give every sign of remaining, simultaneous expressions of the human spirit. He was right, however, in emphasizing that in the modern age science is dominant, coloring every other aspect of life. To be sure, the origins of science are to be sought in antiquity, and have been related by some historians to the experimental element in magic itself. Nonetheless, science as an effective, organized, and creative enterprise is peculiarly the mark of the modern age. Religion, on the contrary, belongs to the ancient past. All the great seminal spirits in religion, Moses, Zoroaster, Buddha, Confucius, Jesus, and Mohammed, are separated from our day by millennia.

When, at the end of the Middle Ages, religion began to lose its dominant position, science emerged in the human arena as a young David, vigorous and self-confident, confronting an aged Goliath, weighed down by the encrusted armor of centuries. For many years, both sides conceived of the relationship between religion and science as one of antagonism. Defenders of the faith maintained that science was man's endeavor to discover the truth through the imperfect instruments of reason and observation and hence was tentative and partial, while religion represents God's perfect revelation of His truth to His children and was infinitely to be preferred. It therefore followed logically that when the teachings of religion were contradicted by science, science was wrong and deserved to be suppressed. The history of the warfare of science with theology, to use the title of Andrew D. White's work, is the story of the fruitless attempts made by organized religion to crush the burgeoning efforts of science, as it strove to break the fetters of outworn notions of reality. Galileo, Copernicus, Mendel, Darwin, Freud, and hundreds of lesser figures each had to encounter the objections of those who believed that it was impious as well as mistaken to subvert the perfect truth of divine Revelation by man's own faltering, imperfect efforts to attain to truth. This view, that science must give way before religion, has so far fallen into decline today that it seems to belong to a bygone age.

Today the roles of victor and vanquished have been virtually reversed, and the contrary view has all but triumphed. What is widely believed, though less commonly stated, is that religion is a farrago of superstition and that science is the proud product of man's intellect. In the contest, therefore, between the darkness of superstition and ignorance, on the one hand, and the bright light of science and knowledge, on the other, it is obvious that science must conquer and religion withdraw ignominiously from the field of battle. This position was widely held in the middle of the nineteenth century, when the world-wide struggle between the protagonists of the evolutionary hypothesis and the upholders of the Biblical account of creation was at its height. It had its tragicomic epilogue three-quarters of a century later in the Scopes Trial in Tennessee. William Jennings Bryan, the defender of the Biblical creation account against the theory of evolution, was not so much refuted by Clarence Darrow, as laughed out of court.

Today the smoke of battle has cleared away, and the intransigeant positions adopted by both antagonists have been largely surrendered. Except for extremist fringes in both camps, who are fighting bygone battles with unabated zeal, the recognition has been growing that a reconciliation of religion and science is both desirable and possible. There has been, however, no unanimity of view as to how peace or, at least, an armistice is to be achieved. One approach has it that religion represents a tissue of hopes based on man's ignorance, while science labors to extend the horizons of man's knowledge. At any given moment, man's universe consists of two areas: the unknown, which is the domain of religion; and the known, which is the field of science. It follows that as science continues its research, the realm of the known grows at the expense of the unknown and the empire of science annexes more and more territory from the kingdom of religion. It is as though two men are sharing a pie between them; the more one takes, the less remains for the other. The ultimate end, therefore, is the peaceful expiration of religion and the total triumph of science.

This conception of the relationship of religion and science is based not merely upon a failure to understand religion, but also upon a misconception of the nature of science itself. Twentieth-century scientific research has revealed the paradox that the increase of knowledge means the increase of ignorance, for each discovery reveals new and unsuspected vistas on the horizon. Thus, as the frontiers of man's knowledge in the fields of astronomy, physics, and psychology have broadened, he has attained to a far better knowledge of reality, to be sure, but with it has come a correspondingly greater understanding of how much he does not know. Thus, a generation ago, the atom, as its name indicated, was regarded as the fundamental and indivisible element of matter, beyond which there was nothing to investigate. Today we know that the atom represents an entire universe of dazzling complexity. Obviously, infinitely more is known about the constitution of the atom than was known in 1900, yet much more is unknown, too. At the turn of the century, human psychology had no conception of the subconscious and its ramifications, as revealed by the research of Freud, Adler, Jung, their disciples, and their successors. Today we know much more about the psychological life of man, but our knowledge has, at the same time, shed light upon unplumbed depths in the human soul. The relatively simple solar system of Laplace, with the sun at the center and the planets circling about it, has today been superseded by an astronomical conception of multiple galaxies, each of limitless dimensions. Our growing knowledge is accompanied by an ever deeper sense of ignorance in what an astronomer has rightly called the mysterious universe. Every branch of science illustrates this truth, which has rendered naive the nineteenth-century hope that as man's knowledge grew, his ignorance would correspondingly diminish. Ignorance is no temporary state that man will transcend in time. It remains, and must remain, a permanent feature of the human situation in the world.

Another and far older method of reconciling the contradictions of religion and science is to keep the antagonists at arm's length from each other. Science and philosophy, it is maintained, are concerned with reason and its conclusions, but religion lies entirely beyond the domain of human intelligence. Faith depends upon an inner light, upon a mystic experience of reality which comes to the religious believer. Reason is useful enough in the mundane concerns of life, but not in the great fundamental issues with which religion is concerned. Thus the Church Father Tertullian justified his belief in the dogmas of Christianity by the slogan, *Credo quia absurdum*—"I believe because it is absurd." He thus lifted the tenets of his faith beyond the reach of reason, where they could be subjected to analysis and criticism.

Now the point need not be labored that many of the most attractive figures in the history of religion have been the mystics and the saints, who eschewed all other paths but the road of faith. They lived solely by the light of their own personal experience, which they felt to be true, without the cold scrutiny of reason. But there are grave perils as well as ineffable delights in the mystic's illumination. This has been attested times without number in the history of religion. Let it be granted that those chosen spirits who can soar on the wings of faith have no need of the footpaths below. But our concern is with the generality of men, who are too diffident, too earth-bound, if you will, too conscious of their own limitations, to lay claim to direct communion with the Most High. They, too, may experience rare moments of exaltation, when they feel a Presence beyond the power of words to describe. But, unlike the perpetual dwellers on the heights, they must descend to the mun-

dane sphere of life's struggle and search, bearing with them only
the memory of the vision and its ecstasy.

The personal encounter of God and man may be the heart of
religion, as we are assured today on every hand—but a living organism contains more than a heart, and religion is more than the
mystic's private ecstasy. Religion believes that it has a truth to
proclaim, and that claim presupposes the faculty of reason and discrimination; it demands obedience to its commandments—and if
the great teachers of religion are to be believed, these are pre-
eminently obligations between man and man—and these require
judgment as well as will. Hence religion must win the concurrence
of the mind as well as the assent of the heart, if it is to come fully
alive.

If the mystic's withdrawal from the world is a path not accessible
to most men, the procedure of placing science in one compartment
of the mind and religion in another, hermetically sealed off from
one another, is fraught with peril. A spirit divided against itself
cannot survive, and an inner conflict must lead to a breakdown.
It is no wonder that in circles which have adopted this method of
"safeguarding religion," fanaticism and hostility toward all those
outside the charmed circle are rampant, traits which are essentially
manifestations of inner warfare, helpless frustration, and gnawing
doubts that cannot be suppressed.

The essential role of reason in religion appears from another
angle as well. The great historical religions have always been collective, both in experience and in expression. That is to say, they
are the outgrowth of the experiences of a group and the embodiments of its outlook. But where a group is involved, there must
necessarily be communication from one man to his fellow and from
one generation to the next, and communication is impossible without a common basis of rationality.

The great monotheistic religions of the West, which are our
primary concern, are all group-religions, embodied in a synagogue,
church, or mosque. Hence they must necessarily stress the *communication* of religious and ethical truth and the *rationality* of what
they seek to perpetuate.

It is false to infer that because religion is marked by a profound
emotional timbre, it is therefore alien to reason. Actually, vital
religion must use the instrument of reason as far as it can lead, and

then go beyond it. Vital religion is super-rational, not anti-rational. That reason is an imperfect guide to the universe is self-evident. But if the world is a *uni-verse*, a unit of being, what man can discover through observation and reason constitutes a significant clue to those aspects of existence beyond the powers of observation and reason to fathom. The known is organically related to the unknown and sheds some light upon it. As we have noted, the Bible is not anti-intellectual. To divorce contemporary religion from reason may confer upon it an immunity from philosophic doubt and scientific contradiction, but it is a spurious and uneasy peace, purchased at a high price. It means isolating it from the world of men's thought and action, and depriving it of any vital role in the arena of man's struggle and achievement.

In sum, it is clear that to solve the problem of the conflict of religion and science by establishing a "no-man's land" between them is no solution at all. Instead, the realization has been growing that both are deeply rooted human enterprises, and that, necessarily, there must be some working relationship between them. Neither a war to the death, nor a sterile armistice between science and religion, can suffice us.

In seeking to establish a peaceful relationship between religion and science, several varied approaches have been attempted. Some advocates of traditional religion maintain that religion and science teach the same truths about the world. Thus it is often maintained that the first chapter of *Genesis*, when properly understood, actually teaches the same as evolution. The six days of Creation may refer to long eras of time. In the words of the Psalmist, "a thousand years in Thy sight are but as yesterday when it is past." The order of Creation in *Genesis* resembles the order postulated by evolution: sea animals, birds, reptiles, land animals, and, finally, man. Thus, these proponents of traditional religion declare, there is no contradiction between the Bible and science.

This harmonization of religion and science is achieved at too heavy a cost. That *Genesis* takes "day" to mean a twenty-four-hour period is clear from the reference to "evening" and "morning" each day of the Creation week and to the establishment of the Sabbath on the seventh day. Moreover, one might ask why it was that no one discovered the theory of evolution in the opening chapter of *Genesis*, before Darwin enunciated his views. It is clear that for nearly thirty centuries, the alleged teaching of evolution in *Genesis* was hardly effective! Moreover, the most important aspect of evolution, which is the recognition that each species is descended from its predecessor in the evolutionary ladder, is, of course, nowhere stated, or even implied, in the Biblical narrative.

There is a more fundamental question: If religion and science teach the same body of truth, what need is there of both disciplines? Saadia, the medieval Jewish philosopher, who presented a similar defense of the role of religion as against philosophy, argued that most persons were slow to learn and imperfect in their understanding, and that therefore religious tradition gave them, in brief and easily comprehensible form, those truths which it would take them a lifetime to achieve through the processes of reason. But even if this contention were accepted, one could argue that today, when scientific truths are widely taught, there is no longer any need for religion. The Biblical story of Creation represents a brilliant aperçu in its recognition of universal law in the world and in its vision of the universe as a cosmos, but its point of departure is unquestionably the scientific knowledge of its own day. We shall see later wherein the abiding significance of the first chapter of *Genesis* resides. It is not to be found in its contribution to biology.

If the relationship of science and religion cannot be one of antagonism, neither can it be that of identity. If they both have value, it must be because they complement, not reduplicate, each other.

At the very outset, we may note the similarity in the approach of both science and religion to reality. As Morris Raphael Cohen pointed out, it is a vulgar error to assume that the scientist begins with the indiscriminate observation of phenomena. Actually, he begins with an idea, a "hunch," or, to use a more respectable term, a hypothesis, which serves as his handle for grasping the segment of the world which he is investigating. Without a working theory, he would be overwhelmed by the number and the complexity of the data before him. Darwin stated that "all observation must be for or against some view, if it is to be of any service." What distinguishes the true scientist from the counterfeit is the former's willingness to modify and, if need be, to scrap his theory in favor of another view, if the objective facts decisively demand it. Yet the history of science is replete with examples of the obstacles which new ideas have encountered in making headway against accepted notions. Religious beliefs are held, as a rule, with greater tenacity, and changes are even more painful. But, essentially, the steps in the process are similar: an original belief, its confrontation with reality, and the consequent modification of the belief.

In an even more fundamental sense as well, religion and science resemble each other. Both rest upon a substratum of faith in a world which is intelligible, because it reflects the operations of an intelligence (whether with a capital I or a small letter is immaterial here). Underlying all scientific activity is the spirit which Einstein described in these words: "What a deep faith in the rationality of the world and what a longing to understand even a small glimpse of it, which makes it worthwhile for a man to spend years of lonely work upon scientific research!"

Faith in the rationality of the world *precedes* scientific research and in turn is supported by it. When, for example, a biologist begins to study an organism, his first question is, what is the function of this particular organ? He takes it for granted that the existence of an organ postulates an activity. In fact, when he finds an organ which seems to be useless, such as the appendix, he assumes that it must have possessed a function in the past, and that today it is a vestigial remains. The chemist Mendeleieff, in his table of atomic numbers, set forth the various chemical elements known in his time, and did not hesitate to postulate that the empty places in his table would ultimately be filled in. His prophecy was fulfilled, but as significant as his foretelling of the few missing elements was the underlying faith that the blocks out of which the universe is built fall into a pattern. That his assumption proved to be true is important, as we shall see, for the nature of the world; that it was made at all reveals the nature of the scientific process.

Belief in the rationality of the world has as its corollary the faith in the uniformity of nature, the universality of its laws. Thus when a chemist publishes the results of his experiments in his laboratory, he is expressing his conviction that what he has discovered in one corner of the earth applies everywhere, and that what is true today held true yesterday and will be valid tomorrow.

Even more fundamental than the faith in the rationality and the uniformity of nature is the assumption that what man sees really exists, that the world about him is not simply an illusion, a phantasy of the imagination. No one can prove that in his waking state man is not asleep, and that what he sees about him is not a dream. Yet all human activity, scientific and practical, is predicated on the belief that, allowing for the distortions and imperfections of man's observation and reason, the real world exists. Solipsism, the view that nothing really exists in the world but I, is universally rejected as a fallacy, not because of any logical demonstration, but because all life and activity would be impossible on that assumption.

Thus science in general rests upon articles of faith of the most far-reaching character. In addition, each science has its own body of special assumptions. It is therefore literally true that *no significant proposition can ever be proved*, unless it rests upon a foundation of beliefs which are not susceptible of proof. Perhaps more than in any other science or branch of mathematics, logic prevails in Euclidean geometry, where every proposition is proved, Q. E. D. Yet, as any elementary student of the subject knows, before the first theorem can be demonstrated, a whole series of axioms and postulates must be assumed, none of which can be proved. Obviously, they are accepted as reasonable, because they seem plausible, but they cannot be demonstrated. So much so that non-Euclidean geometry does not accept them. Yet unless these axioms and postulates were taken for granted, the entire superstructure of Euclidean geometry would be impossible.

Obviously, religion rests upon a series of beliefs which are not subject to logical demonstration, but which its devotees believe to be true. The process of conviction is thus not very dissimilar in both enterprises.

Undoubtedly, the beliefs of religion are not the same as the assumptions made by science. The body of beliefs in religion is considerably more extensive than in science. In part, the reason lies in the fact that religion is concerned with the entire universe, rather than with the segment which man has succeeded in exploring. Moreover, because the beliefs of religion are concerned with the fundamental views of life and death, they will be held with fervor, and surrendered only after considerable anguish and struggle. Yet in both these respects the contrast between religion and science, while very real, is a difference of degree rather than of kind.

It is true that religion attributes the truths which it cherishes to Divine communication, to a process of Revelation, the result of an encounter between God and the prophet, who is then bidden to teach: "Thus saith the Lord." Yet even this ineffable experience is not altogether dissimilar to what science calls intuition. Jung argued that "no scientific discovery has ever been achieved except by intuition." Einstein wrote: "At times I feel certain that I am right without knowing the reason. When the eclipse of 1919 confirmed my intuition, I was not in the least surprised" (*Cosmic Religion, p. 97*). Intuition represents that mysterious inner enlightenment which comes to the most gifted and favored of human spirits.

Thus both religion and science begin with assumptions, with acts of faith. Armed with its respective body of belief, each enterprise goes forth to observe the world about us. Various logical conclusions will emerge, constituting the content of science, on the one hand, and the teaching of religion, on the other. It is, therefore, clear that Tertullian's aphorism, *credo quia absurdum*, "I believe because it is absurd," is far better replaced by the utterance of Anselm, *credo ut intelligam*, "I believe in order that I may understand." Belief must nurture understanding, as surely as understanding must ultimately flower into belief.

The similarity in approach between religion and science is by no means to be regarded as identity. Far more far-reaching and significant are the differences between them. First and foremost is the fact that each science is concerned with some single aspect of reality. For the purpose of understanding the complex universe in which we live, scientific research divides it into specific segments, such as geology, astronomy, biology, chemistry, or psychology. Each segment, having thus been divided for the purpose of analysis, is then subjected to rigorous scrutiny and study. It is this capacity to subdivide which makes it possible for science to conquer. Religion, on the other hand, is concerned with a view of reality as a whole.

Hence, when science is confronted with an insoluble problem, even in its own area, it can afford to confess its ignorance and remain silent. Religion must have a word for the anguished soul walking in darkness, and it must speak now. For as a world-view, religion must reckon with the whole of life, with the unknown as well as with the known, with the immeasurable as well as with the measurable. It must grapple with chaos as well as with cosmos, and it must teach man to face suffering and death as well as to taste the beauty and gaiety of life. What is more, men must be shown

how to enjoy life's pleasures without having them turn to gall and
wormwood. In short, a valid religious world-view cannot do violence to the vast segment of experience which science has comprehended and interpreted, but neither can it overlook the multifarious
elements of the universe which science has not yet mastered. Moreover, there are many aspects of life in the world that are forever
beyond the power of scientific method. There are more things in
heaven and earth than can be weighed and measured; the things
which count cannot be counted.

We are becoming increasingly aware of the reality of that which
is beyond the material. As the atom of matter dissolves into the
electron of energy, so, we are discovering, the intangibles of human
aspiration and fear, achievement and frustration, are realities, concrete forces in their impact on the world of nature and man.

An even more fundamental difference is that science is concerned
with the establishing of facts, not with passing judgment on what
is right or wrong, beautiful or ugly, good or evil. The objectivity
of science is fundamental to its achievement; every aspect of reality
is of equal value for scientific research. Whatever the field of research, it is legitimate so long as it seeks the truth as honestly as
possible. What society does with the discovery, whether it uses it
for life or for death, is no longer within the province of science.
Religion, on the other hand, is fundamentally concerned with value-
judgments, with a scale of ideals and commandments which it sets
before people. Science, in other words, deals with the means and
not with the ends of life, except in the negative sense of ruling out
certain proposed goals as running counter to the facts of man's
nature and of the world. But when there are several possible alternatives, none of which contradicts the facts, science *per se* is
neutral.

When we declare that facts are the area of science and that
values are the province of religion, our purpose is not to separate
the protagonists, but, on the contrary, to make it clear that tension
between religion and science is both inevitable and necessary. Vital
religion, being concerned with reality, must always build upon the
picture of reality disclosed by scientific research. When science
changes its understanding of the universe, religion must necessarily
adjust its vision of the world as well as the conclusions which it
has drawn from it. Does this mean that religion is perpetually at

the mercy of science? The answer is both "yes" and "no." Most scientific progress consists of minute changes in our body of knowledge, which do not affect our over-all view of the universe. But any basic, far-reaching change in the field of science must ultimately affect the world-view upon which religion is based. When the Ptolemaic view of the earth as the center of the universe, with the sun rising in the east and setting in the west, gave way to the Copernican conception of the earth as one of several planets revolving around the sun, the change had tremendous repercussions upon religion's conception both of God and of the role of man in His plan. No wonder the medieval church fought so bitterly against the ideas of Galileo and Copernicus. The evolutionary hypothesis of the origin of species radically transformed the conception of God's role in creation and man's place in the world. The challenge which evolution posed to traditional religion went far beyond the contradiction that it offered to the description of Creation in the opening chapter of *Genesis*. The field of psychology, particularly in the psychoanalytical schools, is still too fluid for any degree of assurance or any real consensus as to its abiding results. Yet it is already clear that it must drastically affect our conception of the nature of man, his impulses, his capacities, and his vices and his virtues, as well as the role of reason as a factor in human character.

In sum, a rethinking of religious fundamentals becomes an inescapable duty, however painful, when any major scientific discovery transforms our conception of reality.

There will be cases, of course, where science itself will be noncommittal with regard to competing theories, or to the conclusions which may be drawn from them, that go beyond the objective evidence. Professor R. A. Millikan, the famous physicist, maintained that "the more he read and studied, the more he was sure about the existence of God." His colleague, the eminent chemist, Dr. Linus C. Pauling, confessed, "My experience has been different, in a sense almost opposite that of Professor Millikan." The knowledge of the physical universe by both men is of the highest order; they diverge in their interpretation of the phenomena. Similarly, it has been argued that the biologic and geologic evidence of evolution simply indicates that one species was derived from another, but does not disclose any direction in the process. Does the scroll of evolutionary development give any evidence of design? There

have been scientists on both sides of the question. Finding design in
the evidence is an interpretation of the data of science which will
impress the observer as more or less plausible, depending on non-
scientific factors in his personality. In a case such as this, religion
is free to choose that particular approach which is most congenial
to its own thinking and for which it believes the evidence is
strongest.

The freedom of choice which religion has between two opposite
readings on the book of science may be illustrated through a Biblical incident. The Book of *Numbers* tells that before the Israelites
were ready to embark upon the conquest of the Promised Land,
Moses sent twelve spies to bring back a report, both as to the character of the country and as to the status of its military defenses.
The spies returned, bringing a majority and a minority report,
radically different in conclusion, though the sum and substance
of the two reports was identical. The ten spies, filled with fear
and cowardice, reported: "The land is indeed beautiful, but it will
prove difficult to conquer." Only the courageous minority of two,
Joshua and Caleb, reported in quite a different spirit: "The land
will indeed be difficult to conquer, but it is worth fighting for."
Similarly, religion is free to choose that interpretation of reality
which is life-giving, rather than the view which breaks down man's
faith in life and his hope for the future. Hence, the religious spirit
sees in evolution striking evidence of a great plan with a great Intelligence directing it along the way. Indeed, it regards its view as
far more plausible than the denial of direction or purpose in the
process.

The right and duty of religious faith to read the book of life
through its own lenses become particularly important whenever, as
is generally the case, science itself offers only a partial clue to
reality. A parable all too congenial to our war-ridden age may serve
to illustrate the true relationship of religion and science. Let us
imagine an army commander confronting a powerful enemy in
a far-flung campaign. In preparing for battle, General Headquarters
sends out scouts to bring back reports concerning the disposition
of the enemy forces, the nature of the terrain, the quantity and
the quality of his supplies, and, if possible, the plans of the foe.
When the intelligence reports are brought back, the commander-

in-chief must coordinate the material, evaluate it, and then plan his strategy. His task is admittedly hazardous and uncertain, because the reports which he receives will at best be fragmentary; few, if any, will be free from some degree of error, and on many of the most important questions he may have no information at all. Yet the commanding general cannot wait for the day when all the information will be at hand, if only because that day will never come. He must decide upon his plan of action for the immediate future. Having no choice, he coordinates the evidence before him, attempts to discount manifest errors, estimates the probabilities with regard to the information which he lacks, and on that basis plans the campaign against the enemy. Obviously, his own temperament and insight will profoundly affect his judgment on the objective facts before him, and will often spell the difference between victory and defeat.

Mankind may be compared to the commander-in-chief, in its long struggle to master a world which it did not create. Each branch of science represents a scout going out into the unknown and bringing back his report on one or another aspect of reality. These presentations are of the highest value, yet they are compounded of truths, half-truths, downright errors, and complete absence of information. From all these reports, man must construct a credible view of the universe, which is his philosophy or religion. Armed with his plan of campaign, man must go forth in the battle of life, which he cannot postpone for the future, because he will not be living forever!

Obviously, the commander-in-chief is dependent upon his intelligence reports for information, and it would be suicidal to ignore them. Yet he must go beyond them and, taking both the known and the unknown factors into consideration, he must stake all his resources on victory. Similarly, for its conception of the universe, religion must turn to the findings of science, which it disregards at its peril. Yet it must go beyond science in its endeavor to find a world-view that will be satisfying and life-giving. The believer stakes his life on his vision of God in the world.

The reason for the tension that has existed in past centuries between religion and science is now clear. At any given moment in human experience, the prevailing conception of the universe as taught by religion will be based upon the scientific conclusions achieved earlier. If, in the interim, science has pressed forward to new frontiers of discovery, it will necessarily come into collision with the accepted religious teaching of the time. Superficially, it will seem that science is attacking religion, but actually it is the presuppositions which religion accepted from earlier science that it is seeking to replace. An enlightened religious approach will therefore find it both a challenge and an opportunity to reconsider its fundamentals and to bring them into harmony with what is true and life-giving in the new advance of science. Religion and science are both partners in man's unending quest for understanding as the key to the good life.

It should be added that even in the quest for objective truth, religion renders significant service. The very existence of a tradition makes it possible to adjust the insights and attitudes of religion to new discoveries without destroying man's sense of continuity. Moreover, the natural resistance of established tradition to a new discovery has value in itself, since it is the nature of every pioneer to go to extremes and to exaggerate the character of his achievement. A conservative influence, like a religious tradition which gives way only slowly before the impact of new and revolutionary ideas, acts as a salutary check upon notions that are proclaimed in the name of science but are beyond its proper purview. The theory of evolution, as preached by some of its early popularizers, was hailed by them as "disproving" God. Freud's view of religion as an illusion, of God as a transformation of the father-image, of morality as a projection of infantile fears—all these ideas represented incursions by a great scientist beyond the legitimate sphere of science. The scientist has a perfect right to have his own religion, theistic, agnostic, or atheistic as it may be. But when he speaks on the issues of life, he should be aware of the fact that it is as a man and not as a scientist that he speaks.

In conclusion, religion, if it is vital, will always be dependent in substantial measure upon science, just as science in turn derives its basic faith and insights from the same fundamental presuppositions that underlie religion. Science and religion, properly comprehended, are neither antagonists nor identical enterprises, but complementary aspects of the human spirit, which needs both in order to see life whole and find it good. Only a religion in which tolerance is linked to warm conviction, and open-mindedness joined to passionate affirmation is worthy of the allegiance of free men. Such a faith, we profoundly believe, may be found, if we seek it in humility and truth. To this basic task we now turn.

GOD

CHAPTER VI

The World and God

A religion without God means playing Hamlet without the prince of Denmark. That is true at least for Western man, where faith in a Supreme Being has always been central in every religious system. Though there have been, to be sure, religions which posited no faith in a Deity, advocates and opponents alike will concede that religion stands or falls with the faith in a Supreme Being outside of man, who governs man's destiny, and with whom man can, in some sense, establish a relationship. Here is the crucial issue: *Is faith in God possible for modern men who are truly conscious of their world, who wish to reckon and not ignore the conclusions of contemporary science and are painfully aware of the evils that darken the horizons of human life?* That is the question, and no dogmatic answer can carry any measure of conviction.

As we have already noted, there is a very articulate school of thought, with a long and respectable tradition behind it, which opposes any rational discussion of the subject. This distrust of the canons of abstract thought and logic, this conviction that belief in God must necessarily be beyond argument or discussion, is often maintained today, as in the past, by men who are themselves richly endowed with the capacity for thought and the gift of expression. In a famous passage, the French thinker, Blaise Pascal, describes his tortured wrestling with religious doubt, until he discovered that what he was seeking was "not the God of the philosophers, but the God of Abraham, Isaac and Jacob." Centuries before his time the Spanish Hebrew poet, Judah Halevi, warned against the blan-

dishments of Greek wisdom, "which produces flowers but no
fruits." His great masterpiece, the *Cuzari*, is a religio-philosophic
dialogue, designed to support his contention that rational demonstration is useless in building the religious life. The same viewpoint
is expressed in the contemporary epigram that religion must be
caught, it cannot be taught.

Undoubtedly, an intellectual discussion on God cannot be
equated with faith in God, and theology is not identical with religion. But a rational conviction of the truths of religion bears the
same relationship to the life of faith that a skeletal structure has
to a living organism. The skeleton is not the body, but without it
the body could not function. Thus a sober analysis of the grounds
for faith in God cannot do duty for a vibrant, deeply-felt religion,
but without it, religion cannot command the assent of the mind, nor
ultimately retain the allegiance of the heart.

Very often, those who oppose the rational approach to religion
try to buttress their position by maintaining that Biblical religion
never argued or demonstrated its fundamental tenets. We have
noted above that this contention rests upon a misreading of the
evidence—the Biblical writers naturally took for granted what no-
body denied; but in all the issues over which men agonized and
differed, they warmly defended their positions, using the canons
of thought native to them. But even if it were true that Biblical
religion was nonrational in expression, that would scarcely suffice
our age, confronted as it is by radical challenges of the greatest
magnitude. It is noteworthy that the medieval religious philosophers, Moslem, Jewish, and Christian, whose loyalty to their respective traditions was not inferior to that of modern exponents
of religion, did not fall back upon the Qoran, the Hebrew Scriptures, and the New Testament, respectively, and use them to justify
a refusal to meet the onslaught of skepticism and doubt. On the
contrary, their encounters with the other side stimulated them and
helped to enrich the content of their own thought. In brief, the
analogy from Biblical religion is mistaken; even if it were not, it
would be no analogy.

Intellectual discussion of such traditional problems as the existence of God is often deprecated from another point of view. There
is no use attempting to prove the truth of religion, the argument
runs, because the effort is doomed to failure. It can only convince

those who are convinced already. Thus, it is maintained, the herculean intellectual efforts of the medieval scholastics proved barren of results. This is quite wide of the mark. The truth is that the work of the medieval philosophers was by no means wasted, even from the modern point of view. Most modern men take it for granted today that God has no physical form, and recognize that the traditional religious vocabulary is to be understood figuratively. These insights are essentially the achievements of the medieval thinkers who, through their canons of interpretation, taught their contemporaries, and the generations to follow, that "the Scriptures speak in the language of men" and that the language applied to God in the Bible is not to be understood as implying that He has any physical form, dimensions or attributes. In their struggle against an anthropomorphic conception of the Deity, the medieval philosophers were carrying to a logical conclusion a process which had begun long before them in the Aramaic translations of Scripture, in Philo, among some of the Talmudic rabbis, and, indeed, in the pages of the Bible itself. This fact, incidentally, is significant in refuting the idea that rational philosophy represents an alien growth in the vineyard of religion, a noxious weed which must be uprooted by the faithful. At all events, today we need not raise the question of any physical form for God. It is, therefore, the rankest ingratitude to disdain the achievements of the philosophers, while appropriating the fruits of their labors.

It is to be expected that many of the problems which confronted them, and consequently the solutions which they advanced, will be irrelevant to our thought today. But much remains that is significant for the modern mind. Even their proofs for the existence of God are of more than historical interest.

Of the four principal categories, several can hardly be regarded as convincing. Such is, for example, the famous "ontological argument" of St. Anselm (1033–1109), which is based on the nature of being. In brief, Anselm argued that every one of us can conceive a totally perfect being, than which nothing greater can be imagined. Now the perfection in this being must necessarily include its existence, for otherwise this perfect being would be less perfect than any object that really exists. Hence this perfect being must be endowed with the attribute of existence—we call it God. Readers interested in the subtleties of logical analysis may follow the fortunes of Anselm's argument in the criticisms of Gaunilon, Aquinas, and Kant and in the defenses of Descartes and Leibniz. While the argument does possess an element of value, most men would admit that merely conceiving of God does not prove His existence. To put it in philosophic language, the transfer from thought to reality, from the conceptual order to the real order, is not justified.

Similarly with the "Twenty-five Propositions" on the existence and incorporeality of God, adduced by the great Jewish thinker Maimonides, or the "Five Ways" of St. Thomas Aquinas, the most influential philosopher of medieval Christendom, who borrowed substantially from his Jewish forerunner. Starting from the generally accepted assumption that every effect has its cause, Aquinas seeks to show that God exists, by calling attention to certain effects in the natural order, which therefore point to God as their cause.

Several of his arguments will hardly seem convincing to the modern mind. Such is his "logical argument," that from "necessity." He notes that all beings in the cosmos are merely possible, that is, they may or may not exist, and therefore they have a limited span of existence, during which they are generated, become corrupted, and finally cease to be. But if there was a time when they did not exist, nothing would exist now, unless we assume one Being whose existence is logically necessary and eternal. That necessary Being is God.

With great acuteness Aquinas also argued from the existence of motion in the world to a motionless Cause, from grades of perfection to a Perfect Source. This approach, which actually goes back to Plato and Aristotle, declares that the changeability and imperfection of all creatures require the assumption of one Being who is responsible for all the motion in progress. Hence, the existence of an imperfect world in motion must imply a perfect, immovable Mover, who is God.

There remain, however, two principal contentions of the medieval philosophers which have significance for the modern mind: the teleological and the cosmological arguments for God. These arguments maintain that at every hand we see an order (Greek *cosmos*), an "arrangement," which reveals a higher aim and purpose (Greek *telos*—"end, goal"). The existence of the design logically implies the presence of a rational Being who is the Designer.

These "proofs" for the existence of a Supreme Being were subjected to devastating criticism by the German philosopher Immanuel Kant in the eighteenth century. Kant argued that since
all our knowledge reaches us through the medium of the senses, we
can know only *phenomena*, the appearance of things, never the
noumena, or their essential nature. Hence it is impossible to prove
the existence of God by logical demonstration, for we can perceive
only His effects, rather than His essence. Actually, Kant's criticism,
which demonstrates that God cannot be proved like a mathematical
proposition, valid though it be, is less shattering in its impact upon
religious thought than originally seemed to be the case. As we have
seen earlier, in every department of human thought, including
mathematics, such absolute demonstrations are impossible without
prior assumptions. Now, if an element of faith must precede all
logical proofs, how can logical proofs in and of themselves be
expected to demonstrate faith in God?

There is another reason why an airtight proof is not to be expected. Wherever we turn, we find the universe, including the life
of man, already a "going concern," far advanced beyond its beginnings. We have no experience of origins, only of operations.
We know nothing and therefore can hazard little more than
guesses regarding the origins of the universe as a whole, or the
solar system, or of the emergence of life, or the appearance of man
on this planet, or the beginnings of speech or thought or music or
society. But God is by definition the Creator, the Progenitor, the
Author and Initiator of the phenomenon of existence and the
process of life, all of which was set in motion long before we
appeared. We totally lack the experience and the perception for
grasping the process of creation. It is, therefore, not to be expected
that we shall discover God in the very moment of the creative act,
beyond cavil or doubt.

Finally, Kant's emphasis upon the idea that only the appearances, and not the essences, of reality are disclosed to man is far
from being as destructive of belief in God as some have imagined.
On the contrary, his contention is in accord with the deepest
insights of Biblical religion. The book of *Exodus*, after describing
the escape of the Israelites from Egyptian bondage under the
leadership of Moses, tells of the Revelation of God at Sinai. The
ecstasy of that exalted moment is followed by an inevitable de-

pression of spirit among the people which leads to the making of
the Golden Calf. Distraught by their betrayal of all the ideals to
which he has dedicated his life, Moses seeks some reassurance from
God that all is not in vain. He therefore asks to be vouchsafed
the sight of the Divine. To this plea, God responds: "Thou canst
not see My face and live; for no man can see Me and live. When
I shall cause My Glory to pass before thee, I shall put thee in the
crevice of the rock and shall cover thy face until I pass. When
I remove My hand, thou shalt see My back parts, but My face
will not be seen" (*Exodus* 32:11–27; 33:12–23).

The passage, though it utilizes simple, graphic terms, like "face"
and "back," as indeed it must, is far from naive in the truth which
it seeks to communicate—man at best can grasp only the reflection of the Divine Glory as revealed in God's activity in the
world; His essence is beyond man's reach. In the "Hymn of
Glory," chanted in the synagogue ritual to the present day, the
poet declares:

> "Men have pictured Thee, but not according to Thine essence,
>   They have imaged Thee according to Thy deeds."

The logician may insist that essences are unknowable; the reflective
observer is satisfied to note the evidence of God's activity in the
world. Actually, the cosmological and teleological arguments of
the medieval philosophers, in spite of Kant's strictures, have gained
in strength with the growth of man's comprehension of the universe, his increasing grasp of its pattern and structure.

What we wish to present is, therefore, not a logical "proof" of
God's existence, but some of the grounds on which the religious
spirit bases its faith in God as King of the universe. It has long
been recognized that the religious approach to reality is far more
satisfactory emotionally than the world-views of agnosticism and
atheism, giving men a sense of at-homeness and a source of hope
and courage. We are not now concerned with these psychological
advantages. We submit that belief in God offers an infinitely more
reasonable interpretation of the universe than rival approaches,
that it is a "truer" reading of the facts than disbelief. Recognition
of God obviously raises substantial problems that cannot be ignored, to which we shall turn subsequently. But the difficulties
faced by a religious interpretation of reality are far more easily

met than the obstacles that are encountered by those who deny
God's existence or doubt it.

At the outset, let it be noted that the distinction which the
medieval philosophers drew between the cosmological argument
of order and the teleological argument of purpose in the universe
arose because they conceived of the universe in static terms.
Similarly, rabbinic thought divided the sphere of Divine activity
into "the work of creation" completed in the past (*maaseh
bereshith*) and "the government of the world" carried on in the
present (*maaseh merkabah*). For modern man, who conceives of
the universe in dynamic terms, order and purpose, cosmos and
process, are one. Past and present and future coalesce to reveal
God as the Lord of Nature.

That nature presupposes a Divine creator was a self-evident
truth to the Prophets, singers, and sages in the Bible: "Lift up
your eyes on high and see who has created all these, who brings
forth their hosts in number, calling each by its name, so great in
strength and mighty in power that not one is missing!" (*Isa.*
40:26). And the Psalmist sang: "The heavens proclaim the glory
of God and the firmament declares His handiwork." In the same
spirit a Hasidic teacher remarked centuries later that just as jewels
remind a lover of his beloved, so man, beholding the beauty of the
world, sees it as a reflection of God. In the ancient world, the
world's existence was tantamount to the existence of God. Even
the nonbeliever who declared "there is no God" (*Ps.* 14:1) was
not denying the reality of God; what he doubted was that God
was concerned with human actions and enforced righteousness in
the world. This was as true among the Greeks and Romans as
among the Hebrews.

It was not until the emergence of modern science that the "self-
evident truth" of the existence of God became a highly debatable
proposition. As science revealed the laws of nature in ever more
abundant measure, scientists became absorbed with the task of
tracing the pattern of cause and effect and adding new links to
the chain. Science seemed to reveal a mechanistic universe, held
firmly in the grip of the iron law of necessity. "I understand,"
said Napoleon I to the astronomer Laplace, "that you have written
a four-hundred-page work on the solar system without once
mentioning God." "God," replied Laplace, "is a hypothesis I

can do without." The positivist Auguste Comte was a little more *galant* in his attitude to the Deity. Mankind had gone through two stages of immaturity, those of religion and metaphysics, when God had bulked large in human thought. Now, in this positivistic age, science would escort God to the frontiers of the universe and bow Him out with thanks for services previously rendered.

Such a position, in which God is irrelevant or entirely expendable, may seem tenable, but only as long as one refrains from asking the ultimate questions. Those whom William James called "the tough-minded" can exercise this self-control. As we have seen, the task of science is to reveal the nature of reality and the laws by which it is governed. Science is dedicated to verifiable truth, preferably by experimentation; it therefore engages in a minimum of speculation about origins and is unconcerned with value-judgments. But scientists are not merely practitioners of science; they are human beings, and these perennial issues continue to intrude upon the thinking of "the tender-minded," whose number is legion. How did it all begin? What agency, if any, set the universe in motion, created life, formed man? What can we infer concerning the Maker from the made?

The argument from design in the universe refuses to die! On the contrary, it continues to gain in vigor and substance as man's insight into the universe continues to grow. The cosmological argument, that the universe reveals design, and the teleological argument, that the world discloses a direction and purpose, have more substance behind them today for the religious believer than in medieval days.

Evidence is constantly growing of a universe that is not only *law-abiding* but *instinct with life*. In the eighteenth century William Paley popularized the view of the world as a wondrously complex mechanism by his figure of God as a "celestial Watchmaker." As the march of science swept triumphantly on in the nineteenth century, men could not be blamed for believing, with Ernest Haeckel, that they had solved "the Riddle of the Universe," and that matter and mechanics were the only realities. Only as the insights of science deepened in the twentieth century did it become clear that matter itself is energy and that the world is best conceived of as a great thought rather than a great machine, a living organism with boundless potentials for growth rather than a lifeless mechanism with rigidly limited processes.

Men find it harder to believe that a dead world can produce life and that chaos and chance can create law and order. The universe, as revealed by astronomy, physics, and chemistry, is an organism rather than a machine, alive and growing and therefore, in a measure, unpredictable. But the harmony and orderliness of nature remain a recurrent miracle.

It seems strange that scientists, who have the most intimate knowledge of the world, are often indifferent or hostile to religious belief. Very frequently, it is the immature faith of outworn doctrines still preached in the church and the synagogue that they reject. But it is undeniable that many natural scientists, though by no means all, are strangers to the sense of awe and wonder before the Creator of the world which they explore so diligently. The reason inheres, in some degree, at least, in the nature of the scientific process. In order to make progress in his chosen field, the scientist cannot assume in advance that any aspect of the subject is unknowable; on the contrary, he must assume that all can be observed, weighed, counted, measured, tested. A gastroenterologist, for example, must be a mechanist if he wishes to understand the functioning of the stomach as fully as possible; he must be a "vitalist" if he wishes to grasp the world of which the stomach is a part. Since man is a creature of habit and his energies are limited, the scientist at times finds it easier to confine his curiosity to the scientific sphere and limit his approach to the world to the dimension of the scientific method, with the result that he fails to see the forest for the trees, the miracle behind the event.

But the miracle is real. Gilbert K. Chesterton gave vivid expression to this truth when he declared that each morning God knocks at the door of the chambers of the sun and says, "Dear sun, please rise!" Our sense of wonder need not be any the less real because we have abandoned mythology and recognize the reign of law. As Alfred Noyes paraphrased the thought of Isaac Newton:

"Whence arises all this order, this unbroken chain of law?
Whence but from some divine transcendent Power?
And Newton from a height above all worlds answered
And answers still, 'This universe

Exists, and by that one impossible fact
Declares itself a miracle; postulates
An infinite Power within itself, a Whole
Greater than any part, a Unity
Sustaining all, binding all worlds in one.
'Tis not the lack of links within the chain
From cause to cause, but that the chain exists.
That's the unfathomable mystery,
The one unquestioned miracle that we know,
Implying every attribute of God.' "

In the three centuries since Newton, science has made phenomenal progress in every direction. No modern poet has surpassed the author of the book of *Job* in his exultation at the variety, power, and beauty of the natural order. Yet the ancient poet had far less evidence of the harmony of the cosmos than has been revealed by modern science. As it progresses, areas of nature or of human experience which previously seemed to be marked by chance and lawlessness, "a land of darkness, like gloom itself, of deep shadows without any order, where the light is as darkness" (*Job* 10:22), are revealed as *plan and pattern*.

The genius of a Newton, a Mendeleieff, a Freud, an Einstein, does more—it is constantly discovering *unity and order* where multiplicity prevailed before. Common observation shows that a feather drifts to earth more slowly than a bar of iron falls to the ground; came the physicists and demonstrated through the law of gravity that both objects obey the same law and fall at the same rate of speed. By dint of extraordinary research the limitless variety of matter in the world was broken down by chemistry into eighty-eight elements (since increased to over a hundred), these being the blocks out of which all material reality is built. This achievement was carried forward by Mendeleieff, who, basing himself on the atomic weights of the various elements, assigned to each an atomic number. When the elements were now arranged in the order of atomic numbers, a table emerged which revealed that the physical universe possesses a structure of extraordinary symmetry. Mendeleieff's atomic table is arranged horizontally, each succeeding element containing one more proton in the nucleus than its predecessor. That is not all. When the elements are read vertically, a remarkable family-relationship among the elements is disclosed, like fluorine, chlorine, bromine, and iodine, or lithium, sodium, potassium, and rubidium. Most remarkable of all was Mendeleieff's discovery that there were gaps in the table, so that it was possible to foretell the existence of unknown elements, and describe their characteristics. Several such elements were subsequently discovered.

To turn from the physical to the psychological realm, intelligent men for centuries had regarded the area of experience which we call dreams as chaotic and meaningless. It was the great achievement of Freud to disclose pattern and meaning in what hitherto had been the crazy quilt of the dreamworld. Whether Freud's specific system will ultimately prevail, or the alternative theories of his opponents or disciples, is immaterial here. What is significant is that here, too, order has conquered disorder. Every science and subscience exhibits instances of the progress of law in areas where chance was previously assumed to exist.

Unless we adopt the solipsistic fallacy and deny that anything exists in the world except our own selves, it is clear that the order which man sees in nature is not an invention, but a discovery; the pattern is not a man-made illusion which he imposes upon the external world, but is inherent in the structure of reality.

That the universe testifies to a Designer is clear not only from the design, but also from *the question of origins*. How did the cosmos arise? Here two divergent answers—and only two—are possible. One may answer that the world is an accident, without plan or purpose, that the solar system of which our earth is a part arose out of the chance collision of masses of matter in space and that the physical elements which make up our environment came into being out of the disintegration of matter or in some other haphazard manner.

Two difficulties confront this view of the world as arising out of accident. In the first instance, the alleged collision of matter must assume that matter had prior existence. And if the question is put: How did this matter arise? one can avoid the assumption of a Creator only by insisting that matter is eternal, had always been there, and therefore no creative act in time was needed to set the universe in motion. The view of eternal matter was the bedrock of naturalistic philosophy in Aristotle, against which the medieval religious philosophers, like Maimonides, fought vigorously. Now, modern physics and astronomy have ruled Aristotle out of court.

According to the principles of thermodynamics, there is a law of entropy which states that there is a continuous flow of heat from warmer to colder bodies and that this flow cannot be reversed, so as to move spontaneously in the opposite direction. Now, if the universe, or the matter in it, were eternal, it would long ago have run down to a condition where all bodies would be at the same low temperature and no energy would be available. Life would then be impossible. In infinite time this state of entropy would already have come to pass. The hot sun and stars, the earth with its wealth of life, are concrete evidence that the origin of the universe has occurred at a fixed point in time, and therefore the universe must have been *created*. It may be added, in this day of nuclear energy, that in a universe which had always existed, no radioactive elements would now be left.

To meet this problem of entropy, various theories have been proposed. Some scientists conceive of the universe as dynamic, and not as static, and declare that it is actually expanding and not contracting. These are questions of great scientific interest. We are concerned to note only that whatever changes must have a fixed point of origin, and, by that token, must be the result of a creative act in time.

Aside from this question of the origin of matter, the assumption that the physical universe is the product of chance is rendered in the highest degree implausible by another consideration. The long arm of coincidence is, of course, a fact. We cannot therefore rule out the possibility that the elements of order in the universe are an accident, but the likelihood is infinitesimal. An analogy may make the point clear. If we walked into a room and found three coins on the floor, making a perfect equilateral triangle, it might conceivably be the result of accident, the coins having fallen from someone's pocket by chance. If we found six coins in a perfect hexagon, the possibility of chance would be more remote. If we saw a hundred coins ranged in lines of ten each, it is still *conceivable* that their position was the result of chance, but the possibility is slight enough to be virtually excluded. The manifold discoveries of modern science have disclosed so much law and order in the universe that only the most determined of minds can seriously maintain that the world arose out of chance.

Let us observe a few aspects of the physical universe. The size

of the earth may seem to be completely irrelevant. Yet, as Frank
Allen points out, if the earth were as small as the moon, with one-
fourth its present diameter, the force of gravity (one-sixth that of
the earth) would fail to hold both atmosphere and water, and
temperatures would be fatally extreme. If the earth were double
its present diameter, it would have four times its present surface
and twice its force of gravity, the atmosphere would be danger-
ously reduced in height, and its pressure would be increased from
15 to 30 pounds per square inch, with serious repercussions upon
life.

Physicists have pointed out that water possesses unique qualities
without which life could not have been sustained. Such is the fact
that water is the only substance that grows lighter as it freezes,
so that life can be maintained under the mass of ice in rivers and
lakes. The miracle grows upon examination. Biologists tell us that
proteins are the essential constituents of all living cells, and that
they consist of the five elements, carbon, hydrogen, nitrogen,
oxygen, and sulphur, with possibly 40,000 atoms in the ponderous
molecule. As there are 92 chemical elements in Nature, all dis-
tributed at random, the chance that these five elements may come
together to form the life-bearing molecule, the quantity of matter
that must be continually shaken up, and the length of time necessary to finish the task can all be calculated. The brilliant Swiss
mathematician, Charles Eugene Guye, has made the computation
and finds that the odds against such an occurrence are 10^{160} to 1,
or only one chance in 10^{160}, that is, 10 multiplied by itself 160
times, a number far too large to be expressed in words. For it to
occur on the earth alone would require 10^{243} years, far more than
two billion years, the accepted age of the earth. Nor could it have
been formed by shaking up or mixing all the material in the universe, because there is not material enough, as du Nouy has emphasized. Finally, this one molecule is not the end, but the beginning of the process, which must find time and room and material
for the infinite number of steps needed to produce all the plants,
fish, birds, and beasts that fill the earth. To try to explain it all
through the mechanism of chance seems preposterous.

Wherever we turn in nature, evidence of plan reveals itself. The
existence of the "water cycle" and the "ammonia-cycle," the
balance of the "carbon-dioxide oxygen cycle" between animal and

vegetable life, all are too complex and too perfectly suited to the
needs of life to be the result of chance, to have arisen within the
limited period of time since life began on this planet.

If the universe had a point of origin in time, it did not begin of
itself. If chance is ruled out by any rational canon, there was a
plan, and its Author may be fairly designated as God. Thus the
cosmological argument of the medievals is far more powerful today
than in their own time. The cosmos being infinitely more intricate
than they knew, the Intelligence which it presupposes is far more
subtle and creative than they imagined. To be sure, the modern
view of a complex world of incredible magnitude creates the new
problem of the relationship of this Creative Power to man and
his hopes, and we shall need to face the issue later. But the belief
in a great Intelligence at work in the universe is by far the most
reasonable interpretation available to us of the miracle and the
mystery of existence.

The feeling of design in the world blends imperceptibly, for the
religious spirit, with the sense of purpose and direction in the
universe, and cosmology becomes inseparable from teleology.

It is one of the ironies of modern cultural history that the theory
of the evolution of species, which a century ago seemed to under-
mine and deny religious faith, actually serves as its cornerstone
today. The implications of evolution for religion are manysided
and far-reaching. Perhaps the most important consequence lies in
the fact that even if the physical universe be eternal (a view which,
we have seen, runs counter to basic scientific principles), evolution
postulates that life did begin at a fixed point in the history of the
earth. It is surely a reasonable assumption that what has an origin
has an Originator.

This consideration does not exhaust the implications which we
may draw from evolution. In the first instance, the theory of
species evolving from one another assumes a tremendous number
of organic changes taking place on each rung of the ladder of life.
Darwin sought to explain the emergence and survival of the
myriads of new types by the theory of natural selection. Thus,
for example, sea creatures existed in the millions until, by accident,
one chanced to grow an apparatus for breathing on land. Then an
environmental change took place, such as the sudden drying up of
a pond for climatic or geologic reasons, and the sea animals found

themselves on dry land. Only the individual equipped with lungs instead of gills was able to survive and propagate his kind. Thus land animals made their appearance. In a similar fashion, natural selection operated to produce all the known variations in species.

It was soon recognized that while natural selection may have played a part, even an important part, in evolution, it could hardly explain the infinite number of changes which must be assumed in the process from the amoeba to the anthropoid apes and man, all within a fixed span of time much shorter than the age of the earth. The theory of "mutations" was therefore evolved, either as a substitute or, more plausibly, as a supplementary device in the evolutionary process. By chance, changes would occur within the genes that would produce new forms, and these might survive by the side of the original types, or in their stead. Whatever advantages the theory of "mutations" has for meeting problems within the field of biology, it does not answer the ultimate question with which we are concerned. Be the mechanism whatever it may, the incalculable number of changes that evolution presupposes must all have occurred within a fixed period of time, which geologists and paleontologists can estimate with some exactness.

Moreover, studies of mutations in many organisms, especially the fruit fly (drosophilae melanogaster), indicate that most natural mutations, far from being beneficial, are actually lethal in character. The majority of the others are defective or at best neutral, and hence are not calculated to increase the vigor of the individual. Dobzhansky has pointed out that "the injurious character of most mutants is not an attestation of inherent perverseness in nature" (*Science*, Vol. 126, No. 3266, 1957), an observation, incidentally, which has implications for the religious valuation of the world. This judgment aside, mutations arising purely from chance are hardly capable of accounting for the boundless variety of life on this planet. Nor is this all. Patau has computed that a mutation conferring a 1% advantage would require one million generations to effect a population breeding true for the new mutation. It is therefore virtually a mathematical impossibility that this infinite number of infinitesimal modifications in a limitless number of living creatures could have taken place within the time limits *purely by chance*.

We may go even further. The striking fact that emerges from

the history of life as posited by the evolutionary hypothesis is
that at each succeeding stage something new and unexpected
emerged which could not have been foretold in the previous level.
The appearance of life itself on a lifeless planet, the growth of
multicellular organisms, the replacement of fission by sexual re-
production which at once multiplied in infinite degree the possibility of variation and progress, the emergence of land animals out
of the sea, the rise of the mammals, the appearance of the primates,
the development of man marked by the development of the hand
as a tool rather than as a means of locomotion, and, finally, the
emergence of reason, speech, and communication—each was not to
be foreseen in the previous stage. The concept of "emergent evolution" seeks to reckon with this phenomenon of novelty in the
evolutionary process, instead of ignoring it.

The contention that the evolutionary process reflects a purposive
Intelligence becomes even more striking when we focus attention
upon man alone. His history is, of course, of far shorter duration
than that of life on this planet, so that the limitless number of
differences, both quantitative and qualitative, which set him apart
from the lower animals must be telescoped into a relatively short
period of time. That this could happen accidentally is hardly likely.
One example must suffice. It has been estimated that the single
change of man's transformation from a quadruped crawling on all
fours to a biped standing erect required the *simultaneous change*
of some two hundred aspects of his bodily structure, nervous
system, and vision; otherwise he could not keep his physical
balance and be able to function in general. One cannot categorically deny the possibility that the haphazard workings of natural
selection preserved through chance produced the variation and
survival of species. But this explanation is infinitely less plausible
than the view of a directive Intelligence for whom, in Kessel's
words, "natural selection is one of the chief mechanisms of evolution, just as evolution is a mechanism of creation."

Evolution, moreover, sees life as a dynamic process, not as a
static cosmos. By that token, the evolutionary hypothesis makes it
possible to restate in modern form the teleological argument for
God. For life is now seen to possess not only law and order, but
also design and direction. On purely scientific grounds, students

of biology have been struck by the fact that evolutionary change
does not strike out blindly in all directions, but tends to show a
steady progression in one direction. To this characteristic they give
the name *orthogenesis*, "right creation." Of the many instances
available, some, like the evolution of the horse's hoof and the
progressive reduction of his toes, are known to every student of
biology. A more inclusive and less familiar instance is afforded by
the well-known physiologist Homer W. Smith (*From Fish to
Philosopher*). The secret of ascent in the scale of life from the
first vertebrate to man, he finds in the kidney's evolution toward
ever greater complexity. It is in the history of this admittedly
important organ that he sees the magnificent pageant of life passing
in a procession which began hundreds of millions of years ago,
during which time thousands of species have come and gone, until
at last man is revealed as nature's masterpiece. One may perhaps
doubt whether any single organ holds the key to the growth of
life, and Smith may well have oversimplified the process. But for
our purposes, the implications of these and other scientific data
are clear.

*The evidence is abundant that as we ascend the evolutionary
ladder from the amoeba to man, we encounter an ever-greater
complexity of physical structure, a corresponding growth in the
specialization of function among the various organs, together with
an increased degree of efficiency, and an ever more developed
nervous system with a heightened degree of consciousness, which
reaches the maximum of self-awareness in man—a breathtaking
sweep upward through the eons of time.*

Having noted the facts as painstakingly and accurately as it can,
science rests. But the scientist or layman who stops at this point
simply refuses to ask the ultimate question. Thus, George S.
Simpson assures us, "As applied to mankind (the interpretation
of the fossil record) shows that we did not appear all at once but
by an almost incredibly long and slow progression. It shows too,
that there was no anticipation of man's coming. He responds *to no
plan* and *fulfills no supernal purpose*. He stands alone in the Universe, a unique product of a long, unconscious, impersonal, *material*
process, with unique understanding and potentialities. These he
owes to no one but himself, and it is to himself that he is responsi-

ble. He is not the creature of uncontrollable and undeterminable forces, but his own master. He can and must manage his own destiny" (*Life of the Past*, New Haven, 1958).

That the process was "incredibly slow" by human standards, and that man is not at the mercy of uncontrollable forces—these contentions may be true, but they are irrelevant. They certainly do not prove the truth of his highly questionable view that there is no plan or purpose and that man stands alone, owing nothing to anyone. On the contrary, the admittedly tentative reading of the book of Science makes it increasingly difficult to believe that an infinite series of meaningless accidents first produced a dead world, which then spawned the complexity and variety of life all about us. Far more compatible with the evidence is the interpretation of reality which recognizes a great Power, whose ways and thoughts are not ours, who creates and directs the universe and has endowed it with its most miraculous attribute, the phenomenon of life.

In sum, evolution, far from dethroning God, as some of its advocates hoped and many of its opponents feared, has extended the scope of His sovereignty. In the Talmud, a Roman matron once asked the sage Rabbi Joshua how the Almighty occupied himself after completing His work of creation. The sage answered, "He is busy arranging marriages between men and women." After experimenting with the project herself and achieving very sorry results, the matron discovered that matching people properly is a difficult task, worthy of God himself. But modern evolution has another answer to the question put by the Roman lady—God is occupied with the creation of the universe which is a never-ending process. This insight was not altogether lacking in the past. In the language of the Daily Prayer Book, "God renews the work of creation each day continually."

In another profound sense, faith in God serves as the foundation for our understanding of the universe. Centuries before the emergence of modern science, polytheism reigned supreme, with its pluralistic view of the phenomena of existence. In that distant period, the opening chapter in *Genesis* boldly postulated one world as the creation of one God. The entire trend of scientific thought has been not merely the discovery of diverse laws operating in various aspects of reality, but of one unifying process underlying them all. The age-old dualism of matter and energy has finally been broken down by modern physics, which has shown that the raw material of the universe is not inert matter consisting of atoms and molecules, but energy, made up of protons, electrons, neutrons, and other particles. The religious believer sees the world not as inert, but as alive, being an emanation of the Living God. Oliver Lodge spoke of the law of continuity, Eddington, of causation as the basic principle of the Universe. The transcendent importance of Einstein's work lies in the discovery that the various forms of matter and energy are not distinct, unrelated systems, but, on the contrary, are interchangeable and therefore constitute a universe. For the religious consciousness, science, too, proclaims the Unity and Glory of God.

God is not merely the abstract principle of unity underlying the variety of nature. He is also the fountain and source of the unity of mankind. The far-reaching consequences of this concept for human life will be spelled out later. Here it suffices to note that the book of *Genesis*, which emphasizes God as the Creator of the universe—"God saw all that He had made and behold, it was very good" (1:31)—is also the source for the doctrine of the unity and dignity of mankind: "This is the book of the generations of man, in the day God created man, in the image of God created He him" (*Gen.* 5:1). No wonder that a second-century sage declared that this verse, rather than the Golden Rule in *Leviticus,* was the most important passage in the Bible.

The faith in one Living God as the Creator of all goes even further. It insists that there is no impassable gulf between inanimate nature and living beings, and no iron wall separating the lower orders of creation from man. Every living thing in the universe can echo the prophet's word: "Have we not all one Father, hath not one God created us!" The impersonal conclusion of modern biological science that man is simply a higher level in evolution was anticipated by traditional religion. We shall note below that a religious ethic therefore is directed not only toward one's fellow men, but toward the animal world and nature as well. The unity of a living universe—that is the corollary of the faith in a Living God.

If nature as a whole testifies to the existence of God, it is man who bears pre-eminent witness to the attributes of his Creator.

The ancients had no difficulty in conceiving of man as the crown of creation, for the earth was the center of their universe, with the sun, moon, and stars having been created to illumine the earth. When the Church fought its long and desperate battle to prevent the acceptance of a heliocentric universe as maintained by Galileo and Copernicus, it was not motivated merely by the contradiction that such a theory offered to the text of Scripture. Basically, it felt that reducing the earth to a minor position as one of the smaller planets revolving around the sun threatened to dethrone man from his unique position as the child of God, the goal and glory of creation.

Undoubtedly, the centrality of man in the universe cannot be maintained today in the simple, naive terms of the past. Yet the idea seems indestructible, and it reappears in new guise, buttressed by scientific considerations. The astronomers have shown that the stars, like the sun, are much too hot to sustain life; there is no sign of life on the moon or on Venus, and though Mars has the climatic conditions necessary for vegetation, they are insufficient for animal life. As Eddington said in *The Nature of the Physical World*,

> "I do not think that the whole purpose of Creation has been staked on the one planet where we live; and in the long run we cannot deem ourselves the only race that has been or will be gifted with the mystery of consciousness. But I feel inclined to claim that at the present time our race is supreme; and not one of the profusion of stars in their myriad clusters looks down on scenes comparable to those which are passing beneath the rays of the sun."

Even if the possibility of life does exist elsewhere in the universe, the earth still remains infinitely precious as one of the areas, indeed the only one known to us, that has fulfilled the goal of the universe, which is life, and that has attained the goal of life, which is intelligence. That the size of a planet is no indication of its importance is too obvious a point to need laboring.

It may be that man is only a temporary embodiment of the Divine creative will, which may yet pass on to higher and better beings beyond our ken. Far more immediate is the peril that man, in the arrogance of his power and the blindness of his selfishness, may wipe himself from the face of the earth. An old rabbinic tradition declares that God created countless worlds and destroyed them before the present universe came into being. Yet even if our world were to suffer the fate of its predecessors, existence would still not be meaningless. Monsignor Ronald Knox expressed the outlook of faith in two charming and witty limericks about a tree standing in an empty University Quadrangle:

IDEALISM

There once was a man who said, "God
Must think it exceedingly odd,
If He finds that this tree
Continues to be,
When there's no one about in the Quad."

A REPLY

Dear Sir:
　　　Your astonishment's odd.
I am always about in the Quad,
And that's why the tree
Will continue to be,
Since observed by
　　　　　　Yours faithfully,
　　　　　　　　God.

The same idea is expressed in the noble synagogue hymn *Adon Olam:*

Lord of the world, the King supreme,
Ere aught was formed, He reigned alone,
When by His will all things were wrought,
Then was His sovereign name made known.
And when in time all things shall cease,
He still shall reign in majesty.
He was, He is, He shall remain,
All-glorious eternally.

Until and unless man is replaced by another creature, the existence of man offers us several significant insights into the nature of God. The cynical epigram of the Greek philosopher Anaxagoras, already quoted, that if horses could speak, they would describe their god in the shape of a horse, embodies a truth unsuspected by its author—*the qualities which exist to any extent in the creature must inhere in greater degree in its Creator.*

Man possesses the highest degree of consciousness of which we are aware. In the Biblical phrase, he holds sway over the fish of the sea, the fowl of the sky, the beasts creeping upon the earth. He possesses in pre-eminent degree the creative capacity, the ability to change his environment instead of being entirely at its mercy. He is blessed with the gifts of reason and speech, and thus has the means of communicating what he has learned to succeeding generations. It is these gifts which make him, in the great Rabbinic phrase, "co-partner with God in the task of creation."

His intellect finds its counterpart in his moral nature—the indestructible yearning in the heart of men after goodness, truth, and beauty. Admittedly, man's *achievement* is limited, but his *aspiration* is limitless. Man is perpetually driven on by a vision of perfection that gives him no peace. Even the worst of men have some standard of the good, by which they try to live. The tyrant, the exploiter, the murderer, the thief, the liar—each seeks to justify his ways to himself and his fellows, however perverted his scale of values. Hitler appeared to his fellow men, and probably to his own psychopathic self, as a liberator of the German spirit, bringing tidings of joy and strength and peace. As Dionysius the Areopagite said, no man consciously adopts evil as a principle of action.

It is a fair inference that the intellectual and moral qualities possessed by man disclose something of the nature of God. Man's traits can be only a partial embodiment of the attributes of his Maker. Man's intelligence, creative capacity, and moral aspirations, halting, inadequate, and fluctuating as they are, must be part of the universe as a whole, for man is linked by a thousand bonds to the lower orders of creation. To regard these qualities as originating with man and as being limited to man alone means to interpose an iron curtain in nature whose unity is everywhere attested. It leaves inexplicable the emergence of these gifts in one tiny corner of a universe otherwise devoid of intelligence, creativity, and goodness.

Religion has preferred a more reasonable explanation for the endowments of man, which the Bible expresses in a graphic and colorful phrase: "God created man in His image." As an image bears a substantial though imperfect resemblance to the live original, so man is a genuine though partial reflection of His Maker. Rabbi Akiba was seeking to praise God when he said: "Beloved is man that he is created in God's image; especial love was manifested to him in that it was made known to him that he is created in God's image." We are here concerned with the converse— God's attributes of intelligence, creativity, and righteousness are attested by their presence in man.

Man's long pilgrimage on earth has yielded him abundant signs of a living God, who, though invisible in the visible world, is abundantly revealed in it. To be sure, scientific theories change, while it is the banner of the eternal God which religion unfurls. But each man can look at the world only with his own eyes and face life with his own understanding here and now. Man cannot be driven into faith by a scientific argument; but he can be helped to find God in the world of nature, in its origins, its growth, and its governance, and to see His hand in its harmony and purpose. Above all, God may be discerned in the nature of man, who, for all his imperfections, possesses qualities that can be described only as divine.

Kant, who demonstrated that man cannot know God's essence, recognized that there are two roads leading to God open to man: "Two things fill my spirit with ever-new wonder and awe, the starry heavens above me and the moral law within me." The medieval Hebrew poet, Judah Halevi, journeying on a stormy Mediterranean from his native Spain on the way to his beloved Zion, sang of three seas, the water, the heavens, and his own heart, all praising his Maker:

The face of the waters, and the face of the heavens, the infinity of sea,
The infinity of night, are grown pure, are made clear,
And the sea appeareth as a firmament—
Then are they two seas bound up together;
And between them is my heart, a third sea,
Lifting up ever anew my waves of praise.

In view of the intimate bond which links God and man, it follows that He must have a deep concern for the direction taken by the human adventure on this planet. God's manifestations in nature, which we have discussed, do not exhaust His role in the world. The great discovery of the Prophets of Israel was the hand of God in history.

CHAPTER VII

God and the Historic Process

Faith in God as the author and governor of nature is not difficult to maintain; the evidence of order and design is widespread
and convincing. It is probably true that today most men in the
Western world profess faith in God, in the sense that the universe
must have a creator. Technically, therefore, atheists are few and far
between. But in ancient times, precisely such a belief was the hallmark of the nonbeliever! Atheism meant not the denial of God's
existence, but of His activity. Epicurus did not doubt the reality
of the gods on Olympus; he denied only that they were concerned
with human affairs. In ancient Israel, the "fool who said in his
heart, 'There is no God'" meant that God was too remote to note
the doings of men, so that men could act corruptly without fear
of the consequences. Eliphaz in the book of *Job* pictures the sinner
as taking refuge in the thought that his actions are outside the
divine range of vision:

> Is not God in the height of heaven?
> And behold the topmost of the stars,
>   How high they are!
> And thou sayest: "What doth God know?
> Can He judge through the dark cloud?
> Thick clouds are a covering to Him,
>   that He seeth not;
> And He walketh in the circuit of heaven."
>
> (*Job* 22:12–14)

The psalmist, looking upon the spectacle of wickedness triumphant and unchecked, cries out:

> Lord, how long shall the wicked,
> How long shall the wicked exult?
> They gush out, they speak arrogancy;
> All the workers of iniquity bear themselves loftily.
> They crush Thy people, O Lord,
> And afflict Thy heritage.
> They slay the widow and the stranger,
> And murder the fatherless.
> And they say: "The Lord will not see,
> Neither will the God of Jacob give heed."
>
> *(Ps.* 94:3–7*)*

There is no need to multiply quotations. Faith in God means more than admission of a First Cause in nature; it is the recognition of God in history that is the touchstone of vital religion. For man to believe in God must mean to believe that God is concerned with men, their deeds, and their destinies.

In the face of the realities of human life, the endless spectacle of war, poverty, and oppression, is such a faith possible for intelligent and honest men? Can one see the hand of God in history without wearing blinders or rose-tinted spectacles? The question becomes even more crucial when we recall that many passionate believers in God declare this world to be the kingdom of Satan and transfer God's reign to another realm. This approach, incidentally, raises more problems than it answers, for it presupposes a God who created the world and then abdicated His power in it to His adversary. But quite aside from this consideration, is not the admission damaging in the extreme, the confession that this world is evil and is not governed by the law of God?

For the answer which we seek, we can do no better than turn to those who first saw the hand of God in history—the Prophets of Israel. How did they arrive at the doctrine, and how did they meet the problems which it raised? We shall then be able to assess their experience and determine whether their faith in the God of history is both meaningful and acceptable to us today.

The writing of chronicles, the cataloguing of battles and booty, of dynasties, defeats, and victories, is nearly as old as the art of writing itself. For centuries it was believed that the destiny of men and nations consists essentially of an accidental succession of incidents, or at best is the repetition of events in identical cycles. So long as these views prevailed, no true history could result. The Greek historians, for all their superb gifts of narrative and characterization, were essentially chroniclers, who recorded the unrelated occurrences as they were alleged to have happened. The concept of history emerged only when men found a pattern and a direction in the ebb and flow of events. As the philosopher Morris Raphael Cohen reminded us, the recognition that there was an underlying meaning to human events was the insight of the ancient Hebrew historians and Prophets.

The Biblical historians, whose works *Joshua, Judges, Samuel,* and *Kings* continue the narratives of the *Five Books of Moses,* are not primarily concerned with political, economic, military, and cultural factors, or even with the interplay of human personality. To be sure, the Biblical books abound in incisive and illuminating comments on all these themes, but however welcome they are to the modern reader, they are by-products of the Prophets' philosophy of history. If their own testimony is to be trusted, they did not achieve their viewpoint through the objective processes of observation and of reason, but rather through the bright light of Divine revelation, "Thus saith the Lord." But whatever the means by which they first arrived at their insight, they did not hesitate to confront their faith with the data of experience. The scientist who makes a discovery through a blinding flash of intuition submits his conclusion to analysis and test by himself and others. Similarly, the prophetic outlook is the resultant of two factors: a passionately felt faith in a God of righteousness, who has created the world and by whose will it continues to exist; and its confrontation by the testimony of observation and experience, through which the faith was refined and deepened. Out of their faith in God, the righteous Ruler of the world, whose sway is universal, they distilled a principle of incalculable significance: the world in which men live and act is based on justice, for that is the will of God. By the side of the law of causality operating in nature, which the Greeks were formulating, the Hebrew Prophets would set what I would call "the law of moral consequence"—*Righteousness leads to well-being, and unrighteousness must end in disaster.* Since God rules everywhere, the principle must apply everywhere,

to individuals, nations, and civilizations. Thus Isaiah (3:10–11)
declared:

> Say ye of the righteous, that it shall be well with him;
> For they shall eat the fruit of their doings.
> Woe unto the wicked! It shall be ill with him;
> For the work of his hands shall be done to him.

A century earlier, Amos had applied the same touchstone of
justice to contemporary world affairs and found in it the key
to the destiny of all the neighboring nations, Syria, Philistia, Edom,
Ammon, and Moab, and of the Hebrews themselves, Judah and
Israel. Amos' younger contemporary, Hosea, emphasized that the
law of consequence was rooted in the universe, by expressing it in
a metaphor drawn from nature:

> For they sow the wind, and they shall reap the whirlwind. . . .
> Sow to yourselves in righteousness, reap in mercy,
> Break up the fallow ground,
> For it is time to seek the Lord,
> Till He come and teach you righteousness. . . .
> Ye have plowed wickedness, ye have reaped iniquity,
> Ye have eaten the fruit of lies.
>
> (*Hosea* 8:7; 10:12–13)

Biblical thought was, however, too honest to rest content with
a faith divorced from life. Passionately committed to the all-
pervasive law of righteousness in the universe, how could it explain
the widespread victory of the forces of wickedness on the stage of
history? The problem was acutely felt by the mightiest intellect
among the Hebrew prophets, Isaiah of Jerusalem. It was he who
declared that the Lord of hosts is exalted in justice and that God,
the Holy One, is sanctified by righteousness. Yet the Assyrian
conqueror, arrogant and cruel beyond description, was treading
all other nations, including Israel, under foot. How could the
spectacle of evil triumphant be reconciled with a just and almighty
God? This agonizing contradiction Isaiah resolved by his profound
concept of "the rod of God's anger." Assyria was pitiful in its
conceit, boasting of its prowess and cleverness, under the delusion
that it was its own will that was propelling it onward in its unrelenting march to power. Actually, however, the world conqueror
was merely an instrument in God's hand, for rooting out the evil

and ushering in the good. Assyria was not the architect of a "new order," but only a scavenger for destroying the old. When its cosmic function would be accomplished, Assyria would pay the penalty for its arrogance against God and its crimes against man. Thus, for Isaiah, the apparent victory of evil did not contradict God's purposes; it fulfilled them.

That militant evil was therefore the rod of divine wrath, the painful yet necessary scalpel for cutting away diseased tissue in the body politic of society—this insight of the prophet, it may be argued, has been validated again and again in the wars, conquests, and revolutions that bespatter the pages of history from ancient times to our own age. It may well be the key to the meaning of the massive tyrannies and rumbles of revolution in the mid-twentieth century.

Another great difficulty confronted the prophetic faith. Belief in the law of righteousness as universally operating in history led to the inescapable conclusion that a sinful people deserved to perish. That meant that Israel, too, of whose sins the Prophets were all too painfully aware and which they never ceased to denounce, was worthy of destruction, since God plays no favorites in judgment. The Prophets loved God, but they loved their people, too, and could not make their peace with this logical but devastating conclusion. This contradiction the Prophets resolved through several ideas which profoundly enriched the concept of God in history.

The first prophet to be confronted by this agonizing challenge was Amos. When he found that the smugly complacent Northern Kingdom of Israel refused even to hear his message, let alone obey his call for spiritual reconstruction, he foretold its annihilation. Yet the total disappearance of his people was an intolerable prospect, not merely because of his natural attachment to his own flesh and blood, but because of his conviction that God's cause needed a spokesman in an idolatrous world. Israel's survival was necessary to God's plan and by that token inevitable. It was clear that the Northern Kingdom was beyond saving. Thereupon Amos transferred his hopes for the future to the smaller and weaker southern kingdom of Judah, and he announced that "the house of Jacob would not be utterly destroyed" (9:8). Israel's God would have His witness in Israel, purged, redeemed, rededicated.

A generation later, his spiritual descendant, Isaiah of Jerusalem, faced the same heart-rending challenge of a righteous God judging His sinful people. Isaiah refined still further Amos' faith that part of the Hebrew people would survive, by enunciating his doctrine of "the Saving Remnant." Not all of Judah, but a part, the best elements of the people, would be saved. Isaiah saw history as a process of the survival of the spiritually fittest, directed by God, who would reveal those capable of regeneration and salvation.

The same challenge, in a far more agonizing form, confronted Isaiah's anonymous namesake, Deutero-Isaiah, a century and a half later. The people of Judah were now in ignominious exile, crushed under the heel of the Babylonians. How to explain the misery and degradation of Israel? It could not be justified simply in terms of Israel's sin, for Israel was surely no worse than its pagan conqueror. Unless these tormenting doubts were met, the people would be plunged into a despair that would be the prelude to its dissolution. This would be an unalloyed tragedy, not only for Israel but for God's cause as well. Even more vividly than Amos, Deutero-Isaiah recognized the need for "God's witnesses" in the world. A bold rabbinic comment spells out the implications of the Deutero-Isaianic metaphor: "Ye are My witnesses, saith the Lord. If ye are my witnesses, I am the Lord, but if ye are not my witnesses, I am not the Lord."

The great prophet of the Exile accordingly evolved his doctrine of the Suffering Servant of the Lord. Israel is not merely God's witness, but man's teacher, who suffers at the hands of the nations because of their moral immaturity. These tribulations are destined to end, when men recognize Israel's true character:

> Behold, My servant shall prosper,
> He shall be exalted and lifted up and shall be very high.
> The nations shall say,
> "Surely our diseases he did bear, and our pains he carried;
> Whereas we did esteem him stricken,
> Smitten of God, and afflicted.
> But he was wounded because of our transgressions,
> The chastisement of our welfare was upon him,
> And with his stripes we were healed.
> All we like sheep did go astray,
> We turned every one to his own way,

And the Lord has placed upon him
The penalty of us all."
It pleased the Lord to crush and afflict him,
Indeed to give his soul to punishment.
He will see his offspring and live long,
And the Lord's purpose will prevail through him.
Because he bared his soul unto death,
And was numbered with the transgressors;
Yet he bore the sin of many,
And made intercession for the transgressors.

(*Isa.* 52:13; 53:4–6, 10–12)

Human progress, particularly in the spiritual realm, is no joy-ride through time, but a process of slow and painful growth, marked not only by the punishment of the guilty, but often, too, by the expiation of the innocent. The drama is on a cosmic scale, and man is fortunate if he is granted even a glimpse of the meaning of events.

Thus the contradiction between a moral God and an immoral world was lessened, even if not solved, by several perennially fruitful insights of the Hebrew Prophets: the recognition of evil power as the instrument for the purging of the power of evil ("the rod of God's anger"), the doctrine of the Saving Remnant, and the concept of the Suffering Servant of the Lord. The last two ideas in particular did much to give meaning to the history of Israel and to make its millennial agony bearable.

But the prophetic contribution to the faith in God in history was not exhausted by these significant ideas. Even when viewed through the prism of these insights, the present order fell tragically short of exemplifying the triumph of God's righteousness. Human suffering was not limited to Israel; all mankind knew war and privation and cruelty. Not only Israel, but all men, were hungering for redemption from evil, and the tragedy was compounded by the fact that faith in God's salvation was noticeably absent among them. To express this universal yearning, the Hebrew Prophets turned to an ancient folk-belief in "the Day of the Lord," which they transposed to a new key. Like most other nations, ancient and modern alike, the Hebrews believed that on some future day their God would arise and grant them victory over their foes. For the Prophets, the God of Israel was the Father and King of all mankind, and righteousness was His goal. Hence they saw all history moving to a great consummation, the establishment of the Kingdom of God on earth. For several of the Prophets, notably Isaiah and Micah, the instrument for God's purpose in the world would be a Heaven-sent King, the Messiah, the anointed scion of the house of David. The Messiah would fulfill the world's true destiny by ushering in freedom and peace, security and brotherhood, for the world. The Messianic age represents the perfect triumph of God's righteousness in an imperfect world.

This faith in the future has so thoroughly entered the warp and woof of modern thought, though often in debased form, that it requires an effort today to realize how revolutionary the prophetic world-view actually was. The ancients generally regarded human life as constantly declining in value, and the Hebrews originally shared this conception. The myths of all nations told of a golden age in the past, and the Paradise tale in *Genesis* reflects the same standpoint. The Greek epic poet Hesiod described human history as consisting of four successive ages, of gold, silver, copper, and iron, and the present was the last and the worst. The Prophets reversed this universal belief by positing the conviction that man's Golden Age lay in the future. Robert Browning was expressing the authentic Hebraic faith when he had Rabbi Ben Ezra say:

> Grow old along with me,
> The best is yet to be,
> The last of life,
> For which the first was made.

How was this Messianic age to be ushered in? Isaiah and Micah envisioned "the end of days" as emerging out of the present, without any radical transformation either in the nature of man or the world. Differences of interest and conflicts of purposes might still exist among men and nations, but they would be resolved, not by recourse to force or fraud, but to the arbitrament of God's law of justice, the sovereignty of which would be universally acknowledged.

In later periods of Jewish history, the objective conditions of group existence became increasingly intolerable, and there seemed to be no end to the sway of evil within the community or to the domination of alien overlords from without. Devout believers in

God's righteousness found it more and more difficult to envisage
the Messianic age as growing naturally out of the present era of
wickedness. Their fervent faith accordingly underwent a far-
reaching change. The Messiah would be no mere mortal king of
royal descent dedicated to establishing universal justice and peace.
He would be a divine or semi-divine being, part of God's plan for
the world from the moment of its creation. In God's own time, the
Messiah would come, and his intervention from on high would be
accompanied by a world-wide cataclysm in nature. This supernatural version of the Messianic faith is to be met with only in
several highly charged visions in the Biblical books of *Ezekiel* and
Zechariah. In post-Biblical literature, the "Apocalyptic" genre, so
called because it purported to "reveal hidden things" concerning
this future era, became dominant. Two Apocalyptic books, incidentally, *Daniel* and *Revelation*, are familiar to Bible readers,
because they entered the Old and the New Testaments, respectively.

The Dead Sea Scrolls shed a tantalizingly imperfect light on the
Messianic faith of some deeply pious communities in Second
Temple Palestine. For these and other sectarians, as well as for the
generality of Jews, the Messiah became increasingly a supernatural
figure endowed with miraculous powers. A special and complex
development of the Messianic idea reached its culmination in the
Christian figure of the Savior, endowed with power to redeem men
from eternal damnation.

Yet even when the natural order seemed most hopeless and the
Kingdom of God most remote, Western religion did not entirely
surrender the older faith that the Messianic age would be ushered
in within the context of normal human experience. Christianity
was not content solely with the doctrine of individual salvation
in the hereafter. In the face of the chaos and cruelty of the present,
the Christian faith looked forward to the Second Advent, which
would adjust the balance of right and wrong on earth. In Judaism,
the emphasis was even more marked. To be sure, man's existence
in "this world" would be miraculously transformed in "the world
to come." That epoch would be so different from men's present
experience that it was beyond men's power to picture, let alone
comprehend. Hence speculation about its nature was labor lost.
The Talmud applied to it the verse in *Psalms:* "No eye has seen it,

O God, but Thine." In the cosmic calendar, however, the establishment of "the world to come" would be preceded by another era, "the days of the Messiah," the lineaments of which men could easily grasp. In the words of a great Talmudic sage, "The Messianic Age will differ from the present order only because of the absence of the tyranny of empires" (*shi'bud malkhuyot*). The enslavement of peoples, the perpetual menace of war, the universal threat of poverty and insecurity—all these consequences of the abuse of power would be lacking in the Messianic era. For this consummation the Jew prayed daily in the *Alenu:*

> We therefore hope in Thee, O Lord our God, that we may soon behold the glory of Thy might, when Thou wilt remove the abominations from the earth and cause all idolatry to cease. We hope for the day when the world will be perfected under the kingdom of the Almighty, and all mankind will call upon Thy name; when Thou wilt turn unto Thyself all the wicked of the earth. May all the inhabitants of the world perceive and know that unto Thee every knee must bend, every tongue vow loyalty. Before Thee, O Lord our God, may they bow in worship, giving honor unto Thy glorious name.

Christians voiced the same faith in the *Lord's Prayer:* "Thy Kingdom come, Thy will be done *on earth* as it is in heaven."

The relative strength of the two motifs in the Messianic faith which we may call the normal and the miraculous varied with conditions and with individuals. But the prophetic faith in the destined establishment of the kingdom of God on earth never died.

However interesting a historical survey may be, this is not our concern here. The basic question is whether there is any validity for us today in the idea of God operating in history, who is manifest both in the present and the future. Is there any rational ground for believing that God is at work in the sorry present and that history is moving toward the consummation of the ideal society in the future?

We profoundly believe this to be the case. The great moral principle of reward and retribution is for us more than a fancy or a hope; we see it as a law of the universe. The law of righteousness which was enunciated by the Prophets may be described as the moral counterpart of a law in the material world called the "principle of impenetrability." This physical law declares that two objects cannot occupy the same space; when the attempt is made to violate the law, as in an automobile collision, disaster results. The prophetic doctrine may be described as "the moral law of impenetrability"; *no individual or group can usurp the right or position of another with impunity; when the effort is made, as in tyranny or oppression, there is moral collision and social catastrophe.*

It is true that at any particular moment in human experience we see far too many apparent illustrations of injustice triumphant,

"Right forever on the scaffold,
Wrong forever on the throne."

But the adverb "forever" in James Russell Lowell's lines is incorrect. The universal lesson of history is that wrong is never permanently enthroned. Here, folk-wisdom, based upon experience, offers the needed corrective of the poet's lines. The Hebrew proverb, "the thief ends on the scaffold," has its parallels in almost every culture, all expressing the conviction that "though the mills of God grind slowly, yet they grind exceeding fine."

The history of mankind reveals a long succession of empires, Egyptian, Assyrian, Babylonian, Persian, Greek, and Roman, each rising from the ruins of its predecessor. Each was supremely confident that its sway would be eternal, yet each in turn was ultimately swept into the discard. Students of the past have traced the decline of these empires and sought to analyze their fall in terms of social, economic, political, demographic, and even climatic factors. Thus the fall of the mightiest empire of all, Rome, has been explained as due in large measure to the gradual expropriation of the small farmers in Italy, through the creation of large estates owned by absentee landlords. As a result of this concentration of wealth, the backbone of the free Roman people was destroyed. In its stead there came into being a class of share croppers in the country and a *Lumpenproletariat* consisting of the plebeian mobs in Rome. No element in the people had any vital stake in the nation, and they were therefore unable and unwilling to defend the State against the barbarian Teutons from without or from the widespread moral corruption and degeneracy at home.

Explanations such as these, when validated by the facts, are most welcome, since they shed light on the historical phenomena involved. The Prophets would not have objected to them; they would have transposed them into a moral key. In the prophetic conception of history, the great empires of the past all crumbled, because they were all built upon oppression, tyranny, and naked power. Reared upon foundations that violated the moral law of the universe, they had no staying power and were doomed to death. Moreover, the Prophets would insist, no past civilization created by man has survived, because none thus far has adequately fulfilled the principles of righteousness. Each social and political structure thus far erected has hoped to prove the exception to the rule by escaping the law of consequence. Each has paid the penalty for its violation by decay and death.

The principle is written large in the history of our times as well. Our century has witnessed the dissolution of the vast empires of Czarist Russia, Imperial Germany, and Austria-Hungary, which seemed impregnable fifty years ago. The principle has been validated in the crumbling of the mighty military machine of Nazi Germany and its Fascist allies in Europe and Asia. The dismemberment of the British Empire has been more gradual, because some measures have been taken here to temper the traditional tyranny of empires by the new and more just formula of a Commonwealth of Nations.

For the religious spirit, the survival of Britain as a major factor in world affairs under the new dispensation is an instance of the prophetic faith that while justice is a universal law, penitence and restitution can avoid the inexorable doom. The more violent break-up of the French Empire in North Africa and the Far East illustrates the instability of evil, when it is unmitigated by the wisdom of repentance.

The violence and brigandage that have irrupted over a large portion of the earth's surface in North Africa, the Middle East, and the Far East pose a major challenge to the West, and are accompanied by excesses that threaten even the positive values of Western civilization. Yet the historian of the future may see in the chaos and conflict of our age the next, pain-fraught step in the process of human liberation, as colonialism breaks down and the dark-skinned peoples are freed from "the white man's burden." Even the feudal overlords and dictators of the Arab world, who are content to let the masses of their people languish in poverty, disease, and ignorance, while they live in luxury and ease, may well have their role in the great plan. The Kassims and Nassers of today would probably be regarded by an Isaiah as the modern counterpart of ancient Assyria, "the rod of God's anger," His imperfect instruments for annihilating evil and ushering in the good.

The great moral superiority of the democratic way of life does not lie in the absence of defects, for it has its abundant share of corruption and inefficiency, and suffers from vulgarity in standards and the tyranny of the mass. The unique promise of democracy lies in the fact that it provides a way of life in which progress toward an ever greater measure of righteousness in the lives of men may be steady and peaceful, sustained by the reasoned will and interest of the entire people, rather than the desires and self-interest of a powerful minority.

If we observe the theatre of history *sub specie aeternitatis*, we may share the faith of the Prophets that the universe of human action is no less law-abiding than the physical world. That God operates in history does not mean that men are therefore relieved of their obligation to struggle and labor for the achievement of justice and peace. God's law does not operate in a vacuum; both its instruments and its objects are men. The Prophets' passionate denunciation of the evils in their day, their unremitting call for a return to the law of God, demonstrates that a vital faith is not an opiate, but a stimulant to action. Faith in God gives men the added dimensions of courage, because it brings them the conviction that the cause of righteousness in the universe must ultimately triumph.

God reveals himself in history not only negatively, through the fall of empires and the decay of national cultures, but also positively, in the progress of civilization. To be sure, the general weakness of religion in the nineteenth and early twentieth centuries brought in its wake the decline of the prophetic faith in God operating in history. Instead, men repeated with relish Napoleon's dictum that "God is on the side of the heaviest battalions." But the magnificent optimism of prophetic religion, its faith in a brighter future for mankind, did not die, largely because of the amazing gains in scientific research and technological invention. Instead, the faith became secularized and emerged in a new and debased form, in the modern theory of human progress, mechanical, automatic, and inevitable. As men's material welfare continued to improve, at least in Western Europe and America, they looked forward to constant progress that would never be halted or reversed. Increasingly, modern men became confident that they had outgrown the older religious view of history and could dispense both with God and His Messiah. The theory of progress reached the nadir of its vulgarization in the litany proposed as a daily exercise by Dr. Emile Coué: "Day by day, in every way, I am getting better and better."

The last three decades of the twentieth century dealt this concept of automatic progress a body-blow. It became difficult to the point of impossibility to maintain this faith after two catastrophic World Wars, and a half dozen "small" wars, grimly highlighted by the wholesale destruction by air raids and the horrors of the atomic bomb. As the great Powers continue to accumulate the instruments for an ever more awesome "massive retaliation," the threat of the extinction of the human race, or, at least, the destruction of modern civilization, has become a grim reality.

The theory of progress has therefore been attacked and ridiculed, with a bitterness that reveals modern man's acute sense of disappointment. Much of contemporary literature and thought reflects the sense of man's innate depravity, the folly of trusting any capacities within him for good, and the conviction that his future is bleak, if not altogether nonexistent.

Here, as is so often the case, we can observe the deep-seated human tendency to leap from one extreme to the other. The doctrine of automatic, unrelenting, and inevitable progress, which is obviously untenable, is only a vulgarization of the faith that the direction of human history is fundamentally upward. If it were possible to plot human development on a graph, there would be no straight line upward; there would be many a plateau and a decline, but the general trend would be toward ever higher levels. If we do not fall prey to the fashionable pose of disillusion and soberly examine the record, a good case can be made out for the contention that progress is real.

By and large, men are happier today than ever before, even if we define happiness in the minimal, pragmatic sense of the absence or reduction of pain. Let it not be forgotten that for the greater portion of human history, most men were physically enslaved, not being able to call their bodies or their children their

own. Man's records go back some eighty centuries. It is less than
a century since serfdom was abolished in Czarist Russia and the
slaves were emancipated in the United States. The glory that was
Greece rested upon the foundation of human bondage, which
Aristotle justified on the ground that unless most men were slaves,
the gifted minority would not be free to develop its creative
potentialities. The long centuries of the Middle Ages were marked
by feudalism, which rested on the base of the serfdom of the
masses. Slavery, as recent studies have indicated, is far from dead
in the twentieth century, but never has so large a proportion of
humankind been free from its toils.

It is fashionable in certain quarters to decry the conveniences
and gadgets of modern life and to extol the beauty and harmony of
the Middle Ages. Yet one sees little disposition among these Cas-
sandras to surrender these material comforts in their own personal
lives. The blessings of modern technology are, to be sure, scattered
in very spotty fashion across the globe. Yet hundreds of millions
of men and women today have access to comforts and luxuries
which were unavailable to kings in the past and which add substantially to the joy of living. One of the most ubiquitous features
of ancient and medieval life was its monotony for most men, who,
being slaves or serfs, were chained to one small corner of the
world, and possessed few pleasures except the grossest. The pleasures and diversions available to modern men, including the fantastic
mobility of our age, produce problems all their own, but it is undeniable that life is infinitely more interesting for modern man
than it was for his ancestors.

Nor is it of small moment that so much of physical suffering
and illness has been conquered or brought under control for
millions. What scale is available to weigh the agony of mothers
through the ages, when infant mortality carried off the majority
of children, or the terror of whole generations in the face of
plagues that devastated entire regions? The substantial increase in
men's life-expectancy, both in civilized and in underdeveloped
countries, cannot be dismissed, in any effort to assess the trend
of human history.

The march of medicine is only one illustration of the truth that
modern man is wiser than his predecessors, if only because he
stands on their shoulders. One may argue that men have thus

far failed to utilize adequately the vastly enlarged horizons of knowledge opened up to them by the progress of the sciences. But it cannot be denied that infinitely more is known today about the world and man than ever before in history. Moreover, for the first time, education is recognized as one of the inalienable rights of man, whatever his race, color or economic level.

In this, the closing third of the twentieth century, it would be hazardous to claim that modern man is better than his forbears. There are so many unknown factors in "character" that it is better to limit ourselves to the area of behavior. Not within living memory has the human chronicle been so crowded with an unbroken succession of wars, acts of genocide, rebellions, terrorism, vandalism and domestic riots as in our day. However, before leaping to the conclusion that man has retrograded, it is necessary to see the picture in perspective. As against these sensational and tragic events should be set the vast reduction in modern times of the incidence of physical violence and cruelty that characterized "normal" relationships between husbands and wives, parents and children, schoolmasters and pupils for centuries in the civilized world and the sheer bulk which cannot be measured.

This is true even in the face of the horrible brutality let loose in the world by Nazism and its imitators. It is not a mere illusion to believe that this dark chapter is only a temporary episode in the history of man, an outbreak of man's insanity that is not likely to be repeated. For the manifestations of violence since the Hitler decade have been informed by a spirit radically different from that of Nazi bestiality. Consider, for example, the upsurge of violence on college campuses and in black ghettos in the United States. These episodes have been flashed across television screens the world over because of their sensational character. Nevertheless, they are still exceptional rather than general. The victims of these outbreaks —and each is a tragedy—are to be counted in the tens or possibly in the hundreds rather than in the thousands or in the millions.

Far more significantly, the difference between latter-day violence and authoritarian bestiality is not merely one of quantity. The recourse to violence in the United States, shortsighted, misdirected and ineffective as it often is, nevertheless stems out of a genuine idealism, out of a hatred of cruelty and oppression. The campus revolt is in part a protest against American involvement in Vietnam, which is felt to be immoral and destructive of all human values. In part, the turmoil in our colleges represents a rebellion against the very genuine evils of impersonality and mechanization characteristic of our educational system. Most of the extremists that have practiced terror in the ghettos—and most of their victims have been blacks—are convinced that they are fighting against the exploitation and brutality visited upon their people for generations. In short, whether men *are* better is an open question; that they *act* better and strive for something better, seems clear.

Hanging over our age is the greatest peril of all time, the threat of war and atomic destruction. Here the race between reason and catastrophe has not yet been decided. It is certain, however, that for more and more men and women the bonds of national loyalties are being pushed farther outward to embrace all of humanity. It is only half a century since the first step was taken toward establishing an instrument of international law among nations. In 1894 The Hague Court for International Justice was created for adjudicating disputes, but only with the consent of both parties and with no power to enforce its decisions. Naturally, only minor issues were referred to it; on major issues the great powers preferred to rely on their superior might. Two decades later the League of Nations came into being. In its Covenant, the League went further, claiming jurisdiction in all disputes in which one party invoked its aid. The League possessed the right, at least on paper, to impose economic sanctions upon the guilty party. In spite of the many limitations under which it labored, the League of Nations was by no means an unmitigated failure.

The next step forward came twenty-five years later in the founding of the United Nations Organization in 1945. It, too, has not fulfilled all the high hopes of its founders, yet in its constitution and achievements it has gone beyond the League. Not only did it absorb and preserve various significant agencies of the League of Nations, like the International Labor Office; it created several other valuable instruments for international cooperation and progress, notably UNESCO. The most important respect in which it went beyond the League lay in its right to employ military force against violators of agreements, a right exercised successfully in the Korean War. Unfortunately, power blocs in the membership of the United

Nations and partisanship in the Secretariat have made the U.N. much less effective in the Middle East recently.

The greatest achievement of the United Nations has lain in creating a forum for argument and discussion which has thus far forestalled the recourse to force by the powerful antagonists ranged on both sides of the Iron Curtain. What has proved equally important, the U.N. has facilitated negotiations among member states on untold issues. In keeping adversaries talking instead of shooting, the U.N. has literally helped to preserve civilization from destruction.

It is worth recalling that from the time that the Constitution of the United States was adopted, establishing an "indivisible union," until the principle was recognized by all the States, there were many hours of grave stress in the American republic and a bloody Civil War convulsed the nation. The present conflict on civil rights demonstrates that full national unity is far from achieved. The triumph of the principle of one world must necessarily be longer and more painful, yet the direction is unmistakable.

CHAPTER VIII

The Language of Piety

"I have abandoned the God of the philosophers and have found instead the God of Abraham, Isaac and Jacob," the seventeenth-century French thinker Blaise Pascal declared. After a long and agonizing intellectual search that had brought him no peace, he concluded, "the heart has its reasons which reason does not know." In this disillusion with the intellectual quest for God, Pascal was not alone. As we have already noted, he had been anticipated nearly five hundred years earlier by the Hebrew poet and thinker, Judah Halevi, who had surrendered the abstract conception of God, debated by the philosophers. Instead, he found the incontrovertible evidence of God in a historic event: His appearance at Sinai before the assembled hosts of Israel as Redeemer and Lawgiver.

Pascal and Judah Halevi gave up philosophy and found religion. Can reason build a bridge to faith? We have devoted considerable discussion in these pages to God as the Creative Power of the universe, revealed by science, and as the Power not ourselves making for righteousness, evidenced by history. Yet a man may give his intellectual assent to these ideas, but may properly ask, "Is this the God of my fathers?" The Cosmic Power in nature, the Absolute of the philosophers, is nowhere to be found in the classic pages of religious literature. The God who appears in the Bible and the Prayer Book is merciful and just, He is wrathful and forgiving, He speaks to man and answers prayer. It was this God whose Law Moses proclaimed, in whose name the Prophets thundered, and after whom the Psalmist thirsted. It was the God of religion whom

Pascal sought so passionately, not the great Abstraction to be coolly contemplated from afar. The two conceptions of God seem poles apart.

Pascal's scorn for the God of philosophy is matched by the disbelief in the God of religion manifested by Morris Raphael Cohen. On Francis Bacon's famous utterance that "A little knowledge may lead a man away from God but a great deal brings him back," Cohen made the skeptical comment, "But it is not the same God to whom he returns."

In the face of so much august authority pro and con, it may seem foolhardy to maintain that Pascal and those who share his views are in error. Yet that is precisely what we suggest. In spite of the difference in approach and mood, we believe that the God of Abraham, Isaac, and Jacob *is* the God of the philosophers, that what the heart has discerned, the mind seeks to buttress through reason, and thus make communicable to other men. The temper of the prophet and the philosopher may be different, but not so totally different as is often assumed. Benedict Spinoza has been described as "God-intoxicated," and Isaiah was a creative thinker of no mean order. But the center about which their universe revolved is the same. A mother who brings a sick child to a physician will look upon the youngster with an emotion of love seemingly absent from the physician's breast, but his objective examination must not be devoid of a genuine sympathy for the child, if he is to succeed in his purpose.

In the preceding chapters, we have sought to indicate the basis for faith in God as being more than a leap in the dark, as Pascal puts it. Nor is faith in God to be justified on pragmatic grounds, as a wager, with everything to win (if God exists) and nothing to lose (if He does not)! We have set forth the grounds on which the religious spirit sees the presence of God in the world of nature and in the affairs of men and nations. Inevitably we have dealt with abstractions, with concepts and ideas. It is true that the world revealed to us by modern science is radically different from the Aristotelian universe accepted by most educated men in the Middle Ages, and the problems confronting us are correspondingly different. Nonetheless, the quest for a rational faith stands in the tradition of medieval religious philosophy, which honors reason as the most distinctive element of man's humanity, as the mark of the Divine image upon him, while recognizing the limitations of man's mind in dealing with a universe always imperfectly known, never completely explored.

Those who today decry the application of reason to religion generally dismiss medieval philosophy as an aberration in the history of religion. What is needed, they insist, is a return to the Biblical faith which was free from the painful lucubrations of philosophers, and which never sought to prove the truths of religion, because it accepted them without question. The God of Scripture was no pale abstraction or cloudy Absolute, but a living Personality, who conversed with men and acted through them.

That God's presence was experienced as real, the Bible makes crystal-clear time and again. The unique relationship of Moses to God is expressed in these words: "To any prophet among you, I make Myself known in visions. I talk to him in dreams. Not so with My servant Moses, so faithful in all My household; I speak to him directly, openly, with no dark sayings, and he sees the very form of the Eternal" (*Numbers* 12:6–8, Moffatt translation). The later prophets all testified to the reality of their encounter with the Divine.

"I saw the Lord sitting upon a seat high and exalted," the youthful Isaiah confessed when he embarked upon his prophetic career. The prophet Ezekiel declared again and again, "The hand of the Lord was upon me." Jeremiah, the most tragic figure among the Hebrew Prophets, in a passage already quoted, has described the drive and the agony of his calling that leave no doubt of the agonizing reality of his encounter with God (*Jer.* 20:7–9).

The God of Scripture is not in need of the evidence of reason. He is alive, active, ubiquitous, and inescapable, as the Prophet Jonah discovered and as the Psalmist learnt:

> Whither shall I go from Thy spirit?
> Or whither shall I flee from Thy presence?
> If I ascend up into heaven, Thou art there;
> If I make my bed in the nether-world, behold, Thou art there.
> If I take the wings of the morning,
> And dwell in the uttermost parts of the sea;
> Even there would Thy hand lead me,
> And Thy right hand would hold me.
>
> (*Ps.* 139:7–10)

We cannot be reminded too strongly of the centrality of experience in religion, rather than mere abstract theorizing. At the same time, there are two perils we must guard against. We must avoid distorting the context and spirit of Biblical religion, and we must not disregard the vast chasm of time and outlook that separates us from the Biblical era. Otherwise, we run the risk of being imprisoned rather than liberated by the Biblical Word.

It is undeniable that nowhere in Scripture do we find any attempt to formulate abstract principles of belief or to erect them into a system of dogma. The painful analysis of concepts which is the task of the philosopher is totally absent in the Biblical writers. There is no attempt to set forth the attributes of God in the schematic form so beloved of theologians, or to demonstrate an ethical code of conduct *more geometrico*, as Spinoza attempted to do. Unlike Socrates, the Prophets did not seek to analyze the meaning of virtue or justice or piety. "He has told thee, O man, what is good, and what the Lord requires of thee, to do justice, to love mercy, and to walk humbly with thy God" (*Micah* 6:8).

All this is true, but it is not the whole truth. The Bible is rich in vivid, concrete images and poor in abstract terms, because the Hebrew mind preferred to deal with the specific rather than the general, but it was not lacking in intellectual power on that account. The syllogism beloved of Western logic will be sought in vain in Biblical thought, which operated "organismically" rather than "logically." But it is obvious, or should be, that the truth or falsity of its ideas is independent of the forms in which they are couched.

Genesis opens with the narrative of the Creation in order to emphasize the unity and the creative power of God. It thus supplies the basis, as we shall see, for the Biblical conception of man, who is its prime concern. God's role in history is never set forth in abstract terms, but is manifested in the Biblical narrative in the concrete. The history of mankind until Abraham, the fortunes of the Patriarchs, and the events that befell Israel in Egypt, in the Wilderness, and later in the Promised Land—all these vividly express the idea of God's government of human affairs, an idea underscored with passion and insight by the Hebrew prophets.

Yet, as we have noted above, general principles are by no means totally lacking in Scripture. Thus the law of righteousness operating in the universe is formulated both positively and negatively:

> Righteousness exalts a nation;
> But sin is a reproach to peoples.

(Prov. 14:34)

> Where there is no Vision, the people perish,
> But he that keeps the Law is happy.

(Prov. 29:18)

No theologian's creed is to be found in the Bible, but the attributes of God are set forth in a theophany repeated several times
in Scripture: "The Lord passed by before him, and he proclaimed:
'Lord, Lord, merciful and gracious God, long-suffering, and abundant in goodness and truth; keeping mercy unto the thousandth
generation, forgiving iniquity, and transgression and sin; and that
not utterly destroying, though visiting the iniquity of the fathers
upon the children, and upon the children's children, unto the
third and unto the fourth generation'" (Ex. 34:6–7).

The Second Commandment of the Decalogue not only forbids
the worship of other gods, but prohibits the making of any image
of the Deity, resembling any being or object in the sky, upon the
earth, or in the water. Some Biblical critics have argued that this
does not deny a physical form to God—it merely denies man's
capacity to know what that form is. Existentially this is a distinction without a difference. If man is forbidden to picture God or
worship Him in any concrete shape, it is tantamount to a denial
of His physical form, at least as far as man is concerned, and no
other being is contemplated in the prohibition! In the profound
passage in Exodus cited in an earlier chapter, in which Moses is
denied the vision of God's presence, the terms used are images symbolic of ideas, concrete embodiments of the truth that God's essence is unknowable to man, while He does reveal Himself in His
manifestations: "Moses said, 'Show me, I pray Thee, Thy glory.'
. . . And He said, 'Thou canst not see My face, for man shall
not see Me and live. . . . It shall come to pass, when My glory
passes by, I will put thee in a cleft of the rock and will cover thee
with My hand until I have passed by. And I will take away My
hand, and thou shalt see My back, but My face shall not be seen'"
(Ex. 33:18–23).

It is worth observing that even the oldest sections of the Bible, like the latest, always stop short of any physical description of the Deity. The Biblical writers pictured His throne, but never His Person, and generally delegated to His messengers or angels the performance of tasks that involve grosser physical activity. Thus in *Genesis*, God announces to Abraham His intention of destroying the sinful city of Sodom, but it is His messengers who carry out the decree.

It is true that the existence of God is never discussed in the Bible, since in the ancient world the existence of gods was never questioned, even by extreme skeptics. This became a vital issue for the medieval thinkers, who were confronted by new challenges from Greco-Arabic science and philosophy. Their solutions are not adequate for us, but the problems are perennial, and there is much that we can learn from them for our day.

The long chapter of medieval religious philosophy, in which Islamic, Jewish, and Christian thinkers participated for centuries, was no blind alley in the history of the human spirit. When Judaism and its daughter religions met Greek thought, the impact was tremendous. On the one hand, Greek philosophy, like that of Aristotle, contradicted some of the basic implications of Hebraic religion, notably the faith in a living, creating God, active in the world. On the other hand, the rationalistic emphasis derived from the Greeks re-enforced the ancient Jewish tendency to remove human traits from the Deity and to conceive of Him in spiritual, non-human terms.

Accordingly, there arose the various representatives of medieval philosophy. The prelude to this development had taken place a millennium before, in the first century B.C.E. Its greatest figure was Philo of Alexandria, who had a tremendous influence on the thinking of the early Church, but whose abiding effect on his own Jewish kinsmen was very slight, largely because of the disappearance of Greek-speaking Jewry shortly after his time. In the tenth century, the philosopher, Talmudist, and Bible scholar, Saadia of Bagdad (882–942), initiated the period of medieval Jewish philosophy, which reached its apogee in Maimonides. Islamic thinkers like Avicenna and Averroes, and Christian theologians like Duns Scotus, Albertus Magnus, and Thomas Aquinas, were, like Maimonides, part of a broad intellectual movement lasting for centuries.

The tasks that the medieval religious philosophers set for themselves were threefold. First, they sought to reconcile religious belief with philosophic truth. Since for most of them there is only one truth and Aristotle was the Divine Philosopher, it meant that the text of Scripture had to be brought into conformity with Aristotelian ideas. This was accomplished by giving the Biblical text an allegorical or symbolic interpretation. In a few, rare instances, the medieval thinker rejected Aristotle's views in favor of the Biblical conception. Thus Maimonides wrote that if he believed Aristotle's conception of eternal matter to be true, he could have reinterpreted the text of Holy Writ to agree with the Master. Since the idea of primal matter seemed to him untenable in its own right, Maimonides rejected Aristotle on this point and held fast to the Biblical teaching of *creatio ex nihilo*, of a God who created the universe out of nothing.

A second, closely related function of medieval philosophy was to purge the conception of God of anthropomorphic traits, of the widespread, indeed inevitable, tendency to picture God in human terms, both with regard to His nature and His activity. This the medieval thinkers achieved by subjecting the text of Scripture to careful analysis and by interpreting all physical references to the Deity symbolically. Thus, Saadia argued, when the Bible speaks of the "mouth of the earth," the phrase is obviously not to be construed literally. Similarly, phrases like "the mouth of the Lord" and "the hand of God" are figurative expressions for God's communication with His children and for the manifestations of His power. Maimonides carried to its highest point the process of eliminating anthropomorphic elements in the God-conception. Uncompromisingly rationalistic, he declared that to ascribe any physical form to the Deity was tantamount to heresy and deprived one of a share in the world to come. It is a striking instance of freedom of thought in religion that on the printed page of Maimonides' *Code* this statement is countered by the comment of a critic and commentator, Rabbi Abraham ben David of Posquières, who wrote: "Better and greater men than Maimonides have ascribed a physical form to God, basing themselves on their understanding of Scriptural passages and even more so on some legends and utterances, which give wrong ideas." So much for heresy!

Maimonides' most significant contribution to the elimination of

physical ideas of God lay in his theory of "negative attributes."
Any affirmative conception of God, Maimonides points out, remains anthropomorphic and by that token is untrue. When we
speak of God as one, as wise, as good, these epithets are necessarily
based upon human experience. "One" means for us a unit in a series;
"wise" conjures up a picture of a human sage; "good" is conceived
of as similar to a mother's love; extend them conceptually as much
as we can, they still remain limited and are inadequate to describe
the oneness, the wisdom, and the goodness of God, which are of an
altogether different dimension. Hence, Maimonides concluded,
the various qualities which we attribute to God are correctly to be
understood as denials of their opposites; God's Unity, Wisdom,
and Righteousness mean that He is "not-many," "not-foolish,"
"not-evil."

The importance of this achievement in eliminating the physical
conception of God cannot be overestimated. Yet, as we shall see,
the religious spirit, when it seeks to give voice to its awe and love
of God, cannot rest content with the denial of negations. It reaches
out for affirmations and insists on praising God for what He is,
not for what He is not.

Finally, medieval philosophy sought to set forth a systematic
theology, by formulating the basic articles of faith. The *Summa
Theologica* of Aquinas was an imposing intellectual edifice that
buttressed the credal formulations so congenial to Christianity with
its emphasis upon faith as the touchstone of salvation. In Judaism,
Maimonides had sought to organize the fundamental doctrines in
his "Thirteen Principles." The all-embracing character of his Creed,
its brevity and clarity, and the authority of its author gave them
wide popularity. Yet here, too, the passion for intellectual freedom
balked at any closed system. Even less distinguished men did not
hesitate to quarrel with both the content and the number of
articles of belief in the Creed of Maimonides, and it never became
an official confession of faith.

Men have often felt that the abstract Deity which emerges from
the speculations of theology is far removed from the Living God
of religion. At times, modern men have doubted, either implicitly
or explicitly, the sincerity and honesty of these medieval thinkers,
or, more charitably, they have explained their activity as the result
of a compartmentalized mind, with faith in one corner and reason

in another, and with no genuine contact between them. These suspicions reveal our own inadequacies. For the great medieval philosophers were all deeply religious men, with sufficient breadth of spirit to encompass what lesser men may find irreconcilable.

Thus the famous medieval work *Fons Vitae* is an abstract philosophical treatise, so free from references to traditional sources that for centuries the religion, let alone the identity, of its author was unknown. Not until the middle of the nineteenth century did it become known that it was the work of Solomon Ibn Gabirol, one of the most passionate religious poets of the Middle Ages. Maimonides himself, unlike other philosophical writers like Saadia and Judah Halevi, was not gifted poetically, but the fervor of his faith is reflected in his *Epistle to Yemen* and other writings.

That an abstract conception of God may go hand in hand with deep personal piety is demonstrated by the medieval "Hymn of Glory." Here the unknown poet succeeds in transmuting into warm emotion "cold" philosophic ideas. That God's essence is beyond human comprehension, that only His manifestations are accessible to man, and that Biblical descriptions of God are metaphors reflecting the variety of His activity in the world—all this is vividly expressed by the poet:

I shall tell Thy glory, though I have not seen Thee,
I shall image Thee and call Thee by name, though I have not known
    Thee.
Thy prophets have imaged Thee, but not according to Thine essence,
They have likened Thee, but only in accordance with Thy works.

They figured Thee in a multitude of visions; Thou art one in all their
    images.
They saw in Thee both age and youth, the hair of the head, now white,
    now black,
Age in the Day of Judgment, youth in the day of battle, a warrior
    mighty in strength.

The hymn ends upon a note of passionate desire for God:

Let my praise be a crown unto Thy head,
And my prayer be right before Thee like incense.
May my outpourings be sweet before Thee,
For unto Thee does my soul yearn.

The mind and the heart are not enemies; among the greatest of men they sustain each other.

If today the medieval thinkers are not our primary sources of religious guidance, it is in large measure a tribute to their achievement. Many of the ideas for which they fought, notably their opposition to the corporeal representation of the Deity, have won once and for all. In other instances, we are no longer troubled by the issues which they encountered, many of which emanated from Aristotle, and have been rendered irrelevant by modern science. But there is abiding value in their conviction that all truth is one, and that religion cannot contradict what reason teaches, because the heart cannot believe what the intellect denies. God may love a broken and a contrite heart; He surely can find no pleasure in a weak and divided mind.

It does not detract from the achievement of Saadia, Maimonides, and their colleagues to point out the limitations in their struggle to eliminate anthropomorphisms. They knew, of course, that human beings would necessarily apply to God words derived from human experience. They were, however, not fully aware that however they might refine the concept of God, the terms of the redefinition would still carry human overtones. This remains true of Maimonides' theory of "negative attributes" as well, for the qualities of plurality, folly, wickedness, even when being negated, remain human, being drawn from men's experience.

A more important drawback in their struggle against anthropomorphism remains to be noted. Perhaps because they were engaged in a difficult battle, the medieval thinkers failed to recognize that the concrete images in which Biblical faith expresses itself are not only inevitable but positively valuable. The principle that "the Bible speaks in the language of men" is not to be regarded merely as a concession to the unintelligent or even as a defect flowing from the limitations of human speech. The vivid language of piety, unprecise though it be, is superior to the painfully exact formulation of the philosopher, in the same degree that poetry is superior to prose. The heartbeat of emotion, the warmth and passion of feeling, find more adequate expression in poetry than in prose.

Nor is this all. Standing midway between prose and music, poetry is able to carry much of the specific content of the former, while possessing overtones that border on the latter. In other words, poetry transcends the narrow limits of meaning and thus is especially suited to give expression to what may not be ineffable but is surely indefinable. Hence the metaphors of religious speech in the Bible and in the Prayer Book are not merely more vivid than the prose of theological doctrine; they are intellectually more adequate. The simple, apparently naive language of traditional piety is not merely more heart-warming. Since at best we can only touch the hem of the garment of reality, it brings us closer to the truth.

Let us attempt to compare the prose and the poetry of religion. In the preceding chapters, we have sought to indicate the evidence for God that the believing spirit finds in nature, in the life of man, and in the workings of human history. We may summarize our conception of God as follows: *God is the creative Power in the universe, who called it into being and governs its unfolding, whose ways are manifest in the laws of nature and the processes of history, through both of which He reveals His unity, creative power, wisdom, and righteousness. From among all his vast creation, God has chosen man and made him more than a creature, by fashioning him in the Divine image, endowing him in some degree with the quest for truth, the striving for justice, the love of beauty, and above all with the capacity for creativity which only man shares with God.*

How ponderous and abstract is this formulation, to which we have been driven by the desire to achieve clarity in thinking! Yet the truth is that this definition does not actually convey more than the brief, vivid, anthropomorphic epithets in religious tradition, which speak of God as Father, as King of the universe, as Master of the world, as the all-Merciful, and as the righteous Judge.

Consider, for example, one of the most familiar terms in the liturgy, *Avinu Malkenu*, "Our Father, our King." The second epithet, "King," indicates His role as Ruler of the world, arbiter of human destiny, and judge of men's actions. The first, "Father," which is a warmer term, stemming as it does from men's most intimate experience, has an even richer aura of meaning. "Father" means progenitor, who creates and endows his creatures with life. It also implies the provider who nourishes and shelters his children. It includes more than physical protection, for a true father rears his children, guides and educates them, and strives to prepare them

for the tasks and responsibilities of maturity. It implies, too, a
mutual relationship between sire and offspring, manifested by love
and concern on the one hand, and by love and respect on the
other.

Moreover, when men call God their Father, they are giving expression to the living paradox of the parent-child relationship,
which is the fountainhead both of suffering and of progress, of sin
and of reconciliation; it suggests that there is both a similarity of
nature between father and offspring which links their destiny together, and a profound difference which expresses itself in a
perpetual tension between them.

The aura of meanings of each epithet is enriched still further by
their juxtaposition in the phrase, "Our Father, our King." An ideal
father's basic attitude to his children is that of love; an ideal king's
fundamental attribute toward his subjects is that of justice. To
our limited human minds these attributes may seem to stand in
opposition, but only because for us love always tends to merge
into sentimentality and justice all too often takes on the lineaments
of vengeance. But God's unique relationship to His creatures is
compounded of both love and justice. The combination of epithets
in the phrase "Our Father, our King" expresses in superb fashion
God's unsentimental love for the creatures that He has called into
being, so that He does not abandon the line of judgment, yet
tempers it with mercy, governing men by law, but offering them
the saving grace of forgiveness. Finally, in placing "Father" before
"King," the religious believer stresses the truth that man's love for
God must take precedence over the duty of obedience.

This whole constellation of religious attitudes, insights, and emotions is wrapped up in one brief invocation, "Our Father, our
King." Is it not clear that the language of unaffected piety may
seem simple but is scarcely naive? When refined and interpreted
by the rigorous thought of the religious philosopher, the language
of the Bible and the Prayer Book proves an incomparable instrument for helping men to experience the Divine Presence. As
Abraham J. Heschel has emphasized, the sense of the power of
words and the sense of the impotence of human expression are
equally characteristic of the religious consciousness. Leo Baeck remarked truly that in the most exalted religious utterance, "the fight
for language becomes the fight against language." It is in this spirit

that the great traditional liturgies are to be understood and participated in. Prayer is poetry, expressing truth beyond the power of prose to exhaust, and, like all poetry and truth, containing intimations too exalted for literalness.

All true worship represents a ceaseless striving to attain to an impossible yet ineluctable goal: to do justice to the Divine dimension of existence and to bring men into contact with God. For the categorical imperative of high religion is always: "Know before Whom thou standest." The Hebrew root *yada*, which means "to know," also means "to love." Knowledge without love is self-delusion; love without knowledge, self-deception. Reason teaches us that we can hope to know God only in part, but piety reassures us that we can love Him with all our heart.

CHAPTER IX

Revelation—God Speaks to Man

In the preceding chapters, we have sought to discover the ways in which God makes Himself known to man, and we have noted that the religious spirit sees Him both as Creator and as Governor of the universe, functioning in nature, in history, and in man himself. Traditional religion has gone much further, however, and maintained that God has made His will manifest in direct revelation to men. According to this doctrine, in ages past God chose men of exemplary character and piety, to whom He communicated His will for men. These messages, put into writing by the Prophets, constitute the Scriptures which are the word of God.

It is undeniable that many modern men, even those who believe in a Supreme Being, find it hard to believe in Revelation, on a variety of grounds which we shall analyze below. So difficult is this concept that there have arisen various modern formulations of religion which seek to dispense with the idea altogether and insist that religion is in its origins a purely human construction, being entirely explicable in psychological and sociological terms. For these thinkers, God may be the goal of religion; He is not its source. Religion is man's aspiration to God, not God's revelation to man.

We are aware of the weighty motives that have led to the abandonment of the traditional concept. Nevertheless, we believe that in this instance, the advocates of religion have uncritically —and unnecessarily—retreated before the challenges of contemporary thought. It is true that certain formulations of Revelation were inadequate even in the past and are totally untenable today. But in surrendering the valid insights to be found in tradition, the modernist has discarded the grain together with the chaff.

As we have already noted, religion stands upon the conviction that God is not merely the Creator of the world, but also the Father of mankind. Ever since the Prophets, religion has maintained that man's ethical ideals, however imperfect and relative they may be, are a reflection of the absolute values which are rooted in the righteousness of God. Now, a just God who wishes His children to practice justice and mercy would surely indicate His will to them. That process of communication is Revelation.

Having asserted this much, an influential and highly articulate school of religious thinkers in our day would refuse to discuss the matter further. They would insist that revelation must be taken on faith and that any effort to analyze the difficulties which modern men encounter with the concept is both futile and unnecessary. Obviously, withdrawing one's convictions from the market place of ideas avoids the perils of competition; the one drawback is that the goods may remain unsold. The objections of modern men to the traditional concept of revelation are not trivial; as in every department of thought, the critic performs an invaluable function in the creative process, for his strictures correct and deepen the content of the idea being discussed.

In some degree, the distaste that many modern men feel for the concept is psychological. The term "revelation" is thoroughly theological in origin and spirit, and modern men are not altogether unjustifiably suspicious of theology, particularly in view of the uses to which it has been put. There is an unmistakable aura of unreality which cleaves to many of the refinements of theological thought, a façade of rational discourse often hiding an amalgam of obscurantism, bigotry, and irrationality. Moreover, theological doctrines, cold and abstruse, seem far removed from the warm, pulsating religious experience. Hence religion and theology are often regarded as opposing forces, the one being the living spirit, the other, the inert body.

The truth, of course, is that if a body without a spirit is a corpse, a spirit without a body is a ghost; a living religion must have bones and sinews as well as heart and soul. As for theological animus, it is not limited to theology; whenever men feel deeply,

there arise the perils of fanaticism and the urge to suppress differences. As we have seen, intolerance stemming from anti-religious
sources has been at least as marked in our day as religious bigotry.
The errors and excesses of theology do not free us from the need
and the duty to think as clearly and as honestly as we can about the
content of religion.

What are the difficulties with Revelation? In the first instance,
men find it hard to believe that the Creator of the universe, vast
beyond our imaginings, would concern Himself with men. The
world is too vast and men are too petty, they feel, for the Creator
to have singled out this one creature on a tiny planet for direct
communication. But to adopt this position really means to be guilty
of anthropomorphism, for we would be conceiving God in human
terms, as being bound by human limitations. It means using our
finite standpoint and limited capacities, as a basis for deciding what
may or may not concern God or be possible for Him. It means
confusing size with significance and mistaking bulk for importance.
Actually, believing that God is concerned with men is far from
unreasonable. For untold aeons, the universe existed, until our
solar system came into being. Innumerable years passed until life
emerged on one planet. Millions more were required until life
appeared on the earth. Hundreds of thousands of years elapsed
until the primitive ancestor of the human race evolved from the
lower creatures. Thus the entire universe represents a cosmic effort, an unending struggle to propagate life and preserve it as the
highest good. It follows that the life and destiny of man, its supreme
culmination thus far, must be of supreme moment to its Divine
Author. Some scientists have speculated that there may be life on
Mars or Venus, on the level of a jelly-fish. Man remains, for the
present at least, the highest flowering of the creation-process; he
stands on the uppermost rung of the evolutionary ladder and is
by that token the supreme bearer of life's potentialities. To put it
into religious terms, man, fashioned in the Divine Image, must of
necessity be of concern to Him whose image he reflects. That man
counts in the universe is a highly reasonable view, though it cannot
be proved; for religion, it remains the deepest conviction.

The concept of Revelation goes further. It assumes that some
individuals and groups have been chosen for Divine communication, while others have not enjoyed the privilege. This, it has been

argued, assumes a kind of favoritism, indeed, a violation of democracy unworthy of God. Those who have claimed to be the recipients of Revelation are stigmatized as suffering from megalomania. The most famous case in point is the doctrine of the election of Israel, which has been a fundamental of Judaism and, in a modified form, is almost equally basic to Christianity. The idea of the Chosen People is effectively mocked in the breathtakingly brief lyric:

> How odd
> of God,
> To choose
> the Jews!

That sentiment has frequently been echoed in Jewish circles. Through the centuries, many Jews have asked in fear and trembling, and often in resentment and bitterness, why this unique destiny was visited upon them. Willingly they would forego both the dignity and the misery that have come in its wake, both the crown and the thorns of chosenness.

Quite aside from the particular claims of Judaism and Christianity, the fact is unassailable that all men are not equally endowed by nature. Shakespeare undoubtedly received a grossly disproportionate share of the poetic genius allocated to Stratford-on-Avon, and the same inequality emerges in every instance of individual superiority. It is the function of the biological and psychological sciences to seek to discover the mechanism which produces talent and genius. Describing genius as a mutation in the genes gives the phenomenon a name, not an explanation. Even if science reveals the how of the process, the why will remain. That these peaks of the spirit appear on the human landscape remains a mystery, part of the Divine plan for a universe which possesses the capacity to produce excellence.

Moreover, the ledger of life is balanced. Creative superiority inevitably brings agony and deprivation in its wake, and the grandeur of genius is compensated for by its misery. All its achievements are outweighed by the sense of inadequacy and unattained goals, which are the hallmarks of true distinction. Beethoven's greatest symphonies died with him.

Be this as it may, this favoritism, if such it be, cannot be negated out of existence. Men are unequally endowed in scientific aptitude and artistic gifts; by that same token they differ in the depth and quality of their spiritual insight, their sensitivity to the Divine call.

It is, of course, perfectly true that any specific claim to revelation may be an example of psychopathology or self-delusion rather than a valid interpretation of reality. It is a truism that such claims have been made by countless individuals and by virtually all religions. But that does not rule out the possibility of authentic revelation. Mental institutions house many an inmate suffering from delusions of grandeur. Whether a young man is a composer of genius or a candidate for an asylum can be determined only by examining his musical work, and it is notorious that there have been cases of violent disagreement in the history of literature, music, art, and science as to whether genius or insanity was at work.

The two great religions of the West have been at one in maintaining that the men whose words have come down in the Bible were authentic bearers of Divine revelation. The third great monotheistic religion, Islam, accepted that claim and built upon it. The medievals were wont to argue that *consensus omnium*, "the general consent," constitutes a valid proof of the truth of religion. This argument is not likely to command assent today. But it should predispose us to examining the record of revelation and decide, as well as we are able, whether the claim may be justified. At least one negative result is clear: the argument of favoritism cannot rule out revelation *a priori*.

Perhaps the most crucial problem with revelation is not so much a logical difficulty as a sense of disquiet, a feeling of discomfort in the face of the mysterious. Revelation is not a "normal" phenomenon, it is not subject to analysis and categorization or even to adequate description. By and large those who have had the experience have sought to describe it in aural and visual terms. It is a voice the prophet hears, a vision his eyes behold. The prophet is called a "seer" through a variety of synonyms (*hozeh, ro'eh*). What is seen and heard obviously belongs to no ordinary dimension of experience.

Pagan religion, which conceived of its gods in human form, sometimes all too human, had no problem here at all. The relationship of gods with humans often took the form of communion, of eating and drinking, even of cohabiting together. There was, accordingly, no problem in the gods' being seen and heard by men. Now, Biblical religion continued to use similar terms for the communication of God with man. This usage was not merely a residue of a more primitive stage of religion. Nor is it simply due to the innate conservatism of language, in proof of which witness such English terms as "ill-starred" and "disastrous," which no longer argue a faith in astrology, or "martial" and "bacchanalian," which do not presuppose faith in the Roman gods of war and wine.

A factor far deeper than habit comes into play. The limitations of human speech inhere in the limitations of human reason. The Bible uses physical terms to describe man's experience of God's revelation, because there are no other terms to use. Yet it is noteworthy that the Hebrew Scripture generally avoids speaking of "seeing God," and when the phrase occurs, the rare and poetic word *hazah* ("envision") is preferred to the common verb *ra'ah* ("see"). Overwhelmingly, the Bible describes God's communications in aural terms ("the Word of the Lord," "thus saith the Lord," "The Lord spoke to Moses"), because of the feeling, which is, strictly speaking, illogical, that hearing a voice is a less grossly material form of contact than seeing a Presence. In sum, the description of revelation is always a metaphor, because poetry, endowed with overtones, is capable of implying more than it sets forth. Its truth lies precisely in its nuances.

Thus the great Revelation at Sinai is vividly described in the book of *Exodus:* "Now Sinai was altogether on smoke, because the Lord descended upon it in fire. The sound of the trumpet became louder and louder; Moses spoke and God answered him with a voice" (*Ex.* 19:18–19). A Talmudic sage was not deterred on that account from declaring: "The Divine Presence never descended earthwards, nor did Moses or Elijah ever ascend to Heaven" (*Sukkah* 5a). In describing the giving of the Decalogue at Sinai, the Hebrew Bible says: "And all the people saw the thunderings and the lightnings" (*Ex.* 20:15). Obviously, "saw" cannot be applied to thunder, which can be heard but not seen. It may well be that the inappropriate verb was chosen expressly to suggest that the perception of the Divine Presence differed in essence from the normal human processes of seeing and hearing.

It is clear that Revelation may be conceived of literally, allegorically, or mystically, but for the religious spirit it remains a *sine qua non*, the source from which the sense of God and the knowledge of His will flow to man.

The Revelation which the Western religious tradition postulates at Sinai was collective, that is to say, an entire people shared the experience. Henceforth, revelation was individual, directed to select men and women, the Prophets. The usage and the etymology of the Hebrew term for "prophet," *nabi*, shed some light on the phenomenon. Originally, the word may have meant "to murmur, mutter," and perhaps it contains an allusion to the primitive modes of ecstatic speech. But whatever its beginnings, *nabi* early developed the meaning "spokesman, mouthpiece of God." The prophet essentially is not a foreteller, but a forthteller, the proclaimer of God's will. Thus Moses is charged in these words: "See, I have set you like God vis-à-vis Pharaoh; and Aaron your brother will be your prophet" (*Ex.* 7:1). The meaning of the term is identical with another utterance: "He shall be a mouth for you and you will be like God for him" (*Ex.* 4:16). The prophet is the spokesman of God.

The Prophets all felt the call as emanating from a Power outside themselves. They speak of hearing a Voice, or feeling the hand of God upon them. Perhaps the most graphic picture of Divine communication is given by Eliphaz, the oldest of Job's Friends:

> "Now a word was stealthily brought to me,
> And my ear received the whisper of it.
> Amid thoughts from the visions of the night,
> When deep sleep falls on men,
> Dread came upon me, and trembling,
> Which made all my bones shake.
> A spirit glided past my face,
> The hair of my flesh stood up.
> It stood still, but I could not discern its appearance;
> A form was before mine eyes;
> There was silence, then I heard a voice."
>
> (*Job* 4:12–16)

The prophets were convinced that there was an objective Reality beyond themselves communicating with them. This is clear from another consideration. Both Moses and Jeremiah heard the Divine call and pleaded in vain with God to be excused from the prophetic mission. Amos indignantly denies that he is a professional practitioner of the prophetic art: "I am no prophet, nor a prophet's son; but a herdsman, and a dresser of sycamore-trees; but the Lord took me from following the flock, and the Lord said unto me: 'Go, prophesy unto My people Israel'" (*Amos* 7:14–15). Of unmatched poignancy is Jeremiah's complaint against his God:

> "O Lord, Thou hast enticed me, and I was enticed,
> Thou hast overcome me, and hast prevailed;
> I am become a laughing-stock all the day,
> Every one mocks me.
> For as often as I speak,
> I cry: 'Violence and spoil';
> Because the Lord's word is made a reproach to me;
> And a derision all day.
> If I say: 'I will not make mention of Him,
> Nor speak any more in His name,'
> Then it is a burning fire in my heart,
> Shut up in my bones,
> That I cannot contain, and keep within me."
>
> (*Jer.* 20:7–9)

The modern psychologist may seek to explain the phenomenon by whatever means he chooses. For the religious spirit, revelation is not a soliloquy, but a dialogue. It is not a man talking to himself, but a communication between God and man, deeply felt, often resented, but not to be resisted. How the spirit works, upon whom it rests, what form it takes may remain a mystery, but the reality is undeniable. Maimonides' definition of prophecy in his *Guide* (*II*, 36) is perhaps the most searching available to us:

> "The real essence of prophecy is an emanation flowing from God, through the active intellect, first upon the rational faculty and subsequently upon the imaginative faculty. It is the highest state of man and the greatest perfection of which the human species is capable. This greatest perfection of the imaginative faculty is by no means attainable by everyone. It is not attained through perfection in theoretical sciences nor through excellence of moral qualities . . . unless the highest possible perfection of the imaginative faculty in its innate originality is joined with them."

J. L. Teicher has called attention to the novelty in Maimonides' emphasis upon "the creative imagination" which must be joined to intellectual and moral excellence as the prerequisites for prophecy. Maimonides proceeds to make it clear, however, that the mere possession of the necessary attributes by an individual does not guarantee that he will become a prophet. Many are called, but few are chosen. An arcanum of mystery remains.

Does not the non-rational and inexplicable character of the phenomenon open the door to a wide variety of abuses? May it not occur that the revelation is non-existent, and that the claims are put forth either through honest self-deception or wilful chicanery? How can a true revelation be distinguished from the counterpart, a true prophet from his false opponent?

These are real issues, with which Biblical religion wrestled. That it could not solve them completely is an indication of the dimensions of the problem. Thus the ninth-century prophet Micaiah ben Imlah prophesied defeat for the armies of Judah and Israel in the war against Syria. When confronted by his opponent Zedekiah ben Kenaanah, who prognosticated victory, Micaiah explained that his adversary was the mouthpiece of a "spirit of deceit" which emanated, be it noted, from the Lord, who had sent it for the purpose of bringing defeat upon King Ahab. A century and a half later, the message of disaster pronounced by Micah the Morashtite similarly was contradicted by happy tidings announced by the professional prophets of his day. Micah went further and denied any authenticity to their message or sincerity to their activity. Instead, Micah explained their motives in materialistic terms, nearly two thousand years before the economic interpretation of history, castigating the prophets "who lead my people astray, crying 'Peace,' when their teeth have anything to bite; but whoever does not feed their maws, against him they proclaim war" (*Micah* 3:5).

How can a true prophet be told apart from a counterfeit? Here, too, no easy answer is available. The book of *Deuteronomy* suggests that a false prophet can be identified by the fact that his prophecy will not be fulfilled (*Deut.* 18:22). Jeremiah, whose prophetic adversaries brought messages far more palatable than his own oracles of doom, argued that only an unpleasant prophecy could be regarded as *prima facie* evidence of its truth, while a

forecast of good tidings simply meant pandering to popular prejudice and should not be regarded as true until validated by events
(*Jer.* 28:7–9). The rather simple criterion adduced in *Deuteronomy* is drastically modified in the same book by the observation
that even when the words of the false prophet are fulfilled, it is
only God's way of testing the people's loyalty to His Law (*Deut.*
13:2–4)!

It is clear that the Bible offers no positive answer to the crucial
issue of determining an authentic revelation of God. Yet a negative
test *is* embodied in the Biblical passages which we have cited:
the truth of a prophet's message is not demonstrated by miracles
that he performs or even by the fulfillment of his predictions. This
insight is elaborated upon by Maimonides. Thus in his *Letter to
Yemen,* he declares that a prophet who attacks the authority of the
Law, or urges the abrogation of the Commandments, thereby con-
victs himself of being a false seer, irrespective of the signs or
miracles associated with his career. The well-known Scandinavian
Biblical scholar of our own day, Sigmund Mowinckel, expresses
the same truth in the modern idiom:

> "The certitude of the experience depends upon whether it
> has a definite content, capable of being apprehended by the
> mind and tested by religious and moral standards."
> (*Journal of Biblical Literature,* 1934, p. 217)

The truth of a claim to Divine revelation thus lies in *no external
sign,* but in the inherent validity of the message, its conformity to
the highest ideals which we recognize as the Will of God. Revelation is therefore no comfortable safe-conduct to salvation, but a
perpetual gauntlet which man must run, an eternally perilous encounter of God and man. It is fraught with danger for the prophet,
as Isaiah discovered:

> "Woe is me! for I am undone; because I am a man of unclean
> lips, and I dwell in the midst of a people of unclean lips; For
> mine eyes have seen the King, the Lord of hosts."
> (*Isa.* 6:5)

It is equally trying for the people, who must decide between the
conflicting demands of diametrically opposing viewpoints, each
of which attacks the other as false and disastrous. From the perspective of history, it is easy today to decide between Micaiah and

Zedekiah, or between Jeremiah and Hananiah, and stamp the former as "true prophets," and the latter as "false," but only because the past is dead and tractable. Whatever pulsates is perilous, for life is a perpetual hazard. To be the recipient of revelation one needs the prophetic afflatus; it requires almost the same level of inspiration to recognize the true revelation and to act upon it. For the Divine purpose is not fulfilled when the word is heard by the prophet. It must reach its destination in the heart and life of the people.

Israel is therefore the people of revelation, not merely because it produced the unique galaxy of men whom we call the Hebrew Prophets, nor even because it created the environment which gave them rise. In the deeper sense, Israel, for all its imperfections, produced the living community in which the Prophets could be heard, be understood in part at least, and find a response.

Biblical religion goes further in conceiving of Israel as the people of revelation. The central event in Biblical tradition is the Theophany at Sinai, when not an individual, but an entire people, heard God's word and committed itself to His service: "Whatever the Lord will command, we shall do" (*Ex.* 19:8). By that act, Israel assumed the role of "a kingdom of priests and a holy nation" (*Ex.* 19:6). Time and again it might fall from its lofty estate, and even rebel against its role, but its irrevocable destiny was to remain the Servant and witness of the Lord and of the truth entrusted to it. Christianity and Islam are at one in affirming the Divine election of Israel. They part company with the mother faith in claiming to be her spiritual heirs.

The "favoritism" that is implied in the Biblical concept of the election of Israel is compounded still further by the rabbinic observation, "All the prophets prophesied in the Land of Israel or about it." Today we are not likely to take such exclusiveness literally; prophets are not limited to one people and one land. Yet the unique position which tiny Palestine occupies in the religious consciousness of three great religions as the habitat of the Bible undergirds the conviction that the Revelation of God was concentrated in large measure within one tiny people, clinging precariously to one small corner of Western Asia, in truth, the Holy Land.

The most fundamental difficulty with the concept of Revelation in our day is peculiarly characteristic of the modern age, though, as we shall see, not limited to it. For the term "revelation" possesses two meanings: it refers both to the process of communication and to the product. In other words, it refers not merely to the encounters between God and man, but to the body of teaching that emerged from their confrontations. For Judaism, the content of revelation is to be sought in the Hebrew Scriptures and the interpretation of Rabbinic tradition. For Catholicism, it is embodied in the Scripture as authoritatively expounded by the Church. For Protestantism, the ultimate authority is the Scriptures as understood by the wisdom and conscience of the individual. It is clear that for all Western religion, revelation is pre-eminently to be sought for in the pages of the Bible.

But this idea, that the Divine revelation was given once and for all, and that the written record needs only to be consulted when guidance is sought, encounters several formidable obstacles. Modern man, unlike earlier generations, possesses a sense of history. He cannot emancipate himself from the recognition that growth and development are characteristic of all life, and that the flowering of new insights and the creation of new institutions constitute man's response to new conditions in an eternally changing world.

This dynamic view of the human spirit stands in sharpest contrast to the static concept which sees Revelation as the proclamation of the will of an eternal God, issued once and for all. Modern scholarship has assembled an impressive body of data documenting the various stages of development in the history of the great religions and thus contradicting the notion of an immutable Revelation. The evidence cannot be refuted; it can only be ignored.

Besides, the modern spirit finds elements in the tradition that it cannot accept as the will of God. The command, "Thou shalt not suffer a witch to live" (*Ex.* 22:17), the injunction to exterminate the Canaanites, or the tale told of the prophet Elisha's curse, which killed forty-two children who taunted him (*II Kings* 2:23–24)—passages such as these affront men's ethical consciousness, which was itself, let it be remembered, nurtured by the Scriptures. Biblical incidents and injunctions such as these were the proof-texts of the village atheist a generation ago, and of such genuinely ethical freethinkers as Thomas Paine and Robert G. Ingersoll.

Another intellectual difficulty for the modern mind is raised
by the Biblical narratives depicting miracles. It is true that the
Hebrew Bible seeks to explain some of the most important in
natural terms, such as the crossing of the Red Sea by the Israelites
at the Exodus. Scholars have pointed out that others, like the stop-
ping of the sun by Joshua at Gibeon, may rest upon a prosaic misreading of a poetic utterance. Moreover, miracles do not play an
important role in Hebrew religion as a whole, nor did they affect
any important principle of belief. Nonetheless, the historical narratives of the Bible, like the Book of *Kings*, described miracles such
as Elijah's replenishment of the widow's cruse of oil and Elisha's
revival of the dead. But if these miracles are not to be accepted
literally, the problem arises with regard to the Scriptures as the
true record of Divine revelation.

Moreover, there are other implications in the traditional concept of Revelation which modern men find it difficult to accept.
If Scripture is a transcript of God's word, everything in it must be
of equal importance. Maimonides was thoroughly consistent in
insisting that the genealogies of Esau in *Genesis* are equally sacred
with the Ten Commandments or the Golden Rule. Few of our
contemporaries could subscribe to such a position today.

It is well-known that the Five Books of Moses contain a considerable amount of ritual commands by the side of ethical teaching and social legislation. Modern men, even if they are disposed
to obey the ritual, do not regard the command, "Thou shalt not
seethe a kid in its mother's milk," as being of equal importance
with "Thou shalt not murder." One may discern the Will of God
in the latter prohibition; it is more difficult to regard the former
in this light.

Some of these difficulties were by no means unknown to ancient
and medieval thinkers. Thus, as will be noted in our discussion
of the role of ritual, the traditional religion recognized that there
were different levels of significance among the various commandments, and it accorded primacy to the ethical over the ritual.
Moreover, the conception of the Bible as the literal word of God
led to a life-giving development in rabbinic Judaism. Since a
message coming directly from the Divine could contain nothing
accidental or superfluous, either in its content or in its form, every
apparently unimportant word and insignificant incident in the

Bible must have a deeper meaning, which interpretation could reveal. The Rabbis were able to find meaning in every jot and tittle of the law, often manifesting a deep ethical sensitivity that blended with their realistic understanding of life and human nature. The imposing development of the Talmud rests upon this method of textual interpretation.

Yet even if some of the difficulties may be softened, the essential problem posed by a literal doctrine of Revelation remains for the modern mind, which has been exposed to the concept of development and growth. In most instances, these difficulties confronting the modern mind are simply ignored by devout believers of the old school. More sophisticated advocates of religion, who are aware of the conflict, seek to meet the challenge in a variety of ways. Some religious teachers concede that development and growth do characterize all aspects of human life, but deny that change is applicable to the area of the Divine. They therefore disregard the evidence amassed by historical scholarship or deny its validity. Another popular procedure is to adopt a modern variant of the medieval doctrine of "the two truths," that may be described as "the compartmentalized mind." The religious apologist may treat the Bible by approved scholarly canons in his scientific research, and then utilize it uncritically in his religious life, hermetically sealing off his beliefs against his knowledge, as far as he is able.

Those who can adopt either of these approaches are, in one sense, very fortunate. They have insulated their religious convictions permanently, and safeguarded them from the corroding acids of free inquiry, doubt, and debate. But there are grave penalties. Insulation against thought means isolation from life. The history of religion underscores the truth that in all its great creative periods it was not set apart from life, but deeply involved in all the intellectual, ethical, and even esthetic currents of the time. Religious progress was the result of the impact of new, challenging, and even dangerous ideas upon the content of tradition. Tradition was enriched because it was attacked; it remained alive because it grew.

Fortunately, the static view of literal revelation is not the only one open to us. It is possible for men who are modern in more than a chronological sense and who have integrated the results of modern science and thought into their world-view honestly to believe in revelation. They can accept it in both senses, as a process of Divine

communication and as a body of teaching possessing permanent
validity. One need not reject the doctrine of *Torah min hasha-
mayim*, "The Torah as a revelation of God," because of an
inability to view it in naive terms. On the contrary, there is available to us a view that is at once more satisfying intellectually and
religiously more profound.

As Franz Rosenzweig pointed out, there are three great moments in the history of the universe, when the divine decisively
penetrates the world, in the acts of Creation, Revelation, and
Redemption. Traditional Judaism found no derogation of the
creative power of God in describing man as "the partner of the
Holy One, blessed be He, in the work of creation." So, too, tradition teaches that the Messianic era depends not only on the will
of God, but also on the acts of men. Thus Redemption cannot
come until "the generation is ready." According to one view, the
Messiah will come when the generation will be totally corrupt, or,
according to another, when the age is completely righteous. Still
other opinions set up other criteria. What is significant is that
Redemption is dependent not merely upon God, but also upon
man.

Similarly, Revelation is not impugned by viewing it as another
aspect of this eternal partnership between God and man. In this
"cosmic symbiosis" God depends upon man as truly as man depends
upon God. Revelation means communication; it requires *two* active
participants. It depends not merely upon its infinite and Divine
source, but also upon its finite and imperfect human instrument.
Indeed, man's role is as important as God's, for unless man hears,
God would be speaking in vain. As Stradivarius says in Browning's
poem, "God cannot make a violin, without Antonio."

Now, God is eternal and unchanging, but man is perpetually
in flux, varying in his capacity to grasp the Revelation of his Maker.
Hence the idea of a progressive and growing revelation is not
merely compatible with faith in its divine origin, but is the only
view that reckons with the nature of the human participant in the
process.

A Hasidic teacher was wont to say that God tempers His message in accordance with the understanding of the people to whom
He addresses Himself, just as a loving father will use "baby talk"
in speaking to his infant. We may suggest a more modern analogy,

to be found in one of the wonders of our time, the electronic transmission of sound. Let us imagine a group of people assembled in a room, and a man addressing them in a normal voice. The auditors, if they possess average hearing, can grasp his words without difficulty. But the naked ear of the audience is incapable of catching the radio waves which fill the atmosphere in the room at the same time. Then a boy brings an inexpensive radio set into the room, and now it becomes possible for the group to hear the sounds emanating from the nearest and most powerful transmitting stations in the vicinity. Nevertheless, the sound waves of distant or weaker stations still remain inaudible until a finer instrument is introduced.

Now, whether the group in the room hears only the human voice of the speaker in their midst, or the wave-lengths of powerful, nearby stations, or the sounds of fainter and more distant broadcasts, depends upon the varying instruments of reception available; all the varied sound waves themselves are to be found within those four walls, whether men are equipped to hear them or not. The objective factor of the sources of sound is unchanged; only the subjective factor of the recipients varies.

That is not all. In no case will the human ear grasp exactly what emanates from the source. Some degree of distortion of the purity of the original sound is inevitable—the finer the instrument, the higher will be the fidelity, but always the receiving instrument affects the timbre and the tone to a greater or lesser extent.

The implications of this modern parable are clear. God is the source of Revelation, but He works through men, whose capacity to grasp the divine truth depends on their personal insight, or, in Maimonides' formulation, upon the extent of their intellectual attainments, their moral quality, and their imaginative faculty. In no slight degree, their spiritual level will depend on the conditions of their age, whose children they inescapably are. Moreover, what they do receive they will refract through the medium of their own personality.

Men will always be hearing the Revelation of God, but never the complete Revelation; what they grasp will be approaching the divine "infinity," but never quite reaching its fullness. Hence, the content of Revelation vouchsafed to men constitutes a growing and evolving body of insights, ideals, and imperatives. God's Word is pre-eminently to be found in the Bible, but the Bible is not co-extensive with God's Word. And this for two reasons. The Divine factor in the Scriptures is intermingled with fallible and imperfect elements that reflect the human aspect—and that is why the Bible speaks with such incomparable power to the human situation. Moreover, the Revelation of God's will was not limited to the Biblical period. The era of the Prophets was the Golden Age of Revelation, but it did not exhaust the process. Hence the Bible is true, but it is not "the Truth, the whole Truth, and nothing but the Truth." That Truth is with God, and the Bible is its repository as apprehended by men.

This view of revelation as a process, in which both participants, God and man, play significant roles, undoubtedly owes much to the modern outlook. Yet it is worthy of note that its roots are to be found in the tradition. The ancient Rabbis sensed the importance of historical and environmental factors when they declared that various sages and saints were denied the Divine Presence, to which they were fitted by personal qualifications, because "the generation was not worthy" (*Sotah* 48b). On the other hand, they recognized that certain ages are marked by unique spiritual perceptiveness: "What an ordinary maidservant saw at the crossing of the Sea in the days of Moses, was not seen by Isaiah, Ezekiel, and all the Prophets" (*Mekilta, Shirata,* chap. 3).

Even more clearly, traditional religion recognized the variable human factor in Revelation. The Bible itself distinguishes between the immediacy and directness of the relationship possessed by Moses and the lesser level of intimacy enjoyed by other prophets, in a passage already cited in another connection. (*Numbers* 12:6 ff.)

This distinction the Rabbis amplify in their striking parable of Moses as a star-gazer with a clear telescope, unlike the other Prophets, who had blurred instruments of vision (*Yebamot* 49b). Similarly, the Talmud compares the Prophet Isaiah to a city-dweller who is familiar with the king and therefore takes him for granted, while Ezekiel is compared to a rustic coming to the capital, gazing in unfeigned astonishment at the unfamiliar spectacle of a royal procession (*Hagigah* 13b). The parable represents a distinction between the levels of inspiration of the two Prophets, as well as an explanation of the difference in their visions.

The prophet Ahijah, who played a significant role in the early history of the Kingdom of Israel, is described by the Talmud as "having seen (the true revelation) but erring in it." In other words, the human factor does not reflect the Divine light; it refracts it through the medium of its personality.

Not only does Revelation vary in content and depth with different individuals, but also it extends over varied periods. In other words, it is not an event, but a process. The theophany of Sinai marked the commencement, not the conclusion, of Revelation, however it is conceived of. In increasing measure, modern scholarship is recognizing that the tradition of the Revelation on Sinai embodies a basic historical fact, without which all the subsequent history of Judaism and, indeed, of the people of Israel is inexplicable. Evidence is mounting for the historicity of Moses and the Mosaic character of the Law, at least in its essentials. But scholarly analyses aside, for the religious consciousness, the first and greatest single hour of Revelation was at Sinai. However, as Rabbinic literature recognized, there were revelations after Sinai as well (cf. Bernard Bamberger, "Revelations of Torah after Sinai," in *Hebrew Union College Annual*, 1941). The relationship between these later stages and Sinai is expressed in an utterance of Rabbi Johanan: "God showed Moses the derivations in the Torah and the derivations of the scholars, and whatever the scholars were to originate in the future" (*Megillah* 19b). The Hebrew verb *hiddesh*, "to create anew," used in this passage, makes it clear that the Rabbis recognized that their function was active, not passive; creative, not repetitive. The same view attains to classic expression in a well-known passage which has often been misinterpreted: "Whatever any gifted disciple was destined to teach before his master was already said to Moses on Sinai" (*Yerushalmi, Hagigah* 1, 76d). Here is a clear recognition that the entire development of religious tradition after Moses is implied in the giving of the Law on Sinai, and that the organic unity binding it all together gives divine sanction to it all.

The continuity of the tradition is one side of the coin; the other is the dynamic character of Revelation, adumbrated in a Talmudic legend at once naive and profound (*Menahot* 29b). Moses in heaven, it declares, found God adding decorative crowns to the letters of the Torah. When he asked the reason for this, the lawgiver was told: "In a future generation, a man named Akiba, son of Joseph, is destined to arise, who will derive multitudes of laws from each of these marks." Deeply interested, Moses asked to be permitted to see him, and he was admitted to the rear of the schoolhouse, where Akiba was lecturing. To Moses' deep distress, however, he found that he could not understand what the scholars were saying, and his spirit grew faint within him. But as the session drew to a close, Akiba concluded: "This ordinance which we are discussing is a law derived from Moses on Sinai," and when Moses heard this, his spirit revived!

The implications of this legend are far-reaching. Tradition is not static—it varies with its human exemplars, but *this dynamic quality contravenes neither its divine origin nor its organic continuity*. Hence the Sages did not hesitate to say: "Matters not revealed to Moses were revealed to Rabbi Akiba and his colleagues" (*Midrash Bemidbar Rabbah* 19:6). It is significant that the same verb "revealed" is used both for the giver of the Law and for its interpreters a millennium and a half later.

It is the function of the scholar to trace the stages in the development of religious tradition and to analyze both the causes and the techniques involved. His concern is with the human element in Revelation, variable and imperfect, influenced by all the factors affecting men. To the extent that this process of "cosmic symbiosis" is human, it may be studied and grasped by the human mind. To the degree that its origin is Divine, it remains beyond the power of the intellect to fathom. Even those who have experienced Revelation can transmit only tantalizing glimpses of the vision which they have seen, pale echoes of the harmonies which they have heard. But as with God himself, so with Revelation—its manifestations in human life are too clear to be denied.

In another fundamental sense, as well, revelation parallels creation. The great creative act that brought the universe into existence began in the dim past, yet the process is never-ending. Similarly, the classic events in Revelation took place in the past, and have been recorded in the words of the Prophets, sages, and saints. But God's communication with man, we may firmly believe, has not ended in time any more than it is limited in space. A Socrates, a Michelangelo, a Bach, a Newton, a Schweitzer, a Herzl, testify to the universality of God's communication with men, to whom He affords a flash of insight into the mystery, the challenge, and the miracle of existence.

The superlative endowment that causes a Shakespeare to issue from some ordinary English farmers, and a Mozart from some moderately talented musicians, we call "inspiration." In restricting the term "revelation" to the sphere of religious and ethical truth, while using "inspiration" to describe other manifestations of genius, we are not yielding to convention. There is a qualitative difference between the two phenomena not to be ignored. God's creative power enters man's spirit in countless areas, such as science, art, music, literature, or the social order, each of which is a segment of existence. All those whom He singles out for greatness in one area or another have been granted His authentic inspiration. But when God reveals a glimpse of His truth, not on one limited aspect of life, but rather on man's total relationship to the universe, when He grants insight into the character of man's nature and duty, the human being that God has chosen as His spokesman has experienced Revelation.

To recognize the true prophet and to heed his call means to stake our lives, and very often the lives of our children and society as a whole, on a decision between the true and the false, the good and the evil. This is fraught with peril; it is literally a question of life and death. Existence is an adventure, sometimes thrilling, sometimes tragic, but always perilous, wherein we must run the risks and win the rewards ourselves.

Human experience bears testimony that through time, God has chosen certain dedicated men and women and made them His instruments for proclaiming His will. These men and women are not passive echoes, but active partners in the process, expressing their own vision of the truth, subject to their own limitations. Nor are we ordinary folk dependent solely upon these revelations of the Divine. The miracles of birth, of love, of death, constitute Divine elements in the pattern of life that surround us everywhere in the universe. Thus it is given to all men to hear the call, "Thus saith the Lord," however imperfectly. No other attribute of human nature so thoroughly justifies man's pretension to having been created in the image of God as his decision to make himself God's partner, either as the bearer or as the recipient of Revelation.

MAN

CHAPTER X

Evil in God's World

According to an ancient rabbinic legend, Alexander the Great, after he had made himself master of the world, was shown a pair of scales. In one cup all the gold and silver which he had amassed was placed, but it was outweighed by the other, which contained a single human skull with the socket of an eye, the symbol of man's limitless desires. When Alexander asked whether there was anything in the world more powerful than either man's achievements or man's desires, he was shown a handful of dust, the sign of death.

Similarly, if we were to place the impressive weight of evidence testifying to the existence of God in one scale, it would be outweighed for many by one hydra-headed fact, the existential tragedy of suffering, the burden of human misery, from which none are free. For untold sensitive men and women, the frail bark of faith has crashed on the hard rock of the persistence of evil in a world allegedly created by a good God.

Many will grant, without pretending to offer a mathematical "proof" of God's existence, that there is convincing evidence of His presence in nature, in history, and in man. The harmony and order of the universe point to a great creative Intelligence, and the processes of history reveal a God of righteousness, governing the destiny of men and nations. Finally, man, for all his imperfections, bears the stamp of his Divine Creator, whose attributes find a pale reflection in His creature.

That so many modern men feel themselves nevertheless unable

to believe in God is not due to any innate contrariness of spirit. On the contrary, they yearn for God, and would gladly believe in Him if they could. With all their hearts they wish that they could feel the presence in the world of a Supreme Being, all-powerful and all-good, but they encounter a great stumbling block on the pathway to God—the widespread existence of evil, the limitless suffering among men, that blots out the glories of nature and turns life into a horror, or at best a trial, instead of a blessing and a joy. The forms of human misery are boundless, penetrating all the relations of men as individuals and as members of society, affecting the lives of nations and races. Evil is manifest in all the protean forms of poverty, oppression, and tyranny. It appears, without the apparent instrumentality of men, in disease, pain, and untimely death. Perhaps its most agonizing form is the spectacle of the suffering and death of children, who are surely too young to deserve such a fate, by any standard that has meaning for men.

When men encounter suffering in their personal experience, their reaction is immediate and powerful, and disbelief is often the result. Because of the strength of their feelings, they imagine that the problem arose with them or their contemporaries. Nothing could be farther from the truth. It is the problem of evil rather than the existence of God that has always been the basic issue in Western religion. This is the fundamental concern of the Bible, with which lawgiver and prophet, psalmist and sage, wrestled. With an honesty that has never been surpassed, the book of *Job,* which Carlyle described as "the grandest book ever written with pen," is devoted to this dark riddle at the heart of existence. The dilemma was put with crystal clarity by Saint Augustine: "Either God cannot abolish evil, or He will not. If he cannot, He is not all-powerful; if He will not, He is not all-good." It is, however, not human suffering as such that creates the full dimensions of the problem, but *undeserved* suffering, what the Talmud calls the question of "Why do the righteous suffer and the wicked prosper?"

The all-pervasive presence of evil in the world provides the basis for the position of the atheist, who denies the existence of God, and of the agnostic, who cannot affirm it. Some thinkers, conscious of all the drawbacks inherent in atheism or agnosticism, have sought to solve the problem of evil by seizing one horn or the other of the dilemma posed by Augustine. Thus some men have surrendered the belief in the goodness of God. Like Hardy, they see the universe as evil, or, like Bertrand Russell, they describe it as totally unconcerned with man's hopes and ideals. Housman expresses his reaction unforgettably in his lines:

> "We for a certainty are not the first,
>   Have sat in taverns while the tempest hurled
>   Their hopeful plans to emptiness, and cursed
>   Whatever brute and blackguard made the world."

Others, unwilling to conceive of God in such terms, have preferred the other alternative—God wills the good, but He is not all-powerful. This is the essence of the humanist position, upon which countless changes have been rung, as in the world-views of such varied thinkers as S. Alexander, H. G. Wells, C. E. M. Joad, and Mordecai M. Kaplan. And William James rejected both horns of the dilemma, when he declared: "God is finite, either in power or in knowledge, or in both."

Undoubtedly, these solutions offer a solution to the problem of evil in the world, to be sure, but at a very high price, *for they create the problem of the existence of good*. If the universe is the result of a malevolent or even of a morally neutral being, what is the origin of all the goodness, truth, and beauty that we do see everywhere in the world? How could a Being lacking these attributes create a life so richly endowed with them? Water cannot rise higher than its source, and man, who is assuredly a creature, points, by the qualities with which he is endowed, to a Being in whom they must inhere in more abundant measure.

On the other hand, if we assume that God is limited in power, how explain the harmony and order pervading the entire universe, the unmistakable signs of a single cosmos? Who created the plus in the world, the regions of reality that lie beyond the bounds of His allegedly limited sovereignty? If God is the sum total only of the forces of good in the universe, or even their source, what power originated the elements in the universe that are not-good? Nor can we meet the problem by the assumption of a Satan who disputes the rule of God, or of an evil Deity like the Persian Ahriman, who struggles for mastery with Ahura Mazda, the god of light, because the world is unitary, not dual, in character, and the same principles operate everywhere. Conscious of these unanswerable objections to a God of limited power, one humanist thinker has argued that it is not the function of religion to offer an explanation of the cosmos. But few men would agree to such a limitation on the role of religion or regard such a concept of God as satisfying.

Thus both alternatives offer no tenable solution to the existence of evil; the original problem in all its urgency remains. Let it be noted at the outset that Hebrew thought, though agonizingly conscious of the existence of evil, steadfastly refused to surrender its faith either in the power or in the goodness of God. Clinging passionately to their God, the Biblical writers succeeded in finding a way in the dark caverns of life. Their most profound contribution to the subject is to be found in the book of *Job*, which will amply repay lifelong study and meditation, far more than can be attempted here.

It is perhaps not astonishing that, like the Bible as a whole, *Job* is more celebrated than known. Because of the complexity of this masterpiece, its basic theme has not been generally recognized. Thus no phrase is less applicable to this manifesto of revolt than "the patience of Job." The understanding of the book has been further complicated because, like other great masterpieces, such as the *Oresteia, Hamlet,* and *Faust,* the basic theme of *Job* had undergone extensive development over centuries, before reaching its present form. The latest stage of the Job tale was utilized by a great poet as a framework within which he could insert his immortal dialogue on man's suffering in God's world.

The outlines of the story are, of course, familiar:

In the land of Uz, there lives a righteous and highly respected patriarch named Job, blessed with all the gifts of God. When the Lord, who is holding court in Heaven, refers with legitimate pride to this loyal servant Job on earth, Satan, the prosecuting attorney in the heavenly assizes, insists that Job's fear of God is motivated by the ample rewards which he has been receiving from God. A wager is struck in Heaven to test Job, and the patriarch is visited by a series of calamities on earth, which rob him of all his possessions and even of his children. Throughout all his afflictions, Job remains steadfast, and no complaint crosses his lips. Instead, he accepts the will of God: "Naked have I come forth from my mother's womb, and naked shall I return. God hath given, God hath taken away. Blessed be the name of God." Then his own person is smitten with leprosy, and his wife, unable to see his agony, tempts him to curse God and die, and thus win release from his torment. Job, however, shows himself as superior to her temptation as to Satan's trials. He rejects his wife's counsel: "Shall we receive the good from God and not the evil?" Job remains silent in his affliction and does not sin. When the news of his suffering reaches three of his friends, princes from nearby districts, they come to comfort him. Stunned by the sight of his misery, they remain silent for seven days. Then Job opens with a soliloquy, a deeply moving lament on his tragic fate, and begs for death to release him from his agony.

Distressing as is Job's situation to his Friends, they find nothing in it to trouble men's faith, for the accepted religious teaching of the day has a ready answer: In a world created and governed by a just God, suffering is the result, and consequently the sign, of sin. Hence, if suffering comes to a man, it behooves him to scrutinize his actions to discover his transgressions. Should he find that he is free from sin, he should wait patiently for vindication, remaining serene in the faith that God's justice will be done. The process of retribution may at times be delayed, but ultimately it will become manifest.

This approach was the distillation of centuries of Hebrew thought which had achieved the faith that a just God rules the world, and then had proceeded to apply it to the destiny of individuals and nations.

In the words of the Biblical psalmists:

> "For His anger is but for a moment,
> His favour is for a lifetime;
> Weeping may tarry for the night,
> But joy comes in the morning."
>
> (Ps. 30:6)

> The Lord is good unto them that wait for Him,
> To the soul that seeks Him.
> It is good that a man should quietly wait
> For the salvation of the Lord.
>
> (Lam. 3:25–26)

A few months previously, Job himself would have had the same reaction. Had it been reported to him during the earlier period of his well-being that some individual had been visited by such devastating blows, the God-fearing Job would have proffered to the victim the same recipe of spiritual self-examination, resignation to God's will, and patient hope for restoration to His favor.

At the outset, therefore, the discussion between Job and his Friends is not a debate. When the Friends come to comfort Job in his affliction, they naturally take it for granted that his faith is unshaken. For even his tragic lament on the day of his birth (chap. 3) is couched in general terms; it is not yet directed against God. Eliphaz, the oldest of the Friends, is certain that all that is required is to remind Job of the basic religious truth that has been momentarily beclouded for him by his suffering:

> If one ventures a word with you, will you be offended?
> Yet who can keep from speaking?
> Behold, you have instructed many
> And you have strengthened weak hands.
> But now it has come to *you*, and you cannot bear it.
> It touches *you* and you are dismayed!
> Think, now, who that was innocent ever perished,
> Or where were the upright cut off?
>
> (*Job* 4:2-3, 5, 7)

Soon enough, however, Eliphaz and his colleagues discover that it is a vastly changed Job that confronts them. Job has undergone a shattering personal experience, but he knows, with the knowledge that defies all the logic of theology, that he is innocent. Thus the simple cause-and-effect relation—sin causes suffering and suffering is the sign of sin—has broken down.

We who have read the tale of the wager between God and Satan in the Prologue know that Job's misery and degradation are part of a cosmic experiment to discover whether man is capable of serving the ideal for its own sake, without the hope of reward. Job has no such inkling. For him, *the accepted religious convictions of a lifetime are now contradicted by his personal experience,* by his unshakable knowledge that he is no sinner, certainly not sinful enough to deserve such a succession of blows as have fallen upon his defenseless head.

Of Job's inner travail the Friends are unaware. Eliphaz, the oldest
and the wisest of the three, proceeds to remind Job of the truths
by which he has lived all his years. It is noteworthy that the
author, whose sympathies are clearly on Job's side, nonetheless puts
into Eliphaz' first speech the fullest and fairest presentation of the
conventional theodicy on suffering. Divine justice does prevail in
the world, the apparent contradictions in the world of reality
notwithstanding. In the first instance, the process of Divine retribution takes time, and so Job must have patience. Besides, the righteous are never destroyed, while the wicked, or at least their children,
are ultimately punished. Eliphaz then describes a vision from on
high which disclosed to him the truth that all men are imperfect,
so that not even a righteous man may justly complain if he suffers.
Moreover, not God, but man, is responsible for sin and suffering,
both of which, be it noted, are expressed by the identical Hebrew
terms ('aven and 'amal):

> Not from the earth does evil sprout,
> Nor from the dust does trouble arise;
> It is man who begets evil,
> As surely as sparks fly upward.
>
> (Job 5:6–7)

That man, and not the universe, is the source of evil is emphasized in the later pseudepigraphic *Book of Enoch,* which is
more consciously theological in character. "Sin has not been sent
upon the earth, but men have produced it out of themselves.
Therefore they who commit sin are condemned" (98:4). Finally,
Eliphaz adds, suffering is a discipline, warning men against sin,
and hence it is a mark of God's love. Ultimately, the righteous
are saved and attain to peace and contentment.

That is not all. In the succeeding cycles of speeches, Eliphaz
adds that there is more to the punishment of the sinner than his
final catastrophe, whether in his own person or in that of his offspring. During the long period of his ostensible prosperity, the
evildoer lives in perpetual trepidation, never knowing when the
blow will fall. His punishment is as long as his life.

In his later speeches, Eliphaz will also emphasize the familiar
traditional doctrine that God visits the sin of the fathers upon
the children, since all the generations constitute a unity. Hence,

justice does prevail, though not necessarily within a single lifetime.

Job has scarcely heard, let alone been persuaded, by Eliphaz' arguments or by the considerably more heated and less illuminating speeches of the other Friends who follow Eliphaz. He has no theory of his own to propose as a substitute for their doctrine, merely his consciousness that he is suffering without cause. He does not claim to be perfect, but insists that he is not a wilful sinner. Against their conventional ideas he sets the testimony of his own experience, which he will not deny, whatever the consequence. As the round of debate continues, Job's fury mounts, as does the helpless wrath of his Friends. His attacks upon their disloyalty, his pathetic description of his physical pain and mental anguish, his indignant rejection of their deeply held faith, serve all the more to convince them that he is a sinner. For what greater impiety is there than for man to lay claim to innocence; what worse arrogance than for him to assume the right and capacity to pass judgment on God?

Bildad, the second of the Friends, paints a picture of the destruction of the wicked, and of the ultimate restoration of the righteous, while he hymns the power of God. Job dismisses this as irrelevant, for he does not deny God's power; it is His justice that he calls into question. Zophar, the youngest and least discreet of the Friends, bluntly summons Job to repent of his secret sins.

Three cycles of speeches are delivered by the Friends, in which the same ideas are reiterated, but with ever greater vehemence. The conventional theodicy, maintained by the Friends, has exhausted itself. As the debate continues, Job is fortified in his conviction that he is right. What he experiences existentially cannot be refuted theoretically; it must be taken into account in any conception of reality.

Job is aware of the contention that morality depends upon faith in Divine justice. If he denies God's justice, how can he maintain moral standards? Job is driven to a desperate expedient, which is to prove one of the great liberating ideas in religion—he cuts the nexus between virtue and reward: righteousness does not necessarily bring prosperity, nor does sin always lead to punishment, as his own tragic experience demonstrates. Hence honest men will tremble at his undeserved suffering, but they will not on that account be deterred from righteousness:

> Upright men are astounded at this,
> Yet the innocent will rise up against the godless,
> And the righteous will cleave to his way,
> And he that has clean hands will grow stronger and stronger.
>
> (*Job* 17:8–9)

The Mishnah is accordingly justified in concluding that Job's righteousness stems from the disinterested love of God and not from fear. Job cannot see how God's ways are justified, but he never wavers in the conviction that in the interim men's ways must be just.

We cannot here trace in detail the poignant crescendo of Job's faith. He turns first to His righteous God and pleads for an "arbiter" (*mokhiah*), to judge the suit between him and God (9:32–35). As the argument continues, Job's plea becomes a conviction that there is, there must be, a "witness" (*edh*) to testify on his behalf. Finally, he reaches the peak of faith. In a moment of mystic ecstasy, he sees his vindication through a Redeemer, who will act to avenge his suffering. The term he uses, *go'el*, means a kinsman, a blood-avenger, who, in earlier Hebrew law, was duty-bound to see that justice was done to an aggrieved brother. In all these appeals, Job is calling to the invisible God of righteousness in whom he passionately believes, to justify him against the visible God of power at whose hands he has suffered. The God in whom Job has faith is more than an impartial judge, or even a witness on his behalf—He is the Redeemer of the righteous:

> As for me, I know that my Redeemer liveth,
> Though He be the last to arise upon earth!
> For from within my skin, this has been marked,
> And from my flesh do I see God,
> Whom I see for myself,
> My own eyes behold, not another's!

But the momentary vision of God arising to redeem him fades; Job cannot permanently hold the ecstasy—

> My reins are consumed with longing within me.
>
> (19:25–27)

As the mystics have taught us, Job's exaltation is followed by a mood of depression, but the impact of his vision is never completely lost. Job's final speech, which contains his lament on his tragic decline, is a soliloquy, spoken to himself rather than to the Friends.

There now appears a brash young character named Elihu, of whom, we are to assume, the dignified elders have previously taken no notice. He has overheard the debate and feels impelled to inject himself into the discussion.

The authenticity of the Elihu speeches has evoked scholarly debate. Without entering here into this discussion, we may point out that these chapters occupy a vital position in the architecture of our book. It is noteworthy that young Elihu is at least as antagonistic to the Friends as he is to Job. Actually, he denies the truth of both positions. The Friends have maintained that God is just and that, therefore, suffering is both the penalty for and the proof of sin. Job has countered by insisting that his suffering is not the result of sin, and, therefore, he charges God with injustice. Elihu accepts the premises, but denies the conclusions of both sides! He agrees with the Friends that God is just, and with Job that suffering may come to the innocent.

How is that possible? Because suffering may come to men as a discipline, chastening them in the face of arrogance, and warning them before they commit sin. That suffering can serve the moral education of man had been indicated in one verse by Eliphaz (5:17), but had been left undeveloped thereafter. Moreover, the great Unknown Prophet of the Exile, Deutero-Isaiah, had utilized it to explain the mystery of Israel's suffering in a pagan world. It is Elihu who makes it central to this thought.

In addition, Job has contended that God is indifferent to man's suffering and therefore is inaccessible to His creatures. This charge Elihu denies. On the contrary, God does communicate with man through dreams and visions, and when these fail, through illness and suffering. This recognition of the uses of pain is the kind of mature insight that would come to a man after years of experience. We therefore believe that the Elihu speeches were added to the book by the author later in his career. But whoever the author, the theme is significant. At every hand, life teaches how frequently smugness and callousness characterize those who are always successful. No wonder it is not easy to tolerate the "self-made man" who worships his maker. If youth is often brash and self-centered, while age is more mellow, it is because frustration and sorrow lead men to a sense of fellowship and sympathy with their brothers.

Elihu's words end as a storm is seen rising in the east. The Lord himself appears in the whirlwind and speaks to Job. The argumentation of the Friends that Job must be a sinner is treated with the silence which it deserves. Nowhere does God refer to Job's alleged misdoings. Instead, the entire problem is raised to another dimension. Can Job comprehend, let alone govern, the universe that he has weighed and found wanting? Earth and sea, cloud and darkness and dawn, snow and hail, rain and thunder and ice, and the stars above—all these wonders are beyond Job.

Nor do these exhaust God's power. With a vividness born of deep love and careful observation, the poet goes on to picture the beasts, remote from man, yet precious to their Maker. The lion and the mountain goat, the wild ass, and the buffalo, the ostrich, the horse, and the hawk, all testify to the glory of God. For all their variety, these creatures have one element in common—they are not under the sway of man, nor are they intended for his use. Even the ponderous hippopotamus and the fearsome crocodile, far from conventionally beautiful, reveal the creative power of God and His joy in the world. Moreover, God declares, were Job able to destroy evil in the world, even He would be prepared to relinquish His throne to him—a moving acknowledgment by God that the world-order is not totally perfect!

The import of the God-speeches in *Job* has been generally misunderstood, because, in accordance with a characteristic feature of Semitic poetry, the theme is not explicitly set forth, but is suggested and left to be inferred by the reader. Commentators usually maintain that Job is finally overwhelmed by the evidence of God's physical power. But that fact Job has conceded time and again during the earlier debate with the Friends, and he has not been cowed into silence on that account. What impels Job to submit now is the essential truth of God's position, which, however, needs to be properly understood. The standpoint of the author emerges under two aspects. The first and minor theme has been expressed by Elihu, as we have seen—suffering frequently serves as a source of moral discipline and is thus a spur to higher ethical attainment. The second and major idea is reserved for the speech of the Lord out of the whirlwind, with the implications being as important as the explicit content.

The vivid and joyous descriptions of the universe in the God-speeches are not mere nature-poetry. They testify that nature is more than a mystery; it is a cosmos, a thing of beauty. The force of the analogy is not lost upon Job. Just as there are order and harmony in the natural world, so there must be order and meaning in the moral sphere. Man cannot fully fathom the meaning of the natural order, yet he is aware of its beauty and harmony. Similarly, though he cannot expect fully to comprehend the moral order, he can believe that there are rationality and justice within it. As Kant pointed out, if it is arrogant to defend God, it is even more arrogant to assail Him. Any view of the universe that completely explains it is by that very token untrue. The analogy of the natural order gives the believer in God rational grounds for facing the mystery of evil with a courage born of faith in the essential rightness of things. What cannot be comprehended through reason must be embraced in love. For the author of *Job*, God is one and indivisible, governing nature and human life. If there is pattern anywhere in the universe, there must be pattern everywhere. As nature is instinct with morality, so the moral order is rooted in the natural world.

One other significant contribution to religion emerges from the Book of *Job*. For the poet who exults in the beauty of the world, the harmony of the universe is important not only as an idea but as an experience, not only logically but esthetically. When man steeps himself in the beauty of the world, his own troubles grow petty, not because they are unreal, but because they dissolve within the larger plan, like the tiny dabs of oil in a masterpiece of painting. The beauty of the world becomes an anodyne to man's suffering.

We may apply Havelock Ellis' description of the function of the artist in general to the achievement of the author of *Job:* "Instead of imitating those philosophers who with analyses and syntheses worry over the goal of life and the justification of the world, and the meaning of the strange and painful phenomenon called Existence, the artist takes up some fragment of that existence, transfigures it, shows it: There! And therewith the spectator is filled with enthusiastic joy, and the transcendent Adventure of Existence is justified. . . . All the pain and the madness, even the ugliness and the commonplace of the world, he converts into shining jewels. By revealing the spectacular character of reality he restores the

serenity of its innocence. We see the face of the world as of a
lovely woman smiling through her tears."

It is before the breath-taking description of nature, the beauty
and mystery of which are the counterpart of the law and mystery
of the moral order, that Job yields up his rebelliousness. His surrender, however, is still a victory, for his wish has been granted:

> I had heard of thee by the hearing of the ear,
> But now mine eye has seen thee.
> Wherefore I abhor my words, and repent,
> Seeing I am dust and ashes.
>
> (*Job* 42:5–6)

To use the language of our day, Job's protest is existential, but it
contributes to a deeper essential religion. Incidentally, the author of
Job does not reject the conventional theology of the Friends out
of hand; he merely regards it as inadequate. What he has added
to religious thought is of central importance—after all legitimate
explanations of suffering are taken into account, a residue of
mystery still remains.

We have presented the ideas of the book of *Job* at some length
because no deeper insight into the issue may be found elsewhere.
With the book of *Job* as a background, we may now seek to
grapple with the problem of evil on our own terms.

At the outset it should be recalled that not all suffering poses a
difficulty, because in large areas of experience it is justified, since
it is the penalty for wrongdoing. We may not be able to share
completely the optimistic faith of some Biblical writers that virtue
is always rewarded and vice invariably punished. But in a very
substantial measure, the principle does operate in life. It may be
true that success is not measured out in exact proportion to one's
deserts, but in general the qualities of reliability, truthfulness, and
diligence win their rewards in the practical world; and, conversely,
the man who cannot be trusted or lacks a sense of responsibility
may enjoy temporary success, but ultimately fails. Even in our
imperfect world there is generally a rough kind of correspondence
between an individual's actions and his destiny. Though we may be
tempted to deny it in an hour of bitterness and trial, by and large
justice does prevail, both positively and negatively.

When we say that "evil is punished," we are, of course, using

human vocabulary to describe a cosmic process. What we mean
is that in a world based on the moral law, the consequence of a
wrong act is inherent and inevitable. This truth the Talmudic sage
Rabbi Eleazar finds in the Biblical verse, "Not out of the mouth
of the Most High do good and evil proceed" (*Lam.* 3:38), which
he interprets to mean, "Of itself, the punishment comes upon the
evildoers and the blessing upon the doers of good" (*Midrash
Debarim Rabba*, chap. 4).

Job's Friends also underscore another aspect of retribution, its
long-range character. All through the years during which the successful malefactor is apparently enjoying well-being, punishment
is at work in the perpetual fear and worry which he experiences,
the gnawing uncertainty as to whether the blow will descend
upon him, and when and how and through whom.

The suffering of the wicked, however painful to behold, does not
do violence to our sense of justice and therefore poses no problem
for faith in a God of righteousness. Even a long delay in retribution, *so long as it finally comes*, would not prove a stumbling
block, great as would be the strain upon men's patience. That such
patience, born of faith, will ultimately be justified by events is
a basic theme in the Psalms:

> God's anger is but for a moment,
> His favour is for a life-time;
> Weeping may tarry for the night,
> But joy cometh in the morning.
>
> (*Ps.* 30:6)

> Resign thyself unto the Lord, and wait patiently for Him;
> Fret not thyself because of him who prospereth in his way,
> Because of the man who bringeth wicked devices to pass.
> For evil-doers shall be cut off;
> But those that wait for the Lord, they shall inherit the land.
>
> (*Ps.* 37:7–9)

It is not the prosperity of the wicked so much as the suffering
of the righteous that challenges the faith in a righteous God, who
rules the universe in justice and truth.

Some religious philosophers, from St. Augustine onward, have
sought to evade the issue by describing evil as being the absence
of good, as darkness is the absence of light. Evil therefore has no

existential reality, and God can therefore not be held responsible
for what does not exist.

As an exercise in metaphysical logic, the attempt may command
respect, but it fails utterly to come to grips with the burning
urgency of the problem. A child who falls over a chair in the dark
is bruised, even though darkness may be described by the physicist
as the absence of light. Whether evil exists positively or negatively,
war, poverty, and disease inflict a massive burden of agony upon
millions of human beings. A youngster left forever crippled by
poverty, a paraplegic tied in a hospital bed for life, a woman dying
of cancer—their unheard cry pierces the walls of any ivory tower
in which a philosopher may take refuge. The reality of evil is a
basic conviction of vital religion. Even Job's Friends do not dare
fly in the face of the facts and nowhere try to comfort Job by
suggesting that his suffering is an illusion.

It is undoubtedly one of the functions of religion to teach men
how to transcend the evils that they cannot transform, to endure
the ills that they cannot cure, but the path does not lie in pretending that the evil does not exist. Those modern cults that offer this
panacea to their devotees are directed to those whose troubles are
self-induced or imaginary. To deny that men's suffering is real,
that it is massive in its proportions and heart-rending in its intensity, is no service to the God of truth.

A vital faith must reckon honestly with the evils of the world,
and particularly with the suffering of the innocent. How can the
existence of these ills of life be reconciled with a good God? It
is significant that while the basic thesis of *Job* is that evil is a
mystery, the book recognizes that our limited intelligence is not
altogether helpless before the mystery. To approach the problem,
we must recognize that evil is a generic term covering many
phenomena. If the problem is to prove tractable, it must be broken
down into its various categories.

What are the major evils of the world? They are fundamentally
three: disease, poverty, and war. As far as disease is concerned,
many of its forms are the result of human acts both of commission
and of omission. Malnutrition, squalor, overcrowding, the failure
to apply preventive medicine or curative drugs—these major causes
of disease are to be laid at the door of mankind. Thus even disease
cannot be stigmatized as completely "an act of God." As for the

other two evils, poverty and war, they are in their entirety man-made. God surely cannot be reproached with making poverty a "natural" and inevitable condition of human existence. We do not live in a world where the heavens above us are bronze and the earth beneath us iron, so that no green thing grows. Ours is not an earth where sunshine, rain, and dew are lacking and life must therefore grow pale and spectre-thin and die. The all-too-typical modern phenomenon of men destroying "surplus" food-stocks is tragic evidence that there is enough food in the world, so that hunger and nakedness are unnecessary. Human poverty is an evil that cannot fairly be charged against God.

As for war, no proof is needed that it is a human invention. Man is virtually the only creature that preys upon his own kind—and that from no real need but because of greed, ambition and—the supreme irony—for the sake of "honor." To describe war as the human counterpart of the struggle for existence in nature is totally false.

As Donald Culrose Peattie has reminded us: "To be sentimental would, in Nature, be suicidal; if there is no compassion in it, neither is there any persecution. You cannot find in nature anything evil, save as you misread it by human standards. Anger blazes in a fight between two bull moose; anger then is a plain preservative measure, as is fear, which is the safeguard of all living. Together, these primary emotions bare the fang, they tense the muscles in the crouching haunch. You may call that hate, if you will, but it is brief and honest, not nursed in the dark like ours. In all of Nature, which fights for life because it loves life, there is nothing like human war.

"We alone are responsible for the existence of cruelty, in the sense of maliciously inflicted pain. This is one of man's inventions —of which so many are already obsolete. . . . In this present agony of mankind, men talk, shuddering, of 'going back to the ways of the beasts.' Let them consider the beasts' way, which is cleanly and reasonable, free of dogmas, creeds, political or religious intolerances. Let no one think he will find in Nature justification for human evil, or precedent for it. Or, even among our natural enemies, any but fair fighting."

In sum, the massive evils in the world, war, poverty, and disease, are, in largest degree, man-made.

However, even if this be granted, we are far from solving our problem; we have merely moved it one step further along. For now a more basic question obtrudes itself: "Why was man created with a capacity to do evil?" Religion finds the answer in the nature of men, to which we shall return later. But some aspects of the theme must be taken into account here.

As we have seen, we do not know why God willed the act of creation. The medieval philosopher who declares that God's full nature includes the creative capacity, the Hindu thinker who insists that God is an artist who needed self-fulfillment, the mystic who suggests that He wanted to express and receive love, the pious believer who maintains that He created everything for His glory in what would otherwise be an empty universe—all are seeking to cast a little light on what remains a mystery. Whatever the motive, God called into being an untold number of creatures, who emerged on this planet, as we now believe, through the evolutionary process. In all this vast creation, God's will prevailed unchallenged. Every living creature obeyed unswervingly the laws of its nature, being governed entirely by its instincts and being totally determined by its environment. Yet in all this universe, the Creator still remained lonely, for He craved fellowship with a being who would possess, if only in part, some of His attributes, so that there could be a sense of true communion, a free relationship between them. Hence God fashioned one creature, man, "in His image, according to His likeness," whom He endowed with Divine reason and creative capacity, including the ability to control and re-create the world.

Now intelligence, the application of reason to a given problem, means the capacity of weighing alternatives and making a decision. But there can be no intelligence in any effective sense, without the freedom of choice among various alternatives, and freedom of choice necessarily includes the freedom to choose unwisely. But since man is morally free, he is by that token responsible for his decisions, be they good, bad, or indifferent. In sum, reason, freedom, and responsibility represent three facets of human nature. Possessing reason, man is free; being free, he is responsible. With few and partial exceptions, the lower animals lack the gift of reason; hence they possess no freedom of choice and are not morally accountable for their actions.

Even in the case of man, the degree of responsibility varies with

the level of intelligence and the extent of freedom which he possesses. An infant may cause some damage, like smashing a vase, but
he is not regarded as a sinner. Only as he begins to grow physically
do we assume a parallel growth in intelligence and consequently
demand an ever greater measure of responsibility.

Why did God create man with the capacity to do evil? The
answer is that if man was to be human, no other course was open—
if he was to possess intelligence, he necessarily had to be endowed
with freedom of choice, and this implies the capacity to choose
evil. Because of this ever-present peril, the Bible issues the call again
and again:

> "Behold, I place before you this day the blessing and the
> curse, life and death. Thou shalt choose life!"

When man, nevertheless, prefers the wrong, as is so often the
case, he invites the penalty inherent in his act, the inevitable consequence of sin. There is a profound truth in the semantic fact that
in Biblical Hebrew, which is rich in the vocabulary of moral conno-
tation, the same terms (such as *'aven*, *'amal*, *'avon*, *het*, and *hattat*)
mean both "sin" and "suffering," both "wrong-doing" and "punishment." The same word represents the act and the consequence,
because they are inseparable. The wrong-doing of man, rooted in
his nature, is the source of most of man's misery. Not God, but
man, is guilty of these evils.

Yet the issue is still not disposed of. If the sinner himself bore
his punishment, our sense of justice would not be troubled. Unfortunately, however, experience demonstrates a tragic bifurcation
between the evildoer and the sufferer—one man sins and another
suffers. Hence, the agonizing cry still remains, "Why do the innocent suffer, while the guilty prosper?" Some men die of hunger
because other men are gorging themselves. A powerful state covets
additional territory belonging to a weak neighbor, and innocent
people are bombed to death. Children grow up in squalid sur-
roundings, surrounded by misery, cruelty, and crime, because other
men grow rich from the rents of slums. Millions perish through
starvation, while "surplus" food is destroyed to maintain profits.

Particularly if we consider the vast underdeveloped areas of the
earth, rather than such advanced countries like the United States, it
is still true, even at the midpoint of the twentieth century, that

those who do most of the back-breaking toil of the world barely can keep body and soul together and live without a ray of hope for security and ease in the future. Contrasting the lot of the prosperous malefactor and the suffering poor, Job cried out:

> One man dies in his full strength,
> Being wholly at ease and quiet;
> His pails are full of milk,
> And the marrow of his bones is moistened.
> And another dies in bitterness of soul,
> And has never tasted any joy.
>
> (*Job* 21:23–25)

Job's passionate protest will continue to re-echo in men's hearts because it is so deeply human.

Yet we are not altogether helpless in facing even the problem of the suffering of the innocent. It is necessary to recall here a principle which is generally regarded as a beautiful ideal or a pleasant conceit. Actually, it is a basic reality of existence, indeed, a grim truth which we cannot elude. Religious teachers have called it "the brotherhood of man." Its full implications are better expressed, stripped of sentimentality, in the concept of the interdependence of mankind. The positive aspect of this principle was expressed by an ancient sage, Ben Zoma. Standing on the Temple mountain in Jerusalem, he saw masses of people streaming up the slopes and said, "Blessed is God, the source of all mystery, who has created all these for my service. How many labors did not Adam have to undergo until he had a piece of bread to eat! He had to plow the ground, sow the seed, harvest the grain, and then thresh, winnow, grind, and bake it, and then only could he eat bread. But when I arise in the morning, I find everything prepared for me!" (*Berakhot* 58a).

This interdependence of mankind, however, is not merely a source of strength to each member of the human race; it is a poignant source of tragedy as well, expressed in John Donne's famous utterance: "No man is an island entire of itself. Each man is a piece of the continent, a part of the main. If a clod be washed away, Europe is the less, as well as if a Promontory were, as well as if a manor of thy friends or these own were. Any man's death diminishes me, because I am involved in Mankind. And therefore

never seek to ask for whom the bell tolls. It tolls for thee."
Bereft of all poetic embellishments, the same truth is implicit in
Benjamin Franklin's dry reminder to his fellow rebels in the
American Revolution: "We had all better hang together, or we'll
hang separately."

John Donne's admonition notwithstanding, each human being
does develop an insular pride. He equates his personality with the
limits of his physique; whatever falls within the territory bounded
by his head at one end and his feet at the other is part of "himself,"
whatever lies outside these boundaries is alien. However flattering
to our conceit this conception may be, the truth is that there is no
disparate individuality in the world. All the members of a given
generation are inextricably bound up with one another. They are
heirs in common of all the contributions of the past, and share the
benefits of the positive elements and achievements of the civilization
in which they live. By the same token, they are responsible for all
its shortcomings and failures, all its errors and sins.

The great Confession of Sin in the traditional Jewish liturgy is
invariably couched in the plural rather than the singular: "For
the sin which *we* have committed before Thee." It thus emphasizes the truth that each human being is accountable not only
for his own personal acts of commission and of omission, but also
for the sins of permission as well, the failings of the society of
which he is a member, the collective transgressions of which he has
acquiesced in by his inactivity, his indifference, or his silence.
Biblical teaching rightly regards the commandment, "Thou shalt
not stand idly by the blood of thy neighbor," as on a par with the
imperative, "Thou shalt not kill." Each individual, in greater or
lesser degree, can mold the weal or the woe of his generation and
is therefore responsible for its shortcomings.

This conception, which may be described as "horizontal responsibility," the interdependence of mankind *across space*, uniting all
men in a given generation, has both negative and positive aspects,
as the Bible recognizes. Thus, according to the Book of *Samuel*, the
entire people is visited by a plague because of King David's sin
(*II Sam.* 24:11 ff.). On the other hand, it is this interdependence
of mankind which makes it possible for the saint, by his presence,
to redeem his sinful contemporaries, as when Abraham sought to
save Sodom for the sake of a righteous minority. Similarly, Eliphaz

promises Job that if he repents and makes his peace with God, he will be able to intercede with Him for sinners and save them:

> Thou wilt then issue a decree, and it will be fulfilled for thee,
> And upon thy ways, light will shine.
> When men are brought low, thou wilt say, "Rise up!"
> And the humble will be saved.
> Even the guilty will escape punishment,
> Escaping through the cleanness of thy hands.
>
> (*Job* 22:28–30)

Nor is this all. Men are linked together also through "vertical responsibility" *in time*, being united in the family-line across the generations of past, present, and future. However humbling it may be to our personal pride, the truth is that each of us is simply a link in a long chain. In completely amoral terms, this is the standpoint of biology. As Weissmann taught, each being is simply a temporary instrument for the transmission of the family genes. Viewed, therefore, *sub specie aeternitatis*, we are not sharply demarcated individualities, but closely interlinked cells of a single organism.

Because most of the Bible antedates the rise of individualism, Biblical thought expresses with clarity and vigor this perception of the interdependence of men, and the doctrine of group retribution that follows from it. Generally it is applied to the nation viewed as a unit, as in the famous passage, which is couched in the plural, in *Deut.* 11:13–17:

> And it shall come to pass, if ye shall hearken diligently unto My commandments which I command you this day, to love the Lord your God, and to serve Him with all your heart and with all your soul, that I will give the rain of your land in its season, the former rain and the latter rain, that thou mayest gather in thy corn, and thy wine, and thine oil. And I will give grass in thy fields for thy cattle, and thou shalt eat and be satisfied. Take heed to yourselves, lest your heart be deceived, and ye turn aside, and serve other gods, and worship them; and the anger of the Lord be kindled against you, and He shut up the heaven, so that there shall be no rain, and the ground shall not yield her fruit; and ye perish quickly from off the good land which the Lord giveth you.

The doctrine of retribution could be held with total conviction, because it arose early in Hebrew history, when man's personal destiny had no existence apart from the clan and the nation to which he belonged.

The Biblical historians, the authors of *Joshua, Judges, Samuel*, and *Kings*, made the doctrine of national retribution the cornerstone of their philosophy of history, explaining the ebb and flow of Hebrew prosperity and disaster in terms of the people's fluctuating obedience or resistance to the word of God. The prophet Hosea, as we have seen, emphasized that the law of consequence was rooted in the universe, by expressing it in metaphors drawn from nature (*Hosea* 8:7; 10:12–13). Hosea's older contemporary, Amos, had applied the same principle of justice as the law of history to contemporary world affairs, and found in it the key to the destiny of all the neighboring nations, and not only of Israel (*Amos*, chaps. 1 and 2).

This conception became embodied in the folk-proverb cited both by Jeremiah (31:29) and Ezekiel (18:2): "The fathers have eaten sour grapes, and the children's teeth are set on edge." The idea received its most powerful religious expression in the famous affirmation that "the Lord visits the sins of the fathers upon the children" (*Ex.* 20:5). It is noteworthy that human agencies are specifically forbidden to act on this doctrine: "The fathers shall not be put to death for the children, neither shall the children be put to death for the fathers; every man shall be put to death for his own sin" (*Deut.* 24:16). It is not a principle of human jurisprudence, to be employed by men of limited life span and vision; it is a Divine law of life functioning in a world created by an eternal God.

We seem to have wandered far from our theme of inquiry, yet actually we have not strayed at all. The interdependence of mankind, for ill as well as for good, which links men through time as well as through space, is the key to much of the suffering of the innocent. From our limited view of disparate individuals, there is sense as well as agony in our cry, "If A sins, why is B punished?" But from the standpoint of God, the question may be meaningless, because A and B are part of the same larger organism. A naive parable may clarify the point. Let us imagine a youngster who is very fond of sweets, who helps himself to four or five servings of his favorite dessert and naturally develops a stomach-ache. If his organs could speak, the stomach might well complain, "Why should I suffer pain, when it was the palate that committed the offense?" From the stomach's limited point of view, the situation is completely unfair. The answer is self-evident to the point of banality. The mouth and the stomach are not independent entities, but are part of a single organism, involved in a common destiny. So, too, all men are involved in one another, sharing each other's sin and bearing each other's penalty.

That human beings suffer for one another is an objective reality, rooted in the world, beyond men's power to change. The interdependence of mankind is, however, more than an impersonal law of man's being. It frequently becomes a voluntary act of his will. Wherever there is love, there is vicarious suffering, freely and gladly borne. As a man increases the number of human beings for whom he feels love and concern—his wife and children, his parents and kinsmen, his neighbors and fellow citizens—he increases correspondingly his vulnerability to pain, because he shares the suffering of those he loves. Nor would he have it otherwise, if only because enlarging the boundaries of loving means deepening the experience of living. No normal father or mother would be willing to be spared the pain, the fear, and the anxiety that flow from the love which he feels for his child. What is true within the family holds true in the larger household of mankind. The crucial distinction is that men are conscious of the link binding them together in the home, whereas they are not yet adequately aware of the larger unit of which they are a part in the world. Yet conscious of it or not, men encounter everywhere the reality of vicarious suffering.

A murderer who pays the supreme penalty visits punishment upon his innocent mother, upon his young children, upon all who are stained by the shame of his wrongdoing. Virtually no man is so thoroughly alone in the world that he can suffer without involving others with him. This law of human existence constitutes part of the existential tragedy of man. To be sure, the doctrine of interdependence of mankind is often professed, but all too rarely taken seriously, but that is the measure of the sin of our age and of its consequences. The physical and moral peril of modern man flows from the fact that he is a citizen of the world and does not know it.

To recapitulate, we have thus far dealt only with suffering which is the consequence of men's wrongdoing. This type of human suffering, as we have seen, falls into two categories. In one, the same individual is responsible both for the act and for its results. In the other, the consequences of the act, be they good or ill, do not necessarily fall upon the individual himself, but upon other members of society, who share an ineluctable unity of life and destiny with him. That vicarious suffering, which is a law of life, includes God himself, is one of the deepest insights of the Judeo-Christian tradition. It is expressed in the Rabbinic interpretation of a passage in *Isaiah:* "In all their troubles, He shares their pain"; and in the Talmudic utterance: "When Israel suffered exile, the Divine Presence went forth into exile with them." In Christianity, it was extended to the doctrine of vicarious atonement. Thus from their individual vantage points, both traditions underscored the truth of the interdependence of mankind, as well as the cosmic interrelationship of God and man.

Suffering is the consequence of sin—that is the heart of the position adopted by Job's Friends in the Dialogue. The great poet who is the author of *Job* expresses their standpoint with all the skill and power at his command *because he believes that it is true. But the Friends' error*, for which they must ultimately seek forgiveness, *is their insistence that it is the whole truth.*

Other facets of the theme, which call attention to the functions of suffering in advancing the quality of human existence, are expressed by other participants in the great Debate in *Job.* Thus Elihu, as we have seen, stresses the educative role of suffering in the formation of character and its preservation. Let it be noted that Elihu does not propose the sentimental argument that suffering ennobles men. It is a highly dubious proposition that suffering makes men better; what it does is reveal them as they really are, stripped of the layers of pretence, convention, and position which ordinarily swathe their lives. Hence, trials often disclose unsuspected sources of greatness in ordinary men and unplumbed depths of weakness in the great and mighty. What Elihu contends is that suffering often acts as a discipline, helping to overcome the fatal human tendency to complacency and arrogance. The Greeks regarded *hybris* ("pride") as the unforgivable crime against the gods. It is the same sin which is punished in the Biblical narrative of the Tower of Babel, and from which the Biblical sage asks to be protected:

> "Give me not poverty or riches,
> Feed me mine allotted bread,
> Lest I be full, and deny, and say: 'Who is the Lord?'
> Or lest I be poor, and steal,
> And profane the name of my God."
>
> (*Prov.* 30:8–9)

Those who have never suffered are all too often insufferable. In Goethe's words:

> "Who ne'er with tears his bread has eaten
> Knows you not, ye heavenly spirits."

It is this disciplinary function which is expressed by the Hebrew term for suffering, *yissurim*, which literally means both "chastisement" and "instruction." It is expressed in the familiar passage, "Whom the Lord loveth He chastiseth, and He speaks like a father with his child" (*Prov.* 3:12). Precisely because of man's reasoning faculty, which permits him to rationalize his basest desires and defend his most indefensible actions, suffering is an indispensable instrument for advancing the moral maturation of men.

To develop humility before God and sympathy with men is theoretically possible to all, but in practice, these virtues generally flower in the soil of suffering. *Non ignara mali miseris succurrere disco*, Dido declares, "Not unknowing of sorrow have I learnt to succor the distressed." To cite one example out of thousands, before Franklin D. Roosevelt was afflicted with poliomyelitis, he gave little evidence of greatness, or even of sympathy for the ill and underprivileged. Viewed from the aspect of history, his affliction, however painful for him, may seem a small price to pay for the emergence of a dedicated leader in the hour of world crisis.

In his masterly biography of Sigmund Freud, Ernest Jones points out: "It was just in the years when the neurosis was at its height (1897–1900) that Freud did his most original work. There is an unmistakable connection between these two facts. The neurotic symptoms must have been one of the ways in which the unconscious material was indirectly trying to emerge, and without

this pressure it is doubtful if Freud would have made the progress
he did. It is a costly way of reaching that hidden realm, but it
is still the only way. That Freud dimly perceived this connection
even at the time, is shown by several allusions to his mode of
working. He did not work well when he felt fit and happy, nor
when he was too depressed and inhibited; he needed something in
between. He expressed this neatly in a letter of April 16, 1896:
'I have come back with a lordly feeling of independence and feel
too well; since returning I have been very lazy, because the
moderate misery necessary for intensive work refuses to appear' "
(*The Life and Work of Sigmund Freud*, vol. I, p. 305).

Illustrations might easily be multiplied of how privation and
disability have proved to be men's steppingstones to greatness.
The phenomenon which modern psychology calls "compensation"
is the method by which suffering becomes an instrumentality for
achievement.

That suffering is a discipline is true of nations as well as of
individuals. The American nation has matured far more in the
four last decades than in all the century and a quarter preceding.
The casualties of two World Wars, the suffering of the Great
Depression, the bloody stalemate of the Korean conflict, and the
horrible threat of atomic destruction have brought to increasing
numbers of Americans a maturity of outlook which is finding
expression in the growing recognition of America's responsibility
to help the undeveloped nations of the world and advance the
cause of world peace and well-being. It is the trials of the twentieth
century that have made it clear to Americans that isolationism,
racialism, and xenophobia constitute the cardinal sins. The process
is far from complete, but the trend is unmistakable.

When startling advances made by Soviet science caught America
off-guard, a reporter as hardheaded as Arthur Krock was prompted
to write a column in the *New York Times*, October 29, 1957,
entitled, "The Spur That Has Won Our Race." His thesis was that
throughout its history, America registered progress only when it
sustained defeat. That suffering is a spur to achievement is a lesson
of human history as a whole. Most human progress is not the result
of disinterested inquiry or idle curiosity, but the response to a basic
lack or a felt need. Necessity is the mother of invention. Man's
primitive ancestors were driven by hunger and cold to discover the

arts of agriculture and cattle-herding. Pain was the great incentive to man's first faltering steps in the study of anatomy, and the practical needs of society led to the beginnings of astronomy and mathematics. Geometry still bears in its etymology the meaning of "land measurement."

The cults that treat suffering as an illusion, and evil as non-existent, may succeed at times in desensitizing their devotees against pain, but they pay a high price. It is fortunate that their success is on the most limited and superficial of levels. Otherwise they would be anesthetizing men against the lacks and failings of the world and, to that degree, would be hindering progress and perpetuating misery. There is deep insight in the Hebrew phrase, "the birthpangs of the Messiah." Not only the advent of the Messianic age, but every act of birth, is accompanied by pain. Every true artist and scientist has experienced within himself the throes of creation. Suffering in all its myriad forms is an indispensable spur to human aspiration and achievement.

Perhaps the most significant aspect of this function of suffering remains to be mentioned. Suffering is an essential element in man's unending struggle against injustice in all its protean forms. It is part of the divine dialectic of history that men refuse to tolerate tyranny only when tyranny becomes intolerable. They do not rebel against evil, so long as it remains within limits that can be borne, and men's threshold of toleration in this respect is notoriously high. That each tyrant refuses to be "reasonable" in his rapacity, that each oppressor learns nothing and forgets nothing, is the saving grace of history, and, by that token, an essential element in the process of human liberation. This truth, be it noted, bears witness to the operation of the law of righteousness in the world.

A few illustrations from history may be adduced. In 1776, when the American colonies were chafing under British misrule, their slogan was, "No taxation without representation." Had King George III been sufficiently enlightened to follow the reasonable counsel of Edmund Burke and conciliate the colonies by permitting them to send a few representatives to Parliament, the bulk of the colonists would have been satisfied, and there would have been no American Revolution. The United States might today still be a colony of Great Britain. If, before the outbreak of the French

Revolution, the king had introduced a measure of reform of the most flagrant abuses, the monarchy might well have survived. Had the Czar of Russia liberalized his government of Russia in 1905 or 1917, he could with impunity have preserved a large measure of his privileges and powers. The tyrant refuses to bend and must be broken—a law of history that is the secret of liberty. It also explains why men must suffer, in order that they may be driven to achieve freedom.

This insight the Bible reveals through the classic epic of liberation—the Exodus from Egypt. In connection with the long-drawn-out duel between Moses and Pharaoh, a striking phrase occurs frequently: "The Lord hardened the heart of Pharaoh." To be sure, Biblical thought, which traces all phenomena directly to God, uses this idiom synonymously with another oft-repeated phrase: "Pharaoh hardened his heart." But the wording of the first phrase enshrines a great truth—the hardening of Pharaoh's heart was as essential an element in the process of Israel's liberation as Moses' stout courage. Had Pharaoh mitigated the rigors of bondage and granted his Israelite slaves a few days' respite in the wilderness, some "extremists" might not have been satisfied, but the masses would have been "reasonable" and returned to their taskmasters. The proof of this contention lies in the fact that this was precisely the reaction of the Israelites a little later when the memory of slavery had dimmed ever so slightly. The Divine plan of liberation demanded that Pharaoh be cruel and unrelenting, so that ultimately slavery might fall.

In sum, suffering performs several indispensable functions in human life—as a force for moral discipline, a spur to creative achievement, and an instrument for progress toward justice and freedom.

We have discussed suffering theologically in terms of sin, and pragmatically as a means for the attainment of higher ends. Evil also may be approached genetically, as the vestigial remains of the lower stages of human evolution. Like the appendix in man's body that is apparently of no value today, although it performed significant functions earlier in his evolutionary career, many antisocial traits that are the source of so much suffering today are remnants of the past, from which man has not yet emancipated himself. Hatred, suspicion, and combativeness are part of man's jungle inheritance necessary for his survival in the past. They are now a hindrance to be overcome, or at least controlled and sublimated.

Underlying our entire discussion is a vivid, indeed painful, awareness of the reality of evil. There have been metaphysical and religious thinkers who have defined evil simply as the absence of good. This approach has been particularly congenial to the mystic. Thus the mystic classic, the *Zohar*, conceives of evil as the disharmony which arose in the universe during the process of creation, when the Divine Judgment was separated from the Divine Mercy. The Kabbalist Rabbi Isaac Luria describes evil as the result of "the breaking of the vessels" which led to the encrustation of the sparks of goodness within hard shells of darkness in the material world. He sees the duty of man as the liberation of these "sparks" and their return to their Divine source. Hasidism perhaps went furthest in denying the reality of evil, when it described evil as simply the lowest rung on the ladder of good, and therefore capable of redemption through man's efforts. It is noteworthy, however, that evil was never dismissed as an illusion. What the mystics taught was that evil was temporary and superficial, and that it needed to be redeemed rather than destroyed. It is one of Martin Buber's most fruitful insights that evil is real, yet capable of redemption, since it is never permanently or completely divorced from the good. The profane, in his words, is the not-yet-hallowed.

This double character of evil has been sensed on the level of ordinary human experience. Men often speak of a trying experience as being "a blessing in disguise." They have found that the perspective of time often reveals the positive value of suffering that has been undergone unwillingly. It is this recognition that often converts suffering into a steppingstone to nobler living.

We must confess that we find ourselves unable to accept the mystic's approach as the full answer to the problem of evil. The suffering of the innocent in painful disease, the death of a child, the cutting off of genius or talent before its fulfillment—all these categories of evil are too agonizing to yield to any of the views already expressed. Here suffering is manifestly not the consequence of the sufferer's sin, being much too cruel to be a fair penalty for error, and much too intense to be justified either as a discipline or as a spur to achievement. Some forms of human suffering we can

understand, however imperfectly. But tragedies such as these are
beyond all the resources of the human intellect. We walk in the
cavern of darkness with only the flickering lantern of reason in
our hand. Without it, we should be plunged into uttermost gloom,
but with it we can see only a little ahead, and often in the shape
of distorted shadows flickering upon the walls. The justifications of
human suffering offered by Job's Friends and by Elihu are not
without merit, but they do not fully dissolve this mystery, to which
only God holds the key. Hence the Lord himself needs to appear
in the whirlwind and speak to Job. The burden of the great God-
speeches, as we have seen, is not to overwhelm Job with the power
of God, but rather to evoke his awe at the spectacle of the beauty
and order of nature, which serves as a clue to the moral order of
the universe. As the natural order is mystery as well as miracle,
so the moral order is miracle as well as mystery. Both are revelations
of the will of God, which man can comprehend only in part, yet
both are capable of evoking man's reverence and joy in life.

Though many of the manifestations of evil in a world created by
a good God of righteousness are within the power of our reason to
grasp, an irreducible core of mystery remains. Here the creative
vision of the artist, the poet, and the musician offers us the only
anodyne from suffering, by bringing us a recognition of the beauty
and harmony of the world. The universe is a work of art, the pattern of which cannot be discerned if the spectator stands too close
to the painting. Only as one moves back a distance, do the scales
and blotches dissolve and the design of the artist emerge in all its
fullness. In the world which is our home, we are too close to the
pattern of existence, too deeply involved in it, to be able to achieve
the perspective which is God's alone. Though we must always be
conscious of the pain of all living creatures and not only of our
own suffering, we can feel that the structure we see is real, and the
lineaments of suffering have their place in the total picture.

To be sure, no neatly articulated system of man can fully comprehend either the grandeur or the misery of existence. Particularly
when tragedy strikes, it is not easy to share Phillips Brooks's cheer-
ful conviction that the checkerboard of life is made up of black
squares on a white background, not of white squares on a black
board. Yet it is then that this faith justifies itself, commended not
merely by the promptings of faith, but also by the voice of reason.

Perhaps the truest word was spoken by a third-century sage, Yannai: "It is not in our power fully to explain either the well-being of the wicked or the suffering of the righteous" (*Abot* 4:15). Nonetheless, we are not called upon to abdicate reason and reflection in pondering on the nature of evil and comprehending as much of it as we can. What still remains a mystery may then be borne with resignation in a world where so much may be experienced with joy. Man's efforts must never cease to transform the evil in the world and reduce its dimensions. Yet what cannot be transformed can be transcended, through the vision of a world which is the handiwork of God.

CHAPTER XI

What Is Man? . . .

"I sought to devote myself to philosophy, but cheerfulness was always breaking in," a contemporary of Samuel Johnson once confessed. A similar incursion has made itself felt in our discussion here. Thus far we have been concerned with transcendental issues, with God and the universe, but at every turn one tantalizing creature has obtruded himself—man. Whether our theme was God as creator, or the meaning of history, or the problem of evil, again and again we have been brought back to the same point.

"What is man?" the Psalmist asked, and answers have been plentiful. Chemists have computed the value of the chemical elements in the human body as worth a little less than one dollar. Biologists have noted man's untold links with the other animals. Psychologists have sought to explain man's nature in terms of primordial, irrational impulses deeply rooted in his spirit and struggling for self-expression in spite of the pressures of society.

Religion is grateful for all the light that scientific research can shed on the subject. Yet it sees no reason for surrendering the Biblical view of man, which was set forth long before the scientific era:

> "God created man in His own image, in the image of God created He him; male and female created He them. And God blessed them; and God said unto them: 'Be fruitful, and multiply, and replenish the earth, and subdue it; and have dominion over the fish of the sea, and over the fowl of the air, and over every living thing that creepeth upon the earth.'"
>
> (*Gen.* 1:27–28)

The first and greatest commentary on this passage in *Genesis* was written not by an exegete or a philosopher, but by a poet. He noted the innate paradox of man's nature—his physical insignificance when viewed against the background of the eternal stars, and his unique endowment as master of creation, a being "little lower than God." For the Psalmist, the greatness of man is his essential attribute.

> O Lord, our Lord,
> How glorious is Thy name in all the earth!
> Whose majesty is rehearsed above the heavens. . . .
>
> When I behold Thy heavens, the work of Thy fingers,
> The moon and the stars, which Thou has established;
> "What is man, that Thou art mindful of him?
> And the son of man, that Thou thinkest of him?"
> Yet Thou hast made him but little lower than God,
> And hast crowned him with glory and honour.
> Thou hast given him dominion over the works of Thy hands;
> Thou hast put all things under his feet—
> Sheep and oxen, all of them,
> And the beasts of the field;
> The fowl of the air, and the fish of the sea;
> Whatsoever passeth through the paths of the sea.
>
> O Lord, our Lord,
> How glorious is Thy name in all the earth!
>
> (*Psalm* 8)

The Biblical conception of man as the crown of creation fashioned in the image of God has often been attacked and ridiculed. Never more effectively than by Bertrand Russell in his *Religion and Science:* "Is there not something a trifle absurd in the spectacle of human beings holding a mirror before themselves, and thinking what they behold so excellent as to prove that a Cosmic Purpose must have been aiming at it all along? Why, in any case, this glorification of Man? How about lions and tigers? They destroy fewer animals or human lives than we do and they are much more beautiful than we are. How about ants? They manage the Corporate State much better than any Fascist. Would not a world of nightringales and larks and deer be better than our human world of cruelty and injustice and war? The believers in Cosmic Purpose make much of our supposed intelligence, but their writings make one doubt it. If I were granted omnipotence, and millions of years to experiment in, I should not think Man much to boast about as the final result of all my efforts."

In the heat of his indignation, Russell fails to note one crucial fact: man is the only creature capable of being indignant at his shortcomings. That man alone is conscious of his ethical limitations means that he is the only animal who is more than animal. Obviously, man's life is fleeting and the stars endure for eons, but the stars are unconscious of man's presence, while man is conscious of the stars. Indeed, man is the only creature on earth who is aware of the existence of heavenly bodies—if we except dogs baying at the moon.

Man alone possesses self-awareness, which bifurcates into conscience and consciousness. It is this truth which *Genesis* expresses in the phrase that man is created in "the image of God." Here, as everywhere, language proves both inadequate and indispensable. The term "image" is a metaphor; it seeks to suggest the kind of relationship to the original that a good portrait bears to the living person. The picture looks like the original, but its similarity is less than identity. "The image of God" implies that the attributes of God are reflected in man in imperfect yet substantial degree.

The precise meaning of the Biblical phrase "the image of God" has been variously interpreted. The Apocryphal work *Wisdom of Solomon* and the medieval mystic and commentator Moses Nahmanides referred it to man's immortality. Some thinkers have pointed out that man alone possesses self-consciousness, the awareness that he is alive and the knowledge that he must die. Generally, it has been equated, as was suggested by Philo and Rashi, with the gift of reason, the capacity to observe reality and to draw rational conclusions. The tenth-century philosopher Saadia suggested that "the image of God" refers to man's dominion over the earth, wherein he resembles his Maker. Both these attributes of intelligence and power may be subsumed under one quality: man's creative capacity. Alone among creatures known to us, man has the ability to transform his environment and to create new objects both in the material and spiritual realm.

To overlook the friezes of the Parthenon, or the *Dialogues* of Plato, the winged words of Isaiah or the sculpture of Michelangelo, to ignore *Hamlet* and *Faust,* or to disregard the work of Newton,

Darwin, and Einstein, gives as unfair and unbalanced a view of man as to forget the tyrannies, cruelties, and oppressions which men have practised upon one another and upon the so-called "lower" orders of creation.

Yet man's inhumanity to man, let it be noted, though far from obsolete, is being practised with ever diminishing enthusiasm and ever more acute pangs of conscience. The widespread disillusion with human conduct in our day is itself an index of the growing conviction that the massive evils of man's contriving today are neither inevitable nor justifiable.

The Biblical conception of man as being created in the image of God is no remnant of antiquated mythology. Long before Darwin, the Creation narrative in *Genesis* placed man in the context of a cosmos which includes and unites all living things. And long after Bertrand Russell, men may find in the ancient Biblical text truths about human nature that transcend the literal. In fact, men have found in it the heart of the Judeo-Christian tradition: the sacred character of life, and the innate and inalienable dignity of each human being.

Eighteen centuries ago, the ancient sages had utilized the same Biblical source as a basis for their conception of man. In dealing with the importance of cross-examination in a capital trial, the *Mishnah* instructs the judges to warn witnesses of the heinous character of false testimony, by stressing the sanctity of each human life. In this connection a homily, at once naive and profound, is introduced which deserves to be cited in full:

> Mankind was created through Adam, a single human being, in order to teach that whoever destroys a single human life is regarded as though he destroyed an entire world, and he who saves a single human life is as though he saved an entire world.
>
> The human race began with a single individual for the sake of peace among all men, so that no man might say, "My ancestor is greater than yours," and to make it impossible for heretics to say, "There are many heavenly Powers!"
>
> Moreover, the creation of humanity through one ancestor proclaims the greatness of the Holy One, Blessed be He. For man strikes off many coins with a single mold and they are all identical. But the King of Kings, the Holy One, blessed be

He, stamps each man in the mold of Adam, and yet no one is identical with his fellow.

Finally, the creation of Adam teaches that each human being is obligated to declare, "For my sake was the world created" (*Mishnah, Sanhedrin,* chapter 4).

An ancient supplemental Rabbinic work, the *Tosefta,* which is contemporaneous with the *Mishnah,* adds another significant inference from the creation of Adam:

> "So that no sinner may say: 'I am a sinner by inheritance, being a descendant of sinners,' and no saint may say, 'I am a saint by virtue of my descent from saints.'"

In sum, the Biblical utterance that man was created by God in His image is the fountainhead of a fruitful and integrated vision of the nature of man:

Each human being is endowed with an innate dignity which makes him not a unit in a statistical table, an atom of dust to be liquidated at will, but a universe, possessing transcendent and ultimate value. Every man, whatever his ethnic origin or racial character, has the rights to life, liberty, and the enjoyment of God's world, rights which are inalienable, having been conferred upon him by God and not by the state or a social contract. Hence these rights, which should be enforced and protected by a just government, cannot be abrogated by human fiat.

Nor is this all. Not merely are all men equal, but their differences are God-given. The eighteenth-century thinkers believed that the distinctions among men in the social, economic, and political spheres should be disregarded, because all groupings are either artificial inventions of priests and tyrants or are the corruptions by society of the pristine innocence of the human race. The ancient Sages saw more truly into human nature, when they recognized the differences among men as God-given, innate, integral to personality. Thus they supplied a religious dynamic for resisting the persistent effort to force all men into a single mold, whether through the brutal force of dictatorship or the mass pressures toward conformity prevalent in industrialized society today.

Finally, the rabbinic outlook insists that no man is innately and eternally evil, and refuses to believe that any man is forever beyond redemption.

This last inference, which is derived from the Biblical narrative of the Creation of Adam, stands, of course, in sharp contrast to a familiar doctrine, which is generally traced back to the same opening chapters of *Genesis*—the conception of the Fall of Man in the Garden of Eden, which placed an ineradicable taint upon all his descendants. It is true that the great classics of the human race derive much of their importance from the fact that they suggest different implications to different readers, beyond their explicit content. It is thus entirely legitimate for Paul to have found in the tale of Adam and Eve's sin in the Garden the basis for his conception of original sin. Because the doctrine has been intimately and persistently associated with *Genesis*, it is often overlooked that no such idea is expressed anywhere in the Hebrew Bible, nor did it ever develop in normative Judaism. Moreover, it is not to be met with even in the New Testament Gospels.

The book of *Genesis* itself notes the punishment meted out to each of the malefactors involved in the Garden of Eden: Adam, Eve, and the serpent. That man remains a free moral agent, capable of victory over evil, is explicitly affirmed in the very next chapter in *Genesis*, where the Lord says to Cain: "If you do well, you will be exalted. But if you do not do well, sin is couching at the door; its desire is for you, but you can master it!" (*Gen.* 4:7). Neither Cain's murder of his brother, nor Lamech's bloody exploits (*Gen.* 4:23), nor men's presumption in seeking to storm Heaven by building the Tower of Babel, nor the wholesale moral corruption of Noah's generation—none of these sins is attributed to the taint of evil going back to Adam's Fall, or minimized on this account.

Centuries later, when the massive power of Roman tyranny seemed eternal and immovable, a sense of despair gripped some circles in Palestine. Their sense of hopelessness found theological expression in the idea that Adam's sin gave his descendants an innate propensity to evil. But even in the Apocryphal and Pseudepigraphical literature which emanates largely from these circles, the doctrine is only slightly hinted at. Only with the Hellenistic *Book of the Secrets of Enoch* does Plato's doctrine of the purity of the soul and the corruptibility of the body make its appearance in Jewish circles. When this Platonic idea is wedded to the conception that sinfulness is inevitable for man and is tied to the Biblical nar-

rative, the doctrine of the Fall of Man emerges full blown, as in
IV Ezra, and later in the *Epistles* of Paul.

This mood, however, never became dominant in traditional
Judaism, which held fast to the faith that each man is master of his
destiny, capable of transforming himself and the world through
his will for good, in which, to be sure, he may count on God's aid.
The Apocryphal book of *II Baruch* gives superb expression to
what was and has remained the basic viewpoint in Judaism:

> Adam is therefore not the cause, save for his own soul,
> But each of us has been the Adam of his own soul. (54:19)

In Christian theology, the towering personality of Paul gave the
doctrine of original sin transcendental importance. It was expressed
in extreme form by Augustine, but was tempered in varying degree
by medieval scholastics, like Aquinas, Duns Scotus, and Abelard.
While the views of Pelagius, who emphasized man's capacity for
good, were ruled out by the Church as heretical, they never disappeared entirely. Catholicism mitigated the rigors of the Augus-
tinian doctrine. It was the Protestant Reformers, notably Luther,
Calvin, and their followers, who stressed the innate depravity of
human nature and declared that sexual desire per se partook of the
nature of sin.

In contemporary Christian thought, the doctrine of original sin
has sustained philosophical and psychological reinterpretation, notably by Niebuhr and Tillich in America. These brilliant theologians
have used the idea in order to counter the easy and unthinking
optimism which prevailed until recently, especially in liberal circles.
Niebuhr in particular has rendered a major service in stressing the
deep-rooted character of evil in human nature and the consequent
difficulties that beset man's efforts to achieve justice and freedom
in society.

Nonetheless, several critical observations are in order with regard to these modern reinterpretations of "original sin." First,
these sophisticated doctrines are not shared among the rank and
file of religious believers, among whom the old concept prevails. Second, the conviction of the predestined and inevitable
corruption of man's nature may be used, even in its new version,
to blunt men's sense of moral responsibility for their actions, and
to persuade them to acquiesce in a corrupt and unjust order of

society. It is noteworthy that this stress upon the innate evil in man has been embraced so enthusiastically by tired liberals and disillusioned radicals, who have lost the zeal and the energy for the struggle for a better world. Undoubtedly, this has not been the approach of Tillich or Niebuhr, but such a conclusion has been frequently drawn by some of their disciples. Finally, the doctrine of "original sin" sharpens the theological problem of the justice of God. For according to this view, God first endows man, the "crown of creation," with a character basically evil, and then proceeds to hold him responsible for his sins.

There is genuine value in a "realistic" view of human nature, but we are not compelled to go from the frying-pan into the fire. A clear-eyed, balanced view of man's nature, that reckons with his virtues as well as his weaknesses, may be found in the outlook of Rabbinic Judaism, which should therefore be of wide general interest. According to this theory, man possesses a good and an evil impulse (*yetzer tov, yetzer ra*) which are perpetually at war in man's soul, and in each situation the act of decision rests with man. Thus the propensity to evil is a deeply rooted aspect of man's nature, but so is the aspiration toward the good. The conception of the "two impulses" avoids both the glorification of the instincts and their denigration, by recognizing that both constitute the natural endowment of man. By that token, human nature in its totality is the handiwork of God, capable of abuse and perversion, to be sure, but also a potential instrument for the service of God and the advancement of the good.

Even when it is conceded that the Fall of Man is not expressed in the Paradise narrative of *Genesis*, it is often maintained that the Bible elsewhere stigmatizes human nature as evil in essence. Two Biblical passages in *Genesis* (6:5 and 8:21), which occur in the narrative of the Flood, are adduced as proof of this thesis. In these verses, God declares, before and after the Flood, that the "imagination (or impulse) of man's heart is evil." Invoking these two passages, George Foot Moore, like other theologians, writes: "The Scripture unqualifiedly declares man's native impulse to be evil."

His august authority notwithstanding, this judgment is the type of error which results from regarding the Bible as a collection of theological proof-texts instead of recognizing it, in Ehrlich's words,

as "a national literature upon a religious foundation." The mis-
understanding that results is the penalty for petrifying literature
into dogma. When seen properly in their context, these Biblical
references to the nature of man as being "evil" are hyperboles,
expressing God's indignation and resignation in the face of the
limitations of human nature. This is clear from a similar use of
yetzer in *Deuteronomy* (31:21) and from the familiar apothegm
repeated several times in Scripture, that "there is no man who
liveth that sinneth not." This judgment the Biblical writers vali-
date by depicting none of the great heroes, Abraham, Jacob,
Moses, or David, as free from sin.

In sum, the Bible regards man neither as a perfect being, nor
as inherently evil. Thus the oldest extant post-Biblical writer,
Ben Sira (second century B.C.E.), conceives of man's nature
(*yetzer*), as Cohon rightly notes, "in a neutral sense, containing
the power to do wrong or right, that is free will." Thus Ben
Sira says:

> God created man from the beginning,
> And placed him in the hands of his *yetzer*.
> If thou so desirest, thou canst keep the commandment,
> And it is wisdom to do His good pleasure.
>
> (*Ecclus.* 15:11 f.)

And again:

> "He that keepeth the Law can control his natural tendency."
>
> (*Ecclus.* 21:11)

That man's nature is neutral remained the dominant view of
post-Biblical Judaism. This is explicitly stated in the rabbinic comment: "God created both impulses, the good impulse and the
evil impulse." Moreover, every element of man's nature, bar
none, can be utilized for the service of the good. Thus the Rabbis
do not hesitate to interpret the great Commandment, "Thou
shalt love the Lord thy God with all thy heart—with both thine
impulses, the evil impulse and the good impulse."

They recognized how often sexual desire becomes a source of
evil leading men to immorality and disaster. Yet long before
modern psychoanalysis, the central role of sex in civilization was

clearly noted: "Were it not for the sexual impulse, no man would build a house or marry a woman or engage in an occupation."

Man is therefore a perpetual battleground between two opposing forces, the impulse toward the good and the propensity to evil, and he is the arbiter in this "warfare of the heart." Even the most powerful of man's instincts is neutral, as is recognized in the Midrashic utterance: "Two impulses God created in His world, the impulses to idolatry and to sexual immorality. The impulse to idolatry has already been uprooted, but the impulse to sexual immorality still remains. God said, 'Whoever can resist the second is considered as though he resisted both.'" Man's misuse of any of his instincts or faculties constitutes his own sin, which can be charged neither to "original sin," nor to heredity, nor to environment.

M. F. Ashley Montagu has expressed the view (*American Journal of Psychiatry*, Dec., 1955, p. 404) that "the evidence indicates that the evil in man is not the cause of his behavior but the effect of the behavior of others upon him." This high optimism is not shared by traditional religion, nor, indeed, is it borne out by the historical experience of the race. The world-view embodied in Jewish tradition would, however, find little objection to his statement: "I know of no evidence which will withstand critical examination that any human being is born with the slightest element of evil within him, whether that evil be called 'original sin' or a drive or tendency to destruction."

It has become the fashion in the modern age to dismiss sin as the figment of a primitive imagination, to be expunged from the vocabulary of educated men. Natural scientists have equated sin with a glandular deficiency or with a psychological maladjustment. Social scientists have explained it away as merely a divergence from the *mores* of one's particular society, as little more than nonconformity to local etiquette. The winds of fashion to the contrary notwithstanding, classical religion has always insisted on the grim reality of sin, man's propensity to it and responsibility for it.

To sin means to rebel against God and the laws of His world. The historian of religion, George Foot Moore, cites the "Westminster Shorter Catechism" for its definition of sin as "failure in the duty which God requireth of man in obedience to His revealed will." Sin is man's omission in rendering that obedience which rests upon the law of righteousness in the universe. In Solomon Schechter's words, "sin taints the divine in man, breaking all communion with heaven." It is a free act of man for which he is responsible. The etymology of the basic Hebrew term for sin, *het*, is significant. It means "missing the mark," a goal for which man should have aimed and which he could have reached. Buber adopts the Hasidic definition of sin as that which cannot be done with the whole being. It is possible to silence the conflict of the soul, but it cannot be uprooted. "Integrity" means wholeness, health, and harmony; sin is conflict, within man and vis-à-vis the world, disharmony and disease of the spirit.

To be sure, modern men find many difficulties with regard to the concept of sin, which has been a foundation stone of traditional religion. Thus Biblical law makes provision for a sacrifice of atonement to be offered for unintentional sin. The question arises, how can an act be regarded as sinful if there was no intent to do evil? The answer lies in recognizing the truth that every act leads to consequences which are inherent within it and inevitable, even if the act is unintentional. If it be true that Sabbath observance, for instance, confers benefits upon man, it follows inescapably that failure to observe it deprives one of these benefits and thus leads to the denudation of the spirit, a loss of serenity, a sense of alienation from the historic community. When there is also a wilful intention to violate the sanctity of a holy day, there is the additional penalty of isolation of the individual from his God. This insight Alice Seligsberg expressed in a letter written to Judah L. Magnes, in which she distinguished between "wrongful" and "sinful" acts. She declared that "even unavoidable wrong for which we are not to blame nevertheless tends to stupefy the heart, and to open the door to sin; and that therefore penance in the form of a purifying sacrifice must be offered by us for our wrongful (though not sinful) omissions of Sabbath observance."

Another difficulty which modern men encounter with the concept of sin is the insistence in tradition that sin encompasses violations of the ritual as well as the ethical imperatives of religion. Men have no difficulty in regarding "Thou shalt not kill" as a Divine, universally binding law. But what about ritual enactments, which exist in all great religions? Are these not man-made laws?

The full answer to this question must await our discussion on the role of ritual in religion. Here one point must suffice. If Revelation is the product of the interaction between the Divine and the human, it becomes less difficult to see in ritual a lesser, but none-theless authentic, element of Divine law, the violation of which is sin. But whatever our concept of the dimensions of sin, the recognition of its reality is vital, not merely for religion, but also for life.

It is therefore clear that the concept of unintentional sin has genuine meaning for the religious spirit in the area of ritual. All the more obvious is the reality of unconscious or unintended wrongdoing perpetrated against one's fellow-man. Religion is right in stigmatizing such acts as "sin," and demanding that the evil be overcome through confession, restitution and penance.

When one recognizes the ambivalent character of human nature, one profound question arises once more, which appeared earlier in our discussion both of creation and of the nature of evil. Why did a good God create a being with a strong propensity to sin and thus expose this creature to suffering? Why was man not created with the quality of sinlessness? If men may be pardoned the presumption of thinking God's thoughts after Him, part of the answer, already stated, is apparent to us. Endowing man with the attribute of reason obviously means freedom of choice, and this freedom, by definition, entails the opportunity to choose the evil rather than the good. Reason, freedom, and responsibility represent three facets of the same reality, when expressed in intellectual, moral, and experiential terms.

This answer, to be sure, merely moves the mystery one step further. Why did God choose to embark upon creation at all? As we have seen, we stand here before the ultimate mystery of the will of God, and all men's efforts to understand it are gropings in the dark. The Hindu philosopher Sankarachaya explains creation as an overflow of God's artistic impulse. Just as an artist is impelled to express his inspiration, which flows over into his work, so God pours His creative energy into His world. Joad objects to the analogy by pointing out that the artist always finds a medium at hand into which he pours his inspiration, and that there-fore the view of God as an artist implies the existence of something else outside of God. Joad's strictures are beside the point, for he fails to recognize that no analogy ever applies perfectly. The Hindu thinker is comparing a human artist and the Divine Creator not with regard to the *process*, but with regard to the *motive*, and here the analogy of the Divine artist is helpful. As far as the process is concerned, God and man are fundamentally different. Man is a "fashioner," a reshaper of pre-existent material. God is the Creator, who calls matter into being and gives it form.

Other attempts have been made to grapple with the why of creation. We have already referred to the view of some mystics who have suggested that creation is an expression of God's love, which sought an object outside of Himself upon which it could be lavished. Others have expressed the view that God's universe was incomplete without man, without the presence within it of the one creature whose affinities with the Creator could assuage the loneliness of God. Closely related is the idea of some religious thinkers that God wished to have at least one being in the universe whose loyalty and obedience to the Divine will would be an act of free choice and therefore an expression of the love of God. The lower animals cannot sin, because they can live only in conformity with their instincts. Only man can master his impulses and thus attain to virtue and the disinterested love of his Maker.

In spite of these and all other attempts to discover the purpose of creation, the mystery remains impenetrable. This inability to pierce this barrier is met with in believer and heretic, in thinker and mystic alike.

What vital religion profoundly believes is that God's creation has a purpose and that it is good. We may conceive of this purpose as we choose, or we may conclude, with Maimonides, that it is forever veiled from human understanding. What we can affirm is the faith expressed in *Genesis:* "And God saw everything that He had made, and, behold, it was very good." In the vast array of living creatures, man has a unique place. His special gifts and vast capacities impose upon him the duty expressed in the Daily Prayer Book: "Blessed is our God who has created us for His glory."

To enhance God's glory is man's duty and privilege, the noblest use to which he can put the gifts of reason and moral freedom with which he has been endowed. Religion sees three great highways by which man can contribute to the glory of God: the path of prayer, the road of ritual, and, above all, the mountain-trail of ethical striving. Before we set out to explore these three highways to perfection, one more ancient stumbling block must be encountered: the age-old paradox of man's freedom and God's knowledge.

CHAPTER XII

The Freedom of Man

In an organic view of life, such as that upheld by religion, certain facets will appear again and again. The attentive reader has undoubtedly noticed how frequently our discussion has pivoted on the central fact of man's capacity to choose freely between various courses of action open to him. This freedom of decision, which is the moral coefficient of man's reason, is the basis of man's responsibility as a member of society. No group life is possible unless each individual is held accountable for his deeds, and such accountability must assume his freedom as a moral agent. Hence, it is life itself, and not merely religion, that insists that man is free.

Man's freedom, however, leads directly to one of the most famous and obvious paradoxes of philosophy—its apparent conflict with the idea of Divine foreknowledge. If God knows all, He knows the future, but a future known is a future determined. If so, how can man then be said to be free? The contradiction is profound, and it is no wonder that some thinkers have sought to grasp one horn of the dilemma and rejected the other. Some teachers have denied man's freedom. They have not only conceded but emphasized that God's foreknowledge implies man's predestination, so that man's fate is predestined for him. That was the position adopted by such varied figures as Mohammed, the medieval Jewish philosopher Hasdai Crescas, and the Protestant theologian John Calvin.

Undoubtedly, this solved the problem, but at a very high cost, for as we have already noted, the moral system demands man's freedom. Hence, later thinkers, both in Islam and in Christianity, sought to moderate, if not modify, the rigors of predestination in their systems of faith. In Judaism, with its strong emphasis on conduct, most Jewish philosophers, like Saadia, Maimonides, and Gersonides, sought to limit God's foreknowledge in one way or another, in order to safeguard the moral freedom and responsibility of man.

In this regard they stood on solid Biblical ground. The Bible, permeated by a profound ethical consciousness, never wavered in its conception of man's freedom. No less than three times, the book of *Deuteronomy* emphasizes the principle:

> "Life and death have I placed before thee, the blessing and the curse. Mayest thou choose life, that thou mayest live, thou and thy seed."
>
> *(Deut.* 30:19; cf. 30:15; 11:26)

The Prophets are at one in urging men to choose the good and reject evil. Thus Isaiah declares:

> Tell the righteous that it will be well with them,
> For they will eat the fruit of their deeds.
> Woe to the wicked—it shall be ill with him,
> For what his hands have done shall be done to him.
>
> *(Isa.* 3:10–11)

In even more passionate terms, Jeremiah castigates the sinner and praises the righteous:

> Thus saith the Lord:
> Cursed is the man who trusts in man,
> And makes flesh his strength,
> Whose heart turns from the Lord. . . .
> Blessed is the man who trusts in the Lord,
> Whose trust is in the Lord.
>
> *(Jer.* 17:5–7)

This in spite of his recognition of the depths and perversities of human nature, which he laments in the same passage:

> The heart is deceitful above all things and very weak,
> Who can understand it?
>
> *(Jer.* 17:9)

Similarly, the teaching of the Wisdom sages in the Bible rests upon the unshakable conviction that man is free to choose virtue and eschew vice.

To revert to our problem, man's freedom as a reality is a conviction that must be maintained by religion and by society, if either is to endure. How can this faith be maintained along with the belief in God's foreknowledge posited by religion?

Real as the challenge is, it is important, at the outset, to avoid the error of assuming that this dilemma exists only for the religious believer and that a nonreligious position would escape the dilemma. Actually, the conflict between God's foreknowledge and man's freedom is inherent in life itself and exists for the nonbeliever as well, except that the terms of the paradox would be slightly modified. Basic to the classical conception of scientific law is the principle of causality that declares that every phenomenon is the result of an antecedent cause. Since man is part of nature, his very being and acting are the effect of an infinite number of prior factors, which determine what he is and does today. But if this principle operates inevitably and universally, how can it be maintained that a man is free to act and to decide on any course of action? Instead of the religious dilemma of Divine foreknowledge and man's freedom, we thus have the philosophic contradiction of determinism versus free will.

Confronted by this dilemma, Spinoza, like some of his religious predecessors, unflinchingly drew the conclusion that only determinism is true and that free will is an illusion. This may satisfy the requirement of philosophic consistency, but it raises grave practical difficulties, of which Spinoza's commentators have been well aware.

If free will is an illusion, it is incumbent upon a rational being to rid himself of the idea. He certainly should be unwilling to live his life on a foundation of error. But once we accept the idea that everything is determined in advance and that no real freedom of choice exists, there is no logical reason—and no incentive—for wrestling with any given problem, for weighing alternatives and for arriving at decisions. If the principle of determinism were taken seriously, it would spell total paralysis of thought and action. Nor does it solve the problem to answer that man is free to consider various possibilities, but that this capacity is itself determined by the factors which shape the individual's constitution. For if the decision is predetermined, such activity is merely a form of shadow-boxing.

Nor is this all. As we have noted, if free will is an illusion, man is not morally responsible for his actions. *Tout comprendre, c'est tout pardonner* would hold true with a vengeance. For if everything is the result of causes beyond man's control, we have no right to upbraid a liar for his falsehoods or punish a thief for stealing, or a murderer for killing. Nor does it make sense to honor a saint for his piety, an artist for his work, a scholar for his wisdom, a scientist for his achievement, or a philanthropist for his benefactions. In sum, society would have no moral right to establish a system of law and order, or demand obedience to its laws, or impose rewards or punishments upon its members.

The practical difficulties of denying free will are highlighted in an incident attributed to the well-known biologist, Jacques Loeb, who was a strong determinist. Professor E. G. Conklin tells: "After Loeb had vigorously denied the reality or possibility of human freedom, he saw his little son running down the steps with a large, open clasp-knife in his hand. At once he shouted, 'Bobby, close that knife. You might fall on it.' I said, 'Now, Loeb, practice your philosophy' and in reply he merely winked one eye at me."

Thus, even in a completely nonreligious context, the paradox of free will versus determinism is real and inescapable. That it takes on a slightly different form in religion is only to be expected.

Philosophers have sought to reconcile the dichotomy through varying approaches and with different degrees of success, the details of which belong to the history of philosophy. Thus Henri Bergson maintained that science deals only with a description of the past, and that scientific laws are merely generalized patterns of what has happened, not predictions of what will or must happen. Thus free will is saved, but the order implied in determinism is sacrificed.

It is noteworthy that in our century, physics, once the most mechanical of sciences, has suggested to some thinkers a way out of the impasse. They have argued that scientific laws are merely statistical averages, telling us, with great exactness, how a *group* of phenomena will react, but incapable of foretelling the path of the *individual* members of the group, who are not determined but "free." A mortality table will, if it is accurate, indicate how many people per thousand will die at a given age, but it cannot forecast or determine which individual will die because of smoking in bed, of cirrhosis of the liver, or of heart disease.

This should, of course, have been clear, as Jacob Kohn has correctly pointed out, even before Heisenberg enunciated the principle of indeterminacy, which declares that one cannot predict the path of any atom, but only that of the mass. Max Born has suggested the more accurate name of "the principle of limited measurability," and Whittaker has called it the postulate of impotence, according to which the position and motion of any particle cannot be predicted with perfect accuracy, because the means of measurement cannot be sufficiently refined, since the position of the observer himself affects the trajectory of the atoms. The astronomer Henry Norris Russell has gone further and suggested that the mechanistic hypothesis of the nature of man is "not an enemy, but an ally of morals and religion" because "determinism enters through the structure of the underlying system, while freedom and responsibility are statistical properties of the assemblage" ("Determinism and Responsibility," in *Science*, Vol. 97, No. 2516, March 19, 1943).

These various theories which have arisen in an effort to solve inner problems of science have, it seems to us, been embraced too enthusiastically by theologians. In the first instance, the phenomena of the physical world are not necessarily convertible into the events of the human situation—at best they offer a suggestive analogy. Moreover, man's present impotence in the face of complex physical phenomena may well yield to further research and render all such theories obsolete. Finally, even if we remain permanently incapable of solving the problem confronting the physicist, the principle of causation still remains the pillar of our scientific understanding of reality, besides being indispensable for the religious world-view. A lawless universe would be a far greater threat to faith in God than a failure to solve the paradox of free will versus predestination.

If the contradiction is to be dealt with at all, it must be from the vantage point of philosophy and religion. Since so many efforts have already been made, we may perhaps be permitted one more attempt to grapple with the problem. It may be suggested that the contradiction arises only because of our incurable human tendency to conceive of God in anthropomorphic terms. Now, anthropomorphism goes far beyond attributing man's gross physical characteristics to the Deity; it applies also to subtler conceptions.

Thus the concept of time has meaning only for finite beings, for whom there is a past which they did not know, a present which they now experience, and a future still beyond their ken. For God who is eternal, past, present, and future have no separate existence. An analogy may be helpful here. For an insect that lives only from sunrise to sunset, a day is a substantial segment of time, indeed, it is coterminous with all of existence. For a flower that flourishes during a summer season, a day is a lesser, though still considerable, period, perhaps one-sixtieth of all existence. For a dog, whose life span is five or ten years, a day is an even shorter interval. For man, whose days are threescore and ten, a day is naturally even briefer. For an elephant or a California redwood, whose life span is greater, a day becomes correspondingly telescoped. It follows that for God, who is eternal, all time is so sharply contracted that past, present, and future become instantaneous. Hence the term "foreknowledge," which means knowledge of the future, is really meaningless when applied to God, for to Him all events are simultaneous. The ancient paradox therefore dissolves and man's freedom is not contradicted by God's foreknowledge, because God does not live in time, but in eternity. Now, whether or not this or any other approach can resolve the paradox of free will versus determinism, it is clear that both elements are grounded in reality.

As we have seen, twentieth-century science no longer is committed to a mechanistic determinism of physical phenomena. The frontiers of research, whether in Einstein's relativity or in nuclear physics, have lent support to the view that the world is best conceived of as a great thought rather than a great machine, a living organism with boundless potentials for growth rather than a lifeless mechanism with rigidly limited processes. More and more thinkers recognize that the universe is the field of interaction between determinism and freedom, or, in the language of theology, between predestination and free will. Whatever is alive in the world is naturally and inevitably the result of anterior factors, and is to that degree determined, but not altogether. There is always an area of freedom where the living creature is master of his fate, free to make his choice between alternatives, able to make or mar his destiny.

The distinguishing mark of all that lives is that it is a blend of law and freedom. It is the essence of life that it can create new life. A universe that is alive can serve as the source of events and experiences which are more than the inevitable consequences of antecedent causes. *Acceptance of the principle of the reign of law, therefore, does not rule out the possibility of freedom*, of the emergence of the new, the unexpected, the hitherto unknown. On the contrary, everywhere there is evidence of what the biologist calls the sport or mutation, what the physicist describes as the emergent, the contingent, and what the religionist sees as the miracle, the hoped-for, the uncounted-on, the answer to prayer.

This is not to surrender the principle of natural law, for to save free will by sacrificing order would be a Pyrrhic victory—religion no less than science must postulate a law-abiding universe. It is merely that we know that the laws of nature are less rigid than was believed in the heyday of nineteenth-century mechanistic science.

These two aspects of reality were sensed by religion, although expressed in its own idiom. Religion has always been conscious of the living tension between law and freedom. The principle of determinism is affirmed by Ben Azzai: "By your destined name will men call you and in your appointed place will they place you and give you what is intended for you. No man can take what is prepared for his fellow and no kingdom can touch its neighbor even by a hair's breadth" (*Yoma* 38b–39a). But the main concern of religion has been to safeguard the principle of man's responsibility. Hence the Talmud declares: "Everything is in the hand of God except the fear of God" (*Ber.* 33b; *Meg.* 25a; *Nid.* 16b). It is, of course, seeking to relieve the contradiction between God's foreknowledge and man's freedom. But its central interest is moral, not theological—all aspects of man's nature and destiny may be determined by factors outside of himself, but one remains inviolate: man's freedom, which is the basis of the ethical life.

Everywhere freedom and determinism interplay. No man is complete master even of his own person, yet neither is he completely at the mercy of extraneous forces. In the words of the sage, Rabbi

Levi: "Six organs, the Holy One, blessed be He, created in man, three are not under his control, the nose, the eyes, and the ears. But three are within his control, the mouth, the hand, and the foot. If a man wants to steal, he can do so, and if not, he can refrain from evil." The physical endowment of the wicked and of the righteous is identical; what disposition they make of it makes the all-important difference: "The wicked are in the power of their heart, the seat of desire; but the righteous have their heart in their power" (*Gen.R.* 67:8; *Pirke de Rabbi Eliezer*, chap. 15). In a dramatic poem, "The Golden Chain," by Isaac Loeb Peretz, Leah, one of the characters, cries out: "Law is a chain. Nature, a rope around one's neck. It strangles, it chokes us; it doesn't let us breathe." To which the rejoinder is made, "And where is mercy?"

God's justice, the law of retribution, of moral cause and effect, is a basic aspect of the Divine nature. But there is another, equally important attribute, His mercy, God's unexpected and undeserved love toward His creatures. The truth of Browning's line, "All's love, but all's law," becomes more striking when it is reversed: "All's law, but all's love." The human mind may not understand how these opposing attributes blend with one another, but life testifies that they do, because both are real. Whether or not we resolve the dichotomy, the religious spirit finds in the laws of nature God's ways, not His limits.

That freedom and law, determinism and free will, causality and liberty, both exist in the universe, is not a contradiction, be it noted, but a paradox. In spite of frequent usage to the contrary, the two terms are not synonymous. A contradiction refers to two opposing statements, at least one of which cannot be true. A paradox consists of two opposing statements, both of which are true, though we may not be able to reconcile them in the present state of our knowledge and insight. The second-century sage Akiba boldly accepted the paradox in its totality when he declared: "All is foreseen, yet freedom is given." In other words—both principles operate in the world. Centuries later, Samuel Johnson similarly seized hold of both horns of the dilemma when he said: "With regard to freedom of the will, all philosophy is against it and all experience is for it."

It is interesting that his biographer, James Boswell, even before he met his famous subject, noted in his private journal: "In support of free will I maintained that Omniscience could not foresee the actions of men; and that it was nobler to create a being with such powers that God knew not how it would act than to create a mere machine, of whose motions he should be certain." Boswell, like Dr. Johnson, was standing on the solid bedrock of religious faith in refusing to attenuate the moral duty of man in the world.

This interaction of freedom and determinism enters into every human action. Once a man makes his decision, whether for good or for ill, he sets into motion factors which assist the goal which he has set for himself, so that his freedom becomes an instrument for determining his destiny. This is the inner truth of such Biblical and post-Biblical utterances as the following:

> Toward the scorners, He is scornful,
> But unto the humble He shows favor.
>
> (*Prov.* 3:34)

> He who comes to defile, the path is opened for him,
> And he who comes to purify, assistance is rendered him.
>
> (*Shab.* 104a; *Yoma* 38b–39a); *Jer. Kid.* 5, 6, 7d)

> Where a man wishes to go, there he is led.
>
> (*Mak.* 10b)

The Rabbinic utterance, "The reward of a good deed is a good deed" (*Abot* 4:2), is famous. It is generally taken to mean that virtue brings its own inherent satisfactions. But we may carry further an insight of Maimonides, who found in this statement a deeper meaning—each good deed we perform conditions us favorably to the next occasion for the practice of goodness. Thus freedom and determinism are constantly reacting upon each other in the creative tension of life.

Living in an imperfect world, men have been led to explain the existence of evil as due to ancestral sin, or to an innate taint in man's nature, or, more fundamentally, to a divided sovereignty in the world between the good and the evil. Thus there arose the Zoroastrian conception of a cosmic war between Ahura Mazda and Ahriman, and the concept of the Kingdom of Satan poised against the Kingdom of God. By and large, however, monotheism rejected these solutions. It wrestled with the problem of evil as well as it was able, without surrendering its fundamental faith in the unity and righteousness of God and the unity and justice of His world. We have seen that while religion did not solve the problem completely, it did succeed in articulating a vision of life which sheds light on this dark corner of existence and makes it bearable.

So, too, with the age-old crux of man's free will and God's foreknowledge or determinism. A vital faith will reckon honestly with the significance of such modern concepts as heredity and environment. It will not be blind to the impact of various current psychological theories about the irrational and the subconscious and of such doctrines as economic determinism. On the contrary, to the degree that they commend themselves as true, religion will seek to utilize them for understanding and elevating man and society. But no matter how it solves the tension between freedom and law, it will maintain its conviction that man is a responsible creature. It will continue to hold aloft the banner of man's inalienable freedom.

CHAPTER XIII

Morality and Its Foundations

The new modern interest in religion derives, as we have seen, from many causes. Probably most men and women who are drawn to religion today are concerned less with the glory of God than with the survival of man. To be specific, they are seeking desperately after a firm basis for morality in an age in which virtually all standards have broken down or are in imminent danger of doing so. Such widely varying phenomena as the irruption of Nazi brutality imitated by dictators and "revolutionary" leaders everywhere, and the reliance upon "the big lie" in international affairs, have their counterpart on the domestic scene. We have only to recall the development of "motivational research" and other advertising techniques, the cult of "personality boys" in political campaigns, the cynical use of propaganda in public affairs and the growth of corruption by elected officials, within government and without. These "class" manifestations are paralleled among the masses in the increase of adult crime and malfeasance, the growth of juvenile delinquency, the spread of sexual misconduct, and the wholesale breakdown of the family. All these signs of the times indicate that a moral crisis of major proportions is at hand.

Like any acute malady, this disease of the modern spirit has been a long time in the making, and many branches of modern science have, rightly or wrongly, had a share in its growth. Modern astronomy undermined man's notion of his centrality in the universe and seemed to find no room in all the vast expanse of space for God and the soul of man. The theory of evolution served to support the notion that man is an animal, scarcely to be differentiated from the lower beasts and governed, like them, by nature's only law—the merciless struggle for existence and the survival of the fittest. Anthropology described the bewildering array of customs and practices to be found among primitive tribes as well as more civilized peoples, and men leaped to the conclusion that morality was merely *mores*, a matter of custom and convention possessing no intrinsic validity or binding power.

Some of the most influential voices of the modern age helped to sap the foundations of morality. Karl Marx argued that in order to perpetuate the inequities of the present economic order, the possessing classes created the moral principles which serve to keep the submerged and exploited masses in check. Contrariwise, Friedrich Nietzsche insisted that morality was the invention of the weaker elements in society, who constituted the majority, in order to control the "superman," who really stood "beyond good and evil" and did not require the canons of love and mercy in governing his relations with others. It need scarcely be added that there were many candidates for the role of "superman," who proceeded to demonstrate their fitness for the august position by trampling conventional standards of morality underfoot.

Finally, Sigmund Freud and his followers suggested that the dynamic factor in human activity was to be sought neither in economics nor in the lust for power, but in the sexual impulse. Morality, for Freud, was the instrument created by society to control this all-powerful impulse, at times driving it underground and suppressing it, at others sublimating it into various cultural forms, like music, art, literature, and science. The mutually contradictory ideas of Marx, Nietzsche, and Freud permeated the thinking of the modern age often at second and at third hand. Thousands upon thousands who had never read a line of their works were nevertheless influenced by them, and began to feel that morality was a relic of a pre-scientific age, rationally indefensible and retained only through inertia.

Throughout the nineteenth and twentieth centuries, men failed to recognize what was really taking place. Modern men were like the spendthrift sons of a hard-working father, who squander the legacy which they have inherited without giving thought to tomorrow. The structure of modern life and progress seemed to be intact, because everything in it was based on the piety and faith of earlier generations. The sense of fair play and the hatred of brute force, the spirit of justice and mercy, the concept of the dignity and rights of men, which infused modern standards of morality, even the extraordinary scientific progress of the age, which, as Einstein pointed out, rested on the faith in the rationality of the universe and the unity of nature—all had their source and sanction in the religious world-view of earlier generations. The modern age was in the position of enjoying the fruits of religion while hacking away at its roots.

The last three decades in world events have made it tragically clear that civilization has reached the point of no return. As we noted at the outset, increasing numbers of modern men have become conscious of the moral peril confronting an age without faith. They have therefore asked the question: Can men build a firm foundation for morality without reference to belief in a Supreme Power? Can men be good without God? The only honest answer is "Yes." It is written large in the lives of countless human beings who call themselves nonbelievers, atheists, or agnostics, whose lives are marked by idealism and human service, by the love of truth and the practice of honor and kindness, often far above the level of devout worshippers in church and synagogue.

The Talmudic sages recognized this truth in one of their most striking utterances. God himself, they said, declares: "I could forgive men if they forsook Me, but kept My law!" And then, as though anticipating our problem, they added, "for the light of the Law would bring them near to Me" (*Jerusalem Talmud, Hagigah* 1, 7). Whatever hopes these ancient teachers had for the future, they regarded the men and women who keep the Law of righteousness, though they ignore God, as fulfilling His will in the present. One recalls Tennyson's lines: "There lives more faith in honest doubt, believe me, than in half the creeds."

Goodness without God is not merely possible; it is a reality in untold individual cases. But the issue goes deeper—Can the ideals of ethical conduct be preserved and transmitted to the coming generation in a society where faith in God has withered and become a mere convention or less? Can the moral code survive the buffetings of circumstance and the blandishments of temptation in an age lacking a religious basis? We are not concerned with special individuals of superior endowment, but with society as a whole. In Edmund Wilson's words, if morality is something *compelling and enduring,* a categorical imperative that must not be violated, what are its sanctions?

What are the alternatives to religious faith? A few decades ago we might have answered that morality is inherent in man, because decency is a natural element of human nature. Hatred of cruelty, love of freedom, consideration for the weak, respect for truth— these traits are innate in man and need no outside prop. Today, no one would seriously maintain this position in the face of the new savagery, displayed not by aborigines in Africa, or by primitives on the frozen wastes of the Arctic, but by masters of civilization, practitioners of science and philosophy, devotees of art and music, lovers of sentiment and *Gemuetlichkeit,* who became transformed into the best-organized band of mass butchers in human experience. Another great people, long slumbering in ignorance and oppression, its noblest spirits held in thrall by a mystic idealism and dreamy hopelessness, threw off its lethargy and became an energetic, hard-boiled nation of remorseless conquerors, mouthing high-flown phrases about justice and peace, while crushing every manifestation of liberty under foot. Nor do the monstrous evils of Nazism and Communism exonerate the democratic world of its moral burdens. Wholesale corruption in government and business, with stealing and murder rampant, the breakdown of family morality and the spread of youthful delinquency and crime—all these affect not a few individuals, but thousands upon thousands of respectable men in society.

The bitter experience of the mid-century teaches that morality cannot be taken for granted as innate and "self-evident." Decency is not an instinct, but an acquired characteristic, which men can shed, and that all too easily.

No lengthy discussion is needed to demonstrate that we cannot depend on the police power of the state to enforce the rules of decent human behavior. It is not morality which rests on the law, but the law which rests on morality. It is obvious that the state cannot enforce a law unless it is believed to be right. When, for good or insufficient reasons, no such conviction prevails, there are not enough policemen, judges, or jails to enforce obedience. In 1857 the United States Congress adopted a Fugitive Slave Act, which required all American citizens to assist in apprehending and returning Negro slaves who had escaped from their masters. Thousands of otherwise law-abiding citizens rejected this law as an affront to their consciences, and pointed to a higher fugitive slave act laid down in Scripture: "Thou shalt not return a slave unto his master. He shall dwell with thee and thou shalt do him no wrong." Against this widespread civil disobedience the government proved powerless. In the twentieth century and on a much lower level, Prohibition was nullified by widespread disobedience and ultimately had to be repealed, after being enshrined as an Amendment to the Constitution. Only when a law is accepted by the vast majority of the people as just, can the state concentrate upon the minority of would-be violators. Ethics is substantially more than a series of traffic regulations for society.

The inadequacy of the power of the state as a basis for morality goes much further. It is possible to place upon the statute books a law making it punishable to beat one's parents, but one cannot enact or enforce a law compelling the honoring of one's parents. Stealing is a crime, but there can be no legal prohibition against envy. Gunnar Myrdal has called attention to the great American dilemma of a nation dedicated to freedom and justice to all, yet practising widespread discrimination on the basis of race, creed, or color. The position of the Negro in the United States constitutes the most striking illustration of the difference between the scope of morality and the power of the law. It is obvious that civil rights legislation and judicial decisions are indispensable instruments in fighting the grossest forms of racial and religious discrimination. Their usefulness, however, depends upon the recognition by the American people that group-prejudice is an evil. Where that conviction is lacking, the statute book is little more than a dead letter, as the struggle for desegregation in the South demonstrates. Constant efforts are being made to institute government or quasi-public censorship of books and plays. Experience has shown that censors fail to prevent pornography and succeed only in imperiling freedom of expression. Morality is too subtle to be grasped by the gross pincers of government. Ethics includes not only overt acts, but also "the duties of the heart," the subtler feelings and attitudes within the spirit of man.

The Talmudic sages, who were both teachers of religion and

legislators for society, were well aware of this truth, when they recognized such subtle categories of sin as "acts exempt from punishment but forbidden," and "deeds free in human law but guilty by Divine law."

Conscious of this truth, many modern men have sought a philosophy for ethics elsewhere. Particularly appealing is the approach of the secular humanist, who declares that morality has no sanctions in the universe, but grows out of the needs of society; being rooted in man's nature, it is binding upon men. Humanism would define morality as a system of regulations that ideally allows for a minimum of conflict and a maximum amount of happiness for man. This is, to be sure, a fair description of morality *in operation*, but it is inadequate as a rationale for ethics on both practical and theoretical grounds.

Let us deal with the practical difficulty first. That man is a potentially moral creature living in an immoral universe, that it is incumbent upon him to live ethically in spite of the hostility or the indifference of the natural world, has been superbly expressed by Bertrand Russell in his deeply moving essay, "A Free Man's Worship," from which we have quoted earlier in this book.

The vision of life as meaningless and doomed to extinction is not subject to logical refutation, only to acceptance or rejection. There undoubtedly are some men who can find in such a standpoint a basis for ethical living, but, one suspects, their number is few. Most men are much more likely to arrive at an opposite conclusion. If our actions do not really matter, and our brief span on earth is meaningless, if life is a sinking ship on which all hands will be lost, why concern oneself with the welfare of others and forego the satisfaction of any desire or goal within our power to achieve? "Let us eat and drink, for tomorrow we die," is at least an equally plausible conclusion to be derived from a philosophy of an immoral universe.

Heroism has always been rare, yet men have been led to extraordinary effort and sacrifice, *but only when they felt that their cause, however weak in their day, would ultimately triumph*. The martyr, as the word's Greek etymology indicates, bears witness to a truth which, he believes, will finally be vindicated. The hope for "fame, the last infirmity of noble minds," as Milton called it, is an act of faith, a deep conviction that high aspiration and achievement are not fated to vanish into nothingness.

The scientist spending laborious days and lonely years in seeking to demonstrate a theory scouted by his contemporaries, the
creative talent in literature, music, and art, the social revolutionary
and reformer battling for human betterment, the religious or social
rebel who declares, with Luther, "Here I stand, I can do no other,"
will never be common. They are not likely to emerge at all from
a world-view that sees all man's ideals of goodness, truth, and
beauty as writ in water, a brief reflection of his own nature,
doomed to perish with him.

Moreover, the humanist basis for ethics suffers from some grave
theoretical drawback. Bertrand Russell declares: "A strange mystery it is that Nature, omnipotent but blind, in the revolutions of
her secular hurryings through the abysses of space, has brought
forth at last a child, subject still to her power, but gifted with
sight, with knowledge of good and evil, with the capacity of
judging all the works of his unthinking Mother. In spite of Death,
the mark and seal of the parental control, Man is yet free, during
his brief years, to examine, to criticize, to know, and in imagination
to create. To him alone, in the world with which he is acquainted,
this freedom belongs; and in this lies his superiority to the resistless
forces that control his outward life." The same feeling is sardoni-
cally expressed in Thomas Hardy's poem, "New Year's Eve," in
which a man remonstrates with God for creating the world in
which we live:

> "Yea, Sire: why shaped you us, 'who in
> This tabernacle groan'—
> If ever a joy be found herein,
> Such joy no man had wished to win
> If he had never known!"

> Then He: "My labours—logicless—
> You may explain; not I:
> Sense-sealed I have wrought, without a guess
> That I evolved a Consciousness
> To ask for reasons why.

> Strange that ephemeral creatures who
> By my own ordering are,
> Should see the shortness of my view,
> Use ethic tests I never knew,
> Or made provision for!"

What Russell calls "a mystery" and Hardy "strange"—the existence of an ethical being in an amoral universe—is much more than that—it is logically untenable. The principle of causation must insist that a creature cannot possess attributes lacking in its matrix— an oak tree can contain nothing that was not present potentially in the acorn. All that exists in man must be implicit in nature, whose child he remains.

There is another philosophical difficulty in regarding morality as man's invention that does not correspond to any objective reality in the world. Such a view creates a dichotomy between man and the rest of creation, setting up an iron curtain in the midst of the evolutionary process. It is an ever more striking conclusion of science that all life is a unit and man is only the highest known element on the evolutionary ladder. Biologists have discovered a thousand links binding him to his fellows a little lower in the scale, physical and psychological. Not only is the nervous system, which is the seat of consciousness, widespread through the animal kingdom, but even the rudiments of a moral system have been noted among some animals. To make morality purely a human construction breaks the pattern of unity in the world, which science is patiently constructing at a thousand points.

To maintain that morality is a purely human invention in an amoral or immoral universe is therefore difficult, raising grave problems in theory. What is fatal, however, is the incapacity of humanism to give men the power they need to struggle and sacrifice for their moral vision—because it lacks the consciousness of victory.

Because of these problems in secular humanism, various schools of thought have arisen that may be described as religious humanism. In opposition to Russell and Hardy, they deny that the world is hostile or even indifferent to man. On the contrary, they insist that the universe is friendly to man's moral aspirations. Thinkers like Henry Wieman and Mordecai M. Kaplan therefore find it necessary to postulate "God" in their world-view. Kaplan has defined God as "the sum total of the forces making for good in the universe." John Dewey, who was further removed from religious tradition, used the term "God" to refer to "the cosmic force latent in conditions that nurture the ideal, as the soil nurtures the seed" (*Cosmic Faith*, p. 51).

In charting its course, religious humanism seeks to avoid the problems confronting both secular humanism and theism. By rooting morality in the universe, the religious humanist seeks to escape the weaknesses of secular humanism that we have just discussed. On the other hand, by equating God with *some* aspects of the universe, rather than with its *totality*, the religious humanist hopes to bypass the problem of evil, the agonizing mystery of suffering in a world created by a good God. Since God is given only "limited sovereignty," He is not to be held responsible for the world as a whole or for the evil in it.

If the standpoint of religious humanism is examined critically, however, it becomes clear that it has not really met the challenges confronting religious faith; it has merely evaded them.

In the first instance, it should be noted that the basic attitude of religious humanism, no less than that of traditional religion, is not subject to "demonstration." For religious humanism is not content to assert that there are *some* elements of good in the world; it maintains that the universe is *basically friendly* to man's aspirations. Now, no man possesses a scale adequate to measure the plus and the minus elements in the world, the good and the evil, and arrive at an empirical demonstration that the light is more pervasive than the darkness. To maintain, as does the religious humanist, that the world is primarily good rather than evil requires an act of faith no easier to achieve than that of traditional religion, expressed in the Biblical dictum, "God saw all that He had made, and behold, it was very good."

Besides, religious humanism does not escape the essential philosophic weakness of secular humanism, which divides the world into "two dominions." The secular humanist builds a wall between the area of the non-moral, which for him is the bulk of the universe, and the area of the moral, which is the limited theatre of man's activity. The religious humanist makes his division elsewhere, but he makes it nevertheless. The world is compartmentalized into the good, where God holds sway, and into the non-good, where He does not.

Moreover, the origin and persistence of evil, incidentally, are left unaccounted for. Some thinkers, like Samuel Alexander, have sought to meet the problem of evil by the conception of an "emergent God." According to this view, God's control over the universe is constantly growing, as evil is progressively conquered. But in this

view, the term "God" has been largely emptied of its meaning—
not God creates the universe, but the universe creates God! As
we have seen, there are additional serious objections to the view
that regards evil as the absence of good, or believes that God is
limited in power, willing the good, but unable to enforce it.

For men to battle against superior odds, to suffer and even to
die for a cause beyond themselves, requires the passionate conviction that evil is a violation of the law of the universe and that "the
earth riseth up against the evil doer." In its desire to bypass the
problem of evil, religious humanism has curtailed the sovereignty
of God, thus conceding far more than was necessary to "His
Majesty's Opposition." Moreover, in assigning to God only the
factors of good in the universe, religious humanism has no answer
with regard to the origin of reality as a whole. One of the most
distinguished exemplars of this school of thought therefore maintains that "the metaphysical conception of God, which depends
upon one's ideas of ultimate reality is not, or *should not be*, the
subject-matter of religion" (Mordecai M. Kaplan, *A New Zion-
ism*, p. 114). But as the words which we have italicized indicate,
most men *do* expect to find a theory of the universe in their
religious outlook. From our entire approach, it is clear that we
regard the cognitive function of religion not only as legitimate
but as basic.

In the attempt to discover a basis for the moral law, we have
found the various competing humanist positions inadequate. If we
penetrate to the inner meaning of Biblical religion, we shall find it
incomparably more satisfying, not only emotionally and pragmatically, but intellectually as well. The universe is governed by this
one Living God who created it and sustains it in righteousness.
The natural order has its counterpart in the moral law—both are
embodiments of God's creative power and goodness. Obeying His
will means living in accordance both with nature and with the
moral law. "Holy shall ye be, for I, the Lord your God, am holy"
is the foundation of morality. Failure to live ethically leads inevitably and ultimately to punishment, which is a human term for
the consequence of running afoul of the laws of the universe.

That the God of nature and the God of the moral law are one
is affirmed by the voice of faith. In the nineteenth Psalm, God is
praised under three aspects, as the Creator of the world, as the

Source of the moral law, and as the motive power behind man's quest for moral perfection:

> The heavens declare the glory of God,
> And the firmament proclaims His handiwork.
>
> The law of the Lord is perfect, restoring the soul,
> The testimony of the Lord is sure, making wise the simple. . . .
>
> Who can discern errors?
> Clear Thou me from hidden faults.
> Keep back Thy servant also from presumptuous sins,
> That they may not have dominion over me; then shall I be whole,
> And free of transgression.
>
> *(Psalm* 19:2, 8, 13–14)

Psalm 104, the great hymn to nature's God, which aroused the boundless admiration of Alexander von Humboldt, describes unforgettably the glories of creation and the recurrent miracles of the world. It then ends with a verse which at first blush seems irrelevant to the theme:

> Let sinners cease out of the earth,
> And let the wicked be no more.
>
> *(Psalm* 104:35)

But whether the verse emanates from the poet or from an editor, it is needed to present the fullness of the Biblical view of God, which, notwithstanding all the difficulties involved, held fast to its faith in Him as the source both of nature and of morality. As we have seen, the magnificent God-speeches in *Job* rest upon the same foundation—God is one in both His manifestations.

When men fall short of the ideals which they profess, conscience intervenes. Henry L. Mencken defined it in a cynical epigram: "Conscience is the still, small voice that tells us that someone is looking." He had only to write "Someone" with a capital, and he would have expressed a truth to which the religious spirit willingly assents—there is Someone, a Divine element, in man's moral consciousness.

To be sure, anthropology has revealed the boundless variety of moral behavior to be found among the tribes and races of men. In any given society, men's standards will reflect the norms of the environment. The discomfort that a cannibal may feel after a luscious repast is more likely to be due to stomach-pains than to conscience-pangs!

Yet it is fallacious to equate conscience with an inner policeman, appointed over us by society, if only because, as Buber points out, conscience often demands action which is in direct violation of the desires and standards of society. The Prophets of Israel, regarded by their hostile and uncomprehending people as enemies of God and of Israel; Joan of Arc, condemned by her own Church as an emissary of Satan; the Doctor Stockmanns, who are attacked as subversives and enemies of society—all the martyrs and heroes of history, who stood their ground against the compact and inert majority, did so because of an inner voice, not an outer pressure.

An important distinction needs to be made here between the *content* of conscience, which may largely, though not altogether, be sociologically determined; and the *existence* of the moral faculty in man, which is a mark of his Divine nature. *What* conscience usually tells most men may be a reflection of the standards in their age, but *that* conscience speaks to them is evidence of the voice of God.

It is, or should be, self-evident that no extant moral or legal system is identical with the moral will of God. All our various codes, from the most primitive to the most advanced, represent man's faltering and imperfect efforts to comprehend the Divine Law in ever greater fullness. As man's understanding of the natural world continues to grow, so does his grasp of the moral imperatives for being. One fundamental difference between these two enterprises of the human spirit lies in the fact that while the greatest progress in understanding nature has been registered in the last few centuries, the great principles of the ethical life were revealed to the prophets and sages relatively early in the history of the human race. The Golden Rule in *Leviticus*, the *Analects* of Confucius, Mencius, and Lao-Tse, the *Paths* of the Buddha, the Beatitudes of the *Sermon on the Mount*, the apothegms of the *Ethics of the Fathers*, the insights of the legists, mystics, and saints of the Middle Ages—all emanate largely from the remote past rather than from eras closer to our own.

It is in the ever-broader range of the application of these laws of conduct, in their extension from the family and the clan to the nation and humanity, in the deepening sensitivity to the dignity and rights of all men, women, and children, in the consciousness of an ever-closer bond uniting the far-flung corners of the earth, that our age has its ineluctable task. There is little need for new ethical principles that will go beyond the highest level of the prophets, sages, and saints of the past. What is desperately needed is the intelligence to understand them and the will to apply them.

Men are more likely to succeed in this crucial enterprise if they recognize that ethical ideals are not principles of etiquette or traffic rules of society, or the trappings of convention, but in truth the pillars upon which the world rests, built into the constitution of the universe. The ethical law is not man's invention, but his discovery, his growing insight into the Creator's will for His creature:

> "Remove from Me the noise of thy songs,
> Nor will I listen to the music of thy harps.
> But let justice well up as the waters
> And righteousness like a mighty stream.
>
> For the Lord of Hosts is exalted through justice,
> And the holy God is sanctified through righteousness.
> *(Amos* 5:23–24; *Isaiah* 5:16)

CHAPTER XIV

Man and His Divisions

At the midpoint of the twentieth century men find themselves more closely linked to their fellows than ever before. The virtual annihilation of distance through improved methods of communication and transportation, accompanied as it has been by fantastically improved instruments of destruction, makes the unity of mankind crystal-clear, but the theory is very far from being translated into practice. On the contrary, the technical progress which has bound men's destinies together seems only to have multiplied the tensions between nations and blocs of nations.

In no small degree, men's despair before these mass aggregations of power has led them to occupy themselves with their own personal lot. Contemporary religion is, accordingly, concerned principally with men's individual fears and hopes, while the "social gospel" has gone into eclipse in our day. Yet it is of the very essence of Biblical religion that it gives at least equal significance to the problems and status of the group. The greatest spokesmen of Hebrew faith, the Prophets of Israel, grappled with the character and destiny of their nation and of humanity as a whole. That emphasis needs to be recaptured today in any faith worthy of the name, for obviously there can be no hope for men if there is no future for man. No world-view is complete unless it offers guidance to modern man with regard to the national and religious groups that claim his allegiance.

We are never fully conscious of the debt which we owe to our religious and cultural inheritance from the past, because so much of it has already been absorbed into our world-view. All too often, therefore, we find the elements of religion either unacceptable or platitudinous; what we do not reject seems to us trite and self-evident. An excellent case in point is afforded by modern man's "future-centeredness," his concern with tomorrow rather than with yesterday. Actually, this attitude toward life is by no means self-evident, nor has it always prevailed. Ancient man saw the past as the Golden Age, when bliss and well-being were his portion; the future he faced with foreboding and dread; as for the present, he saw in it the steady or cataclysmic decline of humanity. This idealization of the past finds its most familiar instance in the Biblical tradition of the Garden of Eden, the sources of which go back to the earliest musings of man on his destiny. Language often preserves clues to early thought. In Biblical Hebrew, "the past" is expressed by terms (like *kedem* or *lefanim*) which means "face," while the future is *l'ahor*, "back." Ancient man stood with his face to the past, and his back to the future.

It was the Prophets of Israel who worked a thoroughgoing revolution in man's thought. They completely reversed the direction of man's ideals, and turned his hopes from the past toward the future. Deeply permeated by a faith in a God of righteousness and power, Biblical religion had an unshakable faith that His cause would triumph. But the actual world about them lacked the necessary attributes of God's kingdom: peace and brotherhood, justice and mercy. That inevitable victory, the advent of which man was both privileged and commanded to hasten, was not visible in the present; it would appear in the future. The future thus became the era of the ideal, the goal of all human striving, the focus of all human hopes. When men's fortunes declined and their hopes suffered a setback, it represented only a temporary regression, a turn in the spiral, the ultimate direction of which remained upward.

For the great Hebrew Prophets, the Kingdom of God would appear at "the end of days" or "End-time." The greatest and most familiar expression of this faith occurs twice in the Bible (*Isaiah*, chap. 2, and *Micah*, chap. 4). It is probably older than either of these eighth-century Prophets, who quoted an earlier seer:

> In the end of days it shall come to pass,
> That the mountain of the Lord's house shall be established
> on the top of the mountains,

And it shall be exalted above the hills.
Peoples shall flow unto it,
And many nations shall come and say,
"Come, let us go up to the mountain of the Lord,
To the house of the God of Jacob;
So that He will teach us of His ways,
And we will walk in His paths:
For from Zion shall go forth the Law,
And the word of the Lord from Jerusalem."
And He shall judge among many peoples,
And rebuke strong nations afar off;
They shall beat their swords into plowshares,
And their spears into pruning-hooks;
Nation shall not lift up sword against nation,
Neither shall they learn war any more.
They shall sit every man under his vine and under his fig-tree;
And none shall make them afraid;
For the mouth of the Lord of hosts hath spoken it.
For as all the peoples walk every one in the name of its god,
We will walk in the name of the Lord our God forever.

At the very outset, the true meaning of the opening phrase, *'aharith hayamim*, "the end of days," should be noted. The words do not refer to the final climax of the human drama before the dissolution of the natural order. That the idiom is very ancient is clear from the parallel in Akkadian (*ina ahrat umi*), and from its use in some of the oldest Biblical poems, like the "Blessing of Jacob" and the "Prophecies of Balaam." It is used relatively rather than absolutely of the future. As the Biblical scholar, S. R. Driver, puts it, the phrase "end of days" refers to the final period within the speaker's perspective, whatever that may be.

Now, obviously, the author of the Vision of the End-time was thinking of the future, even of the distant future. Yet there is no indication that he believed that the new world-order could be ushered in only through a special, supernatural intervention taking the form of a great cataclysm in the natural world. For the Prophet, the Kingdom of God did not depend upon a miraculous transformation of human nature. It would be ushered in when the nations of the earth, *constituted as at present*, would surrender their present attitude of mutual hatred and lawlessness in favor of a new outlook of obedience to the Divine law of justice and peace.

For Isaiah and Micah and their anonymous but influential predeces-sor, the End-time would come to pass without any dramatic catastrophe, but rather as a result of the free conviction of men, voluntarily accepting the law of God as the norm for conduct. The Prophet does not look forward to a Utopia into which men will have been driven by an upheaval of natural forces or by the compulsions of human power, which have scarcely been gentler, whatever the formula, be it the *Pax Romana,* "*Rule, Britannia,*" *Deutschland über Alles*, "the American Century," or "the dic-tatorship of the proletariat." The Prophet's vision rests on faith in man's capacity to achieve the ideal by means of the free exercise of his reason and will.

Herein the Prophets differed from the later post-exilic Apoca-lyptic writers, "the Revealers of Hidden Things," who, as we have seen, despaired of the natural capacities of men to improve their lot and therefore developed the conviction of a supernatural cataclysm as the prelude to the advent of the Kingdom of God.

Today, the same mood of despair over man's nature, evoked by the tragic world situation, has found expression in various schools of contemporary thought, which emphasize man's essential sinfulness and inner corruption, and pin their faith entirely on God's free grace, bestowed upon His unworthy creatures. These contemporary theologians often claim to be the only authentic exponents of "Biblical religion," but they are expounding not the Biblical, but the Apocalyptic faith. When some of these modern theologians deny that man's actions have any role to play in his salvation, they are going beyond the post-Biblical teachers as well, for even to them salvation was an act of cosmic collaboration of God and man.

To return to our theme, the Prophets saw the End-time as differ-ing from the present order principally by the reign of universal peace, and it is in this connection that the Biblical passage from *Isaiah* and *Micah* is generally cited. However, the phrases have become so familiar that their full impact has been lost. In the ancient world, the ideal of universal peace was beyond the ken even of a Plato in his vision of Utopia, as we have seen. For him, mankind was forever divided into Greek and barbarian, with the sword as the final arbiter of human destiny. The Hebrew Prophet may have lacked the dialectic skill of the Greek sage, but it was he who enunciated the ideal of peace which entered the mainstream of Western thought through the Hebrew Scripture and the religions which hold it sacred. Civilized man, aside from such atavisms as Mussolini, are at one in regarding war as evil and peace as the ideal state of society.

Yet even today, while it is recognized that peace is a necessity for human survival, the prophetic faith is lacking that peace is the attainable and inevitable goal of history. The Prophets would never have conceded that mankind is confronted today by a race between world catastrophe and world-order. Their faith in God's government imbued them with the certainty that His will would prevail and humanity would survive. As a later prophet put it, "Not for chaos did He create the earth, but for human habitation."

Had the Prophet not gone beyond the enunciation of the *ideal*, his would have been a memorable achievement. Actually, he goes substantially farther—he indicates the technique for achieving the ideal. He points out that the road to peace lies in the creation of a binding international law, which must be centered in a recognized authority. He does not depend on good will or on mutual love to guard the peace, nor does he expect that all differences of outlook and all conflicts of interest will miraculously disappear in the End-time. Before peace can be a reality, there must be a universal law which shall come forth from Zion, which will be accepted as binding among the nations and will be enforced among them all. The Prophet would have denied the doctrine of national sovereignty, if it is defined in terms of "My country, may she always be in the right, but my country, right or wrong." If government means an agency capable of imposing its will upon its members, the Prophet emphatically believed in world-government under God and His law.

It is noteworthy that he speaks of judging between nations. Judgment means the enforcement of justice. For the Prophet, this Law emanated from the God of Jacob, who, as all the Prophets taught, is the one God of humanity. But irrespective of its source, the character of this international covenant is not legalistic, but moral, rooted in justice and truth and therefore capable of supporting the structure of peace. A Talmudic utterance makes this idea explicit: "Upon three things the world rests—upon justice, upon truth, and upon peace. And the three are one, for when justice is done, truth prevails and peace is established" (*Jerusalem Talmud, Taanith 4:2; Megillah 3:5*).

Unquestionably, however, the most significant contribution for our age to be found in the Prophet's vision of the End-time is one which has been generally overlooked, i.e., his conception of nationalism. Within five short verses, be it noted, the words for "people" and "nation" occur no fewer than seven times—striking testimony of the prophetic belief that national groups will remain as permanent features of human society even in its ideal phase. The bearing of his thought on our age is obvious. For today, nationalism has reached the acme of its power and the nadir of its degradation. It is the basic ill of our age, aside from the economic strife, to which, indeed, it has largely contributed. No greater peril threatens the survival of man than contemporary nationalism, men's total absorption in their own group, the view that all law emanates from one's own ethnic or political unit, that there is no morality applicable to those beyond its limits, and that its interests are to be defended at all costs as the highest good.

What is the remedy for the evils of nationalism? Some have proposed the ideal of cosmopolitanism, the merging and disappearance of all national groupings. Instead of being Frenchmen, Germans, or Americans, men would become citizens of a world state. One nationality, one language, one culture, and, if religion is to survive at all, one faith—this would constitute the common heritage of mankind.

At first blush, such an ideal has an undeniable grandeur and nobility, as the concrete embodiment of the ideal of the unity of mankind. Upon sober examination, however, it becomes clear that if current versions of nationalism are a nightmare, this type of internationalism is an impractical dream.

The history of mankind, both recent and remote, discloses no signs that national loyalty is disappearing, or that nations are seeking to sink their differences in a common world patriotism. On the contrary, the past half-century has seen the creation of a score of new nations, which struggle desperately for their place in the sun. World War I created many independent states in Central Europe. The last decade has seen the emergence of nationalism as a dynamic factor in the Arab world, and in India, China, Burma, and Indonesia. Africa is now seething with rebellious native populations developing a national consciousness. In sum, all signs point not to a diminution of nationalist loyalty, but to its intensification, or at least to its retention, for decades to come.

Nationalism will endure, not merely because of propaganda or the innate corruption of man, but because it draws upon deep roots in the soul of man. It is normal for a man to be attached to the soil where he was born, where he spent the pleasant years of his childhood, and to feel drawn to his own people, with whom he is most familiar. The songs our mother sang, the language she spoke, the festivals of our childhood—these have an appeal beyond words and beyond reason, an appeal which no reasonable man will lightly dismiss.

The goal of a uniform mass of human beings seems, therefore, to fly in the face of reality. But its impracticality aside, if this conception of internationalism could be realized, it would prove disastrous for the human spirit. Of this truth, we should be particularly conscious in an age of growing conformity and colorlessness. National loyalty is the matrix in which all culture is formed. Every cultural achievement of which we have record is particularistic in origin, however universal in goal. Culture is always rooted in a given milieu, drawing its substance from a specific tradition, expressing itself in a given language, and deriving its power from a sense of kinship with a definite people. It is true that Hebrew prophecy, Greek art, Italian opera, German poetry, and English drama "belong to the world." But in every instance, they reflect their ethnic sources and their environmental influences, without which they are inconceivable. If, contrary to all indications, national loyalties were to dissolve, it would spell cultural anemia for the world. To borrow a distinction employed by some thinkers, *civilization*, the science and technology of the world, being impersonal, may be conceivable without nationalism, but not *culture*, which embraces the literature, art, music, and philosophy of the age.

Now, if nationalism is, on the one hand, natural and even essential to the growth of culture, and if, on the other, it constitutes a potential menace to human survival, a tragic dilemma would seem to face the human race: either stagnation or death. Must mankind be condemned to choose between the Scylla of a sterile, colorless cosmopolitanism and the Charybdis of a mad, bloodthirsty nationalism?

Merely to castigate nationalism as evil, as do some moralists of the age, may offer some psychological relief, but as a practical program it is quixotic and doomed to failure. In this area of human conflict, as in others, another solution, at once more practical and more ideal, may be discovered in the Prophets of Israel. In the literal sense of the term, the Hebrew Prophets were the true *internationalists*, believers in the creation of proper relations among nations.

The author of the Vision of the End-time looked forward, not to the elimination but to the "moralization" of national loyalties. Since authority would be vested in the World Law, the nexus binding the members of each people together would not be force, but their common cultural and historic heritage. A nation would be the voluntary association of men and women for the preservation and cultivation of a cherished body of common ideals, practices, and values. This ideal of nationalism as exclusively a cultural-ethnic loyalty has scarcely penetrated the thinking of most men, but it offers the only road to survival for mankind.

Though far ahead of our day, this concept of national loyalty was applied by the Prophets to their own people, which for centuries has embodied this ideal, however imperfectly, being united the world over by no central political allegiance, military power, or geographical contiguity, but only by the consciousness of a common history, faith, and destiny.

The Prophets would insist that the future era has room for all other national groups on the same terms, *a national loyalty, cultural in essence and moral in function*. In George Santayana's words, "A man's feet must be firmly planted in his own country, but his eyes must survey the world." The Prophets went further; their hearts embraced the world.

The Biblical Vision of the End-time is a farsighted interpretation of nationalism, in which love of one's own people and loyalty to humanity represent two concentric circles. The bugbear of dual allegiance, which exercises little minds to the present day, would never have troubled them, because for them, all loyalties, national as well as international, were peaceful in expression and equally subject to the moral law. Hence every Hebrew prophet, from Amos and Hosea to Deutero-Isaiah and Malachi, exemplifies both nationalism and internationalism. Modern thinkers, who deplore nationalism, or seek to ignore it or dismiss it as irrelevant to their conception of the good life, would do well to be instructed by the Prophets of Israel. For the life and work of the Hebrew Prophets is grounded on the conviction that nationalism is not necessarily evil, and, on the contrary, can prove a source of spiritual enrichment in the life of man.

Isaiah and Micah agreed completely with Amos in demanding the same high standard of righteousness from Judah as from Moab, from Israel as from Aram. The conception of an ethical national- ism, implicit in this Vision of the End-time, found its noblest and most concrete expression in Isaiah. Although he saw his people being ground to death in the world war fought between Egypt and Assyria, he foresaw the day when Israel would be "the third with Egypt and with Assyria, a blessing in the midst of the earth; for the Lord of hosts hath blessed him, saying: 'Blessed be Egypt My people, and Assyria the work of My hands, and Israel Mine inheritance'" (*Isa.* 19:24–25).

All signs point to the fact that in the recognizable future, at least, mankind will continue to include a rich variety of ethnic groups. It follows that mankind's best hope lies not in cursing the darkness of nationalism but in lighting a candle from the Prophets' flame, striving to endow nationalism with cultural character and with the discipline of obedience to the moral law. Like all aspects of the secular world, nationalism is not profane; it needs to be made holy.

What of religious differences now so rampant among men? Will the bewildering variety of sects even within a single tradi- tion and the differences in the great communions continue to divide mankind? Is not the truth one? Undoubtedly, many of the differences that are reflected in rival organizational patterns are of purely historical interest today. Nothing is more dead nor more deadly than the theological controversies of yesterday. The trend toward increased unity and cooperation within the sects of Chris- tianity and Judaism, as well as between the great faiths, gives hope that many of the divisions will ultimately disappear.

Yet it would be not merely useless, but stultifying, to anticipate the merging of all religious traditions. The reasons are implicit in our discussion of the fundamental differences between science and religion. Since science is concerned with establishing the facts in a given area of reality, there can ultimately be only one true explanation, no matter how elusive it may prove to be, or how often scientific conclusions may need to be revised. Religion, on the other hand, is concerned with the totality of the universe, great areas of which are unknown, if not forever unknowable. Moreover, its basic interest lies not in establishing the facts, but in enunciating the values that should govern human life. It follows that the subjective element will therefore bulk large in religion, which is rooted in personal or historical experiences and in intangible factors of character, both of the individual and of the group. Variety in religious outlook is of its very essence.

To argue that any one attitude on life is the whole truth is as foolish as to maintain that any one aspect or approach in literature, music, or art rules out all others. Undoubtedly, there is better and worse in religion, according as a given tradition reckons with the truth about reality in greater or lesser degree. One may legitimately speak of higher or lower levels in religion, depending on the values and ideals that a given tradition seeks to inculcate in its devotees and the measure of its success in striving "to perfect the world after the Kingdom of God."

Yet in other respects, the various religions are different as personalities differ, and each can fairly claim to possess some portion of the truth. A man will normally find the faith in which he has been reared, and which has molded his world-view, most congenial to himself. Yet he need not and should not, on that account, deprive himself of the insights which he can find in traditions not his own. Maimonides' injunction, "Receive the truth from whosoever sets it forth," is justified on many grounds, not the least being the fact that all human truth is partial and perpetually in need of correction, whether in content or in emphasis.

Thus the Hebraic tradition, which is the basis of the world-view expounded in these pages, is fundamentally life-affirming; it sees in the phenomena of the natural world the abundant signs of the presence of the Living God. Yet the enjoyment of life's pleasures can easily be distorted into hedonism and degenerate into license and irresponsibility. Here correctives are needed to emphasize the virtues of self-restraint and moderation, and to stress the insignificance of the material aspect of existence. Such a counterbalance is to be found in the ascetic tendencies which exist in all Western religions in some degree. Buddhism goes even further, dismissing the entire fabric of the material world as an illusion, and declaring that the highest goal in life is to attain a level where all desire is absent. As an all-encompassing philosophy of life, the goal of Nirvana is not likely to be acceptable to Western man. The overwhelming material problems that afflict India, its poverty, disease, and overcrowding, may be charged not unfairly to the non-activistic, antimaterialistic world-view that is dominant in India's creeds. Yet as a critique of the excesses inherent in the pursuit of the world's physical blessings, the spirit of Hindu thought is perennially valuable. Western religion, reflecting the temper of the civilization in which it functions, is predominantly activistic, but this trait easily passes over into useless bustle and the fever of motion for its own sake. The stress and struggle of achievement often mask little more than acquisitiveness and greed, so that life is robbed of all serenity and peace. Here Oriental religion, with its stress upon the contemplative life as the *summum bonum*, supplies a much needed balance to the perils of activism. The "truth" lies neither with the West nor with the East, but in a creative tension between the two.

Even within the Judeo-Christian tradition, there are varying and even contradictory emphases, all of which have intrinsic value, and which testify, incidentally, that there is no one royal road to the throne of the Most High. To cite one instance, for centuries there has been a sharp cleavage between the liturgical churches, stressing the resplendent garb of the priesthood, elaborate music, colorful art, and the use of incense and candles on the one hand, and the nonliturgical sects, practising the utmost simplicity and informality in religious worship on the other. Experience has shown that neither approach has a monopoly on truth, that each has its advantages and drawbacks, and that both have often succeeded—and often failed—in bringing the sense of God into the lives of men.

Religious variety is here to stay. The differences which the various creeds exhibit in their world-view and way of life need not be a cause of strife and contention, but, on the contrary, may serve as steppingstones to true tolerance and as means for deepening the life of man.

In the great vision of the End-time quoted above, the Prophet sees God's house established as on a pinnacle, with all the nations flowing toward it, there to seek God's law and obey it. A mountain may well symbolize man's age-old quest for the ideal society. When men set out to conquer a peak, different groups of mountaineers will choose different trails that wind round the mountain slopes. As they inch their way toward their goal, one group of climbers may find itself coming face to face with another, which is headed in what appears the opposite direction, yet in reality they are all striving for the same objective.

In the agonizing ascent of humanity to the New Jerusalem, there are many trails which cross and crisscross one another on the slopes. A narrow view would regard these various paths as opposed to each other. Some of the climbers may indeed be nearer to the peak than others, though even this conclusion is not at all certain until the goal is reached. Each group of travelers, finding the path which it has traversed most familiar, knowing each pitfall and foothold along the way, and recognizing each feature of the landscape, may tend to regard its own trail as the best approach of all. But this is merely a personal reaction. From the vantage point of the Lord's house, all the paths lead upward; what matters is the zeal and devotion with which men make the ascent and struggle toward the goal envisaged by the Prophet: "Men shall do no evil and work no destruction on all God's holy mountain, for the earth shall be filled with the knowledge of the Lord as the waters cover the sea."

CHAPTER XV

Immortality—A Hope That Refuses to Die

Though some may pretend otherwise, virtually no man finds it possible to conceive of a day when he will no longer exist. In a sense not intended by its author, Everyman can echo the words of Hillel: "If I am here, everyone is here; if I am absent, no one is present!" Hence, one of the most enduring beliefs in religion, linking the most primitive and the most advanced forms and finding expression in countless forms and rites, is the all-but-universal conviction that death does not end all for man. Although, as the poet reminds us, death is a bourne from which no traveler has yet returned, and the living have no real experience or observation on the subject, that has not prevented the growth of dogmas and convictions on life after death. Yet it is noteworthy that within the confines of the Biblical and post-Biblical tradition one finds a vast variety of outlook on this theme.

In the Biblical account of creation, man is conceived of as immortal, though it is probable that this is not an inherent quality, but rather an "acquired characteristic"—Adam remains immortal so long as he has access to the fruit of the Tree of Life in the Garden of Eden. The Tree of Life is thus similar to the Golden Apples of the Hesperides in Greek mythology, which conferred immortal youth upon the gods, so long as the food was available; without it they withered and grew old. When Adam sins, the expulsion from Eden accordingly brings mortality in its wake.

Nonetheless, death is never conceived of as total annihilation. The Biblical writers reflect the ancient Semitic idea of a shadowy

238

realm called *Sheol,* where the dead continue a kind of inactive half-existence, a view which has its analogue in the Greek conception of Hades. While a few Biblical passages dealing with *Sheol,* like *Isaiah,* chapter 14, would seem to suggest some distinction between the righteous and the wicked in this nether world, by and large all the "shades" are pictured as existing together, with no differences between them in a realm beneath the earth.

Significantly, Biblical religion never assigned to the after-life an important place in its world-view, and this for several reasons. The most basic factor was the strong emphasis placed by the Hebrew Prophets and Sages upon life in this world. Since God rules, His justice will prevail in the arena of human struggle, failure, and achievement. The theatre where men can fulfill their destiny and duty is here and now—that is the heart of the Biblical call for obedience to God's will.

As we have seen, this prophetic faith was challenged by the widespread evidence of "the suffering of the righteous, and the prosperity of the wicked." The contradiction between life and faith was met in a variety of ways, notably by the faith in group-retribution, the unit being either the family, which survived through the generations, or the nation, whose days were innumerable. Hence, irrespective of their personal fortunes, men could retain their faith that God's justice prevails and could wait for the process to work itself out in human history. The Hebraic faith felt no compulsion to adopt the idea of another life beyond the grave.

The Biblical emphasis upon this-worldly religion was probably strengthened by what Moses and his successors saw of the Egyptian cult of the dead, which was marked by the vast tombs called the pyramids, built by slave labor over centuries, and by elaborate rituals connected with the dead, which absorbed so much of the energies of the living. The other great cultural center of the Middle East, Babylonia, spawned countless magical rites practised by necromancers and witches, in which the Biblical teachers rightly saw an affront to the universal sway of the Living God. Hence Biblical law imposed heavy penalties upon the practice of any such magical arts. Only in the folk-religion of the masses, for whom superstition and fear were not eradicated, did these practices continue to flourish, as indeed they do in our age. The individual's all-absorbing concern with his own personal lot did not yield even to the teaching of official religion.

Nonetheless, the Biblical emphasis upon life and judgment in this world was so powerful that it was never submerged, even when the faith in an after-life developed. The passionate faith of the Prophets in a world in which justice would triumph because God governed history was originally held only by them and a small group of believers. When, as the Prophets had foretold, the two states of Israel and Judah were destroyed in spite of their ostensible prosperity, the people saw in it a vindication of the truth of the prophetic message. Thus, centuries after their lifetimes, the Hebrew Prophets won a total victory, as their faith in the one Living God became the heritage of the entire people. Actually, the Prophets became the instruments for national survival, for only those exiles who accepted the prophetic teachings were able to resist the blandishments of Babylonian assimilation and the lure of resplendent paganism. Only they retained their identity who scorned the multiple deities of the Babylonian pantheon housed in the magnificent temples and shrines of the world capital, and held fast to their faith in the Living God of Israel, whose sanctuary lay in ruins.

This faith in the One God who is the arbiter of history was dramatically re-enforced a few decades later. Cyrus, King of Persia and heir to the Babylonian empire, gave permission to those who so wished to return to Jerusalem and there re-establish an autonomous religious and cultural community. Here was living proof that God was the Redeemer as well as the Judge of men and nations.

The new community was indeed born, and a new Temple filled the site of the old edifice, but the Second Commonwealth was a far cry from the glorious visions of the Prophets, who had foretold the restoration of Israel to universal dignity and honor, with all nations recognizing Jerusalem as the spiritual capital of the world, from which God's law would go forth. Instead, reality disclosed a small, struggling settlement, beset by hostile neighbors, torn by internal strife, under the heel of a succession of foreign rulers, Persian, Greek, Ptolemaic, Seleucide, and, finally and most decisively, Roman. Even the brief and fitful interlude of independence, which lasted less than eighty years under the Maccabees and their descendants, proved scarcely better than the rule of the foreign tyrants.

Yet even in "this day of small things," as the Prophet described the era, faith in the God of righteousness did not waver—it developed a new form of expression. To be sure, it became difficult to hold fast to the Prophets' conviction that the Kingdom of God would emerge out of the present order through the normal processes of history. It seemed obvious that the powers of men were too weak and limited to achieve the redemption of Israel, let alone the regeneration of the world. A far more radical transformation was needed—only a supernatural cataclysm could destroy the wicked now so securely entrenched, and redeem the righteous, now being ground under the heel of the oppressor. The prophetic faith in the triumph of righteousness was driven underground and emerged in a new guise, as an Apocalyptic vision, a revelation intended only for the chosen few, who would know when the Divine judgment would be made manifest. On that day, the world would be shaken to its foundations by the direct and miraculous intervention of God, and the normal order of existence would pass away. A series of catastrophes would come upon the earth, and armies of celestial beings would appear to wage the war against the hosts of evil and destroy them.

During the days of the First Temple, several of the Prophets, notably Isaiah, Micah, and Jeremiah, had conceived of the advent of the Kingdom of God through the instrumentality of a descendant of the Davidic line, who would be the Lord's Messiah, "the anointed," the righteous King.

> And there shall come forth a shoot out of the stock of Jesse,
> And a twig shall grow forth out of his roots.
> The spirit of the Lord shall rest upon him,
> The spirit of wisdom and understanding,
> The spirit of counsel and might,
> The spirit of knowledge and the fear of the Lord.
>
> (*Isa.* 11:1-2)

But in the face of the towering evils of the world, it was no longer easy to believe that a natural figure, a mere human being, could conquer the enemies of Israel and of the righteous. The Messiah was accordingly transformed by the Apocalyptic writers into a supernatural being, endowed with boundless powers. Often he was conceived of as immortal, sitting at the right hand of God. The vision of the Messiah and of his redemptive acts naturally differed with each visionary. The most recent addition to the Apocalyptic literature of the time has come from the Dead Sea sectarians.

Thus the prophetic faith in the Messianic era survived the rigors of an evil age, though transformed into a supernatural key. But another element in human nature now clamored for expression— men's concern with their own personal destiny, and not merely as cells in the larger organism of family, clan, or nation. Here again the earlier Biblical conception of group-solidarity was not surrendered; it was supplemented by a newly articulated interest in the lot of the individual, in his success or failure, his happiness or misery. When, however, the individual becomes the measure of life, the problem of evil becomes infinitely more acute, as we have seen. An eternal people can afford to wait patiently for the process of retribution, however long-drawn-out it may be in human terms, because its life span is unlimited, but an individual is short-lived and his days cannot be retraced. How can the wicked be permitted to prosper and the righteous to suffer on earth and both meet the same fate? This agonizing issue is the theme of the book of *Job*. The profound poet-thinker who is its author found his exalted answer in the acceptance of life and in the insight that the moral order in the universe, like its counterpart, the natural order, has a pattern and meaning though in part incomprehensible to man. He also derived comfort from the conviction that God cares for His creatures, and is not indifferent to man's hopes and fears.

Another thinker of the same period, the skeptical Koheleth, who had also noted the absence of retribution in the world, drew the conclusion that the mystery was entirely insoluble by man and that the only reasonable course in an uncertain and hazardous universe lies in the enjoyment of life, as far as lies within man's power.

As recent research has demonstrated, the Biblical Wisdom writers, who included the author of *Job* and *Koheleth*, were representative of the upper classes of society, the high priestly families, the rich merchants, the landed gentry, and the government officials. Not being acute sufferers under the social and economic *status quo* of their age, they found existence here and now quite tolerable, whatever their philosophic and religious doubts might be. Hence both *Job* and *Koheleth*, like the later Sadducees, who emanated from the same circles, felt no overpowering compulsion to seek a new solution to the problem of suffering, which was making rapid headway among the lower and middle classes of the people.

Ground by poverty and want, exploited by foreign and domestic masters, and subject to all the ills of human flesh, the masses were conscious of their unjust sufferings. Yet God was good as well as all-powerful—where was His mighty hand? The philosophic profundity of *Job* and the skeptical resignation of *Koheleth* were not for them—their souls cried out for a concrete and positive answer, above all, a personal answer.

Out of their anguish of spirit was born the faith that this imperfect world could not be all; that there was another world of truth, where the evils of this vale of iniquity would be righted, the just would be rewarded, and the wicked punished. Judgment after death naturally presupposed that the dead would arise from their graves to stand before the judgment seat of God. Hence, faith in the resurrection of the dead became a cardinal belief both in Rabbinic Judaism and in classic Christianity.

Obviously, this belief that human life did not end in death or even in a shadowy, undifferentiated existence in *Sheol* served admirably to vindicate God's justice. But it did more. It answered the deeply rooted human desire for personal immortality, and mitigated the universal horror of annihilation. The comfortably ensconced Sadducees might scoff and deny this faith in the world to come and in divine judgment in the hereafter. For the masses of the people, the Last Judgment became a passionate conviction, and failure to believe in it stamped one as a heretic.

It has been suggested by some scholars, though denied by others, that foreign influences, like that of Persian Mazdaism, played their part in the emergence of this doctrine of the after-life in Judaism and Christianity. Be this as it may, it is clear that it responded to the deepest aspirations of the people and therefore became basic. Traditional religion now sought warrant for the faith in the hereafter by homiletic interpretations of various phrases in the Five Books of Moses and in a few passages in *Isaiah* (chap. 26), *Psalms* (chap. 17), and *Daniel* (chap. 12), but the real authority of the doctrine derived from passionately felt inner needs of men. Thus the second-century Hebrew Wisdom writer, Joshua Ben Sira, had taught:

> Be exceedingly humble in spirit,
> For man's hope is but worms.

> (7:17)

His Pharisaic grandson rendered the verse into Greek:

> Humble thy soul greatly,
> For the punishment of the ungodly is fire and worms!

Similarly, by the change of one letter, the Greek translator of the Forty-eighth Psalm renders the closing Hebrew phrase "He will lead us eternally" to read "He will bring us to immortality."

The doctrine of judgment after death now developed into a dual conception regarding the realm of the blessed called Paradise, the Garden of Eden, or Heaven, and the land of the doomed, called Gehenna or Hell. By its very nature, this doctrine of the resurrection and the after-life could not be articulated in a single, clear-cut, universally accepted form, though theologians were not deterred from attempting even this task! By and large, this faith continued to be interpreted by each human being in terms of his own insights and limitations, so that it might express the hopes and fears which lived in him.

A history or even an analysis of the various and often contradictory forms that the teaching of an after-life took on in succeeding centuries is not germane to our purpose. Perhaps because the Resurrection of the Savior is the cornerstone of the Christian drama of salvation, the dogma received its greatest elaboration in the works of the Church Fathers and the medieval Christian scholastics and theologians. The classic Christian doctrine of the hereafter found expression in Dante's *Divine Comedy*, with its three sections devoted to a vivid delineation of *Paradise, Purgatory,* and *Hell*.

In traditional Judaism, the same tendency made itself manifest, particularly in the folk-religion, which elaborated every detail of the resurrection, the last judgment, the future bliss of the righteous, and the torments of the wicked. The doctrine of the resurrection of the dead was accepted as basic and was given expression in the Prayer Book, where God is praised as *mehayyeh hametim*, "He who gives life to the dead." Nevertheless, it never succeeded in dislodging the this-worldly emphasis of the earlier Biblical religion. Even the Hebrew phrase quoted above was general enough to permit a variety of interpretations. Nor could the virtual absence of any expression of faith in a judgment after death in the text of the Bible be entirely ignored.

From the Bible and from Rabbinic literature, traditional Judaism now constructed a dual conception of the future destiny of man. The present world-order would be succeeded by "the days of the Messiah," when the injustices now rampant would be righted, and Israel, at present degraded and in exile, would be restored to its true dignity. In the words of the great Talmudic sage, Samuel, "The only difference between 'this world' and 'the days of the Messiah' is that the oppression of empires will cease" (*Berakoth* 34b). Thus the Biblical faith in God in history, expressed in the prophetic teaching of "the Day of the Lord" and "the End of Days," remained alive.

Following the period of "the days of the Messiah" there would be ushered in "the world to come," when the dead would be resurrected, and each man would be judged according to his deeds, winning his due reward or punishment. Yet even here the idea of perpetual torment was ruled out, except for total, unmitigated sinners, and of these Jewish tradition found less than a handful.

Even the generally severe school of the Rabbinic teacher Shammai held that the average sinners would suffer for a twelve-month period in Gehenna, at the end of which they would have been purged of their sins. The disciples of the gentler Hillel declared that they would enter Paradise at once because of the merits of their ancestors and of their children! (*Tos. Sanh.* 13:3; *Rosh Hashanah* 16b) On the other hand, another sage, Resh Lakish, denied the very existence of either Paradise or Hell, and declared that the final judgment would be executed by God's bringing forth the sun from its case, so that its rays would consume the wicked and bring healing to the righteous (*Abodah Zarah* 3b).

A healthy dose of humble ignorance on the entire question of life after death was prescribed in the Talmud, although, to be sure, it was rarely followed: "Said Rabbi Johanan, All the prophecies in Scripture about the future refer to 'the days of the Messiah.' As for

'the world to come,' 'no eye has seen it, except Thine, O God' "
(*Isa.* 64:3).

A view that attained to classic importance in the tradition was
expressed by the Babylonian sage, Rab: "In the world to come
there is neither eating nor drinking, no sexual relations and no
worldly occupation, neither hatred nor envy nor competition, but
the righteous sit with crowns upon their heads and enjoy the
radiance of the Divine Presence" (*Ber.* 17a).

Passages such as these made it easy for the medieval philosopher
Maimonides to interpret the future reward of the righteous as
being entirely spiritual in nature, and consisting of the intimate
communion with God, the capacity to contemplate the Divine
essence at close range, a privilege to which the righteous attain
because of the quality of their lives upon earth. Maimonides went
further. For him, the human soul is not innately endowed with
immortality, but it possesses the power to win immortal life if it
displays knowledge and the love of God while on earth (*Commentary on the Mishnah Sanhedrin*, chap. 10). For this aristocratic
conception which limited immortality to the intellectual and moral
elite, Maimonides was severely criticized by some of his successors.
Thus Hasdai Crescas declared that not intellectual distinction, but
a pious and moral life, constituted the passport to immortality.

The inner-Hebraic religious development that we have traced
above finally emerged in the varied forms of the doctrine of the
resurrection and the after-life. As though it were not complicated
enough, it was cross-fertilized by another influence derived from
Greek thought, which had come into early contact with Rabbinic
Judaism and nascent Christianity. Greek thinkers believed that the
soul, totally spiritual and perfect, was immortal, while the body,
being material, was corrupt and perishable. To be sure, the Bible
frequently referred to the "body" and the "soul," but it did not
treat them as opposed or hostile elements of man's nature. In fact,
Biblical poetry frequently placed the two terms in parallelism,
thus making them both together do duty for "personality" or
"being." These Biblical passages were now read in the light of the
Greek conception of the immortality of the soul, which the philosophers found more "rational" than the Hebraic idea of the
resurrection of the body. Thus Maimonides, who was accused of
accepting only the doctrine of the immortality of the soul, wrote

a special *Treatise on Resurrection*, which did not quite convince the doubters. On the threshold of the modern age, Immanuel Kant and Moses Mendelssohn both competed for a philosophical prize with essays on immortality, the Jewish scribe's son from Dessau winning the prize over the sage of Koenigsberg with his *Phaedon*. Following Plato, Mendelssohn argued that the soul is immortal, because it is incorporeal and indivisible. Actually, as a modern philosopher, Morris Raphael Cohen, insisted rather quizzically, the resurrection is a "more reasonable" assumption to make than immortality. For we do have experience of living beings in whom body and soul are united, but none whatever of disembodied souls!

Be this as it may, the idea that man's soul is pure and immortal was accepted in traditional religion. It found expression in the moving prayer which is part of the traditional *Morning Service:*

> "O my God, the soul which Thou gavest me is pure; Thou didst create it, Thou didst form it, Thou didst breathe it into me; Thou guardest it within me; and Thou wilt take it from me, but wilt restore it unto me hereafter. So long as the soul is within me, I will give thanks unto Thee, O Lord my God and God of my fathers, Sovereign of all works, Lord of all souls! Blessed art Thou, O Lord, who restorest souls unto lifeless bodies."

A striking and witty reconciliation of the two concepts of the immortality of the soul and of the resurrection of the body occurs in a Talmudic discussion. At the time of the Last Judgment, the soul can object that it should not be punished, because it is pure and nonmaterial (the argument runs), and therefore cannot be responsible for the sins committed by the person. At the same time, the body can argue that it is guiltless, since of itself it is inert and incapable of will or action. The answer is given in the form of a parable of two beggars, one blind and the other lame, outside the king's garden, who are eager to sample some of its luscious fruit. Since the blind man cannot see, while the lame one cannot walk, the blind man carries the lame one to the tree and together they commit the trespass. When they are arrested by the king's servants, they disclaim any guilt and point to their respective physical disabilities as proof of their innocence. Undeterred by their protestations, the king orders the blind man to place his lame companion on his shoulders, and then sentences them as a unit to atone for their crime. Similarly, at the Last Judgment God will refute the disclaimers entered by the body and the soul, by uniting them once more into a single organism and then pronouncing sentence upon the whole man (*Sanhedrin* 91a, b).

In whatever manner the two concepts are reconciled, both the immortality of the soul and the resurrection of the dead have remained the official doctrine of orthodox religion, both Jewish and Christian. Modernist interpretations, on the other hand, have generally tended to deny the latter and, with varying emphases, to accept only the former.

With this historical excursus as a background, we may ask: What place do these ideas occupy in a religion for the modern mind? Here, above all, dogmatism is unforgivable, whether in accepting or rejecting the principle. For we lack any experience, however partial, that can guide us with regard to the destiny which awaits men after death. Living men, like their ancestors, can only follow the promptings of their hearts and minds.

One *caveat* is in order here, even more relevant than in other aspects of religious belief. *The fact that men desire immortality does not prove the truth of the doctrine, to be sure, but neither does it disprove it.* There *are* some aspirations in men's hearts that are validated by reality. We must guard against the fallacy of the "nothing-but": "God is nothing but a projection of the Father-image and therefore has no real existence." A child believes passionately that he has a father. Undoubtedly, he wishes to believe it, because the idea is a comfort to him. That, however, does not disprove the idea—he may actually have a father! Similarly, the belief in immortality cannot be dismissed as being an illusion, on the ground that it derives from man's desire for survival and his incapacity to face the annihilation of his personality. Two facts are clear. First, the will to believe is overwhelmingly powerful in this area. Second, men of undoubted mental capacity and intellectual integrity have affirmed their faith in the survival of human personality. Thus, the distinguished medical authority, Sir William Osler, declared: "I had rather be wrong with Plato than right with those who deny altogether life after death" (*Science and Immortality*, p. 43), and the list of those who agree with him could be indefinitely extended.

By way of preface to a modern view, we would do well to recall four basic insights of particular value that are to be found in traditional religion. First is the emphasis upon *living the good life for its own sake* without the desire for reward or the fear of punishment. This principle must be fundamental to a living religion, irrespective of one's attitude toward the hereafter. "O Master of the Universe, I neither fear Thy hell nor desire Thy Heaven," the Hasidic saint, Rabbi Levi Yitzchak of Berdichev, was wont to cry out to his Master. "I desire Thee alone."

Equally vital is the Biblical conviction that *this world is the arena where God manifests Himself and where man can fulfill his destiny*. This view is echoed in Rabbinic thought: "Better one hour of repentance and good deeds in this world than all the life of the world to come, but better one hour of joy in the world to come than all the life of this world" (*Abot* 4:17). For the traditional believer, the full *enjoyment of salvation* is reserved for the world to come, but the *achievement of salvation* is a task to be accomplished in this world. If the ancients, whose understanding of nature's laws and whose control of the natural world were so much inferior to our own, nonetheless gave priority to this world over the next, the implication for modern man is clear. This is the world where man can act to fulfill God's will, and this is the hour that should command his wholehearted concern.

Third, the Bible emphasizes that *children constitute a uniquely satisfying avenue of immortality for men*. "What canst thou give me, seeing that I am childless?" Abraham sorrowfully asks of God, while Rachel petulantly demands of her husband Jacob, "Give me children, for otherwise I die." In discussing the problem of evil we have called attention to the Biblical stress upon the solidarity of the individual with the group, both in time and in space, with his family through time, and with the entire generation of his contemporaries in space. From this truth it follows that whatever other forms of eternal life may or may not be open to man, he does live on, both in his descendants and in the effect that his life and work can exert upon the society of which he is a part. In these very tangible respects, man's immortality is a genuine reality, within his power to achieve.

Finally, there is a bewildering array of conceptions of the afterlife to be found in the religious and literary sources of Western religion, varying from the literal to the figurative, from the grossest and most material to the most spiritual. Yet underlying them all, one principle may be discerned: *the conviction that physical death does not end all for man, that in some sense man's life is indestructible and his spirit is endowed with immortality.*

While the first three attitudes derived from traditional religion may be generally conceded, there will be no such agreement with regard to the last. At this point, each man is free to determine for himself whether he finds it both necessary and possible to believe in personal immortality after death. The decision must obviously be personal, and, by that token, is beyond argument.

Let it be noted that there are deeply moving considerations to buttress this faith in life after death. When men contemplate the boundless suffering of their fellow beings, the wasted opportunities for good, the high gifts that remained unused because of illness or early death, it is no wonder that many are impelled to the conviction that a God, who is wise as well as just, cannot fail to provide somewhere for the tasting of the untasted joys of life, the completion of the uncompleted task, the fulfillment of the unfulfilled promise.

The hope for man's immortality draws support from another aspect of man's nature. All the lower animals are endowed with qualities that find their complete fulfillment in their existence on earth. Their physical attributes and instincts are all admirably suited to their needs, whether it be the ant, the deer, the elephant, or the eagle. None of these endowments are inadequate to the purposes which they serve, nor are any left untapped. All that the creature needs, he has; all that he has, he uses. Man, too, possesses a physical constitution with a basic instinctual heritage, geared to life on the animal level here and now. But man is endowed also with a "plus," for which terms like "spirit" and "soul" come to mind. Whether we employ these words or not, it is undeniable that man possesses aspirations and hopes beyond the limitations of time and space by which he is physically bound. The yearning for the ideal, the panting after the infinite, the perpetual dissatisfaction with the world as it is because of a vision of the world as it can be—are all these specifically human aspects of man's personality destined to remain unfulfilled and finally doomed to extinction?

Considerations such as these re-enforce men's will to believe that loved ones will not be permanently separated, that beauty and goodness are not fated for oblivion. It is obvious that these are promptings of hope, with no conclusive evidence on their behalf, but neither is there any demonstration to the contrary. As James Martineau observed: "We do not believe in immortality because we have proved it, but we forever try to prove it, because we believe it."

It cannot be denied that untold numbers of men and women derive great comfort from their deep faith in immortality. It is equally clear that, particularly in the modern world, so rich in potentialities for realizing man's goals in substantial measure, men are less likely to see in the inadequacies of the present world an argument for faith in the world to come. Hence, the religious believer today finds it easier than did his medieval precursor to hark back to the prophetic faith that Divine justice operates here and now, that the law of consequence penetrates every area of life upon earth and is manifest in every nook and cranny of man's nature. It can scarcely be doubted that in our age faith in the world to come, even for those who accept the doctrine, has become less important than it was in earlier eras.

The belief in immortality remains an area where each individual must confront the wonder of existence for himself, and make peace on his own terms with the mystery of death. He may feel impelled to spell out in detail his hopes and fears, and draw upon the descriptions of the world-to-come to be found in many pages of religious literature. We believe that a man will be wiser to accept the limitations of existence and knowledge that are basic to the human situation, and not seek to peer behind the veil. What form man's deathlessness may take in another realm of being we cannot discover, because it lies beyond the range of our earthly experience. To borrow an analogy from Maimonides, for us to conceive of life after death, an existence necessarily free from physical traits and attributes, is as impossible as for a color-blind person to grasp the colors of a sunset.

The most helpful course for us to adopt is to set forth our own deepest convictions on this issue as one man's view. We believe that the spirit of man is too miraculous to perish utterly. At a thousand points, man has conquered nature; it cannot be that nature can destroy man completely. Moreover, just as man's spirit knows no bounds of space, but is able, through his intelligence, to embrace worlds seen and unseen, so his spirit may well transcend the limits of time, especially since the scientists remind us that time and space are a single continuum. Man's soul, "a portion of God on high," would thus, like its Source, be endowed with the attribute of eternity as well as of infinity. Since man is fashioned in the image of God, he must partake in some degree of this aspect of the Divine. The facet in man's nature which is deathless, the vital spark, the breath of life, we call the soul.

On the issue of man's immortality, humility is the basic virtue and dogmatism the cardinal sin. That man lives on, we may affirm; how he lives on, we cannot know. Koheleth, the Biblical thinker, has told us all we know or need to know: "The dust returns to the earth as it was, and the spirit returns to God who gave it."

MAN AND GOD

CHAPTER XVI

Prayer—Man Speaks to God

As we have had occasion to note more than once, reason and faith are distinct yet mutually dependent activities of the human spirit. Each has its contribution to make to religion, which seeks the allegiance of the mind and the heart. The philosopher may postulate an Absolute Being as a logical necessity; religion affirms the presence of God as a heartfelt certainty, a Being "near unto all who call upon Him in truth." It is this sense of God's intimate concern for His creatures and man's capacity to establish a relationship with His maker which are the essence of the religious approach to God, as distinct from that of the philosopher.

The forms of this communion have differed with the time, the tradition, and the individual, but the sense of this encounter with the Divine has remained constant. In ancient religion, the principal form of this communion was sacrifice, where the worshipper and his god partook of the same food and thus became one. Sacrifice, both animal and human, no longer characterizes modern religion, largely because the Prophets spiritualized men's understanding of God.

At the farthest possible remove from the concrete, material communion of sacrifice is the experience of the mystic. Mystics of all faiths and every age have reported the achievement of an exalted intimacy with God beyond the power of language to describe. A thousand changes have been rung on the Psalmist's ecstasy:

Whom else have I in heaven?
And with thee I desire nothing upon earth.

(*Psalm* 73:25)

But the mystic's encounter remains an ineffable experience, which he cannot describe except by figures of speech that afford no more than tantalizing echoes of soundless melodies. The mystic insists that his experience is both incommunicable and beyond rational analysis; in fact, he regards its ineffability as its great virtue. Be that as it may, it is clear that for the generality of mankind, the mystic vision remains unattainable.

Nonetheless, religion has always insisted that the highway to God is open to every man. He is free to walk the twin paths of worship and of action. Action expresses itself through ritual and through the ethical life; worship, pre-eminently through prayer.

In spite of the much touted reports of the recent revival of religion, the dimensions of the crisis confronting modern religion are highlighted by the decline of prayer as a human experience today; for prayer is the touchstone of living religion. In the words of William James: "Religion is nothing if it be not the vital act by which the entire mind seeks to save itself by clinging to the principle from which it draws its life. This act is prayer, by which term I understand no vain exercise of words, no mere repetition of certain sacred formulae, but the very movement itself of the soul, putting itself in a personal relation of contact with the mysterious power—of which it feels the presence—it may be even before it has a name by which to call it. Wherever this interior prayer is lacking, there is no religion; wherever, on the other hand, this prayer rises and stirs the soul, even in the absence of forms and doctrines, we have living religion."

If we apply this test, we discover that there is little evidence of vital prayer even in the lives of "religious" men and women today. Formerly, daily prayers were part of the regimen of life, for Christians as well as for Jews. Every meal was accompanied by a blessing, as was every important experience of life. Today, prayer has all but disappeared from the personal lives of most people. Where prayer has survived, it is largely public communal worship, and the emphasis is more on rapport with one's fellows than communion with one's Maker.

Untold numbers of men and women who believe in God feel no

need for prayer. They share the sentiment of Voltaire, who was walking along a street with a friend, when a religious procession passed by. To his friend's astonishment, the skeptical philosopher doffed his hat in token of reverence. "M. Voltaire," asked his friend, "have you become a religious believer?" "My dear friend," answered Voltaire, "when God and I pass each other, we salute, but we do not speak."

Even many of those who read their prayers "religiously" do not really pray. For very laudable reasons, they go through the forms of worship, but they rarely undergo the experience of communion with God. If prayer is the heart of religion, the weakness of prayer in our day is a symptom of a major malady, which must be overcome if religion is to be truly alive.

What is prayer? Instead of turning to the analyses of theologians or the descriptions of psychologists of religion, we may take our point of departure from the Bible. The first prayer recorded in Scripture is that of the Patriarch Jacob at Beth-el. When, as a lad, Jacob left his father's home to go toward an unknown destiny, he found himself at nightfall in an open field. With a stone as a pillow, he fell asleep, and in a dream saw a ladder stretching from earth to heaven, with angels ascending and descending upon it. When he arose, Jacob cried out: "How awesome is this place! This is surely the house of God, and this is the gate of heaven." Jacob then proceeded to take a vow of loyalty to God.

We may see in the ancient Biblical incident a symbolic representation of the truth that prayer is a ladder reaching from earth to heaven, from man to God. As there are lower and higher rungs on the ladder, so there are various levels of prayer. He who wishes to revive or introduce the practice of prayer in his life quickly discovers that ascending the first rung is the basic act, and, paradoxically enough, it is the most difficult. As the French proverb puts it, *c'est le premier pas qui coûte*. The problem is twofold. First is the ingrained human tendency to be governed by habit, by patterns of customary behavior, even by inertia, so that every new line of action is painful because it is strange. Second, and even more crucial, the lowest rung on the ladder consists of prayers of petition, in which requests are put to God. This concept of prayer, which proves the major stumbling block for many modern men and women, is rooted in the etymology of the term itself. The

English word "prayer" is derived from the Latin verb *precare*, "beg, entreat," exactly like the German *Gebet*. There are many other factors, as we shall see, that contribute to the decline of prayer; all must be reckoned with, but it is best to deal with first things first.

Yet before we turn to this issue, it should be pointed out that there is more to prayer than petition; the ladder has more than one rung. Even if all the possible doubts and difficulties concerning prayers of petition were sustained, there would be many other values and functions left in prayer. The Hebrew verb "to pray" is derived probably from a root meaning "to judge," and its original meaning may therefore be "to examine or judge oneself." It is true that etymology is a difficult and uncertain science, and words change in meaning during their history. Yet this suggested original significance of the Hebrew word should prevent too narrow a view of the role of prayer.

The difficult question, which theologians call the problem of the efficacy of prayer, actually includes a whole complex of issues. Does man have a right to intrude his own petty desires and limited objectives upon the will of the Almighty? Does the infinite wisdom of God stand in need of the instruction of man? What about the countless instances where men have prayed and have not been answered? None of these problems are new. They have all been recognized ever since men applied their intelligence to religion.

In modern times, with the advance of scientific discovery, the belief in the efficacy of prayer has been confronted by even graver difficulties. As we have had occasion to note in several connections, science continues to reveal in increasing measure the *reign of law in the universe*, disclosing a cosmic order that is marked by a seemingly inevitable and unbreakable chain of cause and effect, underlying all phenomena and events. How can mere words and music, however sincerely or passionately expressed, interfere with the majestic and inviolable laws of the universe? In the words of Omar Khayyam:

> The Moving Finger writes, and, having writ,
> Moves on; nor all your Piety nor Wit
> Shall lure it back to cancel half a Line,
> Nor all your Tears wash out a Word of it.

On the other hand, *science has reduced the dimensions of man* in a world of vast immensity, or rather, in a universe of untold worlds beyond the mind of man to grasp. To be sure, the ancients recognized the pettiness of man in the presence of his Maker. But for them, man was the Divinely appointed lord of the earth, and the earth was the center of the universe, with the sun, moon, and stars created to serve and illuminate it. Today science declares that the earth is one of the smaller planets in our solar system, which is itself one of many. Can man, a mere speck upon this tiny ball, be of concern to the Architect of a limitless universe? Is it not blindness and conceit for man to expect to be heard, let alone to be answered, when he prays?

In the face of so many objections, it is no wonder that so many modern men and women have denied the value of prayer and decided that prayer is at worst a useless, self-deluding exercise, and at best a form of autosuggestion. The basic difficulty confronting faith in the efficacy of prayer has been the conception of the world as governed by immutable law, not to be interfered with by God or man.

The attentive reader will note that we have already dealt with several of these issues in connection with our discussion of such subjects as God in the world and the scientific challenge, the role of man in the universe and the problem of free will versus determinism. It is the nature of an organic body of thought that its elements recur at many points. The reader may wish to review the more extended analysis of these themes above. Here a more cursory treatment must suffice.

As we have seen, it is true that science is constantly revealing patterns of harmony and order in the world. Each new scientific discovery extends the borders of the kingdom of cosmos by annexing to it part of the territory of chaos. Areas of nature or of human experience which previously seemed to be marked by chance and lawlessness are revealed as plan and pattern by the genius of a Darwin or a Mendeleieff in biology, of a Freud in psychology, and of an Einstein in the physical universe. The glory of these achievements of man's intellect offers valid cause for rejoicing and pride. It is important, however, to distinguish between the interpretation that scientists give to their discoveries, which naturally reflect all their personal weaknesses and prejudices, and the objective body of scientific fact. The materialistic view of reality popularized in the nineteenth century has given way in our century to a deeper insight. There is, of course, no unanimity of view among scientists, as among other men, with regard to the implications to be drawn from the admittedly tentative conclusions of science. But more and more thinkers reject the view that "a universe which issues in mind is itself mindless, that a world creative of personality is itself only a dust-storm or a black void."

Now, the distinguishing mark of personality is that it is a blend of law and freedom. Whatever is alive in the world is naturally and inevitably the result of anterior factors, and is to that degree determined, but not altogether. There is always an area of freedom where the living creature is master of his fate, free to make his choice between alternatives, able to make or mar his destiny.

If this is true of all living things, it is even more characteristic of the one being who, as far as we know, represents the highest flowering of personality in the world—man. Man is the result of factors outside of himself, but he is not merely a product of heredity and environment; he is also their fashioner. Man is a creature, but also a creator. This double aspect of his nature the Talmud expresses in the great phrase that man is God's partner in the work of creation. Man, it is true, cannot go it alone, but neither is he a passive, helpless, inert mass of clay. Endowed with the gifts of consciousness and reason, man is fashioned, as the matchless Biblical phrase has it, "in the image of God."

In a universe where man's nature is compounded both of law and of freedom, God, too, is revealed as possessing two attributes. Rabbinic thought graphically described them as the two thrones of the Holy One, the seat of judgment and the seat of mercy, both of which He occupies. Judgment is causation, inexorable and inevitable, but mercy is the opportunity to escape the inexorable and just consequences of the past, a chance to break the iron circle of causality and begin afresh.

We are not seeking to prove that prayers are "answered." In the very nature of things, that is not susceptible of demonstration. Our purpose has been to show that the principle of a law-abiding world—not a "cast-iron" world—does not disprove it either.

Through the ages the experience of millions of men and women has been strong in echoing the Psalmist's conviction: "The Lord has heard my petition; the Lord accepteth my prayer" (*Ps.* 6:10). The voice of faith has insisted that however long the delay and trying the interval, God's answer is forthcoming: "Weeping may tarry for the night, but joy cometh in the morning" (*Ps.* 30:6). Faith proclaims that prayers are answered; reason, if it be truly reasonable and not the superstition of scientists, cannot disprove the promptings of faith.

Belief in the efficacy of prayer encounters another obstacle that claims to be derived from the scientific view of the world. The universe is too vast and man too petty, the argument runs, for the Creator to be concerned with the hopes and fears, the desires and the worries, of a mere speck of dust, an atom of being that we call an individual. That there is a Providence governing the *collective affairs* of mankind at work in the history of the race (*hashgahah kelalit*), is not so difficult to believe. It was the Prophets of Israel who first proclaimed the teaching of God in history and formulated the law of righteousness, working its way out in the world and determining the lot of nations and civilizations. But that there is a God-given destiny that shapes our ends *as individuals*, a Providence concerned with each separate human soul (*hashgahah peratit*), men's minds find difficult, if not impossible, to accept.

Now, paradoxically enough, this difficulty that many moderns experience with prayer is due to an immature conception of God, for once again it is based on an anthropomorphic view of the Deity. The problem arises because we conceive of God in essentially human terms, and so we imagine that His knowledge follows the same pattern as human knowledge. We know that our human minds can grasp only a limited number of details simultaneously; when we increase the number of objects involved, we become hopelessly lost. It is on the basis of this human experience that we decide that God, too, can deal with *generalities*, which are few in number, but cannot grasp a vast number of *particulars*. We fail to recognize that God's knowledge must differ from man's capacity in essence and not merely in degree. It is not merely that He can "know" many more individualities than we can; the entire nature of His knowledge is of another dimension, to which our human experience offers no parallel. To attribute to God the spiritual limitations characteristic of man is only a step removed from that which Maimonides regarded as the basic heresy—assigning human form to the Deity.

In sum, God's knowledge of His world and love of His creatures are of a character totally different from our own and therefore beyond our capacity to grasp fully. Nonetheless, an analogy drawn from human experience, suggested by Dr. Harry Emerson Fosdick, can prove helpful. If an untutored layman wanders into a great engineering plant, where all kinds of machines are operating, with bolts moving, wheels turning, and belts whirring, he sees all the moving parts as one great blur, lacking any individuality. Let an engineer walk into the plant, however, and every bolt and knob, every wheel and belt, has its own character and individual role, because his technical knowledge is infinitely greater. Suppose an illiterate comes into a library; the shelves upon shelves of books that his eyes encounter are for him merely a mass of undifferentiated printed matter. But let a student walk into the same library, and each volume on the shelf has its own vivid personality for him. The greater the scholar, the deeper is his degree of knowledge, and the greater the understanding of the individual elements in the library.

Now, God's knowledge is infinitely deeper than that of the wisest of men. It is a qualitative, not merely a quantitative difference. He knows our past, our present, and our future, and each one of us stands out distinct and unique in God's knowledge and God's love. There is a profound truth imbedded in the fact that in Hebrew the root *yada* means "to love" as well as "to know." "The Lord knoweth the way of the righteous," the Psalmist affirms with the certainty of faith. A dictator, being fashioned of human clay, is unconcerned with individuals; he liquidates and crushes men by the thousands. But for the King of the Universe, every human being is precious: "Beloved is man that he was created in God's image; especial love was bestowed upon him, in that he knows that he is created in God's image" (*Abot* 3:18). To rule out God's knowledge of His children because of the limitations of the human mind is, once again, to commit the blasphemy of making God over in man's image!

The heart of the religious view of life lies in the sanctity of the individual, the dignity and significance of man, of every man, not merely in the mass, but also in the particular. "He who saves a single human life is as though he saved an entire world, and he who destroys a single human life is as though he destroyed an entire world" (*Sanhedrin* 4:5). Religion insists that God cannot be less than man. It declares that each man counts, before God as well as before men.

We have dealt first with "modern" difficulties with prayer, because they are both fundamental and widely felt. But even "the ages of faith" which preceded ours were not naive enough to be free from problems of prayer. Obviously, human experience taught that prayers often went unanswered, that in the very nature of events all prayers could not be answered. An umbrella-seller and an ice cream vendor on a holiday have different prayers for the weather. The Bible tells us that God turned to Abel's gift, but not to the offering of Cain. Religious teachers have emphasized that the prime requisite in worship is sincerity, for any insincere petition is unworthy of attention. But even when a man is sincere, he may find it difficult to concentrate his entire personality upon his goal, to focus completely upon the words which he is uttering, especially if he is following a fixed ritual or order of prayer. Hence, religion has always sought to stimulate "inwardness of purpose," which is expressed by the Hebrew term "*kavvanah*," and which includes both sincerity and concentration in the performance of prayer or ritual.

Absence of sincerity in the worshipper is not the only reason why prayers are unanswered. For one thing, God's answer may be given later. Man is an impatient creature, but God's own purposes have their own time and place. "I prayed to God, but He did not answer my plea," a worshipper complained. "O yes, He did," was the reply. "God's answer was 'No!'" Even the permanent denial of man's petition is often evidence of God's *hesed*, His steadfast love, and is intended for his good. It is not a mark of love for a parent to grant every desire of his child. Modern parents may have expunged the word "no" from their vocabulary; God is too wise and too good for that. The rabbis point out that in the moving prayer which Solomon delivered at the dedication of the Temple in Jerusalem, he asked God to grant the Israelite's prayer only *if it be for his good*, because his faith in God would survive even a rejection. In the case of the heathen, however, whose belief in

God is presumably weak and immature, Solomon asked that his petition be granted, *whatever he asks,* for the sake of God's glory (*1 Kings* 8:38–43; *Tanhuma, ed. Buber, Toledot* 14).

Moreover, to pray concerning what is past is vain. As the Mishnah (*Ber.* 9:3) points out, when a woman has already conceived, it is too late to pray for a male child. A car driver speeding into another vehicle may pray in that awesome moment of crisis, "O God, save me!" But his prayer could not be answered without suspending the laws of gravitation operating in the world and causing widespread chaos and catastrophe. God is no capricious potentate, violating the laws that He himself has promulgated. In Einstein's words, God does not play dice with the universe.

In spite of problems such as these, it remains true that traditional religion has always maintained the efficacy of prayer. Can this belief be retained by modern men? It will be helpful to note at the outset that men have always differed on the processes by which prayers are answered. Some have accepted a more extensive, others a more restricted, view of the power of prayer.

It is universally recognized that prayer has a strong *psychological effect* upon the personality of the worshipper. It need not be labored that prayer brings release to pent-up emotions and creates peace of the spirit by stimulating hope for the best and inducing resignation in the face of the inevitable.

The psychological value of prayer, however, goes beyond these functions of self-expression and relief. If the petition is concerned with the worshipper himself, and *is sincere,* its very expression sets its fulfillment into motion. The irascible father who prays for a better temper in dealing with his children, the untutored youth who prays for wisdom, if the prayer issues from the depths of the soul, will be answered. For the father will be inspired to forbearance, and the youth will be moved to greater zeal in his studies. Nor is this merely a case of autosuggestion, as is often believed. Whatever we propose to ourselves, looking to an improvement in ourselves, takes place in some measure *beyond* ourselves, because the "self" that emerges at the end of the process is different from and better than the "self" that entered into prayer. Obviously, the prayer that cries out, "O God, make me . . ." receives a more direct answer than the one that begins, "O God, give me . . ." because in the former case all the factors which enter into the situation are ready at hand. "Cause us, O Lord, to lie down in peace, and raise us, O God, unto life," the beautiful evening prayer *Hashkivenu* pleads. When it is recited with true inwardness, the peace and contentment for which it prays are forthcoming.

If the prayer is concerned not with our own fortune, but with the lot of our fellow men, it also may receive its answer, *at least* on the psychological level. But most men will agree that if prayers are answered, it must mean more than psychological release. To take one of the most common instances, when a man prays for the recovery from illness of a dear one, at the very outset he knows that his pain, or his fear, will be reduced; he feels better when he has given voice to his desire and hope in word and music. But that is obviously not enough to satisfy an aching and troubled heart. What men want is what Moses asked for his sister Miriam in a brief and poignant phrase, "O God, heal her, I pray Thee" (*Numbers* 12:13). Are such prayers answered? Here we can only fall back upon the testimony of untold thousands of men and women in every walk of life who testify to the healing power of prayer:

> O Lord my God,
> I cried unto Thee, and Thou didst heal me.
>
> (*Ps.* 30:3)

Are all the countless instances in which prayers for health were followed by healing merely cases of coincidence at best, or instances of self-deception at worst? Somehow the answer is too pat to be convincing. That prayers are efficacious has been the innermost conviction of men in every religion, on every level of culture and intelligence.

Moreover, the effect of prayer on illness, in view of the changed spirit of the scientific temper today, need no longer be airily dismissed as an illusion. We should like to suggest that several insights afforded by contemporary medicine and psychology may supply the basis for a scientifically tenable theory as to the process by which prayers for the ill are answered.

The first factor is derived from modern medicine. Increasingly, research has come to the conclusion that *most illness, if not all, is psychosomatic*, that is to say, disease is a disorder not only of the body (Greek, *soma*), but also of the spirit (Greek, *psyche*).

Hence, in greater or lesser degree, the mind, the will, the personality of the patient play a significant role in creating illness. The old doctrine that the body, being physical, is the province of the physician, and that the soul, if there be a soul, is the concern of the priest, and that each realm is independent of the other, rests upon a dichotomy which is increasingly denied by modern religion and science. This distinction between body and soul, which derives essentially from the Greeks, may be useful for purposes of analysis and investigation, as we may speak of the nervous or of the digestive system. But to place body and soul in opposition to one another is a serious error, since both are part of the same unity. Modern medicine has at length discovered that it is not an organ or a physique that becomes ill, but an entire human being, possessing body and soul. Some diseases, once regarded as strictly physical in origin, like ulcers, are today felt to be largely, if not entirely, psychological in origin. The nonorganic factors as against the physical elements vary in significance with each disease and probably with each patient, but they can never be ignored.

The second factor is derived from modern psychology. We are now aware of *the role that the unconscious plays in illness*. On the conscious level the patient is sincerely trying to get well; subconsciously, he may wish to be ill, either because he craves love or attention that he misses, because he is obsessed by guilt feelings that he wishes to expiate, or because he is overwhelmed by responsibilities or tensions which he cannot bear.

When we juxtapose the *psychosomatic character of illness* and its *frequently subconscious motivation*, it becomes clear that whatever can be done to strengthen the psychological will to health of the patient is not extraneous or even peripheral to his situation. It may be as basic to his recovery as the medical ministrations of the physician. When the patient knows that others are praying for him, that they crave his health and well-being, his own desire to get well is fortified and his recovery is speeded. Thus prayer for the ill may find its answer.

It may be hazardous to go even further and invoke a third principle, which, unlike these first two, is still far from general acceptance. We refer to the phenomenon of *telepathy*, the possibility of transferring thoughts and emotions between two persons without written or oral communication between them. There is an impressive and growing body of evidence designed to prove that certain individuals possess a high degree of sensitivity and can therefore be in rapport with others without words passing between them. This would be one step further than the everyday miracle of language, by which we transmit ideas to one another through spoken words, intangible sound-waves impinging upon the auditory organs, being carried by the nervous system to the brain and being translated into ideas. The extensive experiments of J. B. Rhine and his associates at Duke University in "extra-sensory perception" have by no means won universal assent. But it is difficult to avoid the impression that, stripped of exaggerations and hoaxes, telepathy does represent a reality in human experience.

Should this prove to be the case, we may be in a position to understand how *a prayer for the ill, even when the sufferer is unaware of it, may prove effective.* For even such a prayer would establish contact with the patient by impinging upon his subconscious and thus strengthen the factors making for his recovery. In that event, the prayer is helpful, not merely because the patient feels, "I have family and friends who love me and want me to get well." The process may go deeper. By reaching and overcoming subconscious factors within the patient which are fighting against his recovery, the prayer may thus move him along the path of health.

In their great extremities, men have often turned to holy men and asked them to pray for them. Through the ages, the masses have instinctively felt that the prayers of specially endowed individuals, prophets, saints, and sages, had a unique efficacy. "The Holy One ordains a decree, and the saint can set it aside" (*Shabbat* 63a). This age-old conviction may also find its validation in modern psychology. It is a truism that some individuals possess the power of personality to influence and affect their fellows to a degree far greater than others. This would not be the first instance where the wisdom of the simple folk was ultimately vindicated by the reasoned knowingness of the educated.

Telepathy is still subject to argument, but not the psychosomatic character of disease or the role of the subconscious in illness. Underlying our entire discussion is the conviction that an answer to prayer would represent not a violation of the law of nature, but, on the contrary, a utilization of laws of nature, hitherto ignored or unsuspected. It is like walking into a dark room at night and turning on the electric switch. By that act we are not abrogating natural laws, but are changing the physical conditions under which they operate. When a person is fighting a war against illness, he possesses a certain potential of health. He may accumulate some additional units of strength and of will through the power of prayer, and these may be sufficient to turn the tide and carry him over the obstacles in his path to safety and health.

To be sure, the most perfervid believer in prayer will not claim that prayers for the ill always lead to recovery. But he can counter by pointing out that neither does the medicine of the physician nor the scalpel of the surgeon always yield positive results. Since illness is an affliction of the whole body, recovery is speeded when medicine is used to strengthen the body along with prayer to sustain the soul. In achieving this result, the patient's own prayer is most immediate and therefore most efficacious; a little further removed is the petition of his loved ones, of which he is conscious. Yet it is not ruled out that sincere prayer for his health, offered by others of whom he is unaware, may yet play a part in mobilizing the subconscious forces within him for life and health.

In the past, some faith cults have insisted on denying or minimizing the physical element in illness, and persisted in treating sickness exclusively through prayer and other religious exercises. That this approach is mistaken is clear from the true nature of illness. On the other hand, the modern secular age is just beginning to emerge from the opposite error of underestimating the psychic element in illness, in coping with which prayer is our choicest instrument.

In other areas as well, prayer has a direct effect on reality and not merely on the spirit of the worshipper. Ours is an activistic generation, which everywhere demands activity or at least the illusion of activity, and looks with ill-disguised contempt upon meditation and contemplation. Yet the twentieth century affords at least one striking instance of the power of prayer to affect the destiny of a people. The creation of the State of Israel rests upon centuries of Jewish yearning and praying for Zion, which, the religious spirit insists, were not wasted. Prayer nurtured the will to physical and spiritual revival, and thus built the people that built the State of Israel.

Whenever men pray for peace, freedom, and brotherhood, they are setting in motion forces that bring those ideals nearer to fruition. The prayers on the lips of men help create in their hearts the sentiments that they crave. Thinking of his own blindness, John Milton sang, "They also serve who only stand and wait." The modern saint Rabbi Abraham Isaac Kuk pointed out that in Hebrew "standing" is one of the terms for prayer. They also serve who only pray and wait.

To sum up, we may be, in Milton Steinberg's phrase, either minimalists or maximalists in our view of the efficacy of prayer. We may feel that the value of prayers of petition is purely psychological, bringing relief to the pray-er in his distress, or we may believe that prayers impinge directly upon reality and can change the shape of things to come. Whatever our view, however, it is the teaching of classic religion that God's will is paramount and that He needs no instruction from us as to our needs and desires. Hence the medieval Jewish moralist Bachya ibn Pakuda urged men to pray in this spirit:

> O God, I stand before Thee, knowing all my deficiencies, and overwhelmed by Thy greatness and majesty; But thou hast commanded me to pray to Thee, and hast suffered me to offer homage to Thy exalted Name according to the measure of my knowledge, and to make my humble submission unto Thee. Thou knowest best what is for my good. If I recite my wants, it is not to remind Thee of them, but only so that I may understand better how great is my dependence upon Thee. If, then, I ask Thee for the things that make not for my well-being, it is because I am ignorant; Thy choice is better than mine, and I submit myself to Thine unalterable decrees and Thy supreme direction.

There was nothing primitive in the ancient Greek who prayed:

> "King Zeus, grant us the good, whether we pray for it or not.
> But evil keep from us, though we pray for it."

That the Divine will would be done was recognized by pagans like the Roman satirist Juvenal, but what a cold wind blows from his finely chiselled lines!

Nothing, then: shall we pray for nothing?
Let me suggest—leave the gods alone,

Let them determine what will be the most suitable to help us in our
    lives;
They give, not what is pleasant, but what is right for us.

(Tenth Satire, lines 346–50)

But this sense of the inevitability of events can go hand in hand
with a warm and trusting faith in God's goodness. This is clear
from Rabbi Eliezer's brief prayer for wayfarers:

> Do Thy will in heaven above,
> And grant joy to those who fear Thee here below,
> And do what is good in Thine eyes,
> Blessed art Thou, O Lord, who hearest prayer.

(Berakhot 29b)

Because of the recognition of God's will as paramount, traditional Judaism has created the practice of prefacing many prayers
with the formula yehi ratzon: "May it be God's will that thus-
and-so," etc. One medieval thinker went so far as to declare that
there is only one true prayer: "May it be Thy will that Thy will
be done"—and that all others are variations upon this basic theme.
This may be philosophically true, but the heart of faith has always
sought to express the specific emotion of the moment, the burning
need of the hour, the pain and the hope of the day. In the words of
the medieval poet Solomon Ibn Gabirol:

> At the dawn I seek Thee,
>   Rock and refuge tried,
> In due service speak Thee
>   Morn and eventide.
>
> 'Neath Thy greatness shrinking,
>   Stand I sore afraid,
> All my secret thinking
>   Bare before Thee laid.
>
> Little to Thy glory
>   Heart or tongue can do;
> Small remains the story,
>   Add we spirit too.
>
> Yet since man's praise ringing
>   May seem good to Thee,
> I will praise Thee singing
>   While Thy breath's in me.

The mystical classic, the *Zohar*, points out that when the heavenly gates are closed to prayers couched in words, they remain open to prayers expressed in tears (*Terumah*). Never to have wept and prayed means never to have truly lived, never to have stood as a man before God, as a creature before one's Maker.

We have, at considerable length, discussed the value of prayer as petition, not merely because it is the earliest function to arise among men, but because for many persons it remains the most basic. Here our metaphor of the ladder of prayer breaks down. In a ladder made of metal or wood, one can hardly ascend the upper rungs without using the lower ones. Not so with prayer. A man may find it difficult to believe that petitions are answered. He may feel that he has neither the right, the power, nor the wisdom to obtrude his personal desires on his Maker. The great Hasidic saint Rabbi Levi Yitzchak of Berditchev, who never doubted that prayers were answered, was, as we have seen, the author of the passionate plea:

"O Lord of the Universe, I desire not Thy Heaven,
nor fear Thy Hell; I seek only Thee."

Yet even he who, for whatever reason, does not believe in the efficacy of prayer should not hasten to dismiss prayer from his pattern of life. He is far from having exhausted its contents and functions. Above the rung of petition on the ladder of prayer is one which, incidentally, occupies a far larger position in the liturgies of all the great faiths, the function of *thanksgiving and praise*. It is for this reason that the Book of *Psalms*, eloquent in its praise of God for the glory and the harmony of nature and in its thanks for His manifold blessings, is laid under heavy contribution in all Western religion.

The various liturgies of Judaism and Christianity as well as of Islam are replete with epithets of adoration that tend to impress us at times as repetitious and superfluous. In part, the fulsome language of worship is a reflection of the emotionalism and tendency to hyperbole, characteristic of the ancients. But the question still retains its cogency for modern men: Why all this outpouring of praise? There are cynics who have decried this thanksgiving and praise as abject flattery for an Oriental potentate, unworthy of free men. No judgment could be more superficial and more mistaken.

When men thank God and praise Him, they are doing it not for His sake, but for their own.

The process of rearing children offers an illuminating parallel. Why, in raising a child, do parents train him to say "please" and "thank you"? To be sure, the phrases are conventional and are often pronounced in purely mechanical fashion. But what lies behind the convention and what gave it rise? Underlying the ritual of etiquette stands a profound ethical sentiment. The purpose of these formulas of politeness is to remind the speaker that he has no innate claim upon the service or the benefit conferred upon him, that it represents an undeserved blessing, an unexpected plus, for which gratitude is due.

One of the most characteristic goals of religion is the building of a *discipline of thanksgiving*. To this end, Judaism, for example, has created an all-encompassing system of benedictions which it enjoins upon its devotees. Upon partaking of bread or wine, donning a new garment, inhaling a fragrance, experiencing the majesty of a storm, beholding a beautiful woman or a great sage, man is called upon to pronounce a blessing in praise of the King of the Universe, who has thus manifested His goodness and creative powers. The expression of thanksgiving is essential not to the giver, but to the recipient of the gift, because it makes him conscious of the blessings which he enjoys and heightens his delight in these gifts when they are present.

This discipline of thanksgiving in human life proves at least equally valuable when the blessings are lacking. When need or failure, illness or bereavement, comes to us, we are better equipped to face the challenge if we have been trained not to imagine that we have a claim on life, that the world owes us something. When tragedy comes, it is a perfectly normal reaction to cry out in one's pain: "Why did this happen?" There are those who cannot be shaken out of their bitterness, because they regard tragedy as a personal affront to themselves, who had an unlimited account in the bank of life. "How could it happen to *me?*" is their indignant response to the inevitable. Long-drawn-out persistence in mourning is not always a mark of deep devotion to the dead. It often is a banner of war unfurled against life and its Giver; not melancholy, but high dudgeon, is the reigning emotion.

The discipline of thanksgiving, which the ritual of prayer seeks to foster, endows men with humility and a sense of balance. When this gift for seeing oneself properly in the scheme of things exists, one finds a deeper capacity for the enjoyment of life in prosperity and a greater measure of strength to bear affliction in adversity. But where the living sense of appreciation for our blessings shrivels up and dies, either through mere disuse or through the vulgar notion that anything in life can be bought and paid for, the moment of triumph finds us arrogant or blasé, and the hour of trial, weak and lacking in staying power.

A living religion must be a life-affirming religion. It will not glorify misery as the end and purpose of man, nor does it pretend that suffering is an illusion of the mind. It loves life and honors joy as strongly as it respects truth. But because it constantly recalls the Author of life and the Source of joy, it helps man cultivate courage in the face of tragedy. It is noteworthy that in the presence of death, Judaism ordains that a benediction be pronounced: "Blessed be the righteous Judge." The *Kaddish*, which is recited by mourners, makes no mention of the dead. Instead, it reaffirms the faith of the bereaved in God's justice and in the meaning of life. It helps to lift the individual above an exclusive preoccupation with his personal sorrow by associating him with his people's hopes and with the vision of the Kingdom of God and universal peace. It thus takes the suffering human being and leads him gently but firmly up to the next rung on the ladder of prayer—the enunciation of ideals.

Man cannot live for himself alone. To be sure, the individual's hopes and fears, his joys and sorrows, are a fundamental element of religion because they are basic to human life. Nonetheless, each man's own happiness and well-being depend, in large measure, upon the group of which he is a part, his family, his community, his people, his country, and, as the nuclear bomb grimly reminds us, the entire human race. A prime function of religion, even in its darkest hours, has been to make men conscious of the links binding the individual to his fellows. The group to which he belongs includes not merely his contemporaries, who largely determine his destiny, but also the past generations, who are the source of his being and character, and all the future generations, who are the custodians of his hopes and ideals and the guarantors of his immortality.

Prayer serves admirably to articulate men's ideals, to make them conscious of the goals which they profess, and to strengthen their determination to attain them. A study of the prayers in any of the great liturgies will reveal this emphasis upon fundamental ideals of human conduct and aspiration. Thus the Jewish Prayer Book glorifies the Torah as the revelation of God and as the guide to the good life for Israel and mankind. It stresses the ideals of universal peace. It underscores faith in God's government of the world and in the law of righteousness as basic to the universe.

The function of prayer, as of ritual generally, is to keep ideals such as these perpetually in the forefront of our consciousness. Unlike the multiplication table or a chemical equation which needs to be learned only once, the ideals of conduct, both personal and collective, are perpetually threatened by the inundating tides of selfishness, ignorance, and shortsightedness. Thus, there arises the tragic paradox of human behavior: while men recognize that the laws of righteousness and truth are the foundations of society without which life could not go on, there is the perpetual temptation to ignore them or to bypass them in one's own personal experience—whence comes moral disaster.

The exercise of prayer can keep these ideals vividly alive, because it is enriched by a thousand emotional chords, by well-loved words hallowed by the piety of one's ancestors, by the beauty of music more eloquent than speech, by the warmth of fellowship with one's own folk. This sense of fellowship means far more than a common membership in a congregation, or even comradeship with one's contemporaries. It means a feeling of identification with all the past generations, whose spirit lives in us, and a sense of participation in the destiny of descendants as yet unborn. A prayer that has been hallowed by the piety of the past gains in poignancy and power beyond the strength of abstract logic to defend or define.

The knowledge that the ideals we voice are echoed by our brothers brings us more than a warm emotional glow. It sustains our courage in fighting for their realization and strengthens our faith in their triumph. As the tide of petty concerns and meaningless problems sweeps in upon the strand of our lives, it becomes all the more necessary to find an island of refuge, to build a lighthouse of faith, to keep aglow the great goals of human existence. The prayers in which we enunciate our hopes for country, people, and humanity bring us courage, because we know that we are not alone, on earth as well as in heaven.

Thus, rung by rung, men may ascend the ladder of prayer. From the petitions that express the felt needs of their personal lives, they can rise to the level of thanksgiving and praise for the wonders of life and the glories of God's world. Man is, however, no mere passive recipient of God's bounties. In the great Talmudic phrase already cited, the righteous man must be God's copartner in the work of creation. All may be right in God's world; much remains to be done in man's. The affirmation of ideals is one of the most significant functions of prayer, because through it we rise completely beyond our personal selves and are concerned with the totality of mankind.

True religion cannot end with the individual, but it must begin there. To enunciate high-sounding ideals is not too difficult, but to give them grip on our consciences, we must become aware of our inadequacies and failures. A wise and clear-eyed faith will reject the idea of an innate taint in human nature; it will continue to believe that man can achieve the good. Precisely for this reason it will not underestimate the power of the evil impulse in man. "There is no man that liveth and sinneth not," the Bible affirms more than once, and the Mishnah declares: "Envy, lust, and the desire for honor drive a man out of the world" (*Abot* 4:21).

This recognition of the weaknesses to which man is heir need not develop into despair and surrender. Biblical faith insists that man is the prime agent for his spiritual regeneration. He may throw himself upon the mercy of the Heavenly Court only if he approaches God with heartfelt regret for his shortcomings (*haratah*), with explicit confession of his sins (*viddui*), and with a firm determination to return to the path from which he has strayed (*teshubah*). The avowal of one's sins and the plea for Divine forgiveness constitute a special rung on the ladder of prayer, that of the confession of sins—a unique category of petition which arises from a sense of ideals cherished, yet unattained.

It is noteworthy that "repentance" is expressed in Hebrew not by a word like "penitence" or "penance," both of which carry the note of pain and punishment in the Latin, but by the term *teshubah*, "return." This classical Hebrew word, beloved of the Prophets, speaks eloquently of the Biblical faith that when man has sinned, he can return to God and restore the proper relationship of love and awe toward his Father and King.

Beyond all these rungs on the ladder of prayer is another, which fewer men have reached and which words cannot express: the sense of the Divine Presence, when a man feels that he has not only experienced the manifestations of God in the goodness, truth, and beauty of the world, but has actually stood before the *Shekhinah,* the Divine Presence itself.

The effort to give this emotional experience a basis in reason and to relate man's discrete personality to the unity of mankind and of God is made by Victor Gollancz in these words:

> "God was (or should we say, in the more appropriate language of eternity, is?) undifferentiated. But he perceives differentiation, concreteness, Blake's 'minute particulars,' as supreme values. He therefore creates (splits himself up into, produces as emanations?) these concrete particulars. But by a law of reality, multiplicity involves relation, and a concrete particular, if it is to be a concrete particular, must have being and the potentiality for growth within itself. Each particular, therefore, being and growing, must be in relation with every other particular, also being and growing. Now the particulars, not being God (though being of or from God), cannot feel or know perfectly meanwhile—though they can and do have intimations about it—how the value of individual being and growth, and the value of relation, may be realized. . . .
>
> "*God, desiring this consummation* (which may or may not be involved in the historical process), *can help men understand how to live by the intimations he gives them; but he cannot do more than help; for if he did more he would be derogating from the value of individual being, which is the point, as it were, of the whole business.*" (Italics ours.)

Gollancz was here concerned not with prayer, but with the help that God can give to man. In prayer man seeks to elicit this help from God.

Gollancz has sought to express this sense of union with God through rational analysis. On the other hand, the mystics in all great religions have tried to communicate their vision in metaphors, phrases that are rich in meaning for them, but tantalizingly inadequate for others. That is why mystics generally insist that their vision cannot be transmitted in words and that it does not need to be justified by logic. By and large, they have poured out their longing for unison with God and their ecstasy at the consummation of their goal, in poetry, in music—and in silence.

A Hasidic sage was once reproached with being dilatory in his morning prayers, delaying them beyond the hour prescribed by law. "You are right," he answered, "but I cannot help myself. When I rise in the morning, I begin to recite the opening prayer, *Modeh ani lefanekha*, 'I offer thanks unto Thee, O ever living King, who hast restored my soul to me when I awoke. Great is Thy faithful love.' But no sooner have I pronounced the first three words, 'I offer thanks unto Thee,' than I cannot go on. Who is the 'I,' a creature of clay, imperfect, weak and transitory, and who the 'Thou,' eternal and infinite Lord of the Universe? Yet I am permitted to stand and speak before Thee. As I ponder on this wonder I remain lost in silence all day long."

The sense of awe, Albert Einstein declared, the feeling of reverence before the wonder of the universe, is not only at the root of all scientific investigation, but constitutes the noblest emotion of which man is capable. Four millennia ago, the Patriarch Jacob, to whom the Bible ascribes the first recorded prayer, as we have seen, experienced this same sentiment; "And Jacob awoke from out of his sleep and said: 'Surely the Lord is in this place! This is indeed the house of God, and this is the gate of heaven.'"

To attain this sense of God's presence, however infrequently, is no easy task, no one-time achievement, but a lifelong struggle. It is a goal that must be fought for anew each day, against the countless distractions of life, the petty concerns that impede our concentration, the agonizing hours of doubt and loneliness. But the testimony of those who have reached the highest rung on the ladder of prayer is that it is an indescribably glorious experience.

Now vital religion has never regarded this goal as attainable only by an elect few. We have seen that the great religious traditions have made "inwardness in prayer" a perpetual goal for every worshipper and sought to stimulate his power of concentration by every means at their disposal. Undoubtedly, the problem is complicated by the existence of fixed orders of prayer and elaborate ritual systems, and various expedients have been used to meet it, as will be noted below.

Yet the record is clear—when voiced by a sensitive and attuned spirit, the familiar words of the liturgy have taken on wings and ascended to the throne of the Most High. The modern saint, philosopher, and legist, Rabbi Abraham Isaac Kuk, spoke in complete literalness when he declared: "Prayer is for us, as for all the world, an absolute necessity, and the purest of all joys." To experience this joy even at the rarest intervals is worth intensive preparation.

Yet the problem remains. How can one be spontaneous on schedule, or find in well-worn, familiar words the living sense of an immediate experience, which is the goal of prayer? But we must not be hasty in judgment. The man in the next seat who rushes through his prayers may impress us as engaged purely in mechanical exercise, but the truth is that only God and he know how much they mean to him. To be sure, methods of prayer vary radically even within Christianity, from the highly formal structure of the Catholic, the Eastern Orthodox, and the Episcopal liturgies, through the gamut of the nonliturgical patterns of the Protestant groups, to the complete absence of a fixed service, as among the Quakers. The variety includes elaborate vestments, incense, and tapers, and complex musical traditions at one end of the spectrum, and the shouting, dancing, and ecstatic outbursts of the "primitive" church groups and many revivalists, at the other. Moreover, the traditional Jewish method of prayer is different from that of Occidental Christianity. Prayers are not read for the congregation; each worshipper prays himself, often a law unto himself. The spirit of Jewish prayer has never been described with greater justice and insight than by Maurice Samuel: "Anyone who has *davvened* (prayed) with genuinely pious Jews knows, moreover, that *davvening* may be conducted attentively on two levels. On one, the words of the prayer guide the attention of the worshipper; he follows the meaning and puts his heart into it. On the other level, the mood of the prayer, or rather of the occasion, takes the lead. The individual words are then transcended, their meaning is of no importance, the utterance of the lips is, as it were, a genuflexion that accompanies the devotion of the soul.

"Sometimes you will hear a worshipper gabble off the words: 'BlessedaretheythatdwellinThyhousetheyshallpraiseThee-foreverselah!' He begins with a shout and trails off into a subdued drumfire of amazingly precise syllabification, right to the end of the psalm, coming up now and again with an occasional outburst of intelligibility, or pausing here and there for a roulade. You would swear that the man's mind is not on the words—and it is not. Then you would add that his prayer is perfunctory, and you would more often than not be quite wrong. His soul is in the posture of prayer; he may be in the mood of supplication, of adoration, or of humility; he is using the occasion of the common gesture for a private ex-perience; the familiar syllabic exercise is a kind of hypnotic in-duction. *Davvening* is therefore the periodic contact with the re-ligious emotion rather than the formal act of prayer. And the re-ligious emotion is a daily necessity to the pious Jew."

Nonetheless, Judaism, like every religious tradition, has always labored to make prayer meaningful, and to infuse it with inner sin-cerity. Let not your prayer be a fixed routine, but mercy and supplication before God, the Mishnah teaches (*Abot* 2:13).

The historical experience of Western religion demonstrates that elimination of a formal liturgy is not the solution to the problem. The sects, both Christian and Jewish, that have surrendered fixed forms in prayer are not generally marked by greater fervor and devotion than the more ritualistic groups; quite the contrary. As Israel Abrahams points out, "the fixation of times and seasons and formulae for prayer does tend to reduce the prayer to a mere habit. But," he adds: "What can be done at any time and in any manner is apt to be done at no time and in no manner." The prob-lem can be met only by constant striving after inwardness in prayer. The goal never was easy, and it has become infinitely more difficult for modern man, beset by a hundred doubts and a thou-sand distractions. Yet even for him the ancient injunction stands: "Know before whom thou standest."

Even if the goal of true communion with God is achieved only intermittently, it justifies the discipline, the routine, even the long periods when the heart is silent though the lips move, when God seems absent though His name is repeated time and again. The parable told by the saintly Rabbi of Rizin highlights this truth.

In a small village the only watchmaker died, and because the population was small, no new craftsman came to take his place. As time went on, watches and clocks began to lose and gain time, and no accurate timepieces remained. Some villagers accordingly let their watches run down, while others doggedly kept winding theirs each day, though their accuracy left much to be desired. Some time later, a wandering watchmaker came to town, and all the villagers rushed to bring their timepieces for repair. Those watches that had been kept going were easily set to rights. But those that had been allowed to run down were beyond repair, for their mechanism had rusted. The lesson is clear. The spiritual life must be guarded against merely perfunctory exercise, to be sure, but even the routine performance serves as a necessary discipline and the prelude to great moments of exaltation open to every man.

The rungs of prayer which we have thus far described—petition, thanksgiving, the enunciation of ideals, the confession of sins, and communion with God—are to be found in all high religion, being part of the religious experience of mankind. There is, in addition, one more rung on the ladder of prayer which is central to Judaism, but which is vital in every religion which reveres a Scripture as sacred—the practice of study as a mode of worship.

It is of the essence of religion as conceived of in the Bible that communion with God is accessible not only to the esoteric few, the mystics and saints, but, on the contrary, is obligatory upon all, for "God is near to all who call upon Him in truth." At Sinai, God revealed Himself not to one pious soul, but to an entire people, whose qualities ran the full gamut of human character, from hero to knave, from saint to villain, with all the intermediate levels well represented. The Divine revelation is to be found in the *Torah*, "the Law that Moses commanded," which has "become the inheritance of the Congregation of Jacob." Among all peoples, there are richly endowed individuals who have tasted the joy of exploring the frontiers of truth, the ineffable delights of "thinking God's thoughts after Him," but these have been exceptional men, scholars, scientists, and artists. The Jewish tradition has always taught that through the study of *Torah* the experience is possible for all men, each on his own intellectual level. Indeed, it has insisted that it is a universal obligation as well as a universal privilege. Hence the study of *Torah* is a sacred obligation for everyone.

The traditional concept of *Torah*, of course, is not limited to the Five Books of Moses or even to the entire Bible; it embraces the vast reaches of rabbinic literature, in fact, every manifestation of the religious and ethical genius of Judaism, ancient, medieval, and modern. In striking and refreshing contrast to some popular emphases in our day, Maimonides went further and declared that every branch of science that reveals God's ways in the world is part of *Divine Law*.

In the spirit of Maimonides and with apologies to a dictum of Matthew Arnold, vital religion today would interpret the concept of the study of *Torah* to mean striving to know, understand, and live by the best that has been thought and said by all the religious and ethical teachers of mankind. There can be no meaningful revival of religion in general or of prayer in particular, unless it includes as basic the practice of adult study, a concern with the classical sources of religious insight and inspiration, not merely as an intellectual exercise, but as a means of discovering God's will and thus touching the hem of the garment of the Divine.

When men succeed in mastering the full art of prayer, they will have gained an inestimable resource for living with courage, insight, and joy. In the dark hours of trial and suffering which are inescapable in the human situation, prayer helps men to face life without fear or bitterness, knowing that the light will dawn, whether from within or from without. In the days of well-being and prosperity, when men's eyes tend to be blinded by the sunshine, the practice of prayer gives them insight into reality, the capacity to see the Maker behind the made, the Master in His creation. With the deepened sense of thanksgiving one's joy in life grows, as one experiences each day the miracle of creation. In essence, all man's prayers are an echo of the voice of the youthful Jacob at Beth-el: "Indeed, God is in this place, and I did not know it."

CHAPTER XVII

Ritual—Religion in Action

To surrender deeply held convictions and achieve a religious outlook on life is a difficult and painful task. It demands virtues all too rare today, humility, openmindedness, sensitivity, and above all, the capacity to withstand the pressure of conformity and the tyranny of "fashion" and "modernity." Yet there is something far more gruelling than a change in one's ideas and beliefs—a transformation in one's pattern of action, a transformation in the rites and practices by which one lives. This difference explains in large measure why active missionary activity and revival campaigns have been far more characteristic of Christianity than of Judaism, and more successful. For while it is true that "works" are important in the Christian life, greater stress has been traditionally placed upon "faith," as in the great imperative, "Believe on me and ye shall be saved." In Judaism, on the other hand, the emphasis is reversed. While beliefs are highly significant, the credal aspect is not so central as the elements of ritual observance and ethical conduct. The key term in Judaism is not *emunah*, "faith," which, incidentally, means "trust" and "faithfulness" rather than "belief" in the Bible. The operative word is *mitzvah*, "Divine commandment," which refers always to an act prescribed or forbidden. Traditionally, the acts through which men may express their faith and loyalty to God are divided into two categories—"the commandments between man and God," which may be translated into our modern idiom as "ritual," and "commandments between man and his fellow," which is equivalent to the domain of "ethics."

That ritual bulks large in Judaism is well-known. What has often been ignored is that it is indispensable in every vital religion. Thus it is true that early Christianity, as formulated by Paul, embodied a vigorous protest against the Law of Judaism. Yet, as the Church grew and became established, it developed a ritual pattern and a legal system all its own, which are particularly complex and all-embracing in Catholicism, and are unmistakable in Protestantism as well. As for Islam, its similarity to Judaism is striking, including as it does a Scripture, the *Qoran,* which is the Written Law, and the *Hadith,* or oral tradition, upon which the Islamic pattern of life is built.

In our quest for a living religion for moderns, we must therefore deal with the significance of ritual, which has been vigorously attacked as outmoded and no longer necessary. At the very outset it is necessary to disabuse ourselves of several widely held prejudices in this area.

One of the most universal errors, harking back to the anticlerical rationalists of the eighteenth century, is that ritual is the nefarious invention of cunning and greedy priests, who succeeded in foisting this useless and artificial regimen upon the masses of decent and unsuspecting men. One of the most significant findings of modern anthropology is the universality of ritual, which is to be found in the most sophisticated as well as in the most primitive of societies. A given group may have dispensed with any conception of a Supreme Being; nonetheless, it continues to elaborate ritual patterns, as in Ethical Culture or communism. The pageantry of patriotism, the mumbo-jumbo of fraternal orders, the etiquette of social convention—all these indicate that man is incurably ritualistic. Besides, everyday observation makes it clear that when traditional religious ritual is expelled through the door, irrational practices and vulgar superstitions come in through the window.

In different peoples, various aspects of life may become central and develop as the basic feature of their system of folkways. Thus, among the Todas of India, one economic fact has molded their ritual pattern—the worship of the sacred buffalo. Their religious ritual consists of the preparation of its milk, priests are its dairymen, and its Holy of Holies is the cowbells. Among other groups, various social relations occupy this position of centrality. Thus, among some Australian bushmen, the horror of incest is so all pervasive that virtually all members of the tribe are forbidden in marriage to one another. The sectarian Jewish group called the Karaites, which arose in the eighth century as a revolt against the authority of the Talmud, also elaborated the Biblical prohibitions against incest, until virtually all marriages were ruled out for the members of the community and a widespread reformation of these regulations became imperative.

It is clear that ritual is a basic trait of man as a social animal. The reason is not far to seek. John Dewey has pointed out that an ordinary individual has the power to change the *mores* of his group scarcely more than the talk of an infant may modify the language of the family. Basically, ritual is one of the most powerful and pervasive instrumentalities by which society molds the personality of its members to its own ideals. For whatever "cultural" traits may exist in the lower animals with regard to family relationships, as in the case of the ape, or organized economic patterns, as in the case of the ant, or engineering skills, as in the case of the beaver, all are transmitted in the germ-plasm through the mechanism of instinct. In mankind, virtually none of the skills are instinctually transferred; they must all be learnt through the educational process. Tradition is the basic instrument for the transmission of the skills, ideals, and attitudes of society upon which its survival depends, and ritual is a vivid and powerful means for communicating the tradition.

Before seeking to understand the significance of ritual in religion and the life of man, we must clarify some fundamental terms, often misunderstood. An example is afforded by the word "superstition." In its proper use, the term refers to irrational acts which men continue to perform in order to ward off some of the perils inherent in the uncertainties of life. It is an act of fearful tribute to the countless dangers lurking everywhere and generated by unknown powers. It therefore follows that whether a rite is "superstitious" or "religious" can be determined not by observing the act in question, but by analyzing the motive of the actor. Thus, for most people, the avoidance of the number "13" as "unlucky" is purely a superstition, devoid of any genuine religious content. Yet it is theoretically conceivable that a devout Christian, deeply conscious of the fact that in the New Testament narrative the thirteenth participant in the Last Supper was the one who betrayed Jesus, might seek to avoid thirteen guests at a table, as a mark of reverence for his Savior. Maimonides makes this point explicitly in a comment with regard to the Biblical command to affix a small scroll (*mezuzah*) to the doorposts of one's home, when he says: "He who adds the names of angels to his *mezuzah* is not performing the will of God, but, on the contrary, is violating it, because he has made of it an act of superstition." When a ritual act is performed with the hope that it will directly impinge upon reality and bend it to one's will, it is an act of magic, not of worship, not a religious ritual, but a superstition.

Another popular term in our day is "taboo," which is frequently taken to mean any unreasonable prohibition. Since the term is borrowed from the science of anthropology, it must have a precise descriptive meaning, rather than embody a value-judgment. Thus MacDougall has defined a taboo as a prohibition established by a given society that does not seem to be directed to the safety and the welfare of the individual, but rather to that of the community as a whole.

This definition does not seem to us to deal with several of its most important characteristics. One fundamental aspect of a taboo is the fact that a prohibition is laid down without a reason being *explicitly* set forth. That is why men have leaped to the conclusion that a taboo is an unreasonable prohibition. Actually, a taboo may or may not have a basis in reason. MacDougall suggests, for example, that if one tribe among many were to prohibit the use of tobacco on one day of the week, without assigning any explicit justification, the abstinence from nicotine over a period of years would ultimately redound to the health and welfare of the tribe. Another basic element in taboo, overlooked in MacDougall's definition, is that it requires no legal machinery for its enforcement; it is the weight of society, the pressure of public opinion, that supplies the sanctions.

When these factors are recognized, it becomes clear that the categorical prohibitions which we call taboos are essential to human life, because man's imagination has virtually no limits, and "reason" always finds it easy to justify the fulfillment of any desire, even if it runs counter to the welfare of society or to the long-term interests of the individual himself. Hence, any society which would attempt to set forth the reasons for every injunction which it places upon its members would find that many a provision in its code is unenforced and unenforceable. Only the inculcation of taboos, which categorically forbid certain acts that society finds dangerous or undesirable, can succeed in developing proper standards of conduct and making them "second nature" for the generality of men.

The growing incidence of juvenile delinquency and crime in the mid-twentieth century is, in substantial degree, the result of our failure to create such categorical norms of behavior in the younger generation. There has been of late a vigorous protest against the theory and practice of "progressive education." To the degree that the reaction is justified and not merely reactionary, it derives from the recognition that one cannot permit the "reason" that commends itself to children or their arbitrary will to be the sole or determining factor in the content or the techniques of the educational process. A thinker as progressive as Bertrand Russell has pointed out the importance of establishing categorical habits of right behavior in children early in their lives, so that these patterns may become dominant long before the youngsters are in a position to appreciate the motives which led to these compulsions.

These observations are not intended to argue that every taboo is *ipso facto* desirable or necessary, but to underscore the truth that there is an innate wisdom in the growth of human institutions. The fact that a positive or negative injunction is set forth by religion without an explicit rationale does not *per se* mean that it is unreasonable or useless. One of the important areas of religious philosophy, to which many of the greatest minds devoted their energies, from the days of Philo through the medieval thinkers to Franz Rosenzweig in our century, consists of works that sought to discover "the reasons for the commandments." The modern approach will necessarily differ from that of our predecessors, but the effort to discover the vital functions of ritual remains basic to creative religion.

Several insights derived from the history and psychology of religion will prove valuable here. One is the recognition of the significance of symbols in society. Language itself is the most potent system of symbols that man possesses, and the language of prayer, as we have noted, is basically symbolic, attempting to imply through words what cannot be fully expressed. Essentially, rituals consist of symbolic acts and objects which society regards as its *sancta,* its objects of sacred concern. Their significance can scarcely be exaggerated, for a symbol serves as the basis of unity within the group, while permitting diversity of interpretation. What the flag means will differ with the degree of ethical sensitivity of the individual, yet it serves to unite all the citizens, whether in crisis or under normal conditions. Moreover, ritual serves to give dramatic expression to the ideals by which the group lives and which it seeks to perpetuate in the lives of its members, functions which are among the most important in prayer. Hence, prayer is ritual in words; ritual, prayer in action.

Of equal significance in evaluating ritual is the concept of "reinterpretation." This phenomenon explains the paradox, illustrated time and again in anthropology, that a custom may be older than the reason assigned for it. It is characteristic of human development that when society outgrows the reason for a given ritual, the practice is often not scrapped, but given a new meaning, in conformity with the insights and needs of a later day. Failure to recognize the universal phenomenon of reinterpretation has led to the "genetic fallacy" whereby men have passed judgment on the validity of an institution in terms of its origins rather than of its present function.

Two striking examples of reinterpretation may be cited from contemporary Jewish practice. At the Passover Seder, it is customary to pour or spill out a drop of wine from the goblet as each of the Ten Plagues visited upon the Egyptians is mentioned. The basis for the custom undoubtedly lies in the desire to ward off evil, and the act has many parallels in primitive societies. But this lowly origin has been transformed by later Jewish thought into a symbol of lofty universalism. The wine goblet at the Seder represents the cup of Israel's salvation. However, since the redemption of Israel from bondage was achieved at the cost of the suffering of the Egyptians, the cup of joy cannot be full for the Jew as he recalls the misery of his ancient oppressor. Hence, he pours out a drop of wine for each of the Ten Plagues. He is thus imitating the ways of God Himself, for according to Rabbinic legend, the Redeemer of Israel refused to let the angels praise Him when the Egyptian pursuers were perishing in the Red Sea, saying, "My creatures are drowning, and you want to sing praise to Me!"

Another folk-custom which was reinterpreted and which became a symbol of group loyalty is the practice of having the bridegroom break a small glass at the conclusion of the marriage ceremony. The origin of this practice, too, was undoubtedly the desire to drive off evil and malignant spirits, who were felt to be especially potent in so significant and critical an hour. Jewish sentiment today, however, sees in the breaking of the glass a reminder of the destruction of the Temple in Jerusalem and of the breakdown of the national life of Israel, a poignant reaffirmation of the Psalmist's oath: "If I forget thee, O Jerusalem, may my right hand wither, may my tongue cleave to my palate, if I remember thee not, if I do not raise thee up above my chief joy" (*Psalm* 137:5-6). Thus two apotropaic rites of primitive character have become dramatic representations of lofty universalism in one instance and of group loyalty in the other.

Tracing the many-sided origin and development of rituals is a fascinating enterprise. Some are uniquely characteristic of one group; others, arising independently, have analogies in the practice of remote peoples. Frequently, customs are borrowed by one group from another. In rare instances, a custom may arise because of the example of an influential individual, which is followed by the community. It happens frequently that a practice is originally voluntary, and then becomes obligatory, or it may originate in a small segment and spread to an entire people. There are grounds for believing that many of the Jewish laws of purity, like some of the dietary laws, originally arose within the priesthood. They later became part of the practice of an entire people, as the democratic tendencies within Judaism made themselves manifest and all Jews felt impelled to obey the Biblical injunction, "For ye are a kingdom of priests and a holy nation." The widespread traditional custom of covering one's head at worship originally began purely as a voluntary act among the most pious members of society, and then became universal.

Practices also rise and fall in importance. The rite of circumcision, the oldest Biblical commandment, which goes back to Abraham, became the universal mark of Jewish affiliation largely as the result of historical circumstances. There were periods when it was neglected, as the Bible informs us, and eras when the practice was characteristic of most of the surrounding nations. After the Babylonian exile, when Judaism encountered the challenge of the Greco-Roman world which did not practice circumcision, the rite became the symbol of the uniqueness of Judaism vis-à-vis Hellenism and its Roman offshoot. The Syrian Greek, Antiochus IV, in his efforts to make Hellenistic civilization universal in his empire, prohibited circumcision and failed. Three centuries later, the Roman Emperor Hadrian invoked an ancient Roman law against bodily mutilation, as the basis for outlawing the practice. The most civilized writers in Rome ridiculed the custom as barbarous. The reaction was instantaneous—and vigorous. In the language of the Talmud, every commandment for which Israel undergoes martyrdom becomes precious on that account. Thus circumcision, which began as a widespread Semitic custom throughout the Middle East and was not limited to Israel, ultimately became the unique mark of the Covenant of Abraham with God.

While some practices grow in significance, others decline. One of the most striking is the observance of the New Moon Festival in the Jewish ritual. This festival was of great importance in ancient times, probably because of its association with lunar worship. Later it fell into decline, and today it has only a few vestigial remains in the ritual of the synagogue.

Contrariwise, instances are not lacking where customs and rituals that have long disappeared are revived. The Festival of the Drawing of the Water during the Feast of Tabernacles is a case in point. Of this ancient festival, which is described in great detail in the Mishnah, we are told, "He who has never observed the Festival of the Drawing of the Water has never beheld any real merrymaking." For many centuries, the custom remained little more than a memory. In modern Israel, where the quest for water in a parched land has become a matter of life and death, the Festival has been revived, and new rituals have been created for it.

This discussion suffices to indicate that ritual has had a career as rich in variety as human experience itself. The past, to be sure, cannot be dismissed as nonexistent or irrelevant. But its importance must be more than historical, if it is to find its place in a living faith for modern man.

A widespread but erroneous notion, which should be discarded once and for all is that traditional religion regarded ritual as equally significant with ethics. It is true that in some of the oldest Biblical codes, such as "the Book of the Covenant" (*Exodus*, chaps. 20 to 23) and the "Holiness Code" (*Leviticus*, chaps. 19 to

26), both types of laws are intermingled, but this is characteristic of all ancient law and religion, as witness the literatures of Egypt and Babylonia.

However, early in its history, Hebraic religion began emphasizing the importance of the ethical over the ritual and drew the consequences. The Decalogue, which is universally regarded as the noblest expression of Biblical religion, is a striking case in point. The Ten Commandments fall into three categories. Only the first is an article of belief, while the next three are basically ritual. The last six are exclusively ethical. Quantitatively viewed, therefore, Biblical religion emphasized ethical practice as against ritual and belief in the ratio of six to three to one!

Perhaps no religion has a more elaborate ritual than Rabbinic Judaism, yet the Talmud clearly underscored the primacy of ethics. Thus, according to the Mishnah, sincere repentance on the Day of Atonement has the power to bring a man forgiveness for the sins which he has committed against God; as for the sins committed against his fellow men, they cannot be forgiven by the Day of Atonement until he makes restitution to the victim (*Mishnah Yoma*, 8:9). It is an obvious inference that infractions of the ethical law are more severe than violations of ritual law. Even more revealing is a discussion in the Talmud with regard to the basic principles of religion for which a man must undergo martyrdom. While the Talmud declares that the saving of one's life takes precedence over all the commandments of the Torah, including even the Sabbath (*Kethubot* 5a), there are three acts, idolatry, sexual immorality, and murder, which are forbidden even at the risk of death. One of the sages, Rabbi Ishmael, goes further and declares that a man may even practise idolatry under duress in order to save his life, except when the act is public, and it is likely to influence others in society (*Sanhedrin* 7b). It follows that in the hierarchy of values, ethical conduct rates higher even than the Sabbath, the most exalted and fundamental of Jewish rituals. That ritual is a means to an end is explicitly stated in the observation of Rab, the creator of the Babylonian Talmud: "The ritual commandments were given only for the purpose of refining human nature" (*Midrash, Genesis Rabbah* 44:1). It is therefore clear that in traditional religion, ritual is less important than ethics.

Yet ritual remains indispensable for a living religion. Indeed, religious tradition is justified in its insistence upon the Divine character and binding nature of the entire Law, its ritual as well as its ethical aspects. This is the thoroughly reasonable consequence of its faith in Revelation. The *act* of Divine Revelation presupposes that it is the will of God that His creatures know Him and serve Him. The *content* of Revelation, embodied in the Scriptures and in their later interpretation, is, as we have seen, the resultant of God's will as communicated to man and refracted by the human understanding. It must therefore encompass all of life, including both the mode of worship, which is ritual, and the code of conduct, which is ethical.

The obstacles which modern men often encounter in accepting such a view arise from the failure to keep clearly in mind several principles which we have sought to stress—the act of Revelation is an ongoing process, and the content of Revelation is therefore subject to perpetual growth and development. Second, in the hierarchy of values the ethical occupies a higher level than the ritual. At times, a conflict may arise between two commandments, the one ritual and the other ethical, as it may indeed between two ethical injunctions. In either case, the more important imperative will take precedence. But the importance of the ritual needs to be underscored, in this age when ritual has fallen upon evil days.

Ritual performs several indispensable functions in human life. It is, however, more than a means to an end, however exalted. It is an act of communion that man establishes with God, and therefore an end in itself. Seeing in the ritual the command of God, the worshipper feels in the act which he performs a sense of intimacy with his Maker. Ritual becomes more than an instrument for the fulfillment of the ethical; it becomes the highway for the penetration of the religious into secular life—an indispensable instrument for the enhancement of the human spirit.

It has been acutely pointed out by Jacob Agus that mysticism expects the worshipper to speak through the ritual, while rationalism expects the ritual to speak to the worshipper. Perhaps the truth lies in recognizing that both attitudes are justified and the relationship is that of two-way traffic; there must be a movement in both directions.

To evaluate the functions of ritual, we may take as our point of departure the basic viewpoint of one of the most exalted spirits of our time, Albert Schweitzer, who has stressed "reverence for life" as the highest human ideal. It is no diminution of his greatness to note that the concept is rooted in Hebrew religion. The fundamental function of ritual is the hallowing of life. While many pagan religions glorified the instincts of man and gave them virtually free rein, other creeds developed strong ascetic tendencies in an effort to curb the evils inherent in the natural impulses. Vital religion will avoid both extremes, neither surrendering to nature nor suppressing it; its goal is neither the glorification of the instincts nor their vilification, but their sanctification, by making every activity and impulse an avenue for the service of God.

A deeply spiritual attitude toward life, as was characteristic of Hasidism at its best, sees the world divided not into the sacred and the profane, but, in Buber's fine phrase, into the holy and the not-yet-hallowed. It follows that the task of authentic religion is the hallowing of the natural and the moralization of life. Such activities as eating, drinking, resting, sexual gratification, or the enjoyment of fine clothes, the pleasures of a beautiful vista, are not concessions to a man's lower nature. As a Hasidic teacher once put it, "Just as jewels remind a lover of his beloved, so the beauty of the world reveals to man the glory of God." Hence, the beauties and pleasures of life, when properly enjoyed and related to their Divine source, are revelations, nay more, experiences of the Divine. Rest is a necessity for the maintenance of physical vitality, but when an individual observes the Sabbath day, he associates the pattern of his life with the cosmic rhythm of creation and recreation, of labor and rest, and thus makes himself become part of the world process. Eating is essential for the functioning of a living organism, but when the process of absorbing food is hallowed by a benediction of thanksgiving to the Creator of these goods, it becomes a vehicle for experiencing the goodness of life. Sexual activity is perhaps the most powerful impulse of all. When hallowed by a love that has been consecrated in marriage, it makes man literally "God's co-partner in creation." Indeed, every living ritual is a dramatic attempt to enhance some aspect of experience, be it major or minor, by bringing it into conformity with the most basic of all the Commandments, "Holy shall ye be, for I, the Lord your God, am holy."

From this fundamental goal of the hallowing of life flow the four functions of ritual:

1. *The Cosmic or Religious.* These are observances which bind us

to the universe and lend a cosmic significance to the events of our ordinary life. Ritual, when it is meaningful and beautiful, places such occasions as birth, puberty, marriage, and death against the background of a vital universe and its Creator. Primitive man felt that these moments of transition in life were fraught with uncertainty and peril, and so he created *rites de passage*, magical acts designed to ward off evil at these critical junctures. Modern man would be the poorer if he were to lose this feeling of dependence altogether. Through the ritual of a living faith, he transposes fear into awe; blind terror of the unknown becomes a blend of reverence before the mystery of life and trust in its goodness. The events in each human situation no longer remain accidents of animal existence, but become part of the unending miracle of life, suffused with a sense of holiness. Ritual declares, with the unanswerable logic of beauty, that man counts in the universe, that he is not an atom of dust, but a child of God, dependent upon Him, but able to trust in Him.

2. *The Ethical or Social.* It is of the essence of ideals that they must be taught continually, because life, which in the largest sense depends upon them, is always conspiring through a thousand petty devices to defeat man's aspirations for peace, understanding, and justice. As Albert Einstein declared in an address on education: "With the affairs of human beings, knowledge of truth alone does not suffice. On the contrary, this knowledge must continually be renewed by ceaseless effort, if it is not to be lost. It resembles a statue of marble which stands in the desert and is continually threatened with burial by the shifting sand. The hands of service must ever be at work in order that the marble continue lastingly to shine in the sun."

Teachers of every high religion can point to the ethical truths that holy days keep alive before their devotees through the instrumentality of ritual. The mutual responsibility of all men, the brotherhood and equality of all nations, their inalienable rights to physical security and liberty, including freedom of conscience and "spiritual self-determination," the indispensability of law in society —these are some of the ethical fundamentals embodied in the festivals cherished by Judaism. A parallel roster of religious and ethical teachings dramatized by ritual observances can be drawn up for every other great religion.

To teach ideals perpetually and yet avoid monotony is the special function of ritual. For, being symbolic in character, a rite lends itself to many emphases and interpretations while adding color and variety to daily existence. The sacred objects, places, and seasons revered in all religions are rituals symbolizing ethical ideals which can be reinterpreted anew and differently at succeeding occasions and for different purposes, penetrating not to the mind alone, but also to the heart and the senses with even greater power.

3. *The Esthetic or Play Function.* A principal reason for the fact that ritual observance, reverently and meaningfully executed, avoids the pitfalls of monotony is its esthetic character. Ceremony constitutes a source of poetry in life and offers an avenue of play for adults, who, increasingly in our modern civilization, find amusement in mechanical, vicarious, and commercial forms. A religious service offers the adult the opportunity to sing; the Passover Seder, a chance to re-enact a great drama; a Havdalah service at the close of the Sabbath, a bit of pageantry which most grownups find nowhere else.

It is symptomatic of the atrophy of the play function today that adults who seek to reintroduce a religious ceremony into their homes after long disuse are self-conscious and uncomfortable about it at the beginning. It is equally characteristic of the decay of vitality in many modern churches and synagogues that the congregation is a passive and virtually inaudible group of spectators rather than active participants in a religious service. The esthetic, participating element in ritual is all the more essential today for the psychic well-being of the individual and the group.

4. *The Group-Associational.* Finally, it is important to recall that function which so many modern men and women mistakenly regard as the sole *raison d'être* of ritual observance—that it fosters awareness of the group and loyalty to it. It is, of course, obvious that while ethical teaching will tend to be largely similar in all great faiths, and a substantial body of agreement may exist even with regard to beliefs, the "personality" of the religion, its greatest degree of distinctiveness, will necessarily inhere in its ritual, because ritual is the outgrowth of the historical experience of a group, and expresses itself in unique form. One illustration will suffice. Whether a man will wear a *Tallith* or count beads or use a

prayer rug in prayer before the one Living God, will be determined not by objective rational considerations, but in terms of the historic community, Jewish, Christian, or Islamic, to which he belongs.

The preservation, therefore, of a community is in largest measure dependent not upon the credal doctrine or the ethical teaching which it shares, but upon its system of ritual and ceremony. On the basis of this observation, it is frequently assumed that ritual has no other justification. The exaggeration has become a massive error. When teachers of Judaism stress the national or group-associational element in Jewish observances along with the other values inherent in them, they are affirming that whatever strengthens the bond of group loyalty is a good, because the survival of their group and its tradition is a blessing to the world. The same truth applies, of course, to adherents of every religious and cultural group who feel that they possess a message of significance for the world.

It is obvious that the most valuable rituals are those which contribute to the hallowing of life by performing all these functions, the cosmic, the ethical, the esthetic, and the group-associational, and doing them effectively. At times a given practice may perform only one or two, but may do it to such a transcendent degree as to justify its retention. This discussion is not intended to suggest that all practices and customs handed down from the past and hallowed by tradition are sacrosanct and must be retained unchanged forever. There are rituals that have outlived their usefulness, while others are so thoroughly at variance with the contemporary pattern of life as to have lost all power of survival. Nonetheless, it is clear that by and large the ritual patterns which have evolved through the centuries and endured are not easily duplicated or replaced, and should not be lightly discarded.

The roots of ritual are laid deep in the soul of the race. Lest we cavalierly dismiss the ritual impulse as "primitive" and outmoded, we should recall how many of the foundation stones of civilization were laid by our oldest ancestors, lost in the mists of prehistory, such as language, art, government, and the family. Whatever its weaknesses and drawbacks, ritual has not only a long history behind it, but also a significant role before it.

Religion is concerned with man's place in the universe. It must relate man and the accidents of his existence to the mystery and miracle of the cosmos. At the same time, it dare not minimize or postpone the moral imperative to fashion decent men and to build a righteous society. In order to achieve this dual purpose, it must unfurl the banner of the Living God. To keep that faith ever vivid and real, modern man, like his forebears, needs a living ritual.

CHAPTER XVIII

The Re-Judaization of Christianity

In a letter dated April 30, 1944, the young Lutheran minister, Dietrich Bonhoeffer, who was later executed by the Nazis, wrote from his prison cell: "We are proceeding toward a time of no religion at all. How do we speak of God without religion? How do we speak in a secular fashion of God?" One of the most influential of Christian theologians in America, Harvey Cox, initiated a discussion in which he asked the reader to consider "What has happened to the three-letter English word 'God'? Why has it become a virtually useless vocable today?" This feeling, it should not be necessary to emphasize, emanates from men and women who are profoundly and deeply dedicated to vital religion. Yet for them and for many others "God" is dead.

When this new development in contemporary Christian theological thought is observed from the standpoint of the Jewish tradition, a striking conclusion emerges. This desire to avoid the use of "God" may appear revolutionary, even iconoclastic, to Christians, but for Jews it is so familiar it may be called traditional. The entire thrust of Jewish tradition has always been to minimize concern with God and to maximize concern with man. As a result, unsympathetic observers, noting the common Jewish question, "What is the Law?" rather than "What does God ask?" have created the familiar stereotype of Judaism as a lifeless, external legalism, far removed from the fountain of living waters that is its divine source.

When Bonhoeffer asked, "How can we speak of religion without God?" he had only to look to the Hebrew Scriptures for his answer. There is no word for "religion" in the Hebrew Bible. When Cox asked us to dispense with the vocable "God," he was anticipated by the Rabbis of the Talmud, who went so far as to say that God Himself once said, "Would that man forsook Me but kept My law." It is, of course, a fact familiar to every Biblical student that the proper name of the God of Israel, which scholars have reconstructed as "Yahweh," is replaced in reading by the word *Adonai*, "Lord," a step obvious already in the Septuagint, the Greek translation of the Pentateuch dating from 250 B.C.E., which renders it *Kyrios*. But even the substitute term was avoided in post-Biblical times; it was replaced by a variety of surrogates like *Hashem*, "the Name," *Hakadosh Barukh Hu*, "the Holy One, Blessed Be He," *Ribono Shel Olam*, "Master of the Universe," *Abhinu Shebashamayim*, "Our Father in Heaven," and countless others.

The tendency goes far beyond nomenclature. In the Middle Ages when traditional Judaism came into contact with Greek thought—primarily that of Aristotle and secondarily that of Plato —it was greatly stimulated by Greek philosophy. As a result, a completely new vocabulary had to be created in order to deal with these new themes. Now, there was no word for "philosophy" in Hebrew, and so the term *philosophia* was borrowed from the Greek. It is noteworthy that at no time did medieval Hebrew feel the need to borrow another Greek word, *theologia*, "God-wisdom," which Thomas Aquinas utilized in the title of his *Summa Theologica*. In other words, Jewish theologians felt no need for "theology." In this respect, as in so many others, medieval Jewish philosophy was the authentic heir of earlier creative periods, the eras of the Bible and the Talmud. Judaism was always less concerned with the nature of God than with the duty of man.

Obviously, belief and conduct are important in any religion worthy of the name. But the difference in emphasis is unmistakable. While in traditional Christianity the touchstone of salvation is belief, in traditional Judaism it is conduct. This divergence is highlighted in two great universalistic passages. In the New Testament, Paul proclaims, "There is neither Jew nor Greek, there is neither slave nor free, there is neither male nor female; for you are all one *in Christ Jesus*." In the Midrash, we read: "I call Heaven and earth to witness, that whether one be Gentile or Jew, man or woman, slave or free man, the divine spirit rests on each *in accordance with his deeds*."

Rabbinic Judaism possessed a deep faith in life after death and judgment in the world to come. We have already quoted the statement in the Mishnah: "Better one hour of repentance and good deeds in this world than all the life of the world to come, but better one hour of joy in the world to come than all the life of this world." For the traditional believer, the full enjoyment of salvation is reserved for the world to come, but the achievement of salvation is a task to be accomplished in this world. For Judaism, man's duty here and now is the core of religion.

This recognition that God's essence is beyond man's comprehension and should therefore not be man's concern has characterized Judaism from the beginning. A striking illustration, by no means the only one, may be adduced from a passage in the Book of Exodus. After the agonizing disappointment that came to Moses when he came down from Sinai and found that the people had degraded themselves and betrayed him by the orgies around the Golden Calf, he asks to be reassured that the Lord's presence is with him: "And Moses said, 'Show me, I pray Thee, Thy glory.' And the Lord said: 'Thou canst not see My face, for man shall not see Me and live.' And the Lord said: 'Behold, there is a place by Me, and thou shalt stand upon the rock. And it shall come to pass, while My glory passeth by, that I will put thee in a cleft of the rock, and will cover thee with My hand until I have passed by. And thou shalt see My back; but My face shall not be seen.' "

Much more familiar and basic is the prohibition in the Decalogue against any physical representation of the Deity, which is treated as a logical extension of the interdict against worshipping other gods. Even the prophet Ezekiel, who describes the four sides of the heavenly chariot as containing the images of a man, a lion, an ox, and an eagle, is struck with silence when he reaches the climax, "the image of the glory of God."

What implications flow from the trend in contemporary Christian thought that seeks to reduce, if not to eliminate, its traditional preoccupation with God? It seems that the full significance of the movement cannot become clear when it is viewed in isolation from other developments that superficially may seem unrelated to it and to each other. We believe Christian theology today stands at a watershed in its development—that the great process which has been going on for nearly nineteen centuries is drawing to its close and a new era is dawning.

The thesis may be set forth simply as follows: From its inception until our day, Christianity, which arose within the Jewish community, underwent a process of de-Judaization. Today the opposite tendency is making itself felt—a far-flung process of re-Judaization, taking on a variety of forms.

It should be noted that the term "re-Judaization" goes beyond "Hebraization." The latter term means essentially a return to and a renewed emphasis upon the Hebrew Scriptures and their world view. The evidence for this marked tendency in our day is abundant. But the developments we have in mind possess traits that must fairly be called instances of "re-Judaization." First, there is a closer approach to, and a livelier appreciation of, the Jewish interpretation of the Hebrew Scriptures, even when it includes the rejection or the deëmphasis of traditional Christian concepts. Second, there is also the adoption of attitudes and insights that, to be sure, originated in the Hebrew Scriptures but were developed in post-Biblical thought. Third, there is the acceptance of ideas that are not articulated in the Bible at all and are exclusively rabbinic.

The opening chapters of Genesis illustrate this far-reaching change of spirit. The Adam and Eve narrative, with all its implications for the Christian view of human nature, sex, and salvation, is much less frequently invoked today as the basis for the traditional Christian doctrine of the Fall of Man. It is increasingly recognized that finding this idea in Genesis is not *exegesis*, reading out of the text, but *eisegesis*, reading into the text. Moreover, the ability of traditional Judaism to articulate a theory of human nature, truly realistic yet more hopeful than the doctrine of man's innate corruption, is tacitly attracting Christian interest. In point of fact, contemporary Christian moralists, who are concerned with the functions of marriage, are finding the most relevant statement on the subject to be the passage, neglected for centuries, that declares, "It is not good for man to dwell alone." In order to appreciate the full dimensions of the process of this re-Judaization, a brief historical survey is in order.

It is, of course, a truism that Christianity began as a sect within

Judaism. Jesus and the Apostles were all Jews, and their concern was the weal and woe of their own people. This is the key to the understanding of several highly particularistic sayings of Jesus, which are more exclusivist than most rabbinic pronouncements on the subject. It is not accidental that Jesus hailed from Galilee, the hotbed of Jewish nationalism in the Roman period.

It has, of course, long been known that the great basic doctrines of faith and ethics as taught by Jesus in the Gospels were essentially those of the normative Jewish tradition. Jesus' faith in the Fatherhood of God and in the resurrection of the dead, his method of interpreting the text of Scripture, his pattern of religious observance, and his use of parables are all characteristic of Pharisaism. Twenty-five or thirty years ago many other elements of early Christianity were attributed by scholars to non-Jewish sources, Greek or Oriental religion. Today we know that most of these are also authentically Jewish. They were derived from those sectarian groups who wrote the Dead Sea Scrolls. It is, therefore, clear that the debt Christianity owes to Judaism is far more extensive today than was believed a few decades ago; it was derived not only from the mainstream of Jewish tradition but also from sectarian, predominantly Essenic groups, whose life and thought have been rediscovered in the Qumran caves.

The small sect of Judeo-Christians, headed by Jesus' brother James, who observed the Jewish law meticulously, differed from their co-religionists primarily in recognizing Jeshua of Nazareth as the heralded Messiah. They would probably have disappeared in one or two generations were it not for the towering personality of Paul. Paul proudly called himself "a Pharisee, son of a Pharisee," and regarded it as his mission to proclaim the good tidings of his ancestral faith to the world. But, unlike Jesus and the Apostles, Paul lived and was educated in a Greek environment. With him began the Hellenization of Christianity, a process that made it more congenial to the pagan world.

The Hebraic character of Christianity was now broadened or vitiated—the choice of the term depends on one's point of view—or, to use a neutral term, it was complicated by the intrusion of Hellenistic elements. Henceforth, classical Christianity had two sources—one Hebraic, the other Greek. As Gentile Christianity all but submerged the original Jewish-Christian nucleus, the Greek element triumphed over the Hebrew.

The Hellenistic influence endowed Christianity with a speculative character in the succeeding centuries. This trait gained momentum in the subtleties of patristic theology and reached its apogee in the profundities of scholastic dialectic. Because of these tendencies, classical Christianity developed three outstanding characteristics. The first is a preoccupation with dogma, which may be defined in two words as "faith petrified." The second is a concern with heresy, which may be described as "dogma challenged." The third was derived directly from the Aristotelian concept of the immovable Mover and the Greek conviction of the superiority of the static over the dynamic. Hence, traditional Christian theology as elaborated in scholasticism—as distinct from the unreflective piety of the people—was dominated by the concept of God as an immovable figure. Human nature, too, was conceived of as unchanged and unchangeable, as in the classic formulations of natural law.

Inevitably, there resulted a muting of the dynamic concept of history enunciated by the Hebrew prophets and of their faith in the inevitable establishment of God's kingdom on earth. Completely lost to view was the Hebraic concept, spelled out in rabbinic thought, of the world as still being in the process of creation. These three traits—dogma, heresy, and the concept of a static God in a static world—continued to characterize the Christian tradition through the centuries.

Today, Christianity, like all religion, is confronted by a many-faceted challenge—from the secular thrust of our technological culture, from the alleged impact of modern scientific discoveries and philosophic insights, from the overwhelming sense of man's helplessness before monstrous and faceless evils that seem automatic and irreversible, and from the growing challenge of the competing creeds of hedonism and materialism. In the face of so overwhelming an attack, the apparent irrelevance and timidity of organized religion seems to many of its dedicated advocates to threaten its survival. Hence, in many quarters, there issues a call to minimize, if not to eliminate, the Hellenistic factors in the Christian tradition and by that token to revert to its Hebraic origins. It seems clear that this is a call for reversing the millennial process of the de-

Judaization of Christianity in favor of its re-Judaization. This is not a consistent, organized, or even always a conscious movement. It takes on a variety of forms, ranging from moderate to extreme. It encompasses both doctrine and practice, both the life of the Church and its relation to the world. It embraces all branches of Christianity, Catholic, Protestant, and Orthodox. Its representatives include official spokesmen of the Church, as well as individual thinkers.

Thus, the Roman Catholic theologian Leslie Dewart argues that the time has come for Christianity to surrender its Hellenistic modes of thought. He maintains that the traditional Catholic conceptualization of theology is radically out of harmony with contemporary modes of thought. The Hellenistic concepts that frame and express Catholic orthodoxy stand like a petrified forest in a conceptual wilderness, isolated by their frozen fixity from the vibrant ever-growing intellectual life that animates the secular city. The gulf between the conceptualization of Catholic thought and the conceptual patterns of contemporary experience Dewart describes as "Hellenization."

In Protestantism, Jaroslav Pelikan has similarly insisted that Christianity must dispense with the Hellenistic concepts of the past. Perhaps most remarkable is the position of Archbishop Iakovos, the leader of Greek Orthodoxy in North and South America. He calls for the replacing of Greek ideas on the ground that they no longer speak to modern man and he has declared, "We need a new Christianity based on entirely new concepts and terms. Abstract Greek concepts such as God as a Supreme Being have little meaning to youth today. They want more concrete terms. They want concepts that express involvement in the world."

In other instances, the conclusion is not recognized, or at least not explicated. A striking instance occurs in Harvey Cox's *The Secular City*, which is a call for "liberating man from religious bondage." This process, Cox declares, begins with Biblical religion and is marked by three great events in Biblical history. The first is creation, which represents "the disenchantment of nature." Before the Bible, nature was regarded as being magical, indeed divine. Biblical thought insists that nature is secular and that only God is divine. The second event is the Exodus from Egypt, which represents "the secularization of politics." Before, it was taken for granted that the state was holy and the king divine. The Exodus demonstrated that the king of Egypt was a human figure and only God is sacred. The third event is the revelation on Sinai, which represents, says Cox, "the secularization of values," since the prohibition of idolatry in the Decalogue denies absolute value to any ideal except the ultimate. Hence, all human ideals are relative except loyalty to the All-Highest.

In this analysis there are two observations that Dr. Cox does not spell out. One is that all three incidents that set the process of "secularization" in motion are drawn from the Old Testament, and not from the New. The other is even more pertinent to our present concern: in all three cases, the process of "secularization" was carried out fully in Judaism but not in Christianity. For centuries these insights were largely driven underground in Christian life and thought.

Thus, the recognition that nature is not magical or divine but secular is vitiated by the Christian doctrine of human nature. That human nature is sinful and corrupt is an attitude derived from the dichotomy of the flesh and the spirit, which was postulated by Paul and carried much further by Augustine and others. The truth that the state is not divine was undermined by the pagan concept of Caesar as a god, which reappeared in attenuated form in post-Reformation Europe in the doctrine of "the divine right of kings," as in the writings of Robert Filmer, the defender of the royal prerogatives of the Stuarts. Though the phrase sounds Biblical, it is utterly at variance with the early and persistent antagonism to the monarchy in ancient Israel, the stringent limitations on the power of the Hebrew kings, and the castigation in the Book of Kings of most rulers in Israel and Judah as sinners. As for the Biblical prohibition of idolatry, non-Christians at least—and many Christians as well—cannot help seeing the doctrine as gravely compromised by the veneration of Mary and the saints, and the homage accorded shrines, icons, and relics, as well as by the apotheosis of Jesus in the doctrine of the Trinity. When, therefore, Cox is urging the need of secularization if religion is to become relevant, it is a process of re-Judaization he is advocating.

Perhaps the major crisis in our time resides in the widespread collapse of moral standards. The old theologically rooted absolutism in morals becomes totally irrelevant and unworkable in a dizzily dynamic society. The various types of relativistic and situational ethics are worthy of praise for developing a measure of sympathy and tolerance for the members of our rudderless generation. However, it is obviously not to be expected that these schools of thought will supply any real guidance for our contemporaries, since their basis is the denial of binding norms for conduct.

Some thinkers, feeling the need for effective ethical standards, have turned anew to natural law as affording a basis for a theory of conduct that will be conformable to reason and human nature. But natural law, like Christian theology, has two sources, one derived from the Greco-Roman world view, the other, far less known, from the Hebraic tradition. Unfortunately, the former, which is static in its approach, has all but crowded out the latter, which is dynamic in character. As a result, because of its roots in Hellenistic thought and its subsequent history in the Middle Ages, when it was cultivated almost entirely by the Catholic Church, natural law has developed a markedly conservative bias. It manifests an incapacity to reckon with the new insights into the world and the nature of man afforded by science, as its critics have correctly pointed out. Natural law needs to be rescued from some of its friends in order to win over many of its foes. A fresh approach and a new application of the fundamental principles of natural law may well disclose its capacity to help guide modern man out of the moral chaos of our age by pointing the way to a sound basis for ethics that will be truly conformable to reason and will reckon with the complexities of human nature. Here the Biblical, apocryphal, and rabbinic sources of natural law can prove most fruitful in helping to chart the course.

A more obvious instance of the re-Judaization of Christian thought lies in the revision now going on in Christian circles, explicit or implicit, of the traditional concept of human nature. Ever since Paul and the early Church Fathers, Christian theology has emphasized the doctrine of the Fall of Man, particularly since belief in original sin was felt to be the prelude to the faith in Jesus as the Saviour. It is true that the Church later modified the doctrine, in some instances intensifying it, as in the case of Augustine, in others, mitigating it, as in the thought of Aquinas, which was declared authoritative by the Council of Trent. In Protestantism, both Luther and Calvin reasserted several elements of Augustine's extreme position which Catholic scholasticism had modified. But the conception of the nature of man as basically evil, whether maintained in crassly literal form, as in fundamentalism, or in incredibly profound and subtle restatements, as in Tillich and Niebuhr, still remains the official position.

This idea never found any foothold in normative Judaism, which had another concept of human nature—in its doctrine of the two *Yetzers*, "the good impulse" and "the evil impulse," both of which are within the power of each man to control. What is even more significant, traditional Judaism recognized explicitly that the so-called evil impulse may be sublimated, or transposed into a higher key, so as to serve the glory of God and the welfare of man. To cite one classic passage from the Talmud out of several, "Thou shalt love the Lord thy God with all thy heart"—this means with both impulses, the good and the evil impulses.

At the risk of oversimplification, the difference between the Christian and the Jewish attitude toward the nature of man may be put as follows: for traditional Christianity, man sins because he is a sinner; for traditional Judaism, man is a sinner because he sins. But to this observer, at least, it seems clear that in increasing measure Christians are approximating the outlook traditional in Judaism.

This rapprochement is particularly evident in the area of sexual morality and family life, but it goes beyond it. We have before us two contrasting concepts of human nature, either as innately corrupt or as plastic, malleable either for good or for evil. From these attitudes flow two divergent approaches toward ethical conduct and toward the concept of the *summum bonum*. Both emphases, to be sure, are to be found in both traditions. Yet it is fair to say that what is dominant in one is secondary in the other, and vice versa.

In essence, the distinctive ethics of the New Testament is an "ethics of self-abnegation," which regards as the highest form of human conduct the surrender of one's self and the suppression of one's impulses and desires. The traditional Jewish ethic at its best is an "ethic of self-fulfillment," which urges the expression of one's legitimate, indeed God-given, needs and goals as the duty of man. As a logical consequence, the Sermon on the Mount emphasizes the famous principle of not resisting evil. There were historical reasons why, in the difficult period when Christianity arose, this doctrine of not resisting evil by force had so much attraction for morally sensitive men and women. On the other hand, the entire thrust of the Jewish tradition is to oppose evil in all its forms. For most modern people, too, the refusal to resist evil represents not a moral principle but almost the contrary—an invitation to tyranny and oppression. What is undeniable is that historically the ethics of self-abnegation has often led to the acceptance of an intolerable status quo.

It is, therefore, easy to document from the New Testament injunctions to wives to be obedient to their husbands, to slaves to submit to their masters, and to subject-peoples not to rebel against Roman sovereignty. In accordance with its inner logic, the ethics of self-abnegation manifests relatively little concern with the social, economic, and political relations of men. I recall a conversation with the gifted Catholic theologian, John Courtney Murray, who once asked, "What has the Sermon on the Mount to do with contemporary politics?" And he answered, "Nothing." As I pointed out to him at the time, if the question were put with regard to the relevance of the Decalogue, the answer would be, "Everything."

The New Testament ethics of self-abnegation derived its sanction from a negative concept of human nature. That it found a response in the hearts of an entire faith-community, that of the first Christians, is due to the conditions under which the early Church arose. It was an age when the Roman yoke in Palestine was both intolerable and apparently immovable, except by some Heaven-sent supernatural intervention. Jesus and the early Christians, like other sectarian Jewish groups of the first century C.E., were passionately convinced that the end of the natural order was at hand. The Gospels and the Epistles accordingly presented an "interim ethic," expected to last only for the brief period before the great eschatological cataclysm that would usher in a new world. Hence, the New Testament could make extreme demands on human nature for this short interval.

Once it was realized by the Church that the "last days" were not imminent, it became clear that it was not a workable ethic for a perdurable society. Catholic Christianity was compelled to create a corpus of canon law. In our day, Christian ethics is wrestling anew with this problem of establishing norms of conduct in view of conditions and insights unknown in the past. Here, too, the solution lies in the re-Judaization of the Christian outlook.

The most palpable illustration of this thesis lies in the area of sex and family life. We hear a great deal today about "the new morality," which some critics have called "the new amorality." A phenomenon as complicated as modern sexual behavior obviously derives from many factors, social, economic, and cultural. But here religious attitudes continue to be important. It has not been generally noted that "the new morality"—or at least one of the most important patterns within it—represents an inversion of traditional Christian morality. For Paul and many of the Church Fathers sex is basically evil, and if it is not coextensive with concupiscence, it is at least its most prominent element. Ideally, therefore, love and sex should be kept as far apart as possible, for the highest and purest form of love is that which does not eventuate in sexual fulfillment.

The classical Christian outlook on sex as evil has created the concept that the higher love becomes, the less it is involved in sex. Love is holy, but sex is low; love is pure, but sex is unclean. In the Middle Ages, the ideal of knightly love was a love never physically consummated, as in the romance of Tristan and Isolde. Romeo and Juliet are star-crossed lovers whose passion for each other is barely gratified. In the world of reality, Dante and Beatrice, who saw each other only a few times during their lifetime and never established any personal relationship, symbolized the highest type of love attachment.

In the modern period, romantic love has been glorified in song and literature, on the screen and the stage, and has become a dominant element of our culture. In essence, it is a secularized version of the Christian love ideal, for romantic love par excellence is unfulfilled or incomplete love, the passion experienced either before marriage or outside of it.

While traditional morality glorifies love, the modern age glorifies sex and maintains that love is irrelevant and unrelated to sex. Many modern men and women, therefore, have drawn the conclusion that sexual experience is permissible even where there is no love.

What is highly significant in our age of disbelief is that the view of sex as inherently evil persisted even after Christian doctrine lost its hold upon many of its devotees. The conviction that sex is immoral, if not sinful, continues to survive in the world view—and what is even more important, in the emotional makeup, of many non-believers. Many modern men and women who have lost the sense of sin continue to be oppressed by feelings of guilt. It is one of the great insights of modern psychoanalysis that psychological disturbances of varying intensity, running the gamut from minor neurosis to major psychosis, are induced by contradictions in the human psyche between conscious attitudes and subconscious feelings.

It is no accident that our society exhibits a deep-seated schizophrenia—sentimental glorification of "love" on the one hand and widespread pornography, prostitution, and promiscuity on the other. All these unhealthy manifestations have arisen because the sex code preached by traditional religion and embodied in contemporary law all too often runs counter to the promptings of human nature. What has been driven out through the door comes in through the window, with one tragic difference: the visitor is no longer a respectable caller, amenable to law and order, but a surreptitious law-breaker.

The point of view of Jewish tradition in its most creative periods, those of the Bible and the Talmud, differs radically from that of classic Christianity—or, at least, the most influential strain within it. This attitude was expressed with vigor, if not with consistency, by Paul in I Corinthians, Chapter 7:

"It is well for a man not to touch a woman. But because of the temptation to immorality, each man should have his own wife and each woman her own husband. The husband should give to his wife her conjugal rights, and likewise the wife to her husband. . . . To the unmarried and the widows I say that it is well for them to remain single as I do. But if they cannot exercise self-control, they should marry. For it is better to marry than to be aflame with passion. . . . If anyone thinks that he is not behaving properly toward his betrothed, if his passions are strong, and it has to be, let him do as he wishes; let them marry—it is no sin. But whoever is firmly established in his heart, being under no necessity but having his desire under control, and has determined this in his heart, to keep her as his betrothed, he will do well. So that he who marries his betrothed does well; and he who refrains from marriage will do better."

In short, Paul regarded sex as basically evil and marriage as a concession to the lower aspects of human nature, while compounding the contradiction by calling marriage "a great sacrament." This complex of attitudes was reaffirmed by many of the Church Fathers and later theologians, both Catholic and Protestant.

Judaism recognizes sex as an essential and legitimate element of human life. Since God created man with his entire complement of impulses, sex is a manifestation of the Divine. It is therefore neither to be glorified, as in the exaggerations of romantic love, nor denigrated, as in classic Christian theology.

The Bible and the Talmud are frank and outspoken in dealing with the sexual component of human experience. The pages of Jewish literature are free from obscenity and false modesty and from pornography and comstockery, which are essentially two sides of the same coin.

In the medieval mystical treatise *Iggeret Hakodesh*, attributed to Nahmanides, the classic Jewish attitude is clearly and vigorously expressed: "We who are the descendants of those who received the sacred Torah believe that God, blessed be He, created everything as His wisdom dictated, and He created nothing containing obscenity or ugliness. For if we were to say that intercourse is obscene, it would follow that the sexual organs are obscene. . . . And how could God, blessed be He, create something containing a blemish, or obscenity, or a defect; for we would then find that His deeds are not perfect, though Moses, the greatest of the prophets, proclaims and says, 'The Rock, whose work is perfect' (Deuteronomy 32:4). However, the fact is, as it is said, that 'God is pure-eyed, so that He sees no evil' (Habakkuk 1:13). Before Him there is neither degradation nor obscenity; He created man and woman, fashioning all their organs and setting them in their proper fashion, with nothing obscene in them."

Since sex and love are indissolubly linked, the term 'ahavah is used for both the physical and the spiritual aspects of love. The Christian theologians are wont to emphasize the fact that there are two Greek terms for "love," *eros*, meaning "physical love," and *agape*, meaning "charity, spiritual love." The Hebrew outlook, on the contrary, finds it entirely proper to apply the same root, 'ahav, to all aspects of love. The ideal relationship of man to God ("You shall love the Lord your God"), love of one's fellow man ("You shall love your neighbor as yourself"), and the love of man and woman ("How fair and how pleasant you are, O love, with its delights!"), are all expressed by the same Hebrew root. Judaism, then, finds no dichotomy between the physical and the spiritual, and certainly no conflict between them. From this approach flows a whole series of consequences in many troubled and controversial areas.

Thus, birth control becomes a moral problem only on the theory that the procreation of children is basically the one legitimate function of sex relations and that the higher ideal is celibacy, as Paul declared and several recent popes have vigorously reaffirmed. Today, however, Catholic circles are hailing the discovery that the purpose of marriage includes companionship as well as procreation. We can sympathize with our Catholic brothers as they wrestle to overcome the burden of Paul's teaching in this area. But this insight is no recent innovation in Judaism. From its inception, Judaism has always recognized two purposes in marriage, spelled out in the two opening chapters of Genesis. The first is the fulfillment of the first commandment: "Be fruitful and multiply." But the procreation of children, basic as it is, is not the only goal of marriage. In the Bible, Eve is created for Adam before procreation is contemplated, while they are still in the Garden of Eden. The second function of marriage is that of companionship. Actually, it is the only motive assigned in the creation of a helpmate for Adam: "It is not good for man to dwell alone; I will make a helpmate for him."

Judaism regards marriage and not celibacy as the ideal human state, because it alone offers the opportunity for giving expression to all aspects of human nature. Speaking of his celibacy, Paul said, "I would that all men were as I." But when the sage Simeon ben Azzai did not marry, he felt constrained to apologize by saying, "My soul loves the Torah," explaining that he wished to dedicate himself wholeheartedly to study without worldly concerns. His practice was emphatically the exception, not the rule, in Jewish life. The Hebrew term for marriage, *kiddushin*, was popularly interpreted, quite in the spirit of the tradition, as "the state of holiness."

All schools of thought in Judaism, from the most rationalist to the most mystical, emphasized marriage as being the ideal state for human beings. It was also underscored time and time again that all

forms of sexual relationship within the marriage bond, intimate
and private as they necessarily are, are to be regarded as manifestations of the divine and by that token are holy. That companionship, which includes sexual relations, is a legitimate end in itself in
marriage is not merely an implication of the Biblical story but is
explicitly spelled out in the tradition. Rabbinic law teaches that
weak, old, and sterile persons should marry even when there is no
possibility of children. Thus the rabbis could endorse wholeheartedly the sentiment of a modern sociologist: "Sex exists not only for
the propagation of the race, but for the increase of individual
human happiness."

These fundamental attitudes enter directly into the Talmudic
treatment of birth control. In a passage occurring no less than six
times in the Talmud, sanction is explicitly given to the practice of
birth control, where the health of the mother or that of the unborn
child or of another child is imperiled. In the medieval and post-
medieval periods, these attitudes were submerged by the powerful
pressures for group survival. Large families were felt to be necessary to overcome the natural and man-made hazards facing the
Jewish community. But the favorable view of family limitation
expressed in the classical sources was not expunged from the tradition.

Another critical area where contemporary Christian thought
and, even more, Christian practice is discovering the basic Jewish
approach is that of divorce. This graphic symbol of the instability
of modern marriage is a tragic revelation of the mass of human
misery often perpetuated in its name. Nowhere are the inherent
contradictions of the traditional Christian ethic more evident than
here. Marriage is regarded as a concession to the lower aspects of
man's nature. Yet, if the marriage fails, it must be through some
sort of a crime by a "guilty" party against an "innocent" party.
Divorce is therefore a "punishment," at least in theory. Judaism, on
the contrary, regards divorce not as a punishment but as a tragedy,
which is not obviated by refusing to recognize that when love and
mutuality of interests have been eroded, the marriage has failed and
the husband and wife are no longer joined together by God in any
meaningful sense.

The situation may be described from another angle. The contemporary American attitude toward divorce may be summarized

as official severity in law and total laxity in life. It is the consequence of the tragic paradox in attitude that regards marriage as a sad necessity and divorce as a punishment for trying to escape it! Traditional Judaism accepts the diametrically opposite attitude toward divorce. Instead of severity in law and laxity in life, Judaism establishes the contrary balance: the attitude in life toward divorce is strict, thus underscoring the need for the couple to strive earnestly for the permanence of the marriage bond, but the law on divorce is liberal, offering release where life together proves intolerable. All the resources of the tradition, the sanctity of its ideals, and the solemnity of its ritual are invoked to make husband and wife recognize the sacred character of their union. "He who divorces his first wife—even the Temple altar sheds tears for him," the rabbis declared.

In striking out after a new valuation on love, sex, and marriage, contemporary Christian theologians and moralists are discovering new truths in the Old Testament, the implications of which rabbinic Judaism spelled out centuries ago. It is, therefore, no accident that the new Christian attitudes on sexual relations, birth control, and divorce reflect the process of re-Judaization we have postulated. There are other frontier areas, such as illegitimacy and abortion, where Jewish law possesses valuable resources for a modern religious ethic. Even in what is perhaps morally the most crucial area of all, pre-marital and extra-marital relations, there are insights in Jewish tradition that need to be explored. What is clear is that, in this intimate field of concern, our age and, by that token, modern Christianity need to blend a realistic understanding of human nature with idealistic aspiration and an unyielding faith in man's capacity for goodness.

Developments in the practice of the Church, particularly in the conduct of the clergy, also demonstrate the de-Hellenization process at work, coupled with a rediscovery of the Hebraic and, at times, the Judaic components of the Christian tradition. The single most sensational change is the growing involvement of priests, monks, nuns, and ministers in the two major issues confronting America today—war and the racial situation. Increasingly, teachers of religion are becoming involved in the far-flung and complex struggle against political tyranny, social oppression, and economic misery, both at home and abroad. This differs radically from the activity in the fields of social work and philanthropy, which the clergy have traditionally cultivated in the past. This approach also represents a radical break with the time-honored concept of monasticism as a refuge to which sensitive men and women could escape from the chaos, confusion, and cruelty of "the world." This new conception of the role of the clergy in the Roman Catholic Church is far closer to the position of traditional Judaism, which never countenanced the establishment of conventicles for the pious and the learned apart from the world, and whose greatest sons, Hillel, Akiba, Judah Hanasi, Saadia, Maimonides, were deeply involved in the agonies and conflicts of their generations.

The growing demand, thus far rejected by the Vatican, for the relaxation in the rule of celibacy for the clergy derives both from the desire to share directly in the concerns of the world and from a new appreciation of the role of sex in human life. Part of the same process is the new emphasis upon "the collegiality of bishops." The demands that the bishops share authority in the government of the Church with the pope and that the lower clergy be consulted are a radical departure, in fact if not in theory, from what had been the practice of the Church for many centuries. That the Supreme Pontiff is to share the responsibilities of his office with the bishops and even the lower orders is a return to the Biblical tradition. For it will be recalled that in the days of Moses, the Judges, and Samuel the monarchy was opposed as an affront to the kingship of God. Even after the kingship became a *fait accompli* in Judah and Israel the king never enjoyed absolute power, as was the case everywhere else.

The new stress on the role of the laity in the conduct of the Church was highlighted by a recent meeting of laymen in Rome. The conscious evocation of the doctrine of "the people of God" in Catholic circles, though no novelty in Protestantism, goes back to the Biblical injunction at Sinai that Israel be "a kingdom of priests and a holy nation." It finds expression in Moses' hope, "Would that all the people of God were prophets," which he pronounced when Joshua proposed silencing the unauthorized prophesying of Eldad and Medad in the camp.

The demand for involvement in the world, the stress upon deed rather than upon creed, the sense of the dynamism of history, the ethics of self-fulfillment, the realistic yet positive evaluation of human nature, the recognition of sex as a divinely ordained attribute of man—and the willingness to draw the consequences in the arena of life—all these elements of Biblical and post-Biblical Judaism are in the direction in which contemporary Christian thinkers are moving. On the other hand, such Hellenistic elements as a static view of God and history, the conception of the dichotomy of body and soul, the doctrine of man's innate corruption, the stress on dogma and the war on heresy are playing an ever-diminishing role in the thinking of Christians today.

It follows, therefore, that we may be entering upon a new era of ecumenism, on a far deeper level than the exchange of pleasantries or even the recognition of mutual rights in a pluralistic society. Perhaps the day is dawning when Jews as well as Christians will recognize that the survival of Judaism through the ages is not merely an accident of history, that Jews do not constitute what Arnold Toynbee called "a fossilized relic of Syriac society," but that, on the contrary, Judaism still has a vital contribution to make to the world today.

Christianity and Judaism can engage in a truly meaningful dialogue, and the concept of the Judeo-Christian tradition takes on genuine relevance in our day. To be sure, no one tradition has all the answers to the mystery of existence and to the challenge of the human condition. But each tradition can speak significantly, first to its own devotees and then to all men. In this crucial enterprise, the growing tendency in Christianity to return to its roots in the Hebrew Scriptures and the Jewish tradition has a tremendous potential for good.

CHAPTER XIX

The Meaning of Jewish Existence

The far-flung revolution in contemporary Christian life and thought we have described above has its counterpart in a deep ferment within Jewish life today. While the axis in Christianity revolves around faith and morals, in Jewish circles the central areas of concern are the character and significance of Jewish survival and the meaning of Jewish suffering.

It is a truism that the Jewish people has been confronted by the problem of its survival virtually throughout its entire history. As Ahad Ha'am pointed out a long time ago, the nature of this challenge has been twofold. The first is the threat of physical annihilation that has taken on many forms, which we may subsume under the general term of "anti-Semitism." The other is the problem of assimilation, the threat of spiritual decay and extinction. Ahad Ha'am called these two aspects *tsarat hayehudim*, "the problem of the Jews," and *tsarat hayahadut*, "the problem of Judaism." Our calendar reflects this double-barrelled challenge that has confronted Judaism through the ages. Hanukkah celebrates the victory of the Jews against the threat of assimilation, which the Hellenizing King Antiochus tried to force upon the Jewish community of Palestine. Purim, on the other hand, is concerned not with the preservation of Judaism but with the survival of Jews, whose physical annihilation was decreed and almost carried out by Haman. Virtually every generation of Jews had been confronted by one or the other challenge.

It is the melancholy distinction of our age that today both these challenges have attained the apex of their power. Within our own generation we have seen both perils threatening the life of the Jewish community. Within our lifetime the most massive campaign to destroy the Jewish people was undertaken—and all but succeeded. In optimistic movements we are wont to speak of the indestructible survival of the Jewish people. It would be more realistic and accurate to describe Jewish history as the record of the imperfect extermination of the Jewish people.

What has actually happened is that the Jewish people have been exposed to a perpetual process of decimation almost from its very origin. This fact is all too easily illustrated from medieval history. According to the best estimates, there were some four million Jews living in Palestine at the time of the destruction of the Second Temple in the year 70 C.E. In 1170, when the Jewish traveler, Benjamin of Tudela, visited the existing Jewish communities of his time, a record of which he has left in his *Travels*, the Jewish population, after a thousand years of natural increase, stood at one million! Seven hundred years later, in the year 1800, the Jewish population reached four million, where it had been eighteen centuries earlier. What a graphic commentary upon the degree to which disease, starvation, expulsion and massacre wrought havoc with the Jewish community! The increase of the Jewish community to sixteen million, before Hitler, took place within a century and a third, from 1800 to 1933. This growth was tragically reversed by Hitler's success in exterminating six of the seven million Jews of Europe. Destroying six out of every seven of our brothers in Central and Western Europe, he annihilated the great center of spiritual and cultural vitality and leadership for world Jewry.

Now, twenty-five years after the Nazi holocaust, the Nazi philosophy is far from dead both here and abroad. If we ask ourselves, "What of the future?" the prospect is far from optimistic. What Hitler was unable to achieve completely with East European Jewry is now being attempted with very great success by the Communist regimes. The two million Jews of Russia are fighting a manful battle against tremendous odds in order to preserve some sense of Jewish identity in the Soviet Union. But Jewish life in any meaningful sense is being choked to death under communism in Poland and other red satellite states.

Even in the State of Israel, the lodestar of Jewish hope, there are major problems with regard to the spiritual survival of Jews. Recently, a French sociologist, Georges Friedmann, wrote a book with the striking title, "The End of the Jewish People?" In effect, he posed the challenging question: "Are we witnessing the end of the Jewish people simultaneously with the birth of the Israeli nation?" This is by no means a problem of semantics. As a result of the Six-Day War in June, 1967, Israel achieved an incredible victory, with the result that it is today confronted by extraordinary problems of growing magnitude. Guerrilla action on the borders and terrorist activity against civilians both within the country and abroad constitute not a major menace, but a significant strain for the State. But even when the day comes and the efforts of Israel's defense forces are crowned with success, the terrorist attacks are contained, and ultimately it becomes possible to win full loyalty of Israeli Arabs for the State, another problem emerges. Israel today contains a large Arab minority. A sociological study of Israeli Arabs indicates that the death rate among Israeli Arabs fell from 1948 to 1968 from about twenty to six per 1,000, and their birth rate has nearly doubled—from 2.5 to 4.5 per 1,000. If the health and economic conditions under which the Arabs live in Israel continue to improve, as they will, we are likely to be confronted with a situation where a sizeable proportion, if not a majority, of the State of Israel will be not Jews but Arabs.

This prospect, of which Israelis are well aware, creates a tremendous number of problems which are by no means easy to solve. They affect the nature of the cultural milieu of Israel, its economic and social background and *the sense of identity of Israeli Jews* as well. The question will arise: with what group will the coming generations of Israelis identify themselves? Will they be members of the Jewish people or will they, on the contrary, be members of an Israeli nation? No one familiar with Israel today and its heroic struggle for survival can fail to be impressed with the sense of Jewish consciousness and Jewish identification among all Israelis, the youth as well as their elders. There is a strong bond of unity felt by the vast majority of Israelis with Jews the world over, a fact which is sometimes denied, but unjustifiably. But what will happen, not in one, but in two, three and four generations, as brothers become cousins of the second and third degree and the individual experience of the Jews in the Diaspora diverges more and more from the group-experience of the Jews living in the State of Israel? What bond will link them together if the ties of Jewish tradition are loosened?

As for the other important and significant center of Jewish life, the United States, it is threatened by an ominous inner contradiction. While the organized sector of Jewish life, which includes synagogues, centers, schools, fraternal orders, Zionist groups and philanthropic agencies, is survivalist in theory, the life of individual American Jews is, to a large extent, assimilationist in practice. Our collective religious and cultural life, our national institutions, are all officially dedicated to the preservation of Jewish values, but the daily life of Jews demonstrates to what extent indifference and alienation are making inroads. We have only to recall the breakup of the great Jewish neighborhoods of the past, the East Side of New York, the West Side of Chicago, the South Side of Philadelphia, and similar areas throughout our other great cities. There still are districts in which Jews live and new suburban areas are proliferating, but there is an important qualitative difference—once there were Jewish neighborhoods; now there are areas in which Jews live. Those who are old enough to remember the past will recall how much influence the neighborhood itself exerted upon the lives of Jews. The *succahs* that were built in the backyards of the tenement houses, the Sabbath candles in the windows, the funeral processions through the streets, the Torah scrolls being carried at dedications by bearded patriarchs, the chants from the hundreds of little synagogues where services were conducted—these and countless other factors moulded the personality of many Jews who never set foot within the synagogue themselves.

All too little attention has been paid to the phenomenon of linguistic assimilation, the virtual disappearance of Yiddish among the native-born generation of American Jews. For four centuries and more Yiddish was one of the most potent weapons in the arsenal of Jewish survival. In its alphabet and in its idioms, in its earthy wisdom and its echoes of ageless piety, Yiddish was the bearer of Jewish consciousness and the bond of Jewish unity linking believers and non-believers alike through a sense of a common history and a common destiny. This matchless treasure-house of Jewish wisdom has virtually disappeared from the life of nearly all American Jews, except for some elements in the older, immigrant generation.

Today a crisis of mounting proportions exists with regard to American Jewish college youth. It affects many, though fortunately not all, of the most articulate and most creative members of the younger generation. The gravamen of this crisis is not that they attack the structure and content of organized Jewish life, which obviously deserves to be challenged and re-ordered in many respects. Anyone, particularly among the youth, who does not feel impelled to vigorous dissent and protest against the established order, either in American life or on the Jewish scene, is lacking either in mind or in heart or in both. The eye of the storm lies in the fact that there is no common language, no shared body of ideas or sentiments between the youth and their elders, because both groups are Jewishly deracinated. The elders have been the builders and the youth are the products of a Jewishly sterile environment, a background essentially unjewish in any meaningful sense.

Another phenomenon which, notwithstanding the plethora of surveys, has yet to be studied is the outright conversions of American Jews to various forms of Christianity. The practice, both quantitatively and qualitatively, is by no means negligible. One could compile a long list of distinguished men and women born into the Jewish community who have officially adopted various forms of Christianity for themselves and for their children, often following intermarriage. Undoubtedly, there is a variety of motives involved, among which, let it be noted, genuine conviction must also be included!

Intermarriage has, of course, been studied a great deal, because it lends itself to statistical analysis. In his epoch-making study, Eric Rosenthal pointed out that the first generation of American Jews had an intermarriage figure in the city of Washington of 1.4%, which rose in the second generation to 10%, and in the third generation to 17%. This is not as important as another conclusion of his report, the significance of which is often overlooked—the fact that college-trained youth have an intermarriage rate double that of the rest of the population. Today, 85% of all American Jewish youth are attending college and within a decade virtually every American Jew may be getting some kind of college education. This means that we shall have an intermarriage rate of about 35% for the next generation as a whole, without reckoning with an acceleration of the process.

In addition to conversion and intermarriage, there is the wide-spread phenomenon of spiritual alienation by many of our most gifted and creative members, who do not formally leave the Jewish fold. That today Jews occupy a distinguished place in American literature, drama, music and art is too obvious for comment. What is relevant to our concern is that with very few exceptions, the poets, the dramatists and the artists of Jewish parentage have been thoroughly dejudaized, and that their attitude toward their Jewish heritage, of which most of them know nothing, generally varies from indifference to violent antipathy. The great preponderance of Jews who are so visible on the American cultural scene, are Jews only by origin and not by background, choice or commitment.

In sum, the great American-Jewish community of today, num-bering some five and a half million souls, gives every indication—unless all signs fail—of having reached its peak, numerically speak-ing. For the future, we cannot anticipate any growth for the Jewish community and there may very well be a diminution of numbers. This is not necessarily an evil, since the "population explosion" is not an unmixed blessing. Nevertheless, Jewish sur-vival in America—particularly meaningful and creatively satisfy-ing survival—is by no means certain: it remains a great unknown.

The question, therefore, "What meaning is there to Jewish sur-vival?" is far from meaningless—we are dealing with realities. The truth is that Jews have an option today in a free—or at least an open—society as to whether they wish to remain Jews. They feel themselves free to walk out of the Jewish community through one or another of the doors open to them. To be sure, they may find later that the price of admission to the circle of the dominant majority is far higher than they anticipated, in the sacrifice of self-respect, in the loss of integrity, both moral and intellectual, they are called upon to make, and in the damage to the psychologi-cal well-being they bring upon themselves and those nearest to them. But once the step has been taken and the door has been shut, the road to return is barred. The handful of instances where at the cost of great spiritual travail, the wanderer succeeds in coming home, serve only to demonstrate that by and large the process is irreversible. The tragedies can be minimized only in advance, only if our youth and their elders are helped to seek and find their own answers—or at least approaches—to the question of the meaning and purpose of Jewish existence.

At the outset, it should be noted that there have been some Jewish thinkers who have sought to rule this question out as completely irrelevant. One of the most distinguished thinkers America has produced, if perhaps not the greatest of all, was wont to argue that it is meaningless to ask, "Why be a Jew?" "The answer," he said, "is we are born Jews and on that basis we continue to live." Hence, asking the question, he insists, is a pathological symptom, like a man asking, "Why should I continue to live?" Recently, one of the most challenging younger theologians in American Jewry wrote similarly, "Being a Jew has no more role or purpose than being a Frenchman or a German. The unique significance of Judaism in the contemporary world is that it is a sufficient and appropriate way Jews face and share the decisive crisis of existence. Jews have learned in their long history many lessons about life and death. That wisdom has been incorporated into the corpus of Jewish liturgy and literature. Nevertheless, this wisdom does not give us a special role or a special purpose."

Now this position, however emphatically expressed, is, I believe, fundamentally wrong. It is a logical and erroneous conclusion derived from a mistaken premise—the denial of the uniqueness of the Jewish people. This doctrine, religiously expressed as the election of Israel, I consider the foundation-stone of Jewish faith, constant through the centuries of Jewish experience, binding upon believer and non-believer as well. For it is not only an article of belief, but also a valid sociological judgment, confirmed by four millennia of Jewish history. Now it is perfectly true that under normal conditions a people does not ask why it should continue to survive. A Frenchman living in France, for example, ordinarily does not ask himself, "Why be a Frenchman?" But if the Frenchman is living in Ecuador, Egypt or Turkey, and he has children, then he must ask himself, "Should I raise them within French culture? Why should I rear them as Frenchmen rather than as Ecuadorians, Egyptians or Turks?"

It is one of the permanent aspects of Jewish experience that Jewish life has almost never been carried on under normal conditions. What is normal for the Jew is a state of permanent abnormality. Had we been normal, we would have been dead long ago! In the past, there were at least two great occasions when the question of the goal and purpose of Jewish existence came to the fore. Both these events, incidentally, took place outside the land of Israel. The first came shortly after the Exodus, in the desert. When Moses assembled the hosts of Israel at the foot of Sinai, he did not say to them, "You are no longer slaves. You are free to do whatever you wish with yourselves." Nor did he proceed to give them a constitution to carry on their national life *as an end in itself*. According to the words of Scripture, the Jewish people were now commanded to be "a kingdom of priests and a holy nation." Now, a priesthood implies a laity whom the priest serves. By definition, a priest does not minister merely to his own needs but to a community. He is a center that must have a periphery around him. Thus, at the very beginning of their history, Jews were commanded to think not only in terms of self-preservation and their own group interests and identity, but to see their liberation as pointing to a cause beyond themselves.

Eight centuries later, in Babylonia after the destruction of the First Temple, a great Unknown Prophet, conventionally called Deutero-Isaiah, had to wrestle with the agonizing problem of why his people had suffered destruction, degradation and death. Why should the remnants of the people living in exile in Babylonia continue to preserve their identity as Jews? Why not submit to the majority? Why not be absorbed in the resplendent life of Babylonian civilization? Deutero-Isaiah answered the question of Jewish survival once again in terms of a purpose beyond itself: " 'You are My witnesses,' says the Lord, 'and I am God.' " Centuries later the Midrash penetrated directly to the implication of his words in their comment, "If you remain My witnesses, then I am God, but if you cease to be My witnesses I, so to speak, cease to be God."

Moses, who stands at the beginning of the biblical period, and Deutero-Isaiah, who stands near its close, both emphasize the conviction that the survival of the Jewish people is not an end in itself, but is part of a larger purpose beyond itself. It is entirely legitimate, therefore, to seek after a purpose for Jewish survival today. Even the location of the Jewish homeland suggests that it is the fate of the Jewish people always to be on the cutting edge of the human adventure. If Jews were destined to enjoy a peaceful and uncomplicated existence, the Promised Land would have been some remote territory like Alaska or Greenland, or if a warmer climate be preferred, somewhere in the heart of Africa. Instead, the tiny Land of Israel which lies at the crossroads of three continents, Europe, Asia and Africa, has been the most conquered territory in history. Here Jews have been perpetually exposed to all the cross-currents of human culture, being challenged and stimulated by all the blandishments and temptations inherent in their unique position, and threatened by enemies both great and small.

In our day, the problem of the meaning of Jewish existence has become infinitely more agonizing because of the colossal burden of misery and suffering represented by the Nazi holocaust and its aftermath. Those of us who, through no merit of our own, were spared direct contact with the most brutal event in the history of mankind would be obtuse and insensitive if we sought to impose upon the survivors of Nazism our answer to this tragic mystery of Jewish existence. One can not only understand but empathize with those who, having gone through the hell-fires of Nazism, continue to feel the iron of persecution in their own being and are therefore unable to accept any rational approach to this blackest of all riddles.

The dual phenomenon of measureless bestiality by the Nazis and the callousness exhibited by the rest of the world has destroyed for many the faith in a Living God possessing both power and righteousness. Thus, while the "death-of-God" theology may have passed its peak in Christian circles, some Jewish theologians continue to propagate the idea that "God is dead," or at least is moribund. Thus, one Jewish theologian continues to challenge traditional theology with unabated vigor and to insist that there is no God and Israel is His witness. Recently, he declared that "sadly and bitterly" he has come to the conclusion that "the belief in God as the Lord of history must be rejected," and that "Jewish paganism" appears "the most viable religious option available to contemporary Jews." This is no minor change in doctrine. Both in biblical and post-biblical religion the fundamental attribute of God is that He is the Lord of history and not merely the Lord of nature. In fact, as Yehezkel Kaufmann has stressed, it is this characteristic that differentiates the God of Israel from all other deities, far more significantly than does His unity as against the multiplicity of gods in paganism.

Other thinkers, less sensational in approach and iconoclastic in content, insist that the very attempt to find any religious meaning in the Nazi holocaust is blasphemous and that only the *possibility* of a religious response remains. Other articulate victims of the Nazi horror continue to batter at the walls of the citadel of God and to protest against the injustice of His judgment. Underlying these varied reactions is the conviction that traditional theism is capable of only one response to the horror of the Holocaust, to interpret it as a "punitive visitation," a deserved Divine punishment upon the victims. This view, to be sure, is sometimes expressed and even more implied by some official "defenders of the faith." Yet in spite of their august authority this answer, which they propose with sublime self-assurance, is not merely indefensible—it is blasphemous.

We are not, however, compelled on this account to throw the baby out with the bath. Traditional religion possesses resources that reveal it as both more compassionate and realistic than this "straw-man" image of God set up by His official defenders would suggest. The Bible provides the insights for other and profounder responses to the mystery of the monstrous evil of our day, notably in *Deuteronomy*, *Job*, *Genesis* and *Deutero-Isaiah*.

Because of the presence of *Job*, the profoundest book in the Bible, Judaism has always been too clearheaded, too warmhearted, too realistic to accept any of the conventional man-made answers to the problem of evil or to regard them as the final and complete explanation. In the words of Rabbi Jannai in the *Ethics of the Fathers*, "We do not know the reason either for the suffering of the righteous or the prosperity of the wicked." The basic response of the book of *Job* is to be found in the "Speeches of the Lord" out of the whirlwind. In a world which contains so much harmony and order, the Lord of Creation is also the God of history. *The harmony of the natural order suggests that there is a pattern in the moral sphere. Since both are the handiwork of the One Living God, there must be some meaning to human suffering, even if it is veiled from us.* In this respect, the great medieval philosopher Maimonides was following in the tradition of *Job* when he declared that though the purpose of the universe may be hidden from man, we may feel assured that there is a purpose.

Total light is denied us, but some rays do penetrate the darkness. The opening chapter of *Genesis* describes man as created in the image of God. This means, as the greatest Jewish teachers have indicated, that man is endowed intellectually with the power of reason. What is reason in the intellectual sphere is freedom of will in the moral area—and the free will of the individual is the basis for his responsibility to society. In other words, since man has been endowed by God with the power of thinking, he is free to choose between right and wrong. The Torah emphasizes this truth no less than three times in the book of *Deuteronomy*, as in the great call: "Behold, I place before you this day life and death, the blessing and the curse." Every individual, every generation, every group, every society, is confronted perpetually with this basic choice flowing out of the character of man, who is described by the rich and profound biblical phrase, as having been created in "the image of God."

Another insight, likewise derived from the opening chapters of *Genesis*, and emphasized throughout the Bible, is the doctrine of *the interdependence of mankind*. This ethical truth the Rabbis find implicit in the biblical account of the origin of the human race from a single ancestor and in the detailed genealogy of Adam's descendants. Since all men are organically related to one another, when men sin, men suffer. Then the next, obvious question arises: Why is it that some men sin and other men suffer? Why was it possible for the Nazis to commit the most monstrous of crimes and for innocent people to suffer? Biblical tradition would reply that part of the answer lies in the fact that for good and for ill, each human being is not an independent entity but is organically bound up with his fellow man.

The biblical legislator, prophet and sage, are at one in emphasizing the thought that the entire human race, both horizontally across space and vertically through time, is a unity, and therefore one in its sin and in its suffering. It is not at God's door that we can place the major ills of the world: war, poverty and much of disease. Not God, but man, has brought suffering into the world and continues to inflict it upon himself and his fellows.

The prophet Deutero-Isaiah supplies another indispensable insight. Agonizing over the exile and degradation of his people and its apparently imminent destruction, the prophet enunciates the doctrine of the suffering "Servant of the Lord." This people suffers contumely and misery at the hands of the nations because of their moral immaturity, their rebellion against God's law of righteousness, love and peace. The nations of the world have yet to learn that Israel is the messenger, the witness, "the Servant of the Lord," called upon to proclaim the law of justice to all men, to bring light to darkness and set the prisoner free, to be "a covenant to the peoples, a light to the nations." When the nations grow in insight and understanding, Israel's sufferings will end and it will attain to dignity and honor within the family of mankind.

Deutero-Isaiah's approach to the mystery of Israel's suffering has even broader, more universal implications. He is proposing in effect the concept of *vicarious suffering*. This is not a theological dogma, like the doctrine of vicarious atonement, but a datum of human experience which every mother and indeed every parent knows at first hand. When one loves another human being, one is bound to suffer with and for the loved one. When a young man commits a crime, it is not only he who pays the penalty of his misdeed, but all those who are in any sense related to him: his innocent parents, his wife and children, and many others, for all men are brothers in a pitiless as well as a merciful sense.

The awareness of the perilous nature of human freedom, the recognition of each man's interdependence and involvement with his fellows, and the experience of the reality of vicarious suffering —all these aspects of the human condition help to buttress the conviction that the world is not an absurdity and a horror. For it sustains the faith that the harmony of the natural order has its parallel in a meaningful pattern in the moral order. Yet, undergirding and overarching all these efforts to penetrate to the heart of man's suffering in God's world is the recognition that after all has been heard, an irreducible mystery remains—but the mystery can be borne because it encloses the shining miracle of existence.

Understandably, many of those who have had to drink the bitter cup of agony themselves may not be emotionally capable of find balm for their suffering in such doctrines as the interdependence of mankind and the vicarious suffering of the just for the unjust. Yet, these are no comfortable theological abstractions, but stark realities of the human condition everywhere and always. It is only that the stage has grown massive in our day. But men must seek to take insights such as these into account in their view of the universe, less for the sake of God than for the sake of man.

Perhaps other interpretations of the realities of the human condition will commend themselves as more adequate than what has been proposed here. But what seems to me undeniable is that it is not only legitimate but essential to seek and find a meaning and purpose for Jewish existence. This will inevitably entail grappling with the mystery of human suffering in general and the suffering of the Jewish people in particular.

Moreover, the entire history of the Jewish people in the past supports the conviction that it was not simply a form of collective megalomania for Jews to believe that they still have a function to perform in the world. Their contribution to humanity is writ large in the annals of history. The position of the Jewish people in the present suggests that this role is far from spent today. Ten million Jews constitute a tiny minority as against the two billion human beings on this planet who belong to other faiths and cultures, yet there is work for the Jew to do. In religious language, the survival both of the Jew and of Judaism is an essential element in God's plan for the world. The existence of the Jew, indeed his mere survival in the face of towering evil, the preservation of the Jewish identity as a tiny island in a great non-Jewish ocean, is an indication that we live in a world where, all appearances to the contrary notwithstanding, might does not make right and the power of the human spirit does triumph over the forces of physical brutality and strength. In the words of an old prayer, "If we perish who will sanctify Thy name?" The survival of the Jew, like every triumph of righteousness in human affairs, testifies to the fact that we live in a world in which the law of consequence operates and that as surely as there are natural laws in the physical universe, the moral universe has its own laws that cannot be violated with impunity. It is the law expressed in two passages in the book of *Proverbs:* "Righteousness exalts a people, but sin is the disgrace of nations," and "Where there is no prophetic vision, the people perish, but happy is he who keeps the Law."

If the Prophets of Israel were to write a history of mankind and deal with the rise and fall of nations, the result would be quite different from Arnold Toynbee's *A Study of History*. They might conceivably accept a good number of the sociological, economic and political explanations offered by scholars and thinkers for the decline and fall of empires, but behind them all the Prophets would discern another and more fundamental cause. They would maintain that no society has yet endured and no civilization has yet proved permanent because no society and no civilization has thus far been built upon the foundations of righteousness. Each has violated the law of consequence and therefore has fallen prey to destruction.

If there is any merit to democracy and any hope for the survival of the democratic order, it is not because democracy is perfect or efficient, but because it possesses a built-in self-correcting mechanism. Through the ballot box and public opinion, it has within it the seeds of regeneration and the overcoming of its own weaknesses without the necessity for violence and chaos. If the arteries of democracy harden and it no longer has this capacity for peaceful self-regeneration, democracy, like all earlier systems, will be destroyed.

The preservation of the Jew, therefore, is part of the evidence for faith in the principle of the power of the spirit and the victory of righteousness over evil. But it is not only the Jew who needs to survive. Judaism also has a message for the world that can only be indicated here in briefest form. After 1900 years of Christianity and 1200 years of Islam, both of which are derived from Judaism, there is still much in Judaism that is unique either in content or in emphasis, and this particularly in areas where the world is deeply confused and desperately in need of guidance today. Above I have sought to spell out some of the values that Christians are seeking and can find in the Jewish background of their religious heritage.

The Jewish tradition, properly understood and interpreted, can speak to the complex of problem areas in the field of group relations. It does not claim to offer neatly worked-out blueprints for the ills of the world. But it has something significant to say with regard to nationalism, which, as the Prophets indicated, must be cultural in form and moral in expression if it is not to destroy mankind. It is able to offer a theory of religious liberty and genuine tolerance for committed believers deriving from the rabbinic concept of the Noachide Laws.

In its insistence that "all the land is Mine and you are only dwellers and sojourners with Me," and through the entire structure of social legislation embodied in biblical and rabbinic law, Judaism declares that all men have an inalienable right to share equally in the material and spiritual blessings of God's world as a matter of justice and not out of condescension and charity. In the currently most critical area of all, that of racial tension, Judaism would insist that the criterion should be just ends achieved by just means and not the replacement of one set of inequities by one of another hue. As for the most basic aspect of human life, love, sex and family, the Jewish approach to morality can offer sorely needed guidance to our generation. Finally, the entire thrust of the Jewish tradition can aid in the widespread search for a religion that will be secular in the best sense of the term, a faith that will not seek to denigrate the world or escape from it, but will be concerned with the here-and-now, with the life of man, his problems, his agonies, his hopes, his vision of the future.

Speaking to the youth and elders of Israel shortly before his death, Moses declared, "For it is no empty matter for you, but your very life." The rabbis, alert to every nuance of the biblical text, add, "And if it be empty, it is for you that it is empty." In seeking to rally our generation to live in loyalty to the people, the land and the legacy of Israel, we affirm that in Judaism there are values and goals which go beyond the Jewish group. Judaism, when understood in depth and interpreted in sympathy, contains a body of truth, of insights into the character of the universe and its Maker, which the world needs desperately today.

Like all the generations before him, the modern Jew can hold fast to the faith that there is a meaningful and life-giving role for Jews and Judaism in the world. In Bernard Lazare's words, "Being a Jew is the least difficult way of being truly human." Throughout history the Jew has suffered in order to live. He must continue to live, in order to reduce the burden of suffering and thus help bring the day nearer when men will become truly human.

Jewish existence has brought to the Jewish people more than its share of misery and pain. But travail is a prelude to birth. The Jew has been taught by his tradition that life is duty and that duty is joy. He has felt the most intense of all pleasures, that of creation, the sense of being God's co-partner in the building of the world. As he knows all too well, the world is far from perfect, but it is richer in promise and achievement because of his labor and sacrifice.

From his heritage, the Jew has derived a realistic understanding of the limitations of life together with an unconquerable zest for life. The Jew has learned to understand his fellow men and yet to love them as his brothers. What has helped him hold these antinomies in balance has been his sense of humor, his capacity to laugh, to sing and to dance. These gifts of the spirit have been the saving grace of his life in many dark hours.

The Jew has conceived of his earthly existence as a life-long process of going to school and his teachers have been the prophets and sages, the law givers and poets, the thinkers and scholars of Israel from antiquity to the present. The noblest sons of his people, who created the Bible, delineated the contours of the New Jerusalem, in which justice and freedom would be the lot of all men, and universal peace the destiny of all nations. Ever after the Jew has been the captive of that vision, which, he passionately insists, is no dream but a blue-print of the future. In the many volumed *Talmud*, his ancestors fashioned a way of life in which the desires of the body were met while the needs of the soul were heeded. In succeeding centuries the Jew created a rich, variegated literature, both in Hebrew and in the other languages he made his own, notably Aramaic, Arabic and Yiddish. But these achievements did not exhaust his creative energies. He also contributed abundantly to the life and thought of all the peoples with whom he came into contact, enriching the literature, music and art of the world, its philosophy, science and technology, its social progress and economic growth. In Israel, a rich flowering of the Jewish spirit is taking place anew.

Today many of Israel's sons, including those forgetful and even scornful of their heritage, continue in the tradition of their ancestors, who in Heine's words "have fought and bled on every battlefield of human thought." The war for humanity, it need scarcely be said in 1970, is far from won, but the Jew passionately desires to be on hand when the hour of victory comes. There has been suffering and agony for the Jew during the thirty-five centuries of Jewish history, but there has also been the ineffable joy of being truly alive, for, as Justice Oliver Wendell Holmes reminds us, "to live is to function." Life is even more. To live is to think, to feel, to love, to create, to dream. The Jew would not have missed it for the world.

Today this is no longer a self-evident proposition. The growing sense of desperation in our age has driven increasing numbers of youths, both of the under-privileged and of the over-privileged groups, to unfurl the banner of violence as the only effective instrument for gaining attention and "getting things done." It is even being maintained in some quarters that violence is the essence of the American tradition.

Until clear proof is available that the destruction of the universities and other cultural institutions is the only effective way of curing their ills, we reaffirm the position maintained above—what is required is perpetual vigilence in quest of the re-vitalization of institutions. To be sure, there may be more emotional release in the intoxicating wine of violence. Genuine progress is a less heady potion, being compounded of patience and intellectual clarity, respect for differences and humility before the unknown, coupled with a faith in man's capacities and the courage to experiment with the new and the untried.

The record of history, supported by the testimony of common sense, makes it clear that the destruction of the religious "Establishment" will not spell the end of religious institutionalism. It will merely replace it by another set of functionaries and vested interests. The onslaught on religion by authoritarian dictatorships during the Nineteen Thirties did not eliminate the evils, real or alleged, of religion. It merely transferred the allegiance of the masses to the new gods of fascism and communism. The wide-spread disaffection with religion today has not made emancipated philosophers of the people. On the contrary, it has spawned mystical cults and pseudo-Oriental sects, not to speak of occultism, astrology, devil worship, and drug culture.

In every aspect of human life, including religion, there is no shortcut to the New Jerusalem, no substitute for the path of genuine renewal, the goal of which was charted by Rabbi Abraham Isaac Kuk, "The old must be made new and the new must be made holy."

CHAPTER XX

The Ultimate Goal

From the time when man emerged upon this planet as a thinking creature conscious of his own being, he has sought an answer to the fundamental question: What is the purpose of his existence? Closely related is another: What are the criteria of the good life? This deep desire to discover the meaning of life has nurtured man's religious faith, whenever he has been persuaded to accept its view of God's purpose and man's duty. It has also been the fountainhead of his skepticism and unbelief, whenever he could not be convinced of the validity of its interpretation of life. Moreover, man's vision of the good life, whether clearly articulated or not, impels him to perpetual restlessness, an unceasing discontent with the imperfect face of reality, a constant reaching out for more than he can attain and hold fast.

Man has learned much about the world, in the centuries of recorded history, but the ultimate remains a mystery which gives little evidence of dissipating. Today nonbeliever and believer alike are convinced that with regard to the purpose of existence we have made little progress; again, not merely *ignoramus*, "we do not know," but *ignorabimus*, "we shall not know." Here, all ages and temperaments are as one.

The fourth-century Greek poet Palladas of Alexandria seeks refuge from this melancholy thought in the joys of wine:

> How was I born? What place my home?
> So soon to go, why did I come?
> How can I learn from books or men,

When all things are beyond my ken?
I came from naught this world to see,
To-morrow I shall nothing be.

O race of men, from nothing brought,
And nothing worth in deed or thought,
One thing alone contentment gives,
A drug 'gainst trouble while man lives,
The gift of Bacchus, fount divine—
So pour me out a cup of wine.

(Greek Anthology)

The same mystery of existence intrigued the Hebrew thinker
Koheleth, who sought to grasp the truth with the pincers of reason,
but his efforts, too, proved unavailing. Order and beauty were
everywhere in evidence, but the purpose of the cosmos was forever veiled from man:

> I know the concern which God has given men to be afflicted
> with. Everything He has made proper in its due time, and He
> has also placed the love of the world in men's hearts, except
> that they may not discover the work God has done from
> beginning to end. . . .
> Who knows what is good for man in life, during the brief
> days of his vain existence, which he spends like a shadow?
> Who can tell man what will happen under the sun after he
> is gone? . . .
> . . . I saw that though a man sleep neither by day nor by
> night he cannot discover the meaning of God's work which
> is done under the sun, for the sake of which a man may search
> hard, but he will not find it, and though a wise man may
> think he is about to learn it, he will be unable to find it. . . .

(Eccl. 3:11; 6:12; 8:16–17)

It was this bafflement which led the Biblical sage to his insistence
that the enjoyment of life is the only reasonable goal for man.
Like Samuel Johnson, Koheleth was a pessimist with an enormous
zest for living. This sense of mystery induced in Koheleth a brood-
ing melancholy, which is not far apart from that of a believing
saint nearly a millennium and a half later, who lived in a radically
different milieu. The Hasidic Rabbi Bunam of Pshysha found his
beloved disciple Enoch in tears. The Rabbi asked him, "Why are
you weeping?", and Enoch answered, "Am I not a creature of

this world, and am I not made with eyes and heart and all limbs, and yet I do not know for what purpose I was created and what good I am in the world." "Fool!" said Rabbi Bunam, "I also go around thus."

Nonetheless, religion, unlike secular thought, does not remain content with an agnostic position with regard to the goal of creation and the demands of the good life. The rationalist Maimonides declared that though we cannot know God's purpose for the universe, we can and must believe that it has its meaning. His view recalls the utterance of Justice Oliver Wendell Holmes that each man is a soldier in a cosmic campaign, the plan of which he does not know. The mystics, on the other hand, believe that God, seeking an object upon which to bestow His love, called the world into being. God's spirit, unable to brook the unbroken calm of nothingness, called out: "Let there be a universe!" The religious spirit praises the Lord in the hymn, "Blessed be our God who has created us for His glory." Since man is the beloved creature and the child of God, the purpose of his existence is to fulfill the will of his Father in heaven, and thus enhance the glory of God.

What is the will of God and how can man minister to God's glory? Perhaps the finest definition is that to be found in the familiar words, already cited, of the prophet Micah:

"Wherewith shall I come before the Lord,
And bow myself before God on high?
It hath been told thee, O man, what is good,
And what the Lord doth require of thee:
Only to do justice, to love mercy, and to walk humbly with thy God.
(*Micah* 6:6–8)

This threefold imperative, be it noted, is addressed, not to the prophet's countrymen or coreligionists, but to all men everywhere and always. Both the content and the order of the injunction are highly significant.

It may be observed that for the prophet the ethical imperatives of justice and mercy precede the strictly religious ideal of "walking humbly with God." The emphasis upon ethical living as the primary demand of God is fundamental to the Biblical world-view.

The relative order of the two ethical demands is also noteworthy; "doing justice" comes before "loving mercy." Justice is the only firm foundation of group living; without it no stable society, no assurance of peace, is possible. Moreover, justice, not being dependent upon our subjective emotional attitude, is binding upon men in all their relationships, to strangers as well as to kinsmen, toward enemies as well as toward friends. It is a debt which we owe to all human beings, who stand in the same relation to God as we do, as creatures and as children.

Basic as justice is, however, it represents the lower limit of the arc of the ethical life, while it is mercy or love that represents its uppermost point. The Hebrew noun *hesed*, which is generally rendered as "mercy," is more accurately to be translated "loving-kindness" or "steadfast love." To enforce justice alone means to condemn the world to stagnation, for the ceaseless round of cause and effect, of act and consequence, offers no chance for growth and improvement. To practise love means requiting one's fellow beyond his deserts, thus freeing him from the burden of past errors and affording him the opportunity of rising to a higher level of existence. Hence love is the light of the world, the gateway of hope to the future.

Justice and love are mutually indispensable. Justice without love is cruelty; mercy without justice, sentimental caprice. As we have seen, the tension between these two attributes of God reflects both the order and the freedom that characterize His world, the element of stability and the aspect of hope in the universe. In our attitude toward our fellow men, each of us must manifest both these qualities of justice and mercy. Since each man is the center of a complex web of relationships, his duties and opportunities fall into many areas: his obligations to himself, to his family as parent, spouse and child, to his community, to his country, to the world.

In each area, man is perpetually subject to countless temptations, compounded by the weaknesses of his own nature. Moreover, the ethical life is often confronted by the conflicting claims of two ideals, each valid and worthy of allegiance, or by the demands emanating from two areas of relationship, each legitimate and deserving of consideration. Accordingly, spelling out the implications of justice and mercy in human affairs is a complex and difficult task, the function of a work on "ethics," and necessarily beyond the scope of this book. Here it suffices to underscore what should be self-evident: that man's moral conduct remains the touchstone of his sincerity in obeying the call of God. Hence the prophet properly places these ethical imperatives first in his call to man.

It is frequently stated that, according to religion, righteous living is the goal of human existence. Reflection makes it clear, however, that ethical living cannot be the ultimate purpose of human existence, but only a means to an end beyond itself. That purpose is expressed in the climax of the prophetic call, "to walk humbly with thy God," every word of which is freighted with meaning.

"To walk with God" means to be conscious of His presence in every human activity and in every aspect of the world which He has called into being. It therefore follows that the failure to rejoice in the blessings of God's world means to be an ungracious guest in the home where God is host. The enjoyment of life, coupled with the recognition of its divine Source, is not merely every man's right, but every man's duty. However paradoxical it may seem at first blush, the conclusion is inescapable that the enjoyment of life ranks higher in the scale of values than the ethical life, for the ethical life is the means for assuring to all men the enjoyment of life, which is their due.

Why are murder and robbery, deceit and fraud, cruelty and exploitation accounted cardinal sins? Because they deprive the victims of their God-given right to share in such blessings of the world as food and shelter, liberty or leisure. Were the latter not man's rights, the former would not be vices! In more than one period in history it was argued with warmth and sincerity that the suffering of the poor was a blessing, since it prepared them more perfectly for the beatific state in the world to come. For the prophet, no such casuistry is conceivable. For his passionate spirit, justice and mercy are God's imperatives to man, because they are indispensable instrumentalities for man's fulfilling his divinely ordained privilege: walking with God, and seeing His presence everywhere in a world aflame with beauty and aglow with truth.

It is this hierarchy of values, obscurely sensed by the ancients, that may explain the position of a skeptical work like the book of *Ecclesiastes* in the Biblical canon. Undoubtedly, many factors, some even accidental, played their part in the inclusion of this masterpiece in Scripture. Unlike the Biblical legislators, prophets, and psalmists, the skeptical Hebrew sage is not concerned with buttressing faith in God or in urging righteous living upon his readers. But he is stressing the truth that joy in life is a Divine imperative. Even the most pietistic of the rabbis seem to have sensed that, however unconventional the route by which Koheleth arrived at this insight, he was focussing attention upon the highest level of human values, loftier even than the preachment of morality—the enjoyment of life's blessings as the fulfillment of God's will for man:

> Therefore I praise joy, for there is no other good for man under the sun but to eat, drink, and be joyful and have this accompany him in his toil, during the days of his life, which God has given him beneath the sun.
>
> (8:15)

> Go, then, eat your bread with joy,
> And drink your wine with a glad heart,
> For God has already approved your actions.
> At all times let your clothes be white,
> And oil on your head not be lacking.
>
> (9:7–8)

> Rejoice, young man, in your youth,
> And let your heart cheer you in your youthful days.
> Follow the impulses of your heart
> And the desires of your eyes,
> And know that for all this,
> God will call you to account.

> Banish sadness from your heart,
> And remove sorrow from your flesh,
> For childhood and youth are a fleeting breath.

> Remember your Creator in the days of your youth,
> Before the evil days come and the years draw near,
> Of which you will say, "I have no pleasure in them."
>
> (11:9–10; 12:1)

"To walk with God" as the prophet enjoined means to fulfill His will. It embraces the practice of justice and love, but it goes beyond to include the living sense of His presence everywhere in His world.

But the phrase has not yet yielded up all its meaning. "To walk with God" means that man is to recognize himself as God's co-partner, sharing vitally in the task of building and governing the world. This recognition of man's innate dignity as God's co-worker is basic to a proper understanding of his nature, as manifested in his creative activity, his moral responsibility, and his untapped potentialities.

"To walk with God"—but humbly! Is the prophet here warning against the besetting vice of the virtuous—the tendency to self-satisfaction of those who know that they walk with God? "The wicked praises himself, while he blasphemes against the Lord," the Psalmist complains, but the boasting of the sinner is not nearly so common as the self-adulation of the pious. Now, the smugness of those who walk with God is no mere peccadillo, unpleasant but unimportant. To walk with God without humility means to build a wall of arrogance about us, estranging ourselves from our fellow men, who may make no claims to intimacy with Him or who may see Him differently from ourselves. It means to add fuel to fanaticism and to enlarge man's already substantial capacity for hatred and intolerance, by imbuing him with the proud conviction that cruelty and persecution minister to the greater glory of God. No wonder that a Hasidic teacher declared, "Far, far better a sinner who knows that he is a sinner, than a saint who knows that he is a saint." Only if a man walks humbly with God, will he remember that he has brothers, whose dignity is equal to his own.

"To walk humbly with thy God." If this quality is needed in our attitude toward our fellow men, it is the bedrock of man's relationship with His God. To learn the art of humility does not come easy in our age, which is so conscious of man's vast and expanding powers and which has spawned the crass and brutal idolatry of man's self-worship. To walk humbly with God is to recognize that man is not the measure of all things, being neither the center of the universe, nor its creator, but a creature, elevated through God's love to the dignity of partnership with his Maker, so that he may help achieve the Divine purposes, which he can at best only dimly perceive.

Man's humility before God is a shield and buckler against countless evils. It is a protection against the arrogance of the dictator, who justifies his actions both against his own people and against others on the ground that he is answerable to no one and recognizes no law higher than his own will. Few men are likely to attain the dizzy heights of unlimited power, but all men are tempted, at one time or another, to regard their own desires and capacities as the ultimate arbiter and justification of their actions. So, too, we are all destined to descend into the valley of suffering through the loss of our loved ones and, finally, through our own death. To walk humbly with God means to recognize the limitations of man's understanding and thus attain to the wisdom and the courage for resignation:

> For My thoughts are not your thoughts,
> Neither are your ways My ways, saith the Lord.
> For as the heavens are higher than the earth,
> So are My ways higher than your ways,
> And My thoughts than your thoughts.
>
> (*Isa.* 55:8–9)

One final implication flows from the last phrase, "thy God." For all man's weaknesses, his brief hour on the stage of life, his foolish antics, his sorry misdeeds, he alone stands in conscious comradeship with His Maker and can call him, "My God."

A nineteenth-century religious teacher was wont to say: "Each man should carry two stones in his pocket. One should be inscribed with the words, 'The world was created for my sake'; the other, with the words, 'I am but dust and ashes.'" He was unconsciously spelling out the full implications contained in Micah's call to men, "walk humbly with thy God." The Chinese sage Mencius said: "I love life and I love righteousness; if I cannot have both, I choose righteousness." Vital religion believes passionately that man can have both and have them abundantly.